The Life Of The Venerable Anna Maria Taigi, The Roman Matron

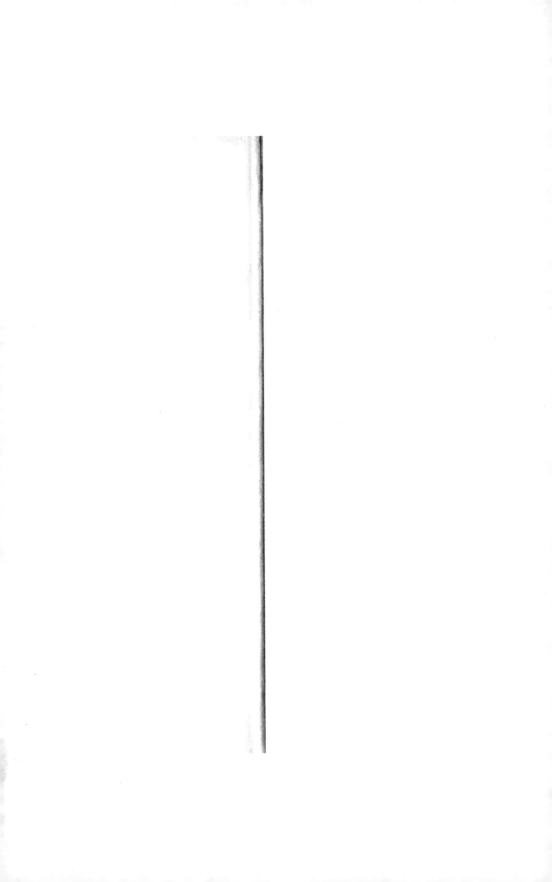

LIBRARY

OF

RELIGIOUS BIOGRAPHY.

EDITED BY

EDWARD HEALY THOMPSON.

———

VOLUME V,
THE VENERABLE ANNA MARIA TAIGI.

The Venerable Servant of God

ANNA MARIA TAIGI.

1769 — 1837.

THE LIFE

OF THE

VENERABLE

ANNA MARIA TAIGI,

The Roman Matron.

(1769—1837.)

EDITED BY

EDWARD HEALY THOMPSON, M. A.

(*With Portrait.*)

NEW YORK:
PUBLISHED BY FR. PUSTET, 52 Barclay Street.

CINCINNATI, OHIO:
FR. PUSTET, 204 Vine Street.

LONDON, ENGLAND:
BURNS, OATES & CO.

1874.

Entered, according to the Act of Congress, in the year 1873, by
ERWIN STEINBACK,
In the Office of the Librarian of Congress, at Washington.

ADVERTISEMENT.

THE only biography of Anna Maria Taigi which has hitherto existed in English is a translation of a work by Mgr. Luquet, the Bishop of Hesebon. This work, written more than twenty years ago, labours under a twofold disadvantage. In the first place, it is incomplete, especially in regard to this holy woman's spiritual gifts; a defect, however, for which the estimable prelate was in no way responsible. Great reserve was imposed upon him with reference to this subject, as appears from his own statement; and in particular he was not permitted to give any account of the extraordinary ... ur by which she was so pre-eminently distinguished — the vision of a luminous orb, or sun, which she beheld for forty-seven years, and in which she saw things past, present, and to come. He was therefore obliged to content himself with saying that the supreme respect which he justly entertained for the Sacred Congregation of Rites, and the commands of the Sovereign Pontiff, prevented him from describing the nature and the greatness of a gift which would fill the faithful with astonishment.

But his work is not only incomplete. It is in many

respects inaccurate, and unfortunately in one very important point, as he himself afterwards regretfully acknowledged : indeed, had it been possible, he would have withdrawn the book from circulation. As allusion is made to the subject of this inadvertence on more than one occasion in the course of the following narrative, it will be sufficient here to observe that Mgr. Luquet composed his work under circumstances unfavourable to the exercise of due discrimination; for, although he had access to a large collection of miscellaneous documents, he had nothing to guide him in the matter of selection, but was left to his own unaided estimate of the apparent evidence on which they rested. He does not seem to have submitted his book to any supervision in Rome ; the Italian Life which bore his name having been translated from his own original work.

Several Lives have since appeared ; notably that of P. Bouffier and, later, that of P. Calixte, both of which are free from the two objections which lie against Mgr. Luquet's publication, having been written subsequently to the introduction of the cause of the Venerable Servant of God, and with the advantage of reference to published extracts from the processes. The latter Life, in particular, is considered at Rome to be the fullest and most correct of any which had then appeared. Both of these biographies have been consulted in the composition of the present volume, as well as an Italian Life by P. Filippo Balzofiore, which, though short, is comprehensive and very accurate ; but the materials have principally been derived from the *Analecta Juris Pontificii*, in which there have appeared at intervals considerable extracts from some of the most important depositions given in the processes.

For details regarding the interment, or, rather, interments, of the Servant God, for on two occasions the body was removed from its place of sepulture, and the state of preservation in which her remains were found at the end of eighteen, twenty-eight, and thirty-one years respectively, reference has been made to a document obtained, through the kindness of a friend, from the Postulator of the cause.

Anna Maria delivered numerous and important prophecies concerning things still future. In consequence of the remarkable way in which all her predictions have been fulfilled which related to what has now become a portion of the past, great interest has naturally been felt regarding them—an interest every day enhanced by the crisis through which the Church and the Holy See are at present passing. These predictions are still reserved under the seals of the Sacred Congregation of Rites; nevertheless, a few have transpired through communications made by persons who during the life of the Servant of God had the opportunity of becoming acquainted with them, and chiefly by Monsignore Natali, the priest who was appointed to receive her revelations. Whatever can be traced to this prelate with certainty may with safety be attributed to her, but he used great reserve and discretion in his confidences. We have been at some pains personally to ascertain what thus might or might not be confidently put forward as a genuine utterance of Anna Maria, and have made the separation accordingly. Predictions which appeared to be clearly traceable to the holy woman herself we have inserted in the text; while other current prophecies, which cannot with equal assurance be referred to her, although they may rest on respectable evidence, we have given in an Appendix; with the addition of a short notice of various similar vaticinations uttered by persons gifted with the spirit of prophecy either in present or past times.

As it is impossible to say, from day to day, what convent, or church, or pious institute at Rome may be sacrilegiously seized, or, as the official phrase is, 'expropriated,' by the usurping Italian Government, it has been thought better to speak of them as they were, without adverting to the present state of things; particularly as that present, with all its wrongs and ravages, will, as all good Catholics confidently hope and believe, soon have become the past: not merely in the ordinary sense of the term, as all present things are momentarily becoming, but in the sense of what is gone and vanished—gone with all its miserable results—and Rome itself, freed from the horde of spoilers now camping within its walls, will have once more recovered its true Catholic character and splendour under the paternal rule of its own Pontiff-king.

In accordance with the decree of Urban VIII., and other Sovereign Pontiffs, we declare that all the graces, revelations, and miraculous facts related in this work have only a human authority, except so far as they have been confirmed by the Holy Catholic, Apostolic, and Roman Church, to whose infallible judgment we submit whatever is written therein ; and that, in giving to the Servant of God, Anna Maria Taigi, the designation of Saint we have no thought of anticipating the decision of the Holy See, which alone has authority to pronounce to whom such character and title rightly belong.

We subjoin the Decree of the Sacred Congregation of Rites in the original Latin, together with a literal translation of the same in the vernacular.

'Decretum Beatificationis et Canonizationis Venerabilis Servæ Dei, Annæ Mariæ Taigi, Tertiariæ Ordinis Sanctissimæ Trinitatis Redemptionis Captivorum.

'Qui potentiam sapientiamque suam ostensurus consuevit ut plurimum per infirma ac stulta mundi atterere sæculi fastum, impiorum elidere molimina, frangere conatus inferorum—is hoc ævo nostro, ubi humana elatio infernæque vires coivisse visæ sunt ad subruenda, si fieri posset, Ecclesiæ fundamenta non modo, sed et ipsius etiam civilis societatis, irrumpentibus undique fluctibus impietatis femellam objecit. Adhibuit ad hoc opus Annam Mariam Antoniam Jesualdam Taigi, honesto quidem loco natam, sed inopem, nuptam vul-

gari viro, familiæ curis implicitam, ac jugi manuum
opere sibi suisque victum quærentem. Eam, quam sibi
elegerat animarum illicem, expiationis hostiam, obsta-
culum machinationibus, malorum deprecatricem, deter-
sam antea sæculi pulvere, arctissimo sibi junxit chari-
tatis vinculo, miris illustravit charismatibus, iisque vir-
tutibus auxit quæ non modo pios homines e quovis
societatis ordine etiam supremo, passim allicerent, bene
vero et impios, omnibusque magnam sanctitatis ejus
inderent existimationem. Hæc porro communis opinio,
quæ totam Servæ Dei vitam exornaverat, cum latius
multo splendidiusque percrebuisset post ejus mortem,
quæ contigit die nona junii anni millesimi octingen-
tesimi tricesimi septimi, in eamdem famam sanctitatis
vitæ, virtutum, et charismatum inquiri cæpit per pro-
cessum ordinaria auctoritate Romæ institutum. Eo
vero condito, ac necessariis omnibus paratis, instante
adm. Rev. Clemente Maria Buratti, cubiculario hono-
rario Sanctissimi Domini nostri Pii PP. IX., causæ
Postulatore, Emus. et Rmus. Dominus Cardinalis Lu-
dovicus Altieri, causæ Relator, in Ordinariis Sacrorum
Rituum Congregationis comitiis ad Vaticanas ædes
infra dicenda die coactis, dubium proposuit: *An sit*
signanda commissio introductionis causæ in casu et ad
effectum de quo agitur? Emi. autem et Rmi. Patres
Sacris tuendis Ritibus præpositi, omnibus accurate per-
pensis, auditoque voce et scripto R. P. D. Andrea
Maria Frattini, Sanctæ Fidei Promotore, rescribendum
censuere: *Signandam esse commissionem, si Sanctis-*
simo placuerit. Die 23 Decembris, 1862.

'De quibus postea facta a subscripto secretario Sanctissimo Domino nostro relatione, Sanctitas Sua rescriptum Sacræ Congregationis ratum habens, propria manu signare dignata est commissionem introductionis causæ Venerabilis Servæ Dei, Annæ Mariæ Taigi, die 8 Januarii, 1863.

'C. Episcopus Portuen. Card. PATRIZI, S.R.C. Præfectus.
'Loco ✠ signi.
'D. BARTOLINI, S.R.C. Secretarius.'

'Decree regarding the Beatification and Canonization of the Venerable Servant of God, Anna Maria Taigi, Tertiary of the Order of the Most Holy Trinity for the Redemption of Captives.

'He who, when He would show forth His power and wisdom, hath been wont for the most part to use the weak and foolish things of the world to confound the haughtiness of man, to frustrate the designs of the impious, and bring to naught the efforts of hell, hath in this our age, when human pride and infernal power have seemed to combine to subvert, if it were possible, the foundations, not only of the Church, but even of civil society itself, opposed a poor weak woman to the floods of impiety bursting in on every side. He hath employed for this work Anna Maria Antonia Gesualda Taigi, born, indeed, of honest parentage, but poor, married to a common man, hampered with the cares of a family, and fain to seek wherewith to support herself and them by the constant labour of her hands. This woman, whom He had chosen for Himself to be an attractor of souls, a victim of expiation, a bulwark against plots, a warder-off of evils by her prayers, He hath first cleansed from the dust of this world, and then hath united to Himself by the strictest bond of charity, hath adorned with wonderful gifts, and hath replenished with such virtues as to draw to her on all sides, not pious persons only, from every rank of society to the very highest, but even the impious themselves, and to inspire all with the highest opinion of her sanctity. Now, this general opinion of men, with which the whole life of the Servant of God had been distinguished, having spread wider and become more notable after her death, which took place on the 9th day of June in the year 1837, an inquiry was instituted into this same report of her sanctity of life, virtues, and gifts, and the process therefore commenced by ordinary authority at Rome. All which being effected, and the necessary preparations made, at the instance of the Very Reverend Dom Clemente Maria Buratti, Honorary Chamberlain of our Most Holy Lord, Pope Pius IX., and Postulator of the cause, his Eminence the Cardinal Luigi Altieri, Relator of the cause, in an ordinary assembly of the Sacred Congregation of Rites, held in the Vatican Palace on the day to be named below, proposed this doubt:—*Whether a commission be nominated for the introduction of the cause in the case and with the object of which there is question?* The Most Eminent and Most Reverend Fathers, appointed guardians of the Sacred Rites, having well and duly weighed all things, and heard what

the Promoter of the Holy Faith, the Reverend Dom
Andrea Maria Frattini, had to say both by word and
in writing, decided that this answer be returned :—
*That a commission be nominated, if his Holiness shall
so please.* The 23d day of December, 1862.

'A report hereupon having been afterwards made, by
the undersigned Secretary, to our Most Holy Lord, his
Holiness, after ratifying the rescript of the Sacred Congregation, was pleased to sign with his own hand a
commission for the introduction of the cause of the
Venerable Servant of God, Anna Maria Taigi, on the
8th day of January, 1863.

       'C. Bp. of Porto Card. PATRIZI,
          'Prefect of the Sacred Congregation of Rites:
            '✠ Place of seal.
    'D. BARTOLINI, Secretary of the said Congregation.'

CONTENTS.

———◆———

CHAPTER I.

ANNA MARIA'S EARLY YOUTH—HER MARRIAGE.

Character of her parents; they remove from Siena to Rome.
She receives a good Christian education. In her thirteenth
year is sent into a workshop. Returns home at nineteen;
her motives for desiring this change. Her love of dress and
amusement. Enters service in the same house with her
parents Her refinement of speech and manners; consequent dangers and temptations. Her conscience roused.
She is advised to enter the married state; her mode of view-
ing the matter. Domenico Taigi; his disposition and manners. His account of the engagement . . . *page* 1

CHAPTER II.

ANNA MARIA'S FIRST YEAR OF MARRIED LIFE—HER CONVERSION.

Renewed indulgence of vanity. Anna Maria's dissatisfaction
with herself. P. Angelo receives a divine intimation respecting her. Her increased uneasiness of mind. Dis-
couraging conduct of a priest; its probable explanation.
The danger of such rebuffs. Anna Maria is led to disclose
the secrets of her soul to P. Angelo . . . *page* 13

A

CHAPTER IX.

ANNA MARIA'S HEROIC CHARITY TOWARDS GOD AND TOWARDS HER NEIGHBOUR.

CHAPTER X.

ANNA MARIA A SHINING EXAMPLE OF ALL THE VIRTUES.

CHAPTER XI.

ANNA MARIA'S DEVOTION TO THE MYSTERIES OF THE INFANCY AND PASSION, AND TO THE BLESSED SACRAMENT.

CHAPTER XV.

CHAPTER XVI.

CHAPTER XVII.

CHAPTER XXII.

ANNA MARIA'S INTERMENT AND RE-INTERMENTS.

CHAPTER XXIII.

MIRACLES ATTESTING THE SANCTITY OF THE SERVANT OF GOD.

APPENDIX.

LIFE

OF THE

VENERABLE ANNA MARIA TAIGI

———◆———

CHAPTER I.

ANNA MARIA'S EARLY YOUTH—HER MARRIAGE.

LUIGI GIANNETTI and his wife, Santa Maria Masi, were
respectable inhabitants of the ancient city of Siena in
Tuscàny ; respectable, not merely according to the con-
ventional acceptation of the word, but in its true and
proper meaning.   Giannetti was universally esteemed
by his fellow-townsmen for his probity ; and his wife,
though she was troubled with an awkward temper, enjoyed that consideration which solid Christian principles are sure to win from good and worthy people.[*]
They had but one child, who was born on the 29th of
May, 1769, and was baptised the following day, receiving the name of Anna-Maria-Antonia-Gesualda.
Her father, who kept a chemist's shop, was, a few years
later, entirely ruined.   The cause of this apparent mis-

---

[*] It is worthy to be recorded of this good woman that, when
at Rome, she had the singular honour of preparing for burial
the body of a saint of our day, the Blessed Joseph Labre.

fortune is not stated; nor is this surprising, for who
would care to chronicle the affairs, adverse or prosperous, of a little tradesman, whose very name would have
long since passed into oblivion, but for the lustre which
his child has reflected upon it? All we know is that
his pecuniary ruin was owing to what is called a reverse
of fortune, which may have been brought on by im-
prudence, but did not carry with it any personal dis-
grace.* These reverses of fortune are, however, in all
cases Providential arrangements, though men are so apt
to regard them simply as untoward accidents. In the
present instance, we can clearly discern the influence of
this event on the future life of Anna Maria. It reduced her to the condition which she was ordained to
occupy, and it brought her to the centre of Christendom,
where God designed to manifest her sanctity and high
gifts to the Catholic world. Giannetti, actuated probably by a natural repugnance to remain, beggared as
he now was, amongst those who had known him in
easy and comfortable circumstances, and hoping, no
doubt, to have better chances of employment in a larger
and richer place, left Siena and repaired to Rome with
his wife and child, then a pretty little girl barely six
years old. Their extreme destitution is evidenced by
the fact that they made the whole journey on foot.

* Anna Maria's biographers have all given a general good
character of Giannetti, and Domenico Taigi expressly testifies
in the processes that he and his wife were good Christians. The
Carmelite Father, Filippo Luigi di San Nicola, Anna Maria's
confessor, who left a deposition inserted in the processes, without saying anything precisely contradictory, does not seem to
take a very favourable view of Giannetti. He speaks of him as
an indiscreet man, who had dissipated his fortune, and says he
was far from being kind to his daughter in her youth. At the
time he knew him, however, Giannetti was probably soured by
misfortune and sickness.

Giannetti found what he sought in the Eternal City, obscurity and work. He and his wife soon procured some daily employment as domestic servants, and were enabled to take a small lodging in the Strada delle Vergini, in the Rione (or quarter) dei Monti. It belonged to the parish of San Francesco di Paula, now known as Santa Maria dei Monti. His first care was to provide for the Christian education of his child, a blessing which in Rome is as free to the poor as the rich. No city, indeed, in the world can boast of an equal number of gratuitous schools for primary instruction as Rome. They are brought, as it were, to the door of every poor family, for one may be met with at almost every turn. Anna Maria was accordingly sent every day to the 'Maestre Pie,' as the good Religious were called who superintended one of these charitable institutions in a neighbouring street, the Via Graziosa. She was a very engaging child and soon won the love of her mistresses, the nuns, who showed their affection in the best way in which they could show it, by cultivating piety in her young heart. They were well seconded at home, where, indeed, she had been early taught to say her infantine prayers with devotion, and often to repeat the sweet names of Jesus and Mary. The husband of Anna Maria, who after her death was called to make his deposition, said he was certain that her parents had given her an excellent education, and had been careful that she should receive all the sacraments proper to her age at the right time. He stated, moreover, that they used to take her daily to hear Mass at a very early hour, and he believed that she was also in the habit of frequent confession. It was at the church of San Giovanni Laterano that Anna Maria received the sacrament of Confirmation, when eleven years of age; and a little later she made her first Communion in her parish church of San Francesco di Paula.

It was a day for which she had longed with all the eagerness of her innocent and loving heart ever since she knew of the blessing in store for her, and at this first visit of our Lord to her soul she was filled with exceeding joy. But, as no particular notice, so far as we are aware, is taken of her first Communion in the processes, we may reasonably conclude that there was nothing manifested by her on that occasion, or at least that nothing was on record, surpassing either in kind or in degree what may not seldom be observed in such Catholic children as are readily disposed to receive devout impressions, and have had the benefit of careful religious training. This advantage she had thoroughly enjoyed, for her mistresses, noting her inclination to piety, had lost no opportunity of instructing her in divine things. She had a quick intelligence and ready apprehension; she also acquired with facility skill in all the various works suited to women, and likely to be serviceable to one of her station in life. Above all, she had an excellent heart, which endeared her to all about her. She had now attained her thirteenth year, and, having made her first Communion, her education was considered to be completed. Her parents accordingly removed their child from school, in order to place her where she could learn a business. They looked out for persons to whom they could safely entrust their treasure, and found two good women, of somewhat advanced age, who lived by the labour of their hands, and had several young girls under their care who, while themselves receiving instruction, assisted their employers in their work. When they had acquired a certain proficiency, their mistresses allowed them a trifling propor-

tion out of their gains; and, as Anna Maria was both
docile and handy, she was soon able to bring her parents a few small coins every week to add to the slender
family purse.

She seems to have been chiefly employed in winding
raw silk in preparation for manufacture; and in this
occupation she continued for six years, giving much
satisfaction to her mistresses. A wish to return home
now arose in her heart. It was prompted by a good
motive, reinforced, however, by one less laudable. She
was anxious to assist her mother, and lighten her daily
toil, and thought she might be of more use in this way
than as at present engaged, for her earnings were very
slight; and then, sooth to say, she was getting a little
tired of winding silk, and hankered after some variety.
The reason is not far to seek: the innocent and pious
child, who is satisfied when it hopes to have pleased its
Heavenly Father and its earthly parents, or those who
stand to it in parental relations, and whose recreations
are as simple as itself, too soon outgrows this happy
state; and then comes a critical time. The world un-
folds upon its view: a child scarce perceives the world,
and does not know what it is even when it casts an eye
upon it; but with youth the eyes are opened, and quite
a new revelation is made to the inner apprehension.
This revelation is simultaneous with a certain development of self-consciousness; indeed, this word perhaps
best sums up what takes place in the young girl's heart.
It becomes to her the source of vanity, and may be said,
generally speaking, to be in her the temptation which
corresponds with that of the passions, which at this
period begin to dawn and gather strength in the youth's
heart, and act as his snare and allurement to draw him
from the paths of virtue.

Anna Maria had arrived at this dangerous season of
life, a season in passing through which the piety of
many who have afterwards become glorious saints has
suffered a partial obscuration or eclipse.   Witness St.
Teresa herself, the Blessed Margaret Mary Alacoque,
and others who might be named.   These holy souls
subsequently applied to their lives at that period epi-
thets which might have misled such as had not other
sources of information.   It is because saints feel so
keenly their former infidelities to grace and deafness to
the call of their Beloved, that they can with all sincerity
use such expressions about themselves as are calculated
to convey the idea that their souls had been stained
with some grievous offence against God.*   Anna
Maria, then, at this age loved dress not a little, though
she had little means wherewith to indulge the taste,
and she wanted to see the world with somewhat more
freedom than was possible while confined in a dull
workshop.   Of course that wish implied what is not
so readily avowed even to self, the desire to be seen.
For who is solicitous to dress smartly and becomingly
for no one's eye ?   To wish to be seen is of necessity
also a wish to please and be admired ; these several

* Mgr. Luquet, Anna Maria Taigi's first biographer, did,
in fact, interpret too literally the terms in which the servant
of God spoke of her past life, and the name of 'sinner' which
she applied to herself.   He consequently accepted without due
examination a false statement with regard to her conduct after
marriage ; accusing her, not only of levity and love of worldly
dissipation, but of the sin of unchastity and conjugal infidelity.
Later he bitterly deplored his mistake.   Anna Maria's daughters
protested against such a judgment of their mother's character,
and all the documents of the processes abundantly prove that
she never arrived at committing a grave offence, however much
her heart may have been allured by the love of pleasure and
amusement.   This remark applies to her life both previous to
and immediately succeeding her marriage.

wishes, which all hang together, being often included under the mere expressed desire for a 'change,' a phrase so commonly heard from the lips of our young women. And how much is implied in that simple word!

It must not, however, be for a moment supposed that Anna Maria had given up her religious practices, or had a thought of offending God, or of overstepping the bounds of Christian modesty; on the contrary, like so many of her inexperienced age, she had not even an idea of the perils which lay hid under the smiling attractions of the world which was captivating her imagination and soliciting her affections. It was agreed between Anna Maria and her parents that she should go into service; and they thought themselves very fortunate when they succeeded in locating their daughter in the same house in which they were themselves employed as domestics; their mistress, who occupied a portion of the Palazzo Maccaroni, consenting to take her as her maid. Nothing could seem better than that she should thus be placed under the eye of her parents and enjoy the advantage of their protection. But if the watchful care of father and mother do not always avail to preserve their children from temptations and perils even in their own homes, much less could the presence of the Giannetti offer a sure guarantee of their daughter's prudent behaviour under another's roof, where, too, they each had their separate avocations. The Palazzo was large, and there were other families lodging in it, with, of course, their visitors and friends frequenting the house. Anna Maria was pretty, and remarkably pleasing. Dress, of which we have said she was fond, sat becomingly on her, and this, combined with manners and diction superior to such as are

usual in girls of her class, was sure to attract the notice
of those whose admiration is dangerous. Anna Maria's
mother, it will be remembered, had seen better days,
and had probably received an education sufficiently
cultivated to secure her from the vulgarity of speech
common among the lower orders ; add to which, that
the accent of the people of Siena and the purity of
language which distinguishes them are remarkable even
in Tuscany, that classic land of the Italian tongue. The
daughter had caught from her mother her native beauty
of language, which added a great charm to her attractive appearance ; for who has not felt that a pretty
face can ill atone for an ordinary voice and a vulgar
phraseology, and that it loses half its grace as soon as
the mouth is opened ?   Anna Maria, then, simple and
uncultivated as she was,—for her education, good in a
religious point of view, had not extended beyond the
merest elements,—spoke and bore herself with a refinement which seemed rather to belong to one of gentle
birth ; a circumstance which, as it added to her attractions, added doubtless also to her perils, as her
lowly condition of life left her devoid of those thousand
safeguards which hedge in the daily path of the well-
born damsel, forming around her a sort of guard of
honour, under the protection of which she may often
carelessly indulge her vanity—not, indeed, without de-
triment to the life of grace within, or to Christian
purity of heart, but, at least, without any immediate
peril to virtue.

We know that Anna Maria was exposed to temptations of this character, while living as a servant in
the Maccaroni Palace, but no details have reached us.
This, however, is of small importance—the imagination can readily supply them ; and besides, it is not a

romance, but a saint's life on which we are engaged, so
that the chief and, indeed, the sole matter of interest is
to know what was the effect on her spiritual state of
being brought face to face with these perils to innocency
which she had neither anticipated nor apprehended.
A word, a look, it may be, revealed to her one day the
danger of her soul and the abyss of sin which was
yawning at her feet: at any rate she saw it, recoiled
into herself, and by God's grace understood whither
her thoughtless levity was leading her. She immediately betook herself to the fortress of prayer, and redoubled her assiduity in the performance of her religious
exercises, as well as her dutiful attention to her parents,
in which, indeed, she had never been wanting. But
this did not suffice her : her strong and ardent mind
was incapable alike of feeble impressions and of half
resolutions ; she had perceived her danger, and desired
to provide against its recurrence. This set her upon
considering her future life; she knew that, although
parents can offer good and affectionate advice, which
comes with great authority from their lips, yet that in
matters so nearly concerning our salvation we must
seek Divine light and the counsel of our appointed
spiritual guides. Accordingly she had recourse to her
confessor, who recommended her to enter the married
state, and bade her pray for direction from above. She
followed his advice, confessed and communicated more
frequently, and, without neglecting her work, allotted
more time to prayer, offering her intentions for the
object she sought, and hoping thus to obtain the grace
of being united to one suited to her in disposition, who
feared God, and with whom she could spend her days
holily. Not a thought nor a desire did she give to the
bettering of her earthly state by marriage ; nay, she

much preferred to wed one who was poor, like herself, and to earn her bread by the labour of her hands. Nor do we hear of the imagination being consulted any more than her temporal interests. True, as we have said, she wished to marry one whose disposition was suited to her own: this was desirable for the sake of married happiness and peace of mind, and for common edification, but of all that is calculated to gratify the fancy we hear not a word; and, in truth, we have reason to think, judging by the choice she made, or, rather, which she considered God had made for her and which she cheerfully accepted, that no such ideas found entrance into her mind. To many this way of considering the question of marriage will appear very unromantic; but in the first place we may observe that the romance of a saint's life — and it possesses, as, indeed, does the interior life of every soul, a touching romance of its own—is to be sought, not in exterior adventitious circumstances, but within. Besides, although the true ideal of a Catholic union need not, and does not, exclude personal liking of a less—as some persons would style it—prosaic character than what is here described, it still remains that the furtherance of highest interests, and not the mere pleasing of eye, taste, or fancy, is the main and the legitimate motive of a Christian marriage. Good Catholics are, indeed, well aware that, in order to enter that state with the blessing of God, they ought to be able reasonably to hope that the marriage union will not only offer no hindrance to their salvation, but prove a means, according to God's order in their regard, for their advance in holiness of life. It was with a single view to this end that Anna Maria looked forward to marriage.

About that time her father had made the acquaintance of a young man named Domenico Taigi, who was
a domestic servant in the Chigi family. He was a
Milanese by birth, and deservedly enjoyed an excellent
character, for he was well-principled, regular in his
conduct, and attentive to his religious duties. To say,
on the other hand, that he had no polish would be to
fall far short of the truth; for he seems to have been
quite uncultivated, and to have had that rusticity of
habits and manners which belongs to the peasant class.
Nevertheless he came of high lineage, being descended
from one of the most illustrious families of Milan, the
Taeggi.* Taeggio, indeed, and not Taigi was the name
by which he always called himself,† and he is thus
entered on the roll of the servants attached to the
house of Chigi. It is not true therefore, as has been
asserted, that Anna Maria made a *mésalliance*, so far
as birth was concerned, in espousing Domenico Taigi;
on the contrary, his original extraction was noble, and
her own parents belonged only to the middle class,
while, as regarded their present condition, they were
on an equality; the advantage being rather in favour

* From documents of the fifteenth century it appears that
the Dukes of Milan conferred special privileges on this family,
a proof both of its high rank and of the estimation in which it
was already held at that time. Other existing documents of a
later date show that high offices of trust were at different times
committed to members of this noble family, which seems to
have been distinguished as much by merit as by rank.

† The corruption of Taigi had its origin with the school-
fellows of Anna Maria's little girls, who were sent, as she herself had been, to the Maestre Pie. Mgr. Luquet, who wrote
the first published Life of the Venerable Servant of God, un-
wittingly adopted an error which had already obtained some
currency. It has thus gone the round of Europe, and the name
of Taigi is now too familiar to Catholic ears for any subsequent
biographer to think of recurring to the correct etymology.

of Domenico, who served a princely house. Yet under
another aspect the union might be regarded as ill-
sorted; for Anna Maria certainly married one who
was her inferior in point of breeding. Education may
bridge over considerable inequalities of birth and station, but the purest blood cannot make amends for
ignorance, coarseness, and vulgarity. A woman mar-
ries the man such as he is, and not his ancestors; and
disparity in cultivation of mind and manners, which in
a married couple must always be a great cross to the
superior, becomes peculiarly trying if, as in the present
case, it is the husband who is the inferior. Indeed, as
a matter of fact, we know that this good man was to
prove a trial to his partner in more ways than one; but
this doubtless entered into God's designs for her more
perfect sanctification.

Domenico's deficiencies, if not his faults, were, however, of a character to be readily discernible; and as
Anna Maria, therefore, with her tact and refinement,
cannot have failed to see them, it is plain that she did
not consider them as furnishing sufficient reason for
rejecting him. He was virtuous and attached to his
religion, and so might be the person whom Providence
had selected for her husband. Accordingly, when he
sought her in marriage, she did not refuse him, but
expressed a desire to ascertain the will of God by
prayer, recommending him to do the same. In this he
readily concurred, and from his statement on oath, when
called to make his deposition, we gather that, like
Anna Maria, he approached the consideration of marriage in a truly Christian spirit. These are his words:
—' When purposing to marry, I made enquiries regarding the servant of God and her family; the result
having been very satisfactory, I decided on marrying

her. She was about eighteen years old, and was in service with a certain lady, called Maria. As I used to carry this lady her dinner every day, the affair was all arranged in a month's time. I asked her in marriage of both her mother and her father, who served in the same house, after having made sure that the young girl would accept me. I know that she prayed to God in order to ascertain His will. I on my part did the same. I also remember that she was dressed decently and suitably. The marriage took place in the parish church of San Marcello within the Octave of the Epiphany. It was the 7th January, 1790.' Domenico's memory must have failed him with respect to his wife's age, for she wanted little more than four months of being one-and-twenty, at the date of her marriage, having been born, as has been stated, on the 29th of May, 1769.

CHAPTER II.

FIRST YEAR OF HER MARRIED LIFE—HER CONVERSION.

DOMENICO TAIGI had found a treasure in Anna Maria. She was ever to him, even during the period preceding her conversion, a loving, faithful, and industrious helpmate. She studied all his wishes, and never from the first was deficient in any duty incumbent on a good and Christian wife. Add to which, she did all with that grace and cheerfulness which lends a charm to the simplest actions. Still it would be a mistake to suppose that the love of dress and amusement was as yet eradicated from her heart. We have heard how Domenico spoke of her attire at the time he asked her in marriage. Serious thoughts were in the ascendant then, and, no doubt, she had ceased to give the same attention as before to the adorning of her person. She would no longer allow her vanity this gratification, for she had recognised its danger; but what she had renounced for her own sake, she was by and by to resume, and with not much reluctance, as it would seem, for that of another. Domenico himself was in fault on this occasion, so far as fault may be found in the pride which a husband very commonly feels in showing off his young and pretty wife to advantage. Fault there is, of course, in all vanity, but this is a form of it which naturally pleads for much indulgence; and there are many in whom, little advanced as they are in the spiritual life, it can scarcely be regarded as deserving of censure. It is in them a natural result of affection, full, indeed, of all that imperfection which belongs to mere nature, but the absence of which would in their case only argue less conjugal tenderness, not greater spiritual perfection. So far in excuse for Domenico's desire to see his wife gaily dressed on festal days and at places of entertainment, where every look of admiration directed to her was sweet to his feelings and flattering to his choice.

But not so was it with Anna Maria. Not only was she acting imperfectly, but she knew it. She felt an inward sting and reproach; the Holy Spirit had not spoken to her soul in vain: for her it was idle to seek excuses, the necessity of seeking which has never even occurred to those who have had less light and no special call of grace. She dressed, it is true, to please her husband; she went to places of amusement, displaying all the beauty of her twenty years enhanced by the ornaments which his affection had bestowed upon her,

and all to please her husband. What more natural?
some will say; or even more commendable? But then,
it must be added, while loving to please her husband,
Anna Maria loved the means,—that is, the dress and
the display,—as well as the end, and her inward Monitor did not fail to tell her so. Besides, God had higher
designs in her regard, with which this easy sort of life
was irreconcilable. For persons thus called not to go
forward is to fall back; with them there is no standing
still. With less favoured souls there may be what
looks like such a stationary condition; their poor efforts
just availing, with the aid of grace, to keep them from
slipping back into positive sin, and to maintain their
spiritual position; like the feeble rower, the strokes of
whose oar enable him to resist being carried back by
the stream, yet are not sufficiently powerful to help him
to make head against its current. But when God sends
a great offer of grace to a soul, we cannot reckon upon
even thus much; for He is not content to have thus
much, and no more, in return for His magnificent liberality. He is a jealous God; He has given Himself
emphatically that designation, and it contains a fearful
threatening of wrath which we can never fathom in this
life, along with a revelation as deep of love unutterable,
incomprehensible! The two—the jealousy and the love
—are counterparts and commensurate. God was pur-
suing Anna Maria with one of those offers of love of
which the most ardent passion of the human heart is
but a faint shadow and type, and she was ignoring it.
She was trying to lead an ordinary life, that is, to fulfil
her essential duties, and at the same time to smile and
frolic through the flowery season of life, and indulge all
that exuberant gladsomeness and love of pleasure which
revels in the hearts of the children of the sunny south.

Surely this might be allowable; it might have been
dangerous once, when she stood alone, but she has an
arm to lean upon now, and a protector to guard her.
How illusory such confidence has too often proved,
when vanity has been allowed its unrestrained gratification, we need not observe, but Anna Maria, happily,
was never to learn this lesson by sad experience. Meanwhile she had no thought of offence or of sin; she
meant only what so many mean without encountering
reproach, either exterior or interior, to be glad and rejoice in the days of her youth. But this was not to be:
God would have her all for Himself and at once, now,
in her youth and her beauty and the freshness of her
heart, or, it may be,—not at all.

It was about a year after their marriage when, on
one bright festal morning, Anna Maria, leaning on her
husband's arm, was wending her way amidst the happy
crowd that was streaming towards St. Peter's. She was
dressed with all the taste and care which her humble
circumstances permitted; nevertheless, her heart was
ill at ease: she knew it was not well with her, and
was secretly conscious that all this vanity, trifling as it
might seem, was displeasing to God. Still she had no
present will to give up the world, and little knew what
a change was about to be worked in her. God, however, at this very moment revealed His purposes to a
holy Religious, P. Angelo, a Servite, who accidentally
passed near her in the crowd. She was entirely unknown to him, and would not have attracted his notice
but for an interior voice which said to him, 'Observe
that woman; I shall place her in your hands. You will
labour at her conversion, and she will sanctify herself,
for I have chosen her, and have called her to be a
saint.' Anna Maria passed on, little suspecting that the

guide selected by God to lead her to the highest paths
of perfection was close beside her, and had even now
received his commission from on high. Yet she may
have received a secret touch of grace, for she had no
sooner entered the Basilica than she went to prostrate
herself before the tomb of the Apostles, where she
prayed with all the fervour of her soul. The inward
voice of God's Spirit now spoke more pressingly to her,
and with more distinct utterance. The light which she
had so often endeavoured, albeit indeliberately, to ex-
tinguish shone with greater clearness, and she could no
longer deceive herself. She had been setting her soul
to sleep, and shutting her eyes to the things of Heaven
that she might enjoy those of earth; she was awake
now, her eyes were opened. The delusive dream had
vanished, and left only bitterness and a cheerless void
in her heart. How many feel this void when worldly
pleasures disappoint them, or bring satiety, as they
surely must at length, who yet never suspect that this
vague yearning is the cry of the soul which has been
created for God and can never rest satisfied with anything short of its supreme and uncreated good. Well,
indeed, it is for them who make this discovery before
they plunge anew into the fruitless search for happiness among creatures.

There was a combat going on in Anna Maria's heart,
but grace was gaining the advantage over nature. No
longer able to endure the inward agitation of her soul,
and convinced that she would never be restored to
peace till some radical change was effected in her, she
resolved to seek this peace in the tribunal of penance,
and, after her visit to St. Peter's, endeavoured to put
her purpose into execution in another church. Here
she entered a confessional, and her first words, afte

c

casting herself on her knees, were, 'Father, behold a poor sinner at your feet.' Whether the priest was hurried, or whatever might be the cause, he treated her in a manner quite foreign to the patience and tenderness which the penitent expects to find in the minister and representative of Christ, an expectation, indeed, rarely disappointed. Having scarcely allowed her to finish her confession, he hastily gave her absolution and dismissed her curtly with these words : 'Go, you are not one of my penitents.'* The explanation which most readily suggests itself, although it does not excuse the repelling behaviour of one who was sitting in the place of the compassionate Jesus, the Friend of Sinners, seems to be the following. Anna Maria, in the light of divine grace, had beheld her soul steeped in worldly affections and following the corrupt bent of nature. She saw also with dismay whither such a path leads, and felt to her heart's inmost core what an evil and bitter thing it was to leave the fountains of living water for the poisonous pool of natural gratification. The interior illumination she had received was doubtless very strong, being proportioned to the high sanctity to which God would lead her. To such heights the depths of humiliation must correspond. Hence her heartfelt designation of herself as 'a poor sinner,' an expression which misled this unknown priest, as it has also helped to mislead others. When, however, the confessor found that she had nothing whereof to accuse herself except what might be regarded as ordinary female offences, such as pleasure in dress, love of admiration, giddy devotion to amusement, and the like, but that

---

* Mgr. Luquet says he refused altogether to hear her confession. This seems highly improbable, and is not borne out by other accounts.

none of these faults had issued in sin of any grievous magnitude, he might possibly be indisposed to spend much trouble on her. He might consider that it was more a case for spiritual direction. He had his own regular penitents; she was a stranger, not one of his flock; such guidance as she desired might be sought elsewhere; and he was not minded to entrench on his time by adding this stray sheep to the number of those who made demands upon it. If this be the true explanation, it serves to account for those strange words of his : ' Go, you are not one of my penitents.'

But whatever may have been the source of the chilling demeanour of this unfatherly priest, which in many a case might have produced most injurious effects, it is clear that in Anna Maria's it was a Providential circumstance overruled for her good. She had not applied in the right quarter; this was not the physician whom God had selected for her, the Good Samaritan who was to probe and bind up the wounds of her soul. She left the confessional, as may be supposed, saddened rather than comforted; and certainly the reception she had met with was most disheartening; it was calculated to create discouragement; and discouragement is one of the most fatal of temptations in the spiritual course : it directly attacks the will, and in the feeble-minded, or in those whose resolve has been feeble, is apt to gain an easy victory. Such moments are always critical : an effort has been made to escape from the world's toils, and it has failed. It was difficult to bring the will to that point ; at last it consented ; and now it would fain break loose again and return by a kind of rebound to what at some sacrifice it had renounced, pleading that it has done all it could and holding itself exonerated from any fresh exertion. The world and its false liberty

never perhaps solicit more powerfully than at such
times, and the devil knows how to profit by the advantage.

Well it was for Anna Maria that she found strength
in her faith and humility to bear up against the temptation, and to resist and triumph over it. Now she
turned anew to God, cast herself on His mercy, and
protested that she would seek nothing henceforth but
His holy will. But to whom should she have recourse?
for it was not an ordinary confession she desired to
make, which any priest might receive ; what she felt to
need was one to whom she could lay bare her whole
heart and conscience, and who would be both willing
and able to act as her spiritual guide. While reflecting
on this subject, she was inwardly moved to address
herself to one of the Fathers who officiated in the
Church of San Marcello. Amongst these Religious she
would surely, she thought, be successful in finding what
she needed. With this intention she entered the church
one day when confessions were being heard, and, observing one of the confessionals surrounded by a large
number of penitents, she concluded that he who had
attracted the confidence of so many must be a true
friend of poor sinners. Accordingly she awaited her
turn among the rest. Now it was the Servite priest, P.
Angelo himself, who was sitting in that confessional.
His eye singled her out among the clustering crowd,
for he had not forgotten the woman whom he had seen
on the Piazza of St. Peter's, and no sooner had she
knelt down than at once, and before she began to speak,
he said, in a voice of paternal kindness, ‘Ah, you are
come at last, soul dear to Heaven! Courage, my daughter! The Lord loves you, and desires to have you all
for Himself.’ These words and the tone in which they

were pronounced were balm to poor Anna Maria's wounded spirit. Still she hesitated at first to appropriate them to herself; for she thought he might have mistaken her for one of his own penitents. P. Angelo hastened to reassure her, telling her that she was not unknown to him, and acquainting her with the intimation which he had received and which he believed had come from Heaven. Then Anna Maria unfolded to him all the secrets of her conscience and the whole story of her past life. What passed in the confessional on that memorable day, which sealed the conversion of this favoured soul, we know not, but its results are known. Anna Maria left the feet of P. Angelo with joy and peace in her bosom and calm serenity on her brow. From this day dates her entrance on the pursuit of perfection,—on that heavenward path from which she was never to swerve, and on which she was to advance without ever casting one look behind at the world which she had renounced.

CHAPTER III.

ANNA MARIA'S LIFE OF SELF-SACRIFICE AND MORTIFICATION.

CONVERSION, as we know, may be understood either of the turning of the soul from the broad way of sinners to the road of salvation, or of the embracing a more perfect way of life. The life of every Christian, if he would keep himself in a state of grace, must be a life involving some occasional sacrifice, be it small or great. For, the very lowest degree of grace being incompatible with a grave offence against God, involving the guilt of mortal sin, the Christian who finds himself in an occasion of temptation to such offence must of necessity sacrifice his natural inclination or fall from grace. The same applies to his obedience to the precepts of the Church—such, for instance, as enjoin abstinence, fasting, and the like—which are, or may be, more or less repugnant to nature, and the observance of which consequently demands some degree of self-sacrifice. Yet the life of Christians generally—ascending from the lowest stage of worldliness and tepidity compatible with the existence of sanctifying grace in the soul, up to the higher ranks of the ordinarily pious, who aspire to something more excellent and really desire to please God, yet are by no means minded to break altogether with the world or to enter on a relentless conflict with self in every form—cannot surely be called a life of sacrifice. Who could give it such a name? The life of even good and pious Christians is often, indeed, one of very much comfort, in which a mild self-indulgence, which escapes notice because of the moderate and, seemingly, reasonable claims to which it restricts itself, has far more part than sacrifice. These pious Christians cannot at any rate be said to have a very hard life; they can scarcely be numbered among the soldiers of Christ who endure hardness; they may rather be compared to those who stay by the baggage, who may possibly have to fight, and hope that they are prepared for such a contingency, but whose ordinary service, as a matter of fact, is not very trying to flesh and blood. The life of the perfect, or of one who ardently aspires after perfection, is, however, an abiding life of sacrifice, realising fully the injunction given by St. Remigius to the first Christian king of France, when he bade him cast away his idols, if he would be converted and receive the grace of baptism. 'Burn,' he said to Clovis, 'what thou hast adored, and adore what thou hast burned.'

Anna Maria's conversion was of this character. True, she was not emerging from paganism, like Clovis, nor was she rising from the depths of sin and moral degradation, like Magdalen; it was rather that, like Ignatius Loyola, and so many other glorious saints of whose conversions we have read, she was escaping from that worldly region whose atmosphere is laden with pride, with the love of pleasure, with ambition, and with all those passions which, freely indulged, destroy souls, and the very inhaling of which is deleterious to the life of grace. Like them, she had foresworn neither the faith nor the love of virtue, but she had been every day offering her little grain of incense to those divinities which the world worships, frivolous vanity and idle dissipation. The fervent convert now burned these idols and cast their ashes to the winds. She broke completely with the past, in order to begin a life of terrible vengeance upon herself for the faults of her youth. Grace had poured a flood of light into her conscience, and in its bright effulgence she had discerned the ruins which sin had made in heart and mind; and so, without delay, she commenced a ruthless war against self in every form. She took the scourge in her hand to drive out everything that desecrated the temple of God within her; and, as sin enters first by the door of the senses, it was on them she made her first attack. On returning home after her confession, she seized the opportunity of finding herself alone to prostrate herself before the Crucifix and inflict on herself a cruel flagellation. Not content with this, she struck her head repeatedly against the floor, exclaim-

ing, ' Satisfy to God, impure head, for so many frivolous ornaments with which you have dared to lade
yourself.' This act of penance she renewed on several
occasions, and more than once with such violence as to
cause the blood to gush from her mouth. P. Angelo,
however, forbade her to continue this practice, enjoining her to restrain her mortifications within the bounds
of discretion. Yet the fervour which had prompted
these indiscreet excesses was very pleasing to God, as
was proved by the extraordinary supernatural graces
which she received on the very threshold of her conversion, and in particular by one which may be considered as unparalleled in the annals of the saints, the
appearance of a luminous disc resembling a sun, in which
she contemplated, as in a mirror, the past, present, and
future, and which she was to behold without intermis-
sion for the remaining forty-seven years of her life.
She also received shortly afterwards, during a vision in
which our Lord appeared to her, the gift of healing by
the touch of her hand ; she was endowed, moreover,
with the power of reading the secret thoughts of others
and of discerning their spiritual state ; she had continual divine locutions, and exhibited in her person all
those phenomena of raptures and ecstasies which so
frequently attend the contemplations of advanced saints,
but are rarely to be met with in persons who have but
just entered on the road of perfection.

If, however, the life of all who aspire to perfection
is a life of sacrifice, a life animated throughout, and
distinguished more particularly in its outset, by a strong
spirit of penance, it was peculiarly so in the case of
Anna Maria, who was of the number of those souls
specially called to offer themselves to God as victims
of expiation. She was deeply conscious from the first

that it was to the life of a victim thus offering itself as
a holocaust that she was invited and urged ; and so
she told her confessor immediately after her conversion.
Accordingly, we shall find the spirit of sacrifice giving
its colouring to the work of grace within her soul during her whole life, and imparting its peculiar character
to her sanctity. The Holy Spirit is wont to communicate to a soul which turns fervently towards God a
secret intimation of its particular attraction. This first
grace is usually the foundation of all the future destinies
of the soul, the seed, so to say, of all future graces.
Divine Wisdom has unerringly chosen for it the path
and the mould in which it is to sanctify itself ; and
the chief office of a director is to ascertain this attraction, in order to encourage his penitent to be faithful
to it and to help to remove all obstacles out of the way
which might impede the operation of the Heavenly
Director. For God has His particular aim and design,
and after that pattern He will perfect the soul, and
after no other. If it choose to follow its own devices,
it will lose its way, and will be cast aside, at least as
respects perfection. Hence the incalculable importance
of fidelity to our particular grace.

Anna Maria's first act was, with her husband's consent, to put away all her vain ornaments, and to dress
herself in common and coarse clothing. In his deposition Domenico thus speaks of this change :—' About
a year after our marriage, the servant of God, being
still in the flower of her youth, quitted for the love of
God all the ornaments she had worn: the rings, the
earrings, necklaces, &c., and adopted the most ordinary
dress she could. She asked my permission, and I willingly granted it, seeing that she was wholly given up
to piety.' He also allowed her to become a Tertiary of

the Trinitarians, and she wore their habit under her other clothes; but of her affiliation to this Order we shall speak hereafter. Along with worldly habiliments, worldly amusements, visits, and even walks of simple recreation were also entirely given up. These last, however, she rather avoided, when she could, on the plea of family and household work or the fatigue occasioned thereby, than absolutely refused; and she was induced subsequently to relax somewhat on this point out of complaisance for her husband and children.

The promptitude and generosity with which Anna Maria responded to the call of God is one of the most striking features in her conversion. She understood from the first the greatness of the gift offered to her: '*Si scires donum Dei*,' said the Saviour to the woman of Samaria, and how few indeed know the extent or greatness of the gift offered to them! we do not mean only the value of the gift which we all receive in our redemption and regeneration in Christ, but that particular gift which God has reserved for each of us, and which He does not fail secretly to proffer to the soul, wooing it thereby to that conformity with His Son for which He has predestined it. Although this gift is not in each case equally great, yet, as proportioned to the capacity of the individual soul, it is ever great and magnificent, like all the gifts of God. He gives liberally and abundantly to all, as St. James[*] tells us; and, if in many cases it seem otherwise, it is not because He is wanting in liberality, but because souls do not deal liberally with Him: they are grudging, niggardly, mistrustful, incredulous, and fail to recognise 'the day of their visitation.' They are not 'straitened' in God, but in their 'own bowels,' as the Apostle[†] up-

[*] i. 5.   [†] 2 Cor. vi. 12.

braided the Corinthians with being. Hence it is that
many Christians take more pains to resist God's grace
than would be sufficient to yield most blessed results,
if bestowed in the right direction. Not that they seem
to themselves to be acting thus—far from it; they are
striving perhaps hard enough to do something, but it is
not what God would have them do; they are striving
to sanctify themselves according to their own notions
and their own tastes. And so the gift of God is
wasted on them, and sooner or later the offer is withdrawn; while of those who accept their gift, too many
do so only after long hesitations or, what is still worse,
never fully and unreservedly. But Anna Maria accepted the Divine offer at once and with a magnanimous spirit; and God was liberal to her beyond all
imagination, as will abundantly appear when we come
to speak of her supernatural gifts.

We have already seen how, after her confession to
P. Angelo, she returned strong in the grace she had received that day in the sacrament of penance, and began
to make instant war upon nature by a severe flagellation and other self-inflictions, which the prudent confessor thought good to retrench. He allowed her,
however, the use of the discipline, hair-shirt, and iron
chain. After the sacrifice of her ornaments, she proceeded to the curtailment of all that could minister
gratification to the taste, and restricted herself simply
to what was necessary for the support of life. To the
fasts prescribed by the Church she added from devotion
others of her own choice; and what fasts were hers!
'I observed,' says her husband in his deposition, 'that
she mortified herself in the matter of food more on
Fridays than on other days—she, who habitually ate
no more than a grasshopper. She did the same on

Saturdays, in honour of the Madonna.' In short, days
of simple abstinence were by her converted into days
of rigid fasting. She often undertook, besides, extraordinary fasts of forty days' duration, or longer; sometimes in order to obtain some grace which regarded the
public benefit, or again for the conversion of some particular person, or for the relief of the suffering souls in
Purgatory. All she took at such times was a little
soup at midday.

Her ordinary practice, when not fasting, was, after
returning from church in the morning, to drink a small
cup of coffee, to which she would add a little bread,
although the latter was often omitted. At dinner a
few spoonfuls of soup and a mere scrap of *bouilli* sufficed her. Towards the close of her life, following a
divine intimation, she entirely abstained from flesh-
meat. As she always stood during meal-time, waiting
from humility on the others, she was able to evade
notice as to what she ate, or, rather, did not eat. She
had thus the opportunity of practising many little
mortifications to the palate without attracting notice :
for instance, in flavouring the soup with cheese, as is
done in Italy, she would remember to forget—if we
may use such an expression—her own portion, and so
would take it unseasoned. In the evening, when the
work of the day was over—and it must be borne in
mind that it is question here of the habitual sustenance
of a woman whose life was one of constant toil—her
supper consisted of a little salad or, at most, a slender
portion out of a dish of small fish, such as the Roman
poor are in the habit of buying, when there happened
to be any on the frugal board ; and even from this
scanty allowance she would subtract something for
the poor. She always reserved for herself what was

worst, placing the best before her husband and children, or giving it to the girls who helped her in her work, and, for a still greater mortification, would often eat what was no longer fresh. This practice was afterwards noticed by her children ; indeed, it is chiefly to the testimony of her surviving husband and daughter, given on oath, that we are indebted for these particulars, which she would herself have been the last to publish. ' My mother,' said one of her daughters, ' used to keep for herself some bits of meat, which she would eat after the lapse of two or three days, in spite of all we said to her, telling her that this meat was spoilt, for it smelt, and had begun to corrupt.' Another eyewitness adds, ' I have seen her take a piece of cod fish which was turned bad, and chew it along with the bones, giving it afterwards to the animals when she had conquered the repugnance of nature.'

And these repugnances were strong in her, as is common in the case of lively, ardent, and sensitive temperaments, whose likings and dislikings are vivid in conformity with their physical constitution. Indeed, before her conversion, Anna Maria showed a marked taste for delicacies, and particularly for sweet things. Domenico, who waited at table in the Chigi family, was often allowed to have a remnant of pastry, or other tempting viand, after the dinner was over ; and, knowing that she was partial to these good things, he used to take some home to his wife, who partook of them with pleasure, their own means not allowing them to indulge in what are generically styled ' treats.' But one who enters on a path of vigorous mortification, such as that which Anna Maria had embraced, has put away ' treats' for ever. Domenico did not in the least understand so radical a change, and continued, when he had the opportunity, to cater for his wife's predilections as before. Anna Maria had no difficulty in receiving with a smile what was thus laid before her, and in thanking her husband affectionately for his recollection of her. Moreover, to satisfy him, she would taste a morsel, just enough, in fact, to tempt her own dormant appetite, that she might the more effectually mortify it by refusing it further gratification, while avoiding at the same time the infliction of any disappointment on Domenico. She would then begin talking of something else, with the view of turning away his attention, and leave the pastry where it was on the table, as if intending to return and finish it; but later, when the circumstance was forgotten, she would take and give it to some one else in the house.

Anna Maria was by temperament extremely subject to thirst, which hard work and the fervour of an Italian summer would aggravate to intensity; nevertheless, in order to mortify herself, she was in the habit of never drinking save at meals, and then with extreme moderation. Even the little she took she would merely sip, never allowing herself the sort of draught which alone satisfies when, not only the mouth is parched, but the whole system languishes from thirst, and its satisfaction is felt to be a craving of necessity rather than the desire for an indulgence. After drinking a drop or two, she would put down her glass and return to waiting on her husband and children. But often and often she would not allow herself even a single drop during the meal. Children have sharp eyes and keen observation, and little Maria would sometimes spy her out and betray her. 'Papa,' she would say, 'see, Mama has never drunk anything;' while her mother hastened to silence the child by reminding her that she ought not to make remarks upon what other people did. When her husband poured out some wine for her she would accept it cheerfully, but took care to mix with it a good deal of water, saying that this made it much more wholesome. Sometimes Domenico would detect her in the act of putting down her glass after first raising it to her lips, and reprehend her for this conduct. 'What are you doing there,' he would say, ' playing with your glass? why don't you drink? Drink at once;' and then with a smile she would obey him.

In the great heats of summer, he would occasionally bring his wife some sherbet or ice to refresh her. These things had been once very acceptable to her, nor would she absolutely refuse them now. Ever grateful to all who showed her kindness, she failed not to thank her husband for any token of affection, but she was also ingenious in devices to avoid profiting by it. Thus, raising the ice to her lips, she would hastily cry out, ' O, how cold it is !' and put it down again. Domenico, to whom the allowing ice to melt in order to render it palatable seemed sheer folly, would shrug his shoulders and, in his rough, coarse way—for with all his good qualities he *was* rough and coarse, and had by no means a good temper—would exclaim, ' What an idiot you are ! You understand nothing about anything.' Probably, as time went on, her husband ceased to interfere with her mode of life in this respect, for P. Filippo di San Nicola, a Carmelite Father, who was her confessor for thirty years, and who made his deposition a year and a half after her death, states that he had known her pass whole weeks without drinking.

Such, then, were Anna Maria's stratagems for subduing nature in respect both of quantity and quality of food. She used to say, ' He who desires to love God must mortify himself at all times and in all things, but chiefly in eating and drinking, because the indulgence of sensuality in this matter was the beginning of all our ills in the garden of delights.' Another of her remarks was, ' The more greedy the ass is'—by the ass she meant the body—' the more needful is it to draw the rein tight.' She used to urge strongly on her children, and on persons who asked her advice, the practice of taking nothing out of meal-times. This was a piece of self-indulgence which she sternly resisted in her own case ; and, trifling as such sacrifices may sound —albeit, implying as they do a daily habit, they demand in many cases a greater amount of self-denial than may at first sight appear— her Divine Spouse deigned to give her special praise for this very act of mortification. He told her that although this denial of the appetite may seem to be nothing, yet God is much pleased with it, and that whosoever would enjoy the sweetness of divine communications and tranquillity of mind must of necessity mortify his palate ; whereas he who satisfies his gluttony renews on his part, so far as in him lies, the bitterness of the Saviour's Passion, who, amongst the other sufferings and insults which He endured from the impious, had to receive their horrible spittle in His divine mouth.

Anna Maria's mortification extended to all her other senses. She guarded her eyes so closely that, as Domenico afterwards testified, notwithstanding her natural vivacity, she never looked in the face of any man save his, her husband's. The strictest modesty presided over her every gesture, whether she were engaged in the common cares of her house or, as in after years was frequently the case, lying on a bed of torturing pain. ' In the midst of her roughest household work,' he said, 'she was dressed as modestly as if she were going to appear in public. In her sufferings she maintained such reserve and circumspection that she seemed like a Religious.' And another deponent said, 'She always kept her eyes modestly cast down, yet without affectation, when conversing with men; one might have imagined that one was talking to a young girl, not to a married woman.' All this was the fruit of that mortification which guarded every avenue of the senses. Over her tongue she exercised the same control. Not only did she not utter one word which could injure the reputation of any one, but she would not suffer in her presence any depreciating remarks. Many a time did she warn her children to correct themselves of the fault of criticising this and that person, although they might do it from pure thoughtlessness, without any tincture of malice, or even from an impulse of zeal, or other apparently worthy motive, or with the view of seeking advice. For she knew well how many are the deceits which nature practises that it may escape from bondage; and no member is so difficult to tame as the tongue.

Not content with thus keeping all her senses in continual subjection, she did not even allow herself the amount of rest which seemed absolutely necessary to enable her to accomplish her various duties. She considered her body to be a rebellious slave, who will submit to the dominion of the soul only so long as it feels the weight of its chains, and so she tasked its strength to the utmost, by night as well as by day. 'My mother,' says one of her daughters, 'scarcely slept at all; she had the habit of staying up to pray, and, as my father used not to come home until the night was far advanced, not perhaps till two or three o'clock in the morning, as soon as my mother heard him coming

D

she would get into bed to avoid being scolded, as she
would have been had he found her still up.' Domenico, however, in fact not unfrequently surprised
her, for in his deposition he says that often, when returning from his service at the Chigi palace towards
three o'clock in the morning, he would find his wife
still praying before the Madonna.   If she was late up
she was also on foot early; for another of her daughters
testified that her mother generally rose before dawn
to go to church, and that she habitually slept no more
than two hours.   Neither did she make up for this deficiency of repose at night by the daily *siesta* which is
commonly taken by people of all classes in southern
countries; for all the witnesses unite in saying that,
while the rest of the family were sleeping after the
mid-day repast, the servant of God used to profit by
this quiet opportunity to read and meditate.   To all
these privations we must add the many austerities which
she practised secretly; the disciplines, the hair-shirts,
iron chains, and other instruments of penance, by means
of which she contrived to give her body no more respite
from suffering than she allowed it from fatigue.

It may, indeed, seem matter for wonder whence she
derived the energy of soul, not to say the physical
strength, to maintain so ceaseless and pitiless a combat
with nature.   How was it possible that she should not
have broken down under so heavy a burden?   There is
but one reply.   Strength is from the Lord, strength of
soul as well as strength of body.   The former she was
daily renewing by intimate converse with God; her
whole soul, open to receive divine impressions, was perpetually imbibing the superhuman force which sustained
her in her holy purposes; while the latter was minis-
tered to her in like manner by Him who had inspired

those purposes. God who gives us to will, gives us also to do when He so pleases. It was not her mere assiduity in prayer, however, which was the source of her strength and perseverance ; it was the purity of intention and perfect interior mortification with which she drew nigh to God which caused the rays of divine grace to penetrate with such warmth and power. There was no mist between her soul and the sun of grace, for she had exercised the same vigilant repression over her interior as over her exterior senses. She watched her imagination to check its wanderings, her will to hinder it from accepting any hurtful satisfaction or indulging in any complacency, her native impetuosity and heat of temper to tame it down to meekness and gentleness, her heart that it might never take delight in the love of creatures, or that, at least, it might love them in God and for God alone.

This inward conflict is not so striking to the observer, and at first sight does not seem so cruel as the exterior mortification. So we are apt to judge, never perhaps having tried either to any great extent; but saints, and spiritual writers who have gathered up the experience of saints, tell us that it is far otherwise. For in the one case the soul is fighting with the body, and undoubtedly the soul is the strongest, and may even yield a little sometimes without undergoing defeat; in the other, it is fighting with itself, and has itself for its enemy. To keep up this struggle, which admits of no truce if we would come off victorious, requires an unrelaxing energy, from which few there are who do not recoil. Yet even the thorough mortification of the exterior senses cannot be achieved without a corresponding subduing of the interior. This double mortification, when effected, which it can only be with divine charity for its motive and accompaniment, is a most sure means of drawing down the choicest gifts from above ; for it is a perfect holocaust of self, and may be compared to that of Elias, which, when laid on the altar of God, was so acceptable that the fire from Heaven descended to consume it.

Anna Maria had well understood the price required for the purchase of perfect love, and she had, as we learn from the processes, made a formal pact with her will never to permit herself any gratification of the senses, or to take any complacency, not merely in what was forbidden or simply dangerous, but in what was allowable and even innocent. She adhered to her resolution, and had her mind continually applied to resisting her inclinations. 'To acquire the love of God,' she said, 'we must always be rowing against the current, and never cease counteracting our own will.' By constantly following this rule herself, she had not only got the mastery over all her passions, inclinations, tastes, fears, repugnances, but had arrived at supernaturalising every interior movement of her soul. How rare is such a victory over self we need scarcely say, nor how arduous to obtain. To offer our external actions to God is nothing to this; although any one who practises a little inward scrutiny will confess that even into actions thus consecrated human motives are very prone to insinuate themselves, or, if not human motives, at any rate the human spirit. How many actions done *for* God can scarcely be said to be done *in* God; but, if the purification of our intention in separate external acts be a difficult undertaking, how much more the consecration of the secret interior acts and movements of the different faculties of the soul! If we doubt this, we have only, on any given occasion when we have not been engaged in some direct act of devotion, to recall what have been the springs of our thoughts and feelings for the last half hour or so, and to consider how much of all that has passed within us, harmless or even good in a way as it may have been, can be referred to supernatural motives or regarded as the response to supernatural promptings. Again, how often shall we be conscious of having been 'rowing against the current'? Drifting with the stream would be a much better description of our habitual condition when not engaged in active reflection; and well it is with us if we so much as keep a look-out for rocks and shoals a-head.

Anna Maria maintained a very strict and special watch over all her natural sympathies and attractions. Every one is sensible of being often more or less the subject of drawings towards particular individuals, drawings for which we cannot always fully account, for they seem by no means precisely proportioned to respective merits or even personal advantages. Such sympathies are part of our nature, as God has made it; they are therefore in themselves quite blameless; but it is scarcely necessary to say that she who was so jealous to preserve her whole heart for God never either yielded to or favoured any such mere growth of the natural heart. Even when these sympathies had for their sole spring the glory of God, and drew her towards those who were actuated by the same pure motive, she moderated the satisfaction she experienced by practising much reserve; on the contrary, if it was question of persons towards whom she felt some natural antipathy, or who had censured or offended her, she behaved with great cordiality and affection of manner; always, however, keeping within the limits

of that prudence, moderation, and modesty which regulated her whole bearing. But more than all this:
Anna Maria knew how to mortify herself even in
spiritual things, and when, after receiving Communion,
her soul was plunged in an ocean of delight, from that
overflowing sensible sweetness of which in the first
years of her conversion God was so liberal to her, she
would, after making her thanksgiving, refuse herself
the joy of remaining longer at her devotions and break
off, in order to disappoint nature of its satisfaction.
If, on the other hand, dryness, weariness, and repugnances assailed her, then, in order to conquer herself,
she would prolong her prayer and, with it, her sufferings ; and God rewarded this heroic generosity of His
servant by a continual increase of the gifts and graces
which He lavished upon her.

It must not be supposed that in what we have said
of the mortifications practised by this holy woman we
have exhausted the subject. Far. from it ; her life was,
in fact, so peculiarly a life of self-immolation, that
every act, exterior and interior, was imbued, so to say,
with the spirit of mortification and sacrifice even to
the last hour of her existence. What we have here
stated may serve, however, as an introductory prelude,
striking the key-note of all that follows in the detail of
her spiritual course.

CHAPTER IV.

ANNA MARIA'S BEHAVIOUR AS A WIFE.

HAD Anna Maria been free from the ties of marriage, there can be little doubt but that her attraction would have led her to the religious life. What her vocation would have been it would be idle to inquire, for vocation is not a matter of our own taste nor even of our attraction; the attraction being not unfrequently sent where the vocation (which is God's call) does not exist. For vocation is not even fitness (as we understand the word), with which it is often confounded in common parlance. It is God's call—no more, and no less. To ask, then, what Anna Maria's vocation would have been, had she not been bound by her marriage, is to ask what it would have been if it had been other than it was. For her union with Domenico Taigi bore all the marks of being designed for her by Divine Providence. It was entered into after prayer and with an entire reference to God's will, and she had never, at the time she contracted it, been inwardly moved or drawn to embrace a higher state. God, in fine, we may well believe, purposed to set before the world in this chosen soul an example of the highest degree of sanctity, not only in the married state—such examples had already been given in all ages of the Church—but amidst what would be generally regarded as the vulgarest cares and the homeliest surroundings.

'It is sufficient' (says P. Bouffier, one of Anna Maria's biographers) ' to read the decree of the Roman Congregation to feel convinced that this mission was special and altogether providential. God willed to use Anna Maria Taigi as an instrument for displaying His wisdom and power in our days and giving to our age a great and solemn lesson.' This age of ours is remarkable for the arrogant self-complacency with which it regards and boasts of its wisdom, science, and progress; 'and behold' (says the same writer), 'God, to confound these proud worshippers of reason and progress, chooses that which is lowest and meanest; He takes by the hand an obscure woman, the wife of a man of toil; and upon one in this lowest stage of the social scale, in this abject and despised condition, as the world esteems it, He showers down His favours with an abundance, a liberality, a prodigality, which fills with wonder even those who are best skilled in penetrating the secrets of God's dealings; and because this poor and unknown woman was faithful to the voice which called her, God replenishes her with His gifts, loads her with His favours, inundates her with His lights, and accords her privileges so extraordinary as to stupefy with astonishment all who are cognisant of them.' For Anna Maria was not only a miracle of sanctity, she was also a miracle of heavenly illumination; she was privileged to read, as it were, in the mirror of the Eternal Wisdom, and thence to derive a knowledge and an insight into things of earth as well as of heaven which puts to shame all the boasted science of the world. She became in the hands of God, 'the soul of her country and of her time;' she was constituted and offered herself as a 'victim of expiation;' she was at once 'the rampart of the Holy See, the oblation of sinners, the consolation of the afflicted, the succour of the poor, the guide of the learned, and the counsellor of priests; she was a theologian, a doctor and mother in Israel, a seer of the ancient days, an inspired prophet, a true wonder-worker!' Such are the enthusiastic terms in which one of her biographers speaks of her, nor will they seem exaggerated to those who are conversant with her life.

Yet, notwithstanding all her exalted gifts, it must be remembered that her state of life in the Christian order was not exalted. It was the married state, which, although honourable, has neither the dignity of the virgin state nor that of the religious by profession, which latter she never had the opportunity of embracing, her husband being destined to survive her. Her position, then, was always that of a wife and a mother, and never rose above it. Now the duties of our state in life, however humble it may be, take the precedence of all others; and we need scarcely observe that had Anna Maria failed ever so little in these duties, or had Domenico and her other relatives and friends who gave their testimony on oath intimated any deficiency on her part in the performance of them, the process for her beatification would have been closed at once. In vain might she have gazed at the 'sun of divine wisdom' for seven-and-forty years, in vain might her hand have had the gift of healing, and her tongue have uttered prophecies, she never could have received the title of Venerable nor have laid any claim to the honours of sanctity. For gifts such as these, which are called by theologians *gratis data*, considered apart from the use made of them by the recipient, do not add to his merit. They are bestowed for the benefit of others, and might even be conferred on one who was not in a state of grace.* Caiphas prophesied; so did

---

* The gifts 'gratis data' are thus defined by St. Thomas: 'Gratia gratis data ordinatur ad hoc, quod homo alteri cooperetur ut reducatur ad Deum.' And elsewhere he says: 'Quia non datur ad hoc, ut homo ipse per eam justificetur, sed potius

Balaam; and even his ass saw a vision and was gifted
with speech to declare it. True, God does not ordinarily impart these gifts save to persons high in His
favour, certainly not in any permanent way; yet, since,
abstractedly speaking, they are not incompatible with
the absence of sanctifying grace, it is evident that they
do not in themselves increase the merit of those who
enjoy them, or necessarily argue their possession of great
sanctity.

Before proceeding, then, to sublimer subjects, we
shall consider Anna Maria in her humble sphere of
wife and mother of a family and in the perfect fulfilment of the duties which that sphere entails. Among
the twenty-one witnesses who had been personally acquainted with the servant of God, and who gave their
testimony as recorded in the processes, the surviving
members of her own family hold an important position.
Domenico Taigi, then ninety-one years of age, was of
the number, as were two of the daughters, Sofia and
Maria, a daughter-in-law, and a grand-daughter. Domenico's evidence is peculiarly interesting, on account
of his simplicity and evident sincerity, as also on account of the precious details of her domestic virtues
which he alone would have been so fully competent to
give, and to which, in fact, he rendered such signal
testimony. It is remarkable that this good man, im-
pressed as he was with the eminent perfection exhibited
by his wife, never apprehended, till she was dead, that
she was a saint in the technical sense of that appella-

---

ut ad justificationem alterius cooperetur.' L. 2, Qu. cxi.
Art. 1, 4. So also St. Bonaventura: 'Nota, quod gratia gratis
data communiter a theologis dicitur gratia, quæ bonis et malis
potest esse communis, et plurificatur in homine secundum mu-
nificentiam largitoris.' (Centiloq. P. iii. s. 35.)

tion. A veil was upon his eyes as long as she lived.
It may help us to realise the possibility of such blindness on his part if we consider the nature of the man,
and compare it with that of his wife. He was (as has
been said) rough, coarse, dull, and ordinary in every
sense of the term. She was delicate, thoughtful, refined,
sensitive. Viewed both intellectually and morally, and
without reference to her exalted sanctity, she was therefore immeasurably his superior. When two persons
thus unequally matched live in close companionship,
the superior mind will take the measure of the inferior,
but the inferior will see only a certain proportion of the
superior. He will not know as he is known. Much
soars above his ken, much lies far beneath the reach of
his perceptions. If this be true of natural gifts, much
more is it the case in regard to spiritual endowments.
Domenico, while quite competent to read the virtuous
and admirable results of holiness exhibited in his companion's conduct, was unable to appreciate the full
merit or character of very many of her actions. Neither
his intellectual nor his spiritual senses were sufficiently
alive for this purpose. He had a glimpse, and little
more than a glimpse, of the fact that she possessed certain supernatural gifts. She herself never spoke on
these subjects to him, she never told him of the mysterious sun which she continually beheld, and, when
occasionally, in spite of herself, she fell into an ecstasy
in his presence, so obtuse were the perceptions of this
worthy man, as we shall find, that he attributed these
seizures to drowsiness or some other bodily affection.
As for her instruments of penance, they were not found
till after her death.

But if there were reasons peculiarly applicable to
Domenico why he should have failed to perceive that

his wife was a saint, we may add, as a general remark, that sanctity tends in its more perfect developments to simplicity. From the first it aims at this virtue, or, rather, at this harmony and blending of the virtues, which results from the dueness of their proportion, and is the special fruit of humility and singlenesss of purpose. But simplicity, from the very unassumingness of its outward form, has a sort of resemblance to what we call the commonplace. Speaking of St. Philip Neri, Father Faber describes the effect which he might have produced upon a foreigner who, hearing of his eminent holiness, had gone to see him : he might have only carried away the impression that he was undoubtedly a very good man, but a man rather to love than revere —kind-hearted, zealous, and a little eccentric, but otherwise commonplace enough. ' Yet,' he says, ' it was the very wonderfulness of his sanctity which caused him to look so commonplace ;' and then he subjoins this startling observation : ' Should we know a saint if we met one ? I doubt it. This is sad to think, but very profitable.'*

An inequality in mental powers and cultivation, such as we have described between Anna Maria and her husband, would alone have proved a considerable trial in married life, but Domenico moreover had a temper very difficult to deal with : he was extremely prone to being what is vulgarly called ' put out ' for very slight causes, and, when he was in this humour, would show it in some such unpleasant fashion as we might expect in a clownish peasant. Besides being irritable, he was also obstinately wedded to his own views and ideas. When once he had taken up some notion it stuck to him like his skin. Argument would

* *Notes on Doctrinal and Spiritual Subjects*, vol. i. p. 387.

have been wasted upon him; indeed, the least objection would throw him into a passion, and contradiction, if persevered in, made him quite intractable. But his wife neither argued with him nor contradicted him. She met his exacting temper and ungracious behaviour with an unvarying and unalterable patience. She always yielded, and when he was angry she was silent. But her silence was far from being of that offensive kind which is sometimes more irritating than a sharp reply, betraying as it does, under the affectation of self-restraint and humility, a certain latent sense of superiority and a covert reproach. Anna Maria's silence was sweet and soothing. When her husband exhibited these tempers her countenance would wear an open and frank expression of cordiality; there would be an eloquent pleading in her looks, which gave no offence because it conveyed no censorious meaning, and betrayed only the desire to win back a smile to his lips. And in this she was usually successful. Domenico, in the absence of opposition, would cool down and regain his equanimity, and then the fear of having distressed his companion, always so good and gentle to him, would make him feel a little remorseful and ashamed of himself; for Domenico, it must be said, had by no means a bad heart. On such occasions, when he had been finding fault with something unjustly, he would say, 'Well, at any rate, do as you wish; as for me, I understand nothing about the matter.' Anna Maria, with exquisite tact, would now take care not to show any consciousness that he had been defeated and had yielded, but in her most caressing voice would say, 'As for me, I should do so and so; what do you think? are you satisfied?' And then Domenico *was* satisfied, and sunshine was restored to the happy home.

Nor was Domenico insensible to this gentle bearing of his wife. By his own confession it had a favourable influence on his temper. 'I often,' he said, 'came home tired, out of spirits and out of humour; she. had the talent of pacifying me by her affability. In short, she knew very well how to be silent and, better still, how to speak when necessary.' And again, 'She knew how to give a charitable warning, and I owe to her the having corrected myself of some faults; she gave this advice with an incomparable sweetness and charity.' She also knew well how to accommodate her tastes to his, and with the best grace, however different they might be. Nothing was dearer to Anna Maria than her religious exercises; nevertheless, if her husband desired the most trifling service at her hands, or wished her to accompany him anywhere, she would immediately leave her devotions. 'My wife was averse to all worldly pleasures,' he says, 'even such as were most allowable. I would sometimes say to her, "Marianna, let us go to such or such a place." She never evinced any disinclination, but acceded to my wishes with a sweet cheerfulness: as, for example, if I wanted to go and see the Fantocini, or some other diversion of the kind. For the love of God,' he also says, 'she often refrained from drinking; but if I said, "Marianna, drink," or, "You have drunk nothing," she would smile, and obey me immediately. I always found her as docile and submissive as a lamb.'

But Anna Maria not only rendered the most exact obedience to her husband in all things, but cordially and sincerely looked up to him as a superior, nay, as an angel-guardian whom God had chosen for her. He was her head, and the head of the family, and, as such, merited interior honour as well as outward respect; and

thus her submission was not a mere dry act of duty, but
the expression of a genuine feeling of reverence. This
it was which imparted to her behaviour the captivating
charm which, rude and uncultivated as he was, had so
powerful an effect upon him. This is clearly apparent
from a few simple and unstudied remarks which occur
in his deposition. It must be observed that Anna
Maria's humble dwelling was constantly crowded with
persons of distinction, both ecclesiastical and lay. It
will, no doubt, seem strange that such should be the
case; but so it was. Her eminent sanctity, her heroic
charity to the sick and suffering, the ecstatic state into
which she so continually passed in different churches,
and, above all, the graces received by those who had
recourse to her intercession and the blessings that ever
attended on the following of her counsels, which were
evidently drawn from some supernatural source—all
these circumstances and other wonders connected with
her had soon begun to attract attention to her in Rome.
She laboured (as we shall find) to remain concealed,
but it was not God's will that she should be hidden.
Obscure, indeed, as respected her state He designed her
to remain till death, but it belonged to the nature of
the mission for which He had chosen her that the great,
the rich, the powerful, the learned should crowd around
her and pay homage to His sublime gifts in her, which
they of her own household, and even her husband himself (as we have seen), scarcely noted. What Domenico, however, did note, and what he was called in
a special manner to record, were her homely, domestic
virtues, and, in particular, her behaviour as a wife. Ex-
emplary as this might have been, it would have wanted
its crowning merit had it been lacking in that cordial
reverence of which we have been speaking, and which

St. Paul so emphatically enjoins* on wives. Domenico felt and knew that he was the object of this reverence. He knew that he was first with her on all occasions. No pre-occupation, not the presence of persons
highest in rank and consideration, could for a moment
cause him to be put by, so to say, or momentarily
neglected. 'It happened to me frequently,' he said,
' when coming home to change my clothes, that I found
the house full; immediately, she would leave everybody,
whatever lord or prelate might be there, and hasten to
me with the greatest cheerfulness and pleasure, that she
might wipe my things and wait upon me, even to the
tying of my shoe-strings. In short, she was my consolation, and that of all the world.'

It is quite affecting, we think, to find this good man
recording these little incidents after the lapse of so
many years. Truly nothing so much contributes to
preserve the freshness of all love as cordial reverence,
but most especially in married life. Many a wife loves
as devotedly as ever, and would not think of disobey-
ing her husband's expressed wishes, but she has ceased
to make him the object of the delicate respect which
the human heart so intensely appreciates, and which
she at first instinctively paid him in return for his preference of her. He feels the change, without perhaps
reflecting on it, and it changes *him* also in his turn.
Assuredly Anna Maria was actuated by motives far
higher than that of merely preserving in her husband's
heart the tenderness of his early affection—fraught as
such preservation is with blessings both to husband
and wife as well as to the family surrounding them—for
with her all the sweet charities of life were imbedded,
as it were, in a wider, deeper, and more comprehensive

* Eph. v. 33.

charity, which included within it all other motives, without extinguishing them, but also without partaking of their imperfections. Respect, then, is the flower, the sweetness, and the guardian of love; and it, moreover, generally obtains from the person who is its object a corresponding and, in some measure at least, a proportional return of respect. Domenico, it is plain, thoroughly respected his wife, not merely when she had become enshrined in memory and invested with the glory which her sanctity cast upon it, but while she was yet upon earth and they were associated in the daily familiarity of common life—that familiarity which proverbially 'breeds contempt,' because it so often reveals littlenesses and lowering imperfections, and still more perhaps because we are so apt to treat each other as common things. If Domenico did not at the time manifest much deference for his wife in his words, he plainly showed his essential esteem of her by his acts. 'The heart of her husband trusteth in her, and he shall have no need of spoils,' says Solomon,* speaking of the 'valiant woman;' and thus Domenico in his deposition says, 'My house was frequented by all sorts of persons, and I could quite shut my eyes, for I knew what my wife was, how she thought, and how she acted.' And again, 'I let her manage everything, because I saw that she acquitted herself perfectly of the task.' We may notice farther that he was able to perceive and to appreciate the moderation with which she exercised this domestic control, never behaving as if her husband had divested himself of his rightful headship in his own family. 'Although,' he says, 'I had given her full liberty, she wished to have my opinion before doing anything unusual.'

* Prov. xxxi. 11.

E

But perhaps his value of her is nowhere more touchingly exhibited than in the following passage, homely
as are the examples which he selects of her excellence,
perhaps all the more touching on that account.   'She
was always,' he said, 'cheerful and pleasant, yet she
had a host of maladies; this, however, did not hinder
her from putting her hand to the work; she looked to
everything, and had hands of gold.   As for me, I did
not give a thought to anything; she made pantaloons
for me and over-coats.   I do not well know how to
express myself: to cut the matter short, I am old, but
if I were young, and were minded to travel over the
whole earth to find such a woman, it would be impossible to meet with her.   I have lost a great treasure.'
The good man seems here to be unconsciously paraphrasing in his simple way those words of Scripture:
'*Procul et de ultimis finibus pretium ejus*—Far and
from the uttermost coasts is the price of her.'   We call
to mind, too, how it is said that ' her husband rose up
and praised her.'*   Domenico rose up and praised his
wife; true, he may have praised her little while they
were living days of toil together under their lowly roof;
such men as he are not much given to express their
feelings—however prone they may be to relieve their
tempers—in words; but after she had passed to her
home of rest in Heaven, then he praised her, and his
praise is recorded solemnly before the whole world.
He even praised her for those things for which, while
she was alive, he had rebuked her; as when he found
her up late at night praying before the Madonna, evidencing thereby that his displeasure proceeded mainly
from anxiety for her health.

Indeed, it is but justice to Domenico to give him

* Prov. xxxi. 10, 28.

credit for having interfered so little with his wife's mode of life, and acceded to so many of her wishes, which at times appeared (as we shall have to notice hereafter) to run counter to his temporal interests and those of his indigent family. Many in his place, united to one whose sanctity not only far exceeded his own, but was of a kind which passed quite out of his sight both in its heights and in its depths—many with an education very superior to his and a nature less rough and unpolished—would not have behaved with half his kindness and forbearance ; for, whatever may be abstractedly thought of it, it is a situation which for obvious reasons practically tries the less perfect as well as the more perfect, who moreover have greater strength to bear up against trials. Her piety seems never to have irritated or chafed him, and this is really no small praise ; for if the merit was chiefly hers, who knew so well by her sweetness how to recommend it, and, above all, never to allow it to interfere with the comfort of his life, still the devil seldom fails to trouble the peace of families by tempting the ordinary Christian to think the extraordinary devotion with which he is brought into close contact excessive, and to tax with indiscretion the unworldliness of the perfect. If so tempted, Domenico deserves the praise of not having given place to the devil, while the unbounded and un-suspecting confidence which he placed in his wife, richly as she merited it, in matters which he could not thoroughly understand, and which from mere fidgeti-ness might have proved very offensive to him, calls likewise for its meed of commendation. For instance, the number of persons of all ranks and conditions who were continually resorting to his house, would have rendered many a man of his sort, who, be it observed,

was not in the least benefited pecuniarily by this continual intrusion, more than fidgety. But he knew
that his wife was always intent on gaining souls to
God, and, giving her credit for this motive, he was
contented to let her do as she pleased, and even to be
ignorant of what she was doing. 'I saw,' he says,
'my poor little house constantly filled with persons of
all classes, and I knew that these persons came to ask
her advice or her prayers. I abstained, however, from
questioning her as to their object in coming, or as to
what she said to them.' We think that this rude man
displayed no inconsiderable amount of delicacy of feeling, as also of kindness, in such abstention.

Another instance of his considerate forbearance may
be noticed where he is speaking, in his deposition, of
the readiness with which his wife would accompany
him to some street show, or such-like amusement,
although he well knew that her heart was set on far
different objects, and quite estranged from all worldly
diversions. No doubt he made this reflection to himself, but, instead of being vexed and discontented, as
selfish persons are apt to be on such occasions, or
choosing to remain ignorant that what was a pleasure
to him was a pain to her, he was contented quietly to
forego his own satisfaction in the matter. For he
adds, 'Having afterwards observed that she went with
me rather to gratify and obey me than to take her own
share of gratification, and that consequently it must be
a sacrifice on her part, I left her in peace.'

Additional instances of Domenico's appreciation of
his wife's excellence will appear when we come to make
further extracts from his testimony in connection with
other subjects. Our immediate purpose here has been
rather to exhibit Anna Maria's behaviour towards her

husband than to give proofs of her husband's regard
and esteem for her.

CHAPTER V.

ANNA MARIA'S BEHAVIOUR AS A MOTHER.

'SEVEN children,' says Domenico, 'were born of our
marriage, four boys and three girls: Camillo, Alessandro, Luigi, and Pietro; Maria, Sofia, and Margherita. Camillo died aged 42; Alessandro, 35;
Luigi, when a year and a half old; and Pietro, two
years and a month. The two younger daughters,
Maria and Sofia, now alone survive, and live with me.
Maria is unmarried, and Sofia is the widow of the late
Paolo Micali of Mantua, Cameriere to his Eminence,
Cardinal Barberini. All these children were nursed by
the servant of God, and scarcely were they born when
she took care to have them baptised, and she was
equally solicitous that they should be confirmed at the
proper time. She taught them the Catechism herself,
as well as to read and write. Morning and evening
they assisted at our family prayers. She was continually thanking God for His blessings, and particularly for having caused her to be born in the bosom of
the Church; and she taught our children to be thankful
to God for so great a favour.'

Further on, Domenico speaks of her assiduity in
preparing the children for all the essential duties and
acts of religion. We will give his own simple, un-
adorned statement. 'The servant of God availed herself of every means to instruct her sons and daughters
for their first Confession and for their first Communion.

She sent one of the girls to make a retreat with the nuns of the Divino Amore before her first Communion; the other was sent to the Bambin Gesù. The boys were prepared by their mother, and made their first Communion at the parish church. Thanks to the vigilance of the servant of God, all the children, boys and girls, led a regular and Christian life; the girls frequented the sacraments once a week, the boys two or three times during the month. She was also careful to procure them the means of earning their livelihood: thús one of them learned the trade of a hatter, the other entered the sèrvice of Mgr. Mastai, Auditor of the Apostolic Chamber.' Another witness gives similar testimony. 'The servant of God,' says this deponent, 'in the care she took of her children was the tenderest of mothers. She wished the boys, on reaching a certain age, to learn a trade suited to their condition, that they might be useful and good men instead of burdens to society. She placed them in workshops which she had ascertained to be conducted in a good spirit. She did not approve the system of our day, in which everybody desires to rise above his station in life, and the education of children is directed with a view to their attaining some civil office or other.' And assuredly the notion, however it may be expressed, whether by the phrase of 'rising in the world,' 'getting on in life,' or 'bettering oneself,' is little in accordance with the spirit of the Gospel; it cannot therefore be matter of surprise that it should not be approved by this pious woman. And yet, as this witness observes, it is the habitual aspiration of our age; indeed, not to desire to elevate ourselves above our condition, if it be a lowly one, is commonly regarded as a token of a mean-spirited disposition, while to aim at rising above it is encouraged

and lauded as a manly and noble enterprise. It may
be objected, however, that such aims and aspirations
are inherent in human nature, and belong to no age in
particular, although social circumstances may modify
the form of their manifestation. This is true, in so far
that ambition and the love of distinction are no novelty
in the world : at all times men have been desirous of
pushing their fortunes and elevating themselves above
their fellows ; but in the ages when society was more
deeply penetrated with Christian principles this desire
displayed itself, at least among the masses, mainly in
each individual seeking distinction by excelling in his
own proper sphere or calling ; and, where great abili-
ties existed, the hope and prospect of advancement
would of course not be absent. But this is very different from an impatient longing to raise ourselves
above the rank in which we were born, and that whether or no we possess the necessary qualifications for
advancement. This latter ambition it is which may
be called a special characteristic of our times, and which
has become the source of a general unrest, the frequent
nurse of discontent, the parent of heart-burnings and
disappointment.

The same witness continues, ' As for the girls, she
sent them to school, taking care that they should be
accompanied by persons on whom she could rely.' The
solicitude with which she guarded the modesty of her
children at the tenderest age appears in the precautions
she adopted with regard to their sleeping arrangements.
She considered that parents could not be too careful in
this matter, and that it was a mistake to suppose that
while children are what people call mere babies, they are
incapable of any hurtful impression. Anna Maria, small
as was her humble home, took care to separate the place

in which her little boys slept from that of the girls; and, in order farther to inspire and foster sentiments of bashful modesty, she gave each child a separate bed, hanging curtains round it for greater privacy. Indeed, she carried her precautions to what some might regard a needless extent: but Anna Maria knew well that bashfulness is the protector of modesty, as modesty is the safeguard of innocence and purity. When the girls became old enough to run on errands, as the phrase is, this careful mother refrained from employing them in this way, convenient as the practice may be to those who have not many hands and feet at their disposal. ' Knowing,' continues the witness before quoted, ' that one of the principal sources of disorder, which often leads to the ruin of young persons, is to let them go by themselves to shops and places of public resort, she never suffered her daughters to be exposed to this danger. She went out herself to make the necessary purchases, or begged a friend of the family, Luigi Antonini,* to do her this service.' She was also very careful that her children should have proper nourishment and be comfortably clothed. In short, she spared no pains which the best mother could take to provide for all the wants, temporal as well as spiritual, of her family. ' If,' says the confessor, ' they have not all turned out as well as she desired, it is assuredly not her fault.' This observation may appear at variance with the testimony given by their father, that they all led regular and Christian lives. Yet the two statements are easily reconcilable. The children may well not have been all

---

* Luigi Antonini was not only the confidential friend of Anna Maria, but also one of her ' spiritual sons,' as those who sought her counsels in the concerns of their souls have been called. He appeared among the witnesses in the processes.

that their saintly mother desired, or all that they might and ought to have been with the advantage of her holy instructions and example, and yet have fallen into no errors sufficiently considerable to render them unworthy of being described in the terms employed by Domenico. And, indeed, that they were on the whole good, though faulty, Christians, is expressly corroborated by what our Lord vouchsafed one day to say to His servant while she was engaged in praying fervently for them : ' I will save your children because they are of your blood, because they are poor, and the poor are My friends. Yes, I will save them, although they have many faults.'

Anna Maria's vigilant guardianship of her children's modesty and virtue was exemplified moreover in the caution with which she proceeded in the matter of their marriages. As is well known, parents of all classes have a much larger share in the choice of partners in life for their children in most European countries than in our own ; their influence in the matter of selection being among ourselves chiefly indirect, while their authority, so far as it goes, lies simply in prohibition. This is not the place to discuss the merits or demerits of either system ; suffice it to observe that the theory prevailing on the continent, that it is part of the parents' duty and province to settle their children in life and provide suitable marriages for them—should marriage be their proper vocation—is founded on a good and true principle, a principle which contrary habits and systems can never entirely eradicate. Nevertheless the foreign system, as very commonly carried out, is liable to great abuses, which mainly spring from two causes : first, that temporal advantages too often influence parents unduly in their choice, to the exclusion both of

higher interests and of personal recommendations, which
latter are not to be undervalued ; secondly, that the
parties themselves have often little opportunity of becoming mutually acquainted, and of thus ascertaining
whether they are suited to each other in tastes, tempers,
or dispositions. Anna Maria, as may well be imagined,
was not likely to be biassed in her selection of a husband for her daughter by worldly considerations ; and,
with true maternal prudence and affection, she avoided
the other abuse, of venturing to unite two young persons without allowing them the means of knowing what
they were about in an affair of such vital importance
to their happiness.

'At the period,' says Domenico, ' of the marriage of
Sofia with Signor Micali, in order to have time to ar-
range everything and that the future married pair might
become acquainted with each other, the servant of God
permitted the said Micali to frequent the house for
about two months previous to the marriage, and to converse with Sofia, always however in her presence.' To
many this precaution may wear a formal and prudish
appearance, accustomed as they are to the widely different practice prevailing in this country. But we would
remind them that in no country do strict Catholics,
not to speak of saints, approve of those caressing famili-
arities which amongst ourselves are commonly regarded
as the almost necessary, and certainly permissible, accompaniments of the affianced relationship and to which
solitary interviews offer so much opportunity and encouragement. Domenico proceeds to say, 'No other
young man frequented our house with a view to marrying our daughters :' from which it is plain that Anna
Maria's anxiety for the happiness and temporal welfare
of her children did not induce her to seek husbands for

them, or to incur the risk of those casual attachments, formed solely by frequent and intimate association, which too often lead to the union of persons in every way ill matched. Their future she committed to God in prayer, as she had her own, and when the occasion arose used her consummate prudence, enlightened by divine grace, to insure a good and safe decision. 'When the two boys wished to marry,' says her husband, 'the servant of God made inquiries respecting the young persons whom they desired to take as their wives; and, the accounts having been favourable, she gave her consent, as I also did; the wedding-feast consisted in a simple family meal.'

It seems almost needless to say that the obedience which Anna Maria had always required from her children she strictly exacted from them towards their father; and moreover they had under their eyes the example of the filial respect which their mother continued to pay towards her own parents, as we shall have occasion to notice. She also punished them when necessary, but always with moderation, as her husband testifies : 'she saw with pain,' he says, 'parents carried away in their anger to strike their children on the head, and would try to prevent them when prudence allowed her to interpose.' 'The servant of God,' he adds, speaking of his wife's obedience to the fifth commandment, 'never inflicted a bodily injury on any one, neither did she harm any one with her tongue.' She was watchful also to prevent any such harm accruing to others in her presence, and especially in that of her children, and avoided, as far as possible, admitting into her house persons who by their conversation might scandalise one of these little ones; and, as even ordinarily good people will sometimes be careless as to what they say in the

hearing of children, falsely imagining that they have
no ears or attention for remarks of a worldly or equi-
vocal character, that they will not understand them, or
that no evil impression will be produced by what they
thus casually overhear, this vigilant mother took care
to check all such levity and indiscretion, which, indeed,
was distressing and hateful to herself. An enemy also
to all censorious conversation, as we have already observed, she specially abhorred it when ecclesiastics were
its subject. 'Ill fared it,' says Domenico, 'with any
who criticised a priest or spoke of our Holy Father with
scant reverence; she instantly administered a reproof,
giving as her reason that the Pope is the Vicar of Jesus
Christ, and that priests are His ministers.' 'In speaking of ecclesiastics,' observes Cardinal Pedicini, 'she
used to say, "They are God's ministers, and therefore
always worthy of our respect: at the hour of death,
whom shall we need save the priest?"' Her children
were also taught by her example to show personal reverence to the consecrated servants of our common
Lord. 'The ministers of God,' says Domenico, 'were
the object of her profoundest veneration. When a
priest visited us, I remarked that she rose and went to
kiss his hand;* she also made our sons and daughters
kiss it with the greatest respect. This she did likewise
when in the streets she met any priest with whom she
was acquainted, kissing his hand publicly with the utmost reverence.' Thus it was that Anna Maria taught
her children betimes to venerate those who hold God's
place in regard to us, a lesson which childhood readily
learns, and still more surely imbibes from the parent's
example.

* This practice, we need scarcely say, is not unusual among
a devout Catholic population; as, for example, the Tyrolese.

Truthfulness, again, was a virtue which she strictly inculcated. 'I never,' says her husband, '"heard the least untruth from her lips, nor detected her in the slightest artfulness; she reproved servants energetically on this point, much more the children.' But it was not only by instruction and example that Anna Maria trained her children to the love of virtue and holiness; under her roof they lived in a very atmosphere of piety. One may say that religious influences were silently brought to bear upon them at every hour of the day, and reached them through every sense. The Taigi occupied a small house which was situated in a lane running into the Strada Sdrucciolo. It was furnished, as may be imagined, in the plainest and simplest manner, but the moment you crossed the threshold, you might observe that cleanliness and order reigned throughout the humble dwelling. No one can have failed to notice how much a judicious order tends to satisfy the eye, and how cheerful and attractive a room may be made to look by mere arrangement, although it may contain no one article of furniture in itself either costly or beautiful. This is because order is one of the essential elements of beauty, and the love of it is a reflex of a divine attribute. There is no confusion in any work of God : confusion is therefore antipathetic to our minds, created as we are to the image of God. The obscure dwelling, then, of which Anna Maria was the soul and presiding spirit was distinguished by this charm, which even poverty itself does not preclude ; but it was much more than orderly : you felt that you were entering a sanctuary. The family is from God, it is of divine institution, and the home is its abode. This makes home a sacred place ; and sacred it is in the hearts of thousands to the dear affections and charities of domestic

life, around which countless sweet and tender recollections gather as years roll on: but with how many is it
nothing more! Yet the Christian home has, and ought
to have, a sacredness surpassing that which any earthly
affection, however pure and good, can impart. The
family under the law of grace is the nursery of souls for
God; it is therefore a sanctuary wherein high mysteries
are enacted: God is forming His elect in its bosom.
Hence its outward appearance and regulation should
speak, not only of earthly comfort, of kind human affections, and sweet human recollections, but of the everlasting home, the blessed mansion of our Heavenly
Father and of the great family of the saints, His children
and our brethren, who await us there. Upon the walls
of the Taigi's dwelling, arranged with a taste which the
heart not seldom teaches, hung the pictures of their
holy patrons; not costly pictures certainly, but devout and well-chosen, and such as inspired devotion.
Amongst them conspicuous was the King of Saints, our
dear Lord upon His cross; at the end of the room was
a little altar, the family oratory, with the Good Mother,
the Madonna, before whose image a lamp was kept constantly burning, notwithstanding the poverty of the
family. There also you might observe the candles of
the last Purification feast, and the palms of the last
Holy Week, which had received the Church's blessing,
and the holy water, which puts devils to flight, helps
to purify from venial stains, and attracts the loving
protection of God's good angels. This little altar Anna
Maria had set up even before her conversion and in the
first days of her marriage.

But if the religious aspect of this house was calculated to impress the mind of any casual observer, how
deep must have been the mute influence exercised on

the inmates by the continual sight of holy symbols and
the dwelling among objects which have the perfume of
the Church's benediction on them. But this was not
all : it was the bearing and behaviour of her who ruled
and ordered the house, and regulated the daily life observed therein, which so peculiarly hallowed it and gave
to it almost a conventual character. 'She had established the habit,' says Domenico, ' of saying upon entering the house, " *Sia lodato Gesù e Maria*—Praised be
Jesus and Mary;" it was also her "*Buon giorno*" ("Good
morning") to us, which she said bending her head with
deepest reverence.' The pious mother also awoke her
children by calling on the holy names of Jesus and Mary
at their bedsides, that their first thought might thus be
secured for God and Eternity; then, as soon as they
were dressed, all together prayed at the little altar,
thanking God for the protection granted during the
past night, and begging a blessing on the labours of the
day.* She herself rose daily at a very early hour, while
all were yet in their beds, to prepare herself for Communion ; and after arranging everything and leaving
directions with her old mother, who lived with them,
as to what she should do in any contingency that might
arise, she went to Mass, returning home after having
made her thanksgiving. Every occupation of the day
had its appointed hour, and the Holy Name of God was
invoked before entering on it. She gave frequent
utterance to ejaculatory prayers while engaged in her
work; these aspirations were like so many sparks escaping from the inward furnace of her heart, and must

---

* The pious usages here mentioned remind us of those suggested by F. Ratti in the first chapter of his little book entitled
*The Good Mother of a Family occupied with her Children in
the Practice of Christian Piety*. (Burns.)

have had a sanctifying effect on all who heard them.
Then again, the blessing of God was reverently implored
on each meal; and when the labours of the day were
ended, either before or immediately after supper parents
and children clustered together to read some Life of a
Saint or other devout book; the observations suggested
and the conversations which sprang out of the subject
forming the evening recreation of this truly happy
family.

Before seeking repose, they were once more assembled before the little altar, when the Rosary was
always said in common; after which she offered, as her
husband states, 'many other prayers to her holy patrons.'
Elsewhere he specifies in more detail some of her devotions on these occasions. ' She was very devout,' he says,
' to the angels, particularly our holy angel-guardians, to
whom she prayed morning and night. She also addressed herself to the Sacred Heart of Jesus, to the holy
Apostles, St. Joseph, St. Francis, and others; in short,
she had an infinite number of holy protectors and pro-
tectresses, whom she invoked after we had said the
Rosary together. She prayed for the Holy Father, for
the cardinals, for all priests, for benefactors, for the
conversion of sinners, as also for that of heretics, for
the sick, for the exaltation of Holy Church, for the
whole world, for the living and the dead, and even for
bad tongues' (these would seem to have been her
peculiar aversion, since Domenico singles out this act
of charity for special notice): 'all these prayers were
said together every evening.' Yet the good man was
not wearied: far from it; for he adds, in his simple
way, ' and this seemed a Paradise to me.'

Such were the devotions practised by this pious
mother in her family. She also provided that all

should, as far as was possible, profit by the public devotions of the Church, especially on festival days ; and would often take her girls by turns with her when she went to visit some one or other of the many sanctuaries of Rome, selecting in preference that which was dedicated to the saint whom the Church specially honoured on that day. Domenico seems willingly to have joined her in these acts of piety whenever his laborious life of constant domestic service permitted him. 'Frequently,' he says, ' on festival days, when I had a little liberty, we used to go together to Holy Benediction and the holy Rosary at the Minerva with our family ; in the evening, we used often to go to the Quarant' Ore, where the Blessed Sacrament was exposed. Such were our diversions.' He elsewhere mentions how exact she was in her way of keeping and making her children keep the feast days of obligation. ' On working days,' he says, 'she toiled, washed, and performed all her household business, with an activity which might have fatigued four persons, but the feast days she employed in praying and in having books of piety read to her. She heard several Masses ; and, when the children returned from the parish catechising, she took them to some church, generally the Minerva, to be present at the sermon, and again at Rosary and Benediction. In the course of the day she did only what was strictly necessary ; that is, she made the beds and did the needful cooking ; and she took care that the festival should be hallowed by every member of the family.'

As all know who have frequented Rome, there are very joyous and somewhat uproarious popular diversions at certain seasons of the year, particularly during the Carnival. But, even when occurring at less objectionable times, not only were these noisy demonstrations of frolic and mirth distasteful to Anna Maria herself, but she did not like them for her children. She knew too well the engrossing and evil effect of that wild thoughtless abandonment to vain joy which fills the heart of youth, when pleasure seems running riot in every bosom and dancing in every eye; she remembered too well how sad, empty, and sick, as respected heavenly things, the soul was left after partaking of such inebriating draughts of enjoyment; and so she would fain have kept all she loved and prized away from similar temptations and satisfied with the sober joys of home. When, therefore, Domenico wanted to go and witness some gay amusement of this kind and desired that his wife and family should be of the party, if she could gently dissuade him, she would remain at home; but if not, and he persisted, then she cheerfully consented to accompany him with all the children.

It must not be inferred, however, from this reluctance to join in any public diversion that Anna Maria was stiff or gloomy with her young family, or discouraged innocent recreation and mirth. She knew that children must have some amusement, but she wished it to be of a simple and harmless character. Children, in fact, naturally find most enjoyment in such diversions; it is generally their parents and elders who first cultivate in them a taste for entertainments which bring with them a hidden peril. The child, even the grown child, left to its own native bent, loves to revel amongst the cowslips or the fragrant hay, or to take a merry country ramble, and finds a keener relish in such disportings than it does at first in the more artificial amusements to which it is often heedlessly introduced. Accordingly, Anna Maria would occasionally herself vite her girls to make an excursion outside the town, a great pleasure to all young people, but especially to the sons and daughters of poverty, cooped up habitually within the narrow precincts of their small, crowded dwellings in bye-lanes and corners. She would always, however, strive to combine a pious object with this ramble of recreation. Some church or shrine used to be the goal, where, along with their mother, the children paid their devotions with a freshness and a fervour which such little pilgrimages are wont to kindle. Then they made a rural repast,—it was a light one,—consisting generally of chestnuts and a little wine, which the mother had brought with her, knowing that nothing so delights the young as a meal *al fresco.* One of these parties on a solitary occasion, probably from some unexplained motive of convenience, took place on a Friday. There was no sin in this certainly; the precept of abstinence was not broken, and the amusement was of a very sober kind, and such as did not exclude pious thoughts; yet she who was called to follow not a rule of duty alone, but one of perfection, which draws its law, manifested by interior suggestions and inspirations, from a whole class of feelings and motives which are brought to bear very feebly on ordinary Christians, or to which they do not much attend, was reproached by her Heavenly Spouse with having chosen for recreation the day which is consecrated to the memory of His Passion. It is needless to say that she was mindful never to do the like again; and even her children, following her example, abstained from indulging in such diversions on the Friday.

That she was not only willing that others should be mirthful, but that her gravity operated as no cold hindrance to innocent gaiety, is proved also by Dome-

nico's deposition. By nature Anna Maria had been
extremely lively, nay, even ardent and impetuous ; the
impetuosity, indeed, had been all tamed down, and the
ardour diverted into a higher channel, but her sweet,
joyous cheerfulness had never deserted her, although it
was nourished now on more genuine food and sprang
from a purer fountain. 'She spoke of God and of holy
things,' says her husband, 'without becoming wearisome, like some of your devout people, who always
want to talk about themselves and their piety in order
to make a parade of their devotion. She adapted herself to all conversation on innocent and indifferent subjects, and she laughed at the jokes that might be made
when at table ; but she was so prudent, that she knew
how to turn the conversation insensibly to the things
of God, and we were caught without perceiving it.'
Domenico, in his artless simplicity, seems here to have
hit upon as near a definition of a bore as can well be
given, an animal whose genus we all instinctively recognise without being able well to state wherein its
essence consists. The tongue speaks out of the abundance of the heart, but when the soul within abounds in
self, it is self which it pours forth, whatever may be
the subject. Not that all persons who contrive to be
tiresome on good and profitable subjects ostensibly aim
at magnifying their own virtue, but perhaps they value
their advice a little too much, if not themselves, and
at any rate like to hear themselves talk. This is quite
sufficient to make others dislike to listen to them.
Their hearers, accordingly, resent and detest the intrusion, even when they cannot consciously assign the reason. We more than doubt if any saint ever was or could
be tiresome. Saints, it is true, may have but one note,
but that note contains all harmonies ; they may talk of

one thing alone, but that one thing so engrosses their own attention that they have lost sight of themselves. Anna Maria's heart was overflowing with what was the unceasing object of her own contemplation, and on the altar of divine love she had made a perpetual holocaust of that self-love which is hateful to men as well as to God. Other witnesses, well-acquainted with her, have testified that she was disinclined to speak of worldly matters, but that when she could freely lead the conversation to heavenly things her face beamed with happiness. Scarcely had she opened her lips to speak of the goodness of God and pronounced the Holy Name of Jesus, her sweet Saviour, when immediately the interior fire which consumed her manifested itself in every feature of her face, and she appeared all inflamed and as one transported with a holy intoxication.

Such were the influences under which the children of Anna Maria were brought up. But we shall not have completed our view of her as mother of a family until we have also regarded her in the cognate capacity of mistress of a family, which shall be the subject of the next chapter.

CHAPTER VI.

ANNA MARIA AS MISTRESS OF A FAMILY.

In speaking of Anna Maria as a wife and a mother a good deal has incidentally been said or implied of her conduct as the 'materfamilias,' the mistress of a household, and hers, we shall find, was by no means a small one, exclusive of her numerous children. A few re-

marks, however, remain to be added with respect to
her admirable behaviour in this capacity.

Industry and economy will at once suggest themselves as necessary duties in her who rules the house,
provides for its necessities, and controls the application
of its means. Those means were in the case of the
Taigi very small. Domenico received only six *scudi**
a month for his service in the Chigi palace, so that
without very prudent management, the resources of the
family would have been quite insufficient for its decent
maintenance. He had, as we have seen, handed over
the whole administration of the funds to his wife, and
he had no cause to repent having done so. While taking
care that every one had sufficient and well-prepared food
(always excepting herself), she practised the strictest
frugality and economy, not merely on the ground of
necessity or for prudential reasons, but from higher
motives ; waste and extravagance being in all cases reprehensible. ' The expenses,' her husband says, ' were
well regulated according to needs ; she let no one want
for anything, but at the same time she was frugal, in
order to avoid bad habits.' We have already seen his
testimony to the vigour and activity with which she
acquitted herself of her numerous labours ; nevertheless
all was performed with the greatest nicety. ' She did
all,' he says, ' with the utmost exactness, and she worked
exceedingly well. In short,' he adds, ' she was an incomparable woman for all her good qualities.' And
again he says, ' For the love of God she made herself
the servant of all. She might have had herself waited
upon, since I almost always kept a servant for her, but
she set her hand to everything in order to serve others ;'
and then he goes on to state what we have already

* The Roman *scudo* is reckoned as being worth about 4s. 3d.

mentioned, that she always stood and attended to the rest while they sat at dinner. Her servants (for later, when she was visited with a complication of infirmities and painful complaints, it became necessary to have a second domestic) she treated with the utmost kindness. She was most careful that they should receive good and abundant nourishment. She used to give them their breakfast herself, and reserved for them their full share from the midday repast. When, in after years, she was often helplessly confined to her bed, so anxious was she that they should have enough that she would make them take their meals in her presence. ' She treated the servant-girls like sisters,' are Domenico's words ; 'besides their monthly wages, which she paid punctually, she made them little presents for any additional trouble that occurred ; these girls,' he adds, 'showed very little gratitude, nevertheless she overlooked it all through a spirit of charity ; she instructed them in religion, and often took them with her to Mass on festival days.'

Speaking of her strict observance of the seventh commandment, Domenico thus alludes to her punctuality in paying her debts :—' Not only did she pay what she owed, but I remember that, if in her daily reckoning with Luigi Antonini she remarked an error of a *soldo*, she would take care to return it before breakfast.' (Luigi Antonini, it will be remembered, was the friend who executed her little commissions.) ' At the time she was making stays for the nuns of S. Domenico e S. Sisto, she restored even a scrap of thread which remained over and above. She contracted no debts, for she never stepped beyond the length of her leg; but, if constrained to incur some trifling debt, she warned the tradesman before buying, and hastened to pay him

without waiting for his application.' But, while so
strictly just in her dealings, she also took care that her
own family should not be defrauded either in the quantity or the quality of the articles she purchased.

Difficult times came, when the armies of the French
Republic forcibly occupied the Eternal City,* and, the

* We cannot resist quoting from the pages of a modern
historian the following account of the entry of General Berthier
into Rome at the head of the troops of the French Directory,
in the year 1798, recalling as it does so forcibly late events.
Unlike the generals of Victor Emanuel, this agent of the Revolution acted with regret, and accomplished his odious mission
reluctantly. Its effects were none the less disastrous. 'He
(Berthier) entered Rome on the 15th of February, the anni-
versary day of Pius VI.'s exaltation, proceeded to the Capitol,
and proclaimed the Republic, calling on the names of Cato and
Brutus. Rome had its Directory, composed of seven members
—all deserters of the Pontifical cause—and of a Secretary.
named Bassal, a former Curé of Versailles, an apostate and a
regicide. People were well aware that the army of Berthier
was marching to seize a rich prize; and a multitude of birds of
prey, low speculators, Jews, agents of the Directory, had accompanied it and rushed into the Eternal City. An immense pillage
took place. The Vatican was rapaciously plundered: palaces,
villas, all the galleries, all the churches, pictures, statues,
antique vases, cameos, sacred vessels, sacerdotal vestments,
fell into the hands of the French Republicans charged with the
task of "regenerating" Rome. Berthier deplored, but could
not prevent these depredations. Masséna presided over the
spoliations. From time to time the "Marseillaise" was sung
round the tree of liberty, planted on the Capitol. Braving the
menaces with which he was assailed, strong against iniquity
and injustice, the Venerable Pius VI. refused to give up the
temporal sovereignty. His life was spared, but he saw himself
loaded with humiliations and insults; he was pitilessly robbed
of his furniture, his ornaments, his valuable library. Some
days later, the agents of the Directory notified to Pius VI. the
orders they had received to remove the Pope from Rome; and
on the 2d Ventôse (20th February) the venerable Pontiff found
himself compelled to quit Rome, which he was never to see
again. Dragged from his palace in the middle of the night, he
was placed in a carriage and taken to Viterbo; at Siena they

Chigi family having removed to Paris, poor Domenico
lost his monthly six crowns of wages. 'My poor wife,'
he says, 'full of courage and energy, animated me to
put my trust in God. In order to feed our numerous
family, she learnt how to make women's shoes, as well
as stays, and worked night and day. The Lord blessed
her labours, so as to enable her not only to provide
bread for the household, but to succour a multitude of
poor who had recourse to her charity. It is true that
her work would not have sufficed to meet such great
needs, nevertheless it brought her into relation with
the nuns of S. Domenico e Sisto ; and, as the Queen of
Etruria* was in their house at that time, her Majesty

---

permitted him to stop, and reside awhile in the convent of
St. Augustine; later he removed to the Carthusian monas-
tery of Parma.' All who are conversant with the history of
those times are acquainted with the subsequent sufferings, imprisonment, and exile of the Pontiff. The Directory had required the Grand Duke to banish the Holy Father from his
dominions ; he nobly refused, and his refusal cost him his states.
The French Republic, not knowing what to do with their prisoner, removed him into France, ill as he was and suffering
from painful ulcers in his legs. In this almost dying state, he
was borne over the Alps, after receiving wherever he passed the
sympathising homage of the Catholic people of Italy. Even in
France itself, where every effort had been made to decatholicise
the population, the passage of the august prisoner was an ova-
tion. 'France,' says the author from whom we quote, 'regained her fervour at the sight of this Anointed of the Lord,
crowned with thorns like his Master.' He died in exile and
imprisonment at Valence on the 29th August, 1799. Gabour,
Histoire de France, tom. xix.

* So called by anticipation. This princess was Maria Luisa,
daughter of Charles IV., King of Spain. By the treaty of Luné-
ville, concluded in 1801 between the French Republic and Austria, the grand-duchy of Tuscany was erected into a kingdom,
that of Etruria, and conferred on Louis of Parma, a prince of
the house of Bourbon, to whom Maria Luisa was married.
After his death, which occurred in 1803, she governed his do-

became acquainted with the servant of God.' To
Anna Maria's connection with the Queen of Etruria,
we shall recur by and bye; at present we limit ourselves to our immediate subject, her management of
domestic affairs. A terrible famine afflicted Rome during those miserable days. 'I remember also,' continues
Domenico, 'that at the epoch of the Roman Republic
[this was in 1798] the corn failed, and Rome found itself in one moment lacking bread. It became necessary
to wait amid the throng of people at the baker's; and
my poor wife, whose health was so delicate, would remain courageously whole days exposed to the cold and
wind, that the family might not suffer want.' This
was in order to receive a share in the public dole which
was made daily to the poor during the dearth.

Everything that she did, however arduous, was performed with the same heavenly calm as if it had been
mere common work, or, rather, with far greater tranquillity than others perform their ordinary business. No
eagerness was ever displayed by Anna Maria, no spasmo-
dic energy; there were no vociferations and exclamations, none of that affected bustle which so often accompanies, though it in no way expedites, the dispatch of work
when some more than usual call is made for exertion.
All such manifestations are ebullitions of self, the off-
spring of impatience, vanity, the desire to attract attention, or the mere result of natural impetuosity. 'Activity' (says the author of that beautiful little work,
The Divine Sequence) 'is one thing; hurry is an-

---

minions, as guardian of her infant son, until 1807, when she
resigned her authority, in pursuance of a stipulation entered
into between France and Spain. In 1808 the kingdom of
Etruria was absorbed by the French Empire and divided into
three departments.

other. The former is consistent with the greatest
peace and calm; the latter is the result of imperfection
at least, and often of actual sin. We cannot think of
the good angels as hurried; but we can, alas! constantly of ourselves, or of the devils.'* Anna Maria
did her work, whatever it might be, for God, and so
she always performed it to the best of her ability, great
things and small alike, and very peaceably, a condition
of doing well and also of doing quickly. Neither did
she ever aim at anything extraordinary or unusual; she
took such measures and adopted such means as any
prudent, hard-working woman in her class might have
done. What was extraordinary in her actions of this
class must be sought, not in their substance, but in the
manner of their performance. Domenico probably intends to allude to this character of quiet moderation
with which she went through her toils, and to the simplicity which pervaded all she did, when, after speaking of her laborious diligence, he subjoins, 'Nevertheless, she was opposed to all excesses in the matter of
exertion; by which I mean that I never perceived that
she allowed herself to be carried away by presumption,
ambition, and vain-glory. . . . She joined patience to
humility; and I may say that her whole life was a prolonged and most painful exercise of patience.'

No one can reflect upon the picture presented to us
of this humble woman, thus calmly occupied at her
daily work, without recalling to mind Her who not
only offers us the type of perfect womanhood, but is
herself immeasurably the highest of pure creatures, and
yet whose life on earth was almost entirely spent in the
apparent exercise of a round of common duties. We
cannot refrain from giving here another and a longer

* P. 68.

extract from the work of which we have just spoken.
'We are all and each of us so impregnated with evil,
we are so saturated with our own sins and the sins of
those about us, that we fail to realise the sublime and
exquisite beauty of daily life, with its round of ordinary
occupations, as lived and performed by a perfectly holy
being. We have woven our passions into every act
and every thought, we wake with their hot breath on
our lips, we break bread with our sin-soiled hands, we
hew wood and draw water in the covetousness of our
nature; and the exquisite, tender, and pathetic beauty
of ordinary daily life escapes our perception. If we
would learn to see it, we must study Mary. He who
did not abhor the Virgin's womb will make the scales
fall from our eyes, if we set ourselves quietly and deliberately to contemplate Her whom He chose to be
His Mother. The dignity of life, which we are apt to
miss in our graceless scuffle with ourselves and with
others, will gradually dawn upon us. And that, not
as life in the wilderness, not on the top of a pillar,
nor yet in its glorious but exceptional phases, as an
apostle, as a martyr, or even as a confessor; but life in
its most simple elements, its least striking developments, its least dazzling surroundings. Life, in short,
as Mary lived it; and as Jesus chose and fashioned it
for His Mother, and thus fashioning it for her who is
the culminating point of creation, He has sanctified
life in the aspect that it offers to the multitude. He
has made all things pure to those who live in purity.
He has hidden Himself behind the simplest accidents
of life. "He standeth behind our wall, looking through
the windows, looking through the lattices."* He has
left a blessing on our daily path, like the perfume of

* Cant. ii. 9.

hidden violets by the side of the dusty road. *Where* we seek Him, *there* we shall find Him ; for He is not far from every one of us, and He has given us His own pure and Virgin Mother to go hand in hand with us through the routine of existence. It all resumes itself in this : that simplicity and secrecy are strength, while multiplicity and multifariousness are a loss of power, as they are a loss of dignity. When God will reveal Himself to man, He hides Himself in the bosom of a virgin. When He would show us a perfect human being, He places her in an obscure village, and to men's eyes she betrays nothing extraordinary. All beginnings of great things are little. All beginnings of good things are simple. Nothing really great ever began by assuming a great name, or proclaiming its commencement with a flourish of trumpets. The largest rivers flow from the most hidden springs. We are still searching for the sources of the Nile ! God's ways are the same always and everywhere. And they are a constant and silent protest against the bustling vain-glory of men, against the hurry and scramble of our mode of life ; our ill-tempered eagerness and indiscriminate hurry. A large, deep-drawn, wide-embracing hopefulness, and a steady, uninterrupted but unhasteful effort, will alone convert nations and peoples, diminish the reign of evil, and translate into action our daily and hourly prayer, " May Thy Kingdom come." '*

If Anna Maria did not favour any extravagant application of strength and vigour, which, after all, can be practised only by fits and starts and entails a proportionate, or, rather, disproportionate, expenditure of time devoted to the recruiting of overtaxed powers, not to speak of the moral collapse sure to follow these un-

* *The Divine Sequence*, pp. 65-7.

natural bounds of feverish energy, she far more than made up for this by always keeping on at her work. This patient perseverance is a far greater tax on fortitude, and every other moral quality which sustains us in bodily labours, than are the most strenuous occasional efforts. Nay, the very body, our animal nature itself, prefers the latter method, and would far rather be overcharged for a brief space, and then lie down, like a wearied beast, and take its fill of rest, than subject itself to unremitting, though moderate, toil which, if it does not break down the strength, wears and consumes it. Anna Maria was never idle : Cardinal Pedicini mentions that he never entered her house—and he was a daily visitor for many years—without finding her engaged in her domestic avocations ; and when she was too ill to move about, and the most torturing sufferings nailed her to her bed, her hands were still busy mending the household linen or some article of clothing.

We have said that the humble dwelling of the Taigi harboured other inmates besides their own immediate family. After their marriage, Domenico had offered a home to his mother-in-law, and she lived with them till her death. This not only brought an additional individual to be fed and clothed out of their small means, but introduced a fresh temper, not of a very agreeable nature, into the narrow domestic circle. Camillo and his young wife also continued, for some time after their marriage, to live under the paternal roof. It is not always easy, even in the largest houses, for families thus circumstanced—that is, where two generations live together—to maintain an unbroken state of harmony. Often the old will think the young neglectful or wanting in respect, and the young will regard the old as tiresome and exacting ; how much

more trying, therefore, must such an association be
likely to prove where the different, and perhaps incon-
gruous, members are necessarily crowded together in a
limited space and in juxtaposition all the day long!
But Anna Maria knew how to deal with these difficulties, and by her gentle influence to preserve family
union and concord. In addition to those we have
mentioned, her father, although he did not live with
them, constantly frequented the house. Ruined in circumstances as he had been in early life, he was now
equally so in health, and the chief object of his visits
was, it would appear, to obtain little indulgences and
delicacies which he was unable to procure for himself.
A certain false pride, which seems to have formed an
element in the poor man's character, prevented him,
however, from showing much appreciation of any kindness he received. We give Domenico's own simple
account. 'Her father,' he says, 'who from easy circumstances had fallen into great poverty, often came to
the servant of God for help ; with my permission, she
used to give him things to eat which he was fond of,
and even a few small coins to purchase what he fan-
cied ; from pride of nature, he showed little gratitude
for these attentions. In the last years of his life he
was attacked by a horrible leprosy, and the servant of
God washed and combed him with the greatest patience, and did him all the good that lay in her power;
when he fell dangerously ill, she rendered him all the
assistance she was able, saw that all the sacraments
were administered to him, and, after his death, had
Masses offered for him and the Rosary said in common
for the repose of his soul. She fulfilled the same duties
towards her mother, whom I took into our house, and
whose wayward temper long exercised the patience of

my poor wife. It seems as if God had given her parents
of this sort in order to put her patience to the proof.
She attended on her mother for many years with incomparable respect and affection. She gave her the
choicest things she was able to provide for her, showed
compassion to her, cheered her, in a word did everything to satisfy her. Observing that this old woman
liked to have a little pocket-money, Anna Maria did not
fail to gratify her in this respect, although she was
not allowed to want for anything. Finally, when she
was taken ill, my wife hastened to have the sacraments
administered to her, which was always one of her first
thoughts in cases of sickness; after her death, she took
charge of the body, fulfilling the same duties of charity
as she had previously done in the case of her father.'

While the family consisted only of Anna Maria,
her rude, but good-natured husband, and children, who
could readily be taught to respect their grandmother,
and accommodate themselves to her peculiarities of
temper, the maintenance of peace and harmony was a
comparatively easy task. But as years rolled on the
children became men and women, and Camillo, as we
have said, brought home his wife to take her place in the
family circle. This young woman seems also to have
had a temper of her own and rather domineering pro-
clivities. Such a one was sure not to get on well with
the cross-grained old· dame who sat at her father-in-
law's fireside, and whom age had probably not rendered
less testy. Neither was it likely that she would always
show the perfect docility of a daughter to her mother-
in-law. The relation is a somewhat delicate one at
times, even in foreign lands, where the authority of
parents over their daughters-in-law, particularly when
they live with them, is recognised in a manner to which

in England we are strangers. But Anna Maria was
equal to the occasion. 'She knew how, by her marvellous prudence,' says her husband, 'to make a heavenly peace always reign in the family, although we
were many in number and with very different disposi-
·tions; above all, at the time that Camillo, my eldest
son, lived with us, during the early days of his marriage; for soon he went to occupy the lodging which
his master, Mgr. Mastai, had provided for him. The
daughter-in-law was of a humour very difficult for any
to deal with, because she wanted to command as mistress; but the servant of God knew so well how to restrain all within their proper limits, and this with so
much affability, that all I could say on the subject
would be very little. I do not know how to explain
myself: her manners had a charm which irresistibly
compelled one to satisfy her, and it was always for the
advantage of holy peace and of the family. I let her
regulate everything, for I saw that she acquitted herself perfectly of the task. If she saw anybody dis-
quieted, she said nothing, but waited till the mind had
calmed down; then she gently led the person to reflect, and gave good advice regarding patience and
humility. These little squabbles were rare, because
my wife was so prudent that she no sooner perceived
any slight difference arising, whether between her old
mother and her daughter-in-law, or others, than she
hastened to stifle the quarrel with a kindness which
served to cement peace and harmony still more strongly.'
He adds that in the case of illness of any member of
the family she was prodigal of her care, giving up for
the time, if necessary, both her daily Mass and her
other devotions. The family was further enlarged
when the widowed Sofia returned, with her six chil-

G

dren, to her parents' house, at which time their increased numbers rendered a change of abode imperative.

Much more might be added with reference to Anna
Maria's behaviour in her domestic life and in her conduct with regard to the temporal interests of her family,
which will find its appropriate place when we come to
speak of her different Christian virtues, and in particular of her sublime hope and confidence in God and
her heroic charity. For the present, the sketch we
have given, imperfect as it is, may suffice. And imperfect it is in more ways than one, not only by its in-
completeness, which we hope in a measure to supply
elsewhere, but because, having for the present done no
more than make a passing allusion to the supernatural
life she was interiorly leading, and to the extraordinary
gifts of which she was the recipient, while thus engaged in the most homely of occupations, the picture we
have given is wanting as yet in a feature which greatly
enhances its sublimity. Not that, as we have said,
these gifts were in themselves merits, but because the
humility, the simplicity, and the homeliness, suited to
her humble position, which were so remarkably manifested in her, receive an additional value in our eyes
when we view her as the recipient of such splendid and
singular graces. Moreover, it should be kept in mind
that those marvellous communications and astound-
ing graces with which this holy woman was favoured
did not follow upon a long previous life of holiness,
but were vouchsafed to her from the very first days of
her generous turning to God. Neither did they come
gradually : they were a rich dowry bestowed upon her
at once, and on the very threshold of her course. Her
ears heard divine locutions, her hand received the gift

of miraculous healing, in those early beginnings of a
sanctity which seemed born mature; her eyes beheld
that sun of divine wisdom—which was only to be
extinguished when they opened on the glory of the
beatific vision—ere yet the penitential tears of her conversion had dried upon her cheeks. Surely this reflection cannot but add greatly to the admiration with
which we regard Anna Maria Taigi engaged in what
we are apt to call the plodding avocations of a life of
toil, and busied in the quiet performance of the common
domestic duties which fall to the lot of the wife and
mother in the poor man's family. Nevertheless it was
in the perfect fulfilment of these and other Christian
duties, and not in her possession of those glorious
privileges, that she was laying up a store of merits before God and earning the crown prepared for her by
the Just Judge.

CHAPTER VII.

ANNA MARIA'S HEROIC FAITH; AND HER DEVOTION TO THE BLESSED TRINITY.

WHAT the root is to the tree, and the foundation is
to the building, the theological virtue of faith is in the
Christian life. But faith must be distinguished as of
two kinds, habitual faith and actual faith. 'Habitual
faith is that theological virtue which inclines us to believe the mysteries of God, on account of His revelation; and actual faith is the act or operation proper to
this habitual faith. . . . This habitual faith is often in-
active, and, as it were, set to sleep in the greater part
of the faithful, because it is not exercised by the acts

proper to it, and thus it is of little profit in this state,
like a sword which remains in its scabbard without
being drawn. But when it produces its acts, and is
actually exercised by the consideration of its proper
objects, then it is efficacious and active, and produces
admirable effects for the good of the faithful. . . . To
follow the act of faith and operate conformably to the
inclination it leaves in the heart, this is to vivify faith ;
according to what the prophet says : "*Justus ex fide
vivit*—The just man liveth by faith."* He is speaking
of this actual faith in exercise, because hence it is that
the man draws and preserves the life of his soul, which
consists in grace and in all kinds of exercises of piety
and devotion. In like manner he acquires the life of
glory for eternity, because, thus vivified, faith becomes
meritorious ; as on the other hand it is dead, as says
the Apostle St. James, when its acts are not produced :
"*Fides sine operibus mortua est*—Faith without works
is dead."† . . . Such is the faith of the greater part of
Christians, who make no reflection from morning till
night on the truths revealed by God to enlighten and
guide them amidst the darkness of this world ; hence
they perform all their works from human motives and
reasons drawn from self-interest, acting only through
concupiscence and passion. In them faith is dead, in-
active and profitless, seeing they make no more use of
it than if they did not profess it ; whence it follows
that their life is pagan rather than Christian, being in
no way influenced by the spirit of Jesus Christ.'‡

What is true of too many to this excess, is true in
a lesser degree, varying indefinitely, of the great mass

* Habac. ii. 4.   † ii. 20.
‡ Bail, *La Théologie Affective, ou Saint Thomas en Médi-
tation*, tom. iii. med. x.

of Christians. Few of their actions, comparatively, are
the immediate fruits of faith, prompted by supernatural
motives and animated by them during their performance.
Yet this precious gift of faith, when received into a soul
and allowed to act with its full vigour, is able to trans-
form a sinner into a saint, even in a moment of time.
Witness the thief on the cross, and Magdalen at the
feet of her Saviour. For though it is charity, not faith,
which unites the soul to God and produces sanctity in
it, nevertheless a living faith is the principle of sanctity.
Even as the sight and knowledge of corporal and material things is the principle of the love we bear them,
and if we knew them not by a natural light we could
not love them, so also is it with the spiritual sight and
with spiritual love. 'Hence, as this love is necessary
to us, the sight and knowledge are equally so; and as
this sight and this knowledge are supernatural, we can
have them only by faith.'* Thus our Lord, after saying of Magdalen, 'Many sins are forgiven her, because
she hath loved much,' turned to the penitent herself
and said, 'Thy faith hath made thee safe.'†

To be converted, then, to God truly, the soul must
see and accept by faith, the condition of its producing
an act of love. But the fulness and fervour with which
such conversions are effected in souls differ widely: in
some, this process is from the first, although genuine,
more or less languid and lacking in warmth; in others,
the pristine fervour is suffered afterwards to cool and
die out. Anna Maria offers a striking example of the
precise contrary in both respects. Hers was one of
those conversions in which the power and energy of
faith are signally exemplified. As a proof of this, we
have to note the generosity with which she entered at

* Bail, tom. iii. med. ix.   † Luke vii. 50.

once on a life of rigorous penance. It would be an insufficient account of the matter to impute this generosity to mere ardour of disposition and high natural courage. True, it needed both ardour and courage to enter on such a course; but something more was needed for perseverance. This something more was her strong faith. 'The penitent and suffering life which she embraced before the world in the flower of her years,' says Cardinal Pedicini,* 'and in which she persevered until death, is

* Carlo-Maria Pedicini, born at Benevento in 1760, belonged to the noble family of that name. He studied at Rome, entered the priesthood, and was made a Roman Prelate. He filled successively several offices in the service of the Holy See. Pius VII. made him coadjutor to Mgr. Quarantotti, Secretary of Propaganda. When this last was created Cardinal in 1816, Mgr. Pedicini became the actual Secretary. He was made Cardinal by Pius VII. on the 23d of March 1823, and subsequently Prefect of Propaganda and Vice-chancellor of the Roman Church by Gregory XVI. He was acquainted with the V. Anna Maria Taigi for more than thirty years, and was in the habit of visiting her almost daily until his own occupations, as Secretary of Propaganda, became too constant to allow of his continuing the practice. She had been commanded by her confessor, under obedience, to manifest everything to Mgr. Pedicini concerning the extraordinary graces she received, as he was himself unable to visit her as often as was desirable. In 1815, Mgr. Pedicini appointed, at the recommendation of Mgr. Strambi, a priest of Macerata to replace him, who continued to discharge the office of spiritual confidant to the servant of God until her death in 1837. Cardinal Pedicini died six years after the V. Anna Maria, and his epitaph in the Church of San Lorenzo in Damaso justly praises his piety, integrity, charity, and the order with which he performed all his actions. The Cardinal had drawn up a long statement, collected from his notes, of all he had personally known of the life and virtues of Anna Maria, lest death should remove him before the inquest commenced, as was in fact the case. This document accordingly was inserted in the processes, where it fills near a thousand pages. P. Calixte has inadvertently asserted that Cardinal Pedicini was raised to the purple in 1814: this statement is clearly inaccurate.

an indubitable proof of the lively and heroic faith
which animated her.' In the light of faith she had
seen what she herself was and what God was; and
that sight never left her. She lived in it and of it.
'A lively and continual faith in the presence of God,'
says the Cardinal, 'produces a holy life in whosoever puts this truth in practice. It sanctified Abra-
ham, on whom the Lord enjoined this exercise : "*Am-
bula coram me, et esto perfectus*—Walk before me,
and be perfect."* This presence of God, he testifies,
was with Anna Maria in all her actions even the most
simple and indifferent. The Divine goodness had im-
pressed this maxim, which guided the father of the
faithful, deep in her mind and heart from the very beginning of her special call to the life of perfection. We
have seen how admirable was her correspondence to that
great grace; so admirable, that God imparted to her a
testimony of His love which is unparalleled in the lives
of His most favoured servants, the permanent vision of
the mysterious sun already mentioned. Nor was this
all : she was conscious also of being directed in her
slightest actions by a divine voice. 'She had God
always present before her in all her actions,' writes the
Cardinal, 'whether by reason of the mysterious sun of
which I have spoken, or of the divine voice which continually directed her in her least actions in the most
surprising and extraordinary manner. Hence we may
conjecture what was the progress of her faith, which was
more and more stimulated by the excitations to which
I have alluded, and by the direction of the Holy Spirit.'
God is not used to impart great and exceptional gifts
where He knows they would not meet with adequate
correspondence. In such cases they could, indeed, but

* Gen. xvii. 1.

serve to the condemnation of the unhappy recipient.
The All-knowing and All-good God, while giving or
withholding according to His sovereign pleasure, observes a certain order and measure which we cannot fail
to recognise, and in bestowing His graces has regard to
the capacity of each; that capacity being, in fact, but
the preparation of heart duly to correspond with the
gift bestowed : for who can limit the degree of grace
of which any soul is capable? Viewed in the light of
this truth we are struck with amazement at the bare
imagination of what must have been the lofty capacities
of the soul of this holy woman, to whom He communicated and manifested Himself in so extraordinary a
manner, and the fidelity to grace which merited for her
the permanence of these gifts. But of this enough for
the present.

There was nothing for which Anna Maria felt more
gratitude than for the gift of faith. 'Many times she
undertook,' says the same witness, 'penitential exercises
in order to obtain the grace to know what she could do
to testify her thankfulness to God on account of the
gift of faith which He had vouchsafed to grant her.'
Heresy* being the vice opposed to faith, it was the object of her cordial detestation. 'She manifested,' says
her confessor† in his deposition, 'a profound repulsion

* Heresy is a term which by some is used rather vaguely,
and by others never used at all, as not being fitted for fastidious
nineteenth-century ears. Heresy, then, it may be observed,
does not consist in, and is not identical with, simple error concerning divine truths, which may be involuntary. Heresy is
defined as 'a voluntary error of the understanding against a
truth of faith, maintained with obstinacy by one who makes profession of the religion of Jesus Christ.' Bail, tom. iii. med. xi.

† P. Filippo-Luigi di San Nicola, a Carmelite of the Convent
of Santa Maria della Vittoria at Rome, to whom allusion has
already been made. He dictated in writing an account of the

to maxims which persons tainted with heresy would sometimes advance in her presence, or who took the most holy names of Jesus and Mary in vain. She hastened to repair the offence done to God by the most fervent and tender ejaculations, and, if she had no authority to correct these unhappy persons, she prayed for their conversion, and asked pardon for them of God.' This she would also do if she heard blasphemies uttered in the streets, by insolent or drunken men, whom she could not admonish. On such occasions she might be seen to shudder through her whole frame, like one who feels a sharp physical pain. 'She detested,' continues P. Filippo, 'every doctrine and every maxim not conformable to the decisions of the Holy Catholic Church; by faith rooted in her heart, she believed firmly all the divine mysteries without any doubt, and would have willingly shed all her blood for every article appertaining to them.' And again he says, 'Reflecting on the precious grace which she had received in baptism, she never ceased to thank God for it, as for a signal benefit of His love ; hence proceeded the joy which filled her heart when she heard of heretics returning to the faith, and of Jews and infidels embracing it. On the other hand, she felt an extraordinary grief when she heard

---

servant of God about a year and a half after her death. An indult of the Cardinal Vicar Ordinary of Rome had granted permission to collect the attestations of persons of advanced age. Wishing to give to his relation the value of a juridical deposition, P. Filippo made at each session a profession of the Catholic faith, took an oath, and appended his signature to every page in presence of twelve witnesses. When the juridical process was opened in 1854, the relation of P. Filippo was presented amongst other documents intact, and still invested with the seals attached to it sixteen years previously. It was inserted in the process.

of any offence against God ; hence her continual prayers
for the conversion of sinners. Many a time she offered
herself to God to endure every kind of suffering, and
even to shed her blood, that her Heavenly Spouse might
be known and loved by all men. These fervent offerings brought her many crosses and pains. Thus was
verified that which was frequently told her by God, that
she should be a martyr for the faith, but by a martyrdom different from the ordinary, longer and more meritorious, because it would consist both in bodily sufferings and in terrible mental pains. The divine voice
repeated on several occasions, "Thy life for the maintenance of the faith is a long martyrdom." And again,
"This is why I have many times told thee that I had
chosen thee to place thee in the rank of the martyrs." [*]

Anna Maria was constantly impelled to introduce
in conversation the subjects on which she was habitually pondering. But as she did this, not from a
human eagerness, but by a divine movement of grace,
it was with a simplicity which rendered them always
acceptable. 'Anna Maria,' says the confessor, 'had the
talent of intermingling the maxims of faith with the
most ordinary subjects of conversation without the
smallest affectation, and so naturally that one could see
that it proceeded from the deepest sentiments of her
heart.' The same was the case when she had to speak
of temporal things with a view to consoling others;
she was always reverting to the element in which she
breathed. 'As one,' says P. Filippo, 'who seeks treasures in the bed of the ocean, and who must now and
then raise his head above water to breathe the vital air,

* This communication is expressed in the Italian by a distich:

'Per ciò Io t' ho più d' una volta detto:
Nel numero de' martiri t' ho eletto.'

so Anna Maria felt the need of raising herself from time to time above worldly interests in order to inhale the vivifying air. She raised her mind and her heart to Heaven and to the truths of faith which were her life.'

Her exceeding devotion and reverence for all that appertained to the faith was the necessary consequence of the sublime degree in which she possessed it. From this source flowed the love and veneration with which she regarded, and the priceless value she set upon, all the sacraments of the Church. She had the most lively faith in the sacrament of penance, receiving it with the most perfect compunction, and she would have wished, especially during the closing years of her life, to confess always before receiving Communion; 'but, knowing the tenderness of her conscience,' says the confessor, 'I enjoined her, under obedience, to communicate daily and confess every week; and she submitted.' She used to recommend frequent confession to all over whom she had any influence; suggesting this practice to her husband with much sweetness, but enjoining it on her children with authority. She availed herself of every opportunity to lead the sick whom she visited to cleanse their souls and reconcile themselves to God in the sacrament of penance; and confession also was the first thing she urged upon any of her own house who were taken ill; for she was very desirous that this sacrament should be received while as yet the mind was fully alive, and before the malady had made much progress. In like manner she manifested her profound respect for the sacraments of Confirmation and Extreme Unction, and the high value she set upon them, by having some of her children confirmed while still under the usual age, because they were in danger of death, and by her promptness in causing both her father and mother to be anointed with the holy oils in their last sickness. Of her burning love for the greatest of all the sacraments, the Adorable Sacrament of the Altar, we shall speak at large hereafter.

Anna Maria's deep reverence for the least of God's commandments sprang also from the strength and liveliness of her faith ; and this remark equally applies to her observance of the precepts of the Church, in regard to which she was so zealous that, when a dispensation from fasting was rendered necessary, on the score of health, for any member of the family, she would desire to have it in writing from the confessor, not being content with a mere verbal permission. The same faith made her regard and treat with exceeding respect all those things which are called ' the sacramentals' of Holy Church, and which become to those who duly prize them the channel of so many benedictions. Holy water, a deep value for which seems always to have distinguished souls of high sanctity, she specially esteemed ; and with the sign of the cross, that other great Christian weapon against the powers of evil, she frequently armed herself, not limiting its use to those customary times when all habitually make it, but employing it on many others—such as when coming in and going out of her own doors ; she also blessed her children's beds with this holy sign. Agnus Deis, blessed candles, and the relics of saints were similarly the objects of her reverential devotion ; and she could not bear to see any blessed object, such as a rosary, or a holy picture, left in the hands of little children, too young to understand the respect due to them, and who only make playthings of them. Her devotion to the Blessed Mother of God, and to the Saints and Angels, will find

its more appropriate notice elsewhere, and we shall also
defer all reference to her temptations against faith till
we come to speak of her interior trials.

We have already had occasion to remark on her
veneration for the priesthood. 'She honoured bishops,
cardinals, religious, priests, and nuns,' writes P. Filippo,
'and prayed incessantly for them, particularly for her
own confessor, to whom she manifested her whole conscience. She ever paid an unquestioning obedience to
the minister of God; if he enjoined or forbade anything, she submitted, and that, too, although his judgment might not be conformable to the supernatural
lights she received from above : I ascertained this frequently, in order to put her faith and obedience to the
test.' Her obedience to her confessor was, indeed, so
entirely based on faith that she would never have
thought of contradicting him or disputing any point
with him, still less of quitting him for another, however saintly, from whom she might have hoped to receive much help and consolation. If, therefore, she
changed confessors several times, it was owing to no
caprice on her part, but was the result of divine direction, either signified to her immediately or imposed by
circumstances.*

* 'As confessors, she had 1. A Servite Father, P. Angelo.
2. A Passionist, who was selected for her by Mgr. Strambi;
she used to go very early in the morning to him for confession,
but the great distance of the Church of SS. John and Paul interfered a little with the discharge of her domestic duties; besides, a pain in her legs which then attacked her made her
understand that it was not the will of God that she should continue this practice; the confessor with regret advised her to
address herself to some priest in her own neighbourhood. She
accordingly chose 3. the Abate Salvatori at San Ignazio, and
kept to him for several years, which were marked by a multitude of heavenly favours; but, as he made everybody ac-

As it may be supposed, Anna Maria's devotion to the Holy See and her veneration for the august head of the Church were unbounded. She never spoke of the Holy Father but in terms of the deepest reverence. Faith made her discern so clearly Him who is represented in His Vicar as He is in no other authority upon earth that she frequently gave utterance to her feelings, when hearing of the Sovereign Pontiff, in these emphatic words: 'He is God upon earth'*—expressions at which aliens from God's Church take scandal, because, in their blindness and ignorance, they cannot understand them, and think that whoso uses them is deifying a man. Anna Maria's own conduct would suffice to disprove so absurd a charge, for in proportion to her realisation of the incomparable grandeur of the office filled by Christ's Vicar was her keen sense of the duty of the faithful to offer continual prayers in his behalf. She was, indeed, continually praying for him,

---

quainted with her, without using any reserve, she was no longer able to enjoy a moment's freedom, whether at home or in church ; by a command from above, to which the confessor conformed, she had to quit him, and placed herself in the hands of P. Fernando, a Discalced Trinitarian, of the Convent of the Quattro Fontane ; and him she had also to leave some time afterwards. Finally, by a divine disposition she addressed herself to the undersigned P. Filippo Luigi, Discalced Carmelite at Santa Maria della Vittoria ; she confessed to him for thirty years and more.' *Deposition of P. Filippo.*

* When that holy woman, Mother Margaret Hallahan, was at Rome, we read that she once remarked, 'I am afraid of saying what I felt about the Pope, lest I should scandalise people. I wanted to kneel there and look at him for hours. There was all that was grand and powerful on earth—the man before whom kings were as nothing ! And when I heard him sing Mass I cannot express what I felt : *it was the god of the earth prostrate in adoration before the God of Heaven !*' And again she wrote, 'I cannot see the Pope without emotion. *He seems so truly to represent God upon earth.*' *Life, by her Religious Children,* p. 430.

and beseeching the Lord to deliver him from the snares
of his enemies, with which then, as now, he was surrounded. For this end 'she offered to the Eternal
Father,' says her confessor, 'the Precious Blood of
Jesus Christ, to which she was very devout, her fervent
prayers, the persecutions, crosses, and maladies which
God had sent her in more than usual abundance, not
to speak of the penances which she imposed upon herself. What did she not do in this respect, and what
did she not obtain! How grateful Rome ought to be
to her,' he exclaims; 'one day, please God, this will
be known! When she offered herself to God for the
peace of the Church, she knew that these offerings were
to cost her an aggravation of sufferings, maladies, and
persecutions, because the Divine Justice exercised Itself
upon her.'

She was left in no doubt on this point, for heavenly locutions had apprised her of it. We shall have
to return to this subject when we come to speak of her
as a victim of expiation; at present we advert to it
simply in illustration of her ardent love for the Church
of God. This love sprang from the vivid spiritual perceptions which she had by faith; for faith is 'the
evidence of things which appear not,' and reveals them
as they truly are, making the soul to realise their proper value; a truth of which the eleventh chapter of
St. Paul's Epistle to the Hebrews contains so magnificent an exposition. This might seem to be the place
to allude to the many miracles of healing which she
wrought, as exhibiting the extraordinary power of her
faith. That she possessed that eminent faith which is
numbered among the gifts *gratis data*,* we have her

* The gifts *gratis data* are thus enumerated by St. Paul in
his first Epistle to the Corinthians (xii. 8-10): 'To one by the

confessor's testimony; but as theologians generally refer
miracles, not to the gift of faith, but to that of healing,
or of miracles, we abstain here from citing them as
instances.*

Although we have deferred speaking of Anna Maria's
devotion to the Blessed Sacrament, as well as to our
Lady, the Saints, and Angels, till we come to dwell
more particularly on her special devotions, yet this place
seems peculiarly fitting for allusion to a devotion which
was in her so prominent from the first: we mean devotion to the Blessed Trinity; and this on account of

---

Spirit is given the word of wisdom; and to another the word of
knowledge, according to the same Spirit. To another faith in
the same Spirit; to another the grace of healing in one Spirit;
to another, the working of miracles; to another, prophecy; to
another, the discerning of spirits; to another, diverse kinds of
tongues; to another, interpretation of speeches:' in all nine.
    * 'By the grace *gratis data* of faith, some understand that
faith which is the mother of miracles, because it produces them
all. . . . Such a faith is excellent, because, besides theological
faith, it includes an heroic faith. . . . But in reality this faith
belongs to the 4th or 5th grace *gratis data*, wherein prodigies
are spoken of. Others by the (gratuitous) gift of faith understand the gift of professing and preaching intrepidly the mysteries of our holy faith; but it does not appear that this gift
implies, beyond theological faith, anything more than a great
constancy and fortitude in openly professing the holy faith, or
a great zeal in promulgating it. . . . I shall adhere, then, to the
Angelical Doctor in stating that faith, as a grace *gratis data*,
consists in a supereminent certainty of the truths which belong to our faith, not in order to their belief, but in order to
their manifestation to others and for the instructing them well
therein. . . . The grace of faith consists in the infused virtue of
faith (which theologians rank first), without which none can be
just or can be saved. . . . The grace (*gratis data*) of faith consists in a most eminent assurance which God adds by His light
to the common faith, in order to render the subject apt to instruct others concerning the Catholic verities of faith, which are
the first and infallible principles of Catholic doctrine.' Scaramelli, *Direttorio Mistico*, vol. i. pp. 64, 5.

the preëminence of that 'royal dogma of the faith,' as
Father Faber emphatically calls it, and the 'queen of
all mysteries,' nay, the very 'Object of our faith,' in a
sense in which no other is. 'There is not a movement
in the whole Church,' says the same spiritual writer in
his work on *The Blessed Sacrament*,* 'not a doctrine
or a rite, or a ceremonial, or an exercise of jurisdiction,
not an energy of power and of benevolence, but, rightly
interpreted, is an act of worship of the Most Holy and
Undivided Trinity.   There is not a church opened, a
sacrament administered or received, a sacrifice offered,
or a devotion practised, the honour and the glory of
which does not reach to the Holy Trinity.'   Yet while
adoration of the Blessed Trinity forms thus the sum
and substance of all Christian devotion, nevertheless a
prominent and special devotion to this Mystery of all
mysteries, the head and fountain of all the rest, is not
usually a characteristic of the commencement of a life
of perfection.   It is rather the goal to which the per-
fected soul tends, and in which it rests as its· centre,
when it has been so blessed as to attain to it. 'What
proves,' says one of her biographers, 'that Anna Maria
was raised betimes to the heights of the supernatural
life, is the devotion which she had, from the earliest
period of her conversion, to the mystery of the Holy
Trinity.   Assuredly this great and profound mystery
merits the adoration, veneration, homage, and worship
of all Christians, because it is the first of all mysteries,
the source and term of all the others ; yet experience
teaches us that the greater number even of pious persons fail to reach these heights.   The *cultus* of this
mystery is reserved for souls of no· common order,
souls whose courage and generosity permit them to as-

* Pp. 285, 6.

H

cend high enough to gaze in contemplation, through the
obscurities of faith, on the august abysses of the Unity
of our God in the Holy Trinity of Persons. Anna
Maria descended and mounted alternately, passing and
repassing from the sublimities of contemplation to the
simplicity of practice.'* This holy woman had been
divinely invited to these lofty heights. Her confessor
tells us that one day, when she was praying in the
church of the Carmelites, before an altar where a picture representing the Most Holy Trinity was exposed,
she heard, being rapt in an ecstasy, the voice of her
Lord inviting her to the adoration of this great Mystery.
This divine locution greatly intensified the attraction
which already drew her loving heart to a worship of
which (as Father Faber tells us†) one of the leading
characteristics is tenderness.

It was Anna Maria's great devotion to the Blessed
Trinity which prompted her when, after her conversion, she desired to become a Tertiary of some religious
order, as the nearest approach to the religious state
which she, as a married woman, could make, to select
that of the Discalced Trinitarians.‡ On being ques-

* P. Gabriel Bouffier, *Vie de la Vénérable Servante de Dieu,
Anna-Maria Taigi,* p. 93.

† *Notes on Doctrinal and Spiritual Subjects,* vol. i. p. 3.

‡ The Order of Trinitarians for the Redemption of Captives
was founded by St. John of Matha and St. Felix of Valois, and
formally approved by Innocent III. in 1198. An association of
lay-persons, to aid the Brothers in their charitable labours and
to join with them in honouring in a special manner the Ever-
Blessed Trinity, was formed later by the saintly founder, and
erected into a Third Order by Pope Honorius III. on the 7th
May, 1217. 'This institute,' says Mgr. de Ségur, 'is not a
simple confraternity; it is a genuine order, as the Holy See has
formally declared. "We decree and declare," says Pope Benedict XIII., "that the Third Order [of the Trinitarians] is truly
and properly an order, including within its unity seculars living

tioned by her confessor, P. Angelo, as to her motives
and object in becoming a Tertiary, she replied that her
motive was an ardent desire to offer herself to the Lord,
so as to belong to Him irrevocably. 'I should desire,'
she said, 'to be before Him a real and constant victim
for all the sins committed in the entire world against
the Divine Majesty.' She already understood her mission. 'It is well,' he rejoined; 'God assuredly wills
this of you—that you should be a religious in the midst
of the world.' Having obtained her spiritual father's
sanction, the next thing was to gain her husband's permission, which, as we have seen, he granted; it being
understood that the Fathers received her only on the
condition that she should continue to perform the duties
of her secular state as a wife and a mother. She was
received in the church of the Convent of San Carlino.*
One of the Fathers, P. Giovanni of the Visitation, a
man of eminent virtue, who was afterwards created
Minister General of the Discalced Trinitarians, thus

---

in the world. It has its own rule, its novitiate, its profession,
and a habit of a particular material and form."' The Tertiary,
in short, is one who lives as a Religious in the world, so far as
this is possible. The Trinitarian Tertiary engages to live in
the world the life which is proper to the Trinitarian Religious;
a life of poverty, penance, and humility, but, above all, a life
of active and disinterested charity towards his neighbour, the
exact opposite of the worldly life, which is one of avarice, sensuality, selfishness, and pride. Special indulgences have been
granted to this order by successive Pontiffs, all applicable to the
souls in Purgatory. Pius IX., by a rescript of the 22d March,
1847, renewed and added to them.

　* San Carlino alle quattro fontane, one of the four Trinitarian Convents of Rome. The Trinitarians at San Carlino
were Spaniards. The Chapel of San Carlino, or little St. Charles,
was dedicated to St. Charles Borromeo, and was so designated
to distinguish it from larger churches in Rome of the same
name.

refers to the ceremony in his juridical deposition. It will be observed that it contains an instance of the prompt and perfect obedience which she always paid to her confessors. 'Anna Maria was in a state of great fervour; the sensibility of her heart and the ardour of her devotion were excited to the highest point by the novelty of this ceremony, so moving in itself, but, more than all, by the prospect of the total self-despoilment which she was about to make, at the foot of the altar, of all that she had loved in the world, in order to put on for ever the insignia of poverty and penance. From the very commencement of the ceremony she experienced through her whole being an extraordinary commotion. In vain did she strive to check her tears and sobs, and to repress the boundings of love and the burning sighs which arose within her. Nothing seemed capable of calming the agitation of her mind. The voice of obedience had alone this power. P. Fernando, who was giving her the holy habit, had been her conessor, at least at intervals. He commanded her to cease those exterior movements of devotion, which interfered with the good order of the holy function. At once all agitation ceased, to the great surprise of the assistants, and the Venerable passed instantaneously from the involuntary demonstrations of an unaccustomed fervour to a state of perfect tranquillity, in which you could no longer perceive in her countenance aught but the sweet shining of a heavenly ecstasy, and during the whole remainder of the ceremony, which was pretty long, she continued to maintain the most perfect recollection. One could nevertheless discern through it what must have been the secret operations of grace in her soul. All the fortunate witnesses of this scene were affected to tears. From that time they conceived the

highest opinion of Anna Maria, and regarded her as a
holy soul, to whom God had accorded great privileges.'

It will be noticed that the case was widely different
from what might have borne a practical resemblance to
it in the natural order. A person moved even by a
sincere fervour to abandon herself to unchecked demonstrations of an excited character might, very likely, at
the admonition of a priest, have possessed sufficient
self-command to check these natural ebullitions; but
the result would probably have been a certain temporary abashment, and, even if calm gravity had taken
the place of fervid excitement, she would not have instantly passed into another state of devotion equally
striking and far more unusual. For Anna Maria seems
at once to have experienced a change which He who
inwardly prays in the faithful could alone have operated; an ecstatic state of calm interior union being apparently substituted, without the intervention of an
instant of time, for that of sensible devotion with all
its irrepressible external manifestations.

From the moment that Anna Maria was thus bound
more closely to the service of God through her affiliation to a religious order, her charity knew no bounds,
and her mortifications and penitential exercises were
restrained only within such limits as the discretion of
her confessor imposed upon her, and to which she always submitted. The desire to imitate Jesus Christ
Crucified and to unite herself intimately to Him became now, more than ever, the one prevailing occupation of her mind. P. Calixte (himself a Trinitarian
and one of Anna Maria's most approved biographers)
says that it was shortly after she had been received as
Tertiary that, prostrate one day at the foot of the Crucifix, in her little oratory, after inflicting on herself a

severe discipline, she first beheld that mysterious sun which was to accompany her through life. All accounts agree in stating that she saw it first while thus engaged, and that it occurred during the early days of her conversion. Her confessor bade her ask of God an explanation of this extraordinary phenomenon, and she received for answer: 'This is a mirror which I cause you to see, that you may understand good and evil.'* Her confessor then enjoined her to beg God to withdraw this gift, and communicate it to virgins in monasteries rather than to a married woman. Anna Maria again obeyed; but our Lord was not well pleased with the command which had been given her, for He replied that God is free to do as He wills; that no one ought to be presumptuous enough to wish to penetrate His secrets; and that the confessor ought to limit himself to performing his duty and not go beyond it. The light of the sun (which we shall hereafter describe) was at the beginning of the colour of flame and the disc itself like dead gold. But in proportion as Anna Maria made progress in virtue its brilliancy increased, until, although she was fortified to behold its splendour, it exceeded, as she said, that of seven suns.

Anna Maria used to perform with utmost punctuality all the exercises of the association, and endeavour by every means in her power to propagate the devotion. She paid frequent visits to the Church of the Trinitarians, where she would offer the most fervent prayers for those Christian slaves who were groaning in bondage to the infidels, and often obtained their liberation, as was supernaturally revealed to her. 'She joined to prayer,' says Cardinal Pedicini, 'special penances in

---

* 'Questo è uno specchio che io ti faccio vedere, perchè tu capisca il bene e il male.'

addition to those which she habitually performed, mortifications both spiritual and corporal, visits to the Seven Basilicas, prolonged fasts, pilgrimages barefoot to the holy Crucifix of San Paolo fuori le mura, of which I have been many times the eye-witness in company with her confessor. In the first years she had often to write letters; she began them with the Name of the Trinity: "Praised be the Holy Trinity," &c. If, when visiting the sick, she was requested to make the sign of the cross upon them, or to let them touch the Madonna which she wore on her heart, she never failed to call with reverence on the Most Holy Trinity to obtain by the merits of the Virgin the desired grace.'

Such, then, and far greater than we can say, was the faith of Anna Maria, and such her devotion to the great primal Object of faith, the Ever-Blessed and Adorable Trinity.

CHAPTER VIII.

ANNA MARIA'S SUBLIME HOPE AND CONFIDENCE IN GOD.

HOPE, the second of the theological virtues, while it resembles faith in the distinctive character of these virtues, namely, in having God for its immediate object, differs from it in this, that it disposes the will to hope in God, whereas faith is a virtue which resides in the understanding, which it illuminates and elevates to believe that God is, and that all that He has revealed is most true. Hope, then, resides in the will, to raise it to an expectation of God, looking to receive from Him eternal happiness in the possession of Him. Ne-

vertheless, the two virtues are closely united ; hope
having its roots, so to say, in faith, which enlightens
the mind to know that man's beatitude is in God; that
it is his ultimate end ; that God calls him thereto, and
gives him the means which suffice for its attainment.
This knowledge moves the will to raise itself towards
God and to look forward to the possession of Him
hereafter ; and, because of itself it could not reach so
high, God infuses the divine virtue of hope into the
soul to fortify its natural weakness in this expectation
and aspiration. Hope prompts also many other acts in
the soul with reference to God, as the object of its desire, but this expectation may be regarded as its proper
and distinctive character. Moreover, even as faith
which moves the understanding to believe in God as
its first and principal object, inclines it also to believe
many other things, external to God, which He has revealed, thus also the second theological virtue, which
moves the will to hope for God as its prime and principal object, disposes it also to hope for many other
goods which proceed from God, and which are sub-
servient to the accomplishment of man's beatitude or
are means to its attainment.* As the soul is also in
man joined to a body, in union with which body he
has to work out his salvation, and as this body has
certain needs, the supply of which are conditions of its
life, divine hope produces, secondarily, a confidence
that God will give what is needful in this respect, so
long as it is His pleasure to prolong the period of our
probation on earth. He who has given the greater
will assuredly give the less : such is the nature of the
Apostle's argument when he says, 'He that spared
not even His own Son, but delivered Him up for us

* See Bail, *La Théologie Affective*, tom. iii. med. xii.

all, how hath He not also, with Him, given us all
things?*

Regarding the sphere of hope, then, as embracing
all these various objects, we will dwell awhile on the
sublime degree in which this great servant of God possessed this virtue. As faith does homage to God's
truth, so hope honours His goodness towards us, and
His fidelity to His promises, which assure to us our
reward through the instrumentality of specified means,
even as the act of hope we. make expresses. These
means, as all know, whereby grace, the remission of
sins, and eternal blessedness in the possession of God
are to be attained, are the merits of Jesus Christ; but
under this comprehensive head is implicitly contained
all which the merits of the God-Man have won for us :
the precious and abundant treasure of assistance and
encouragement in our heavenward path which He purchased for us by His Blood ; the patronage of His Immaculate Mother, whom He has given to us for our
mother also ; the intercession of His saints ; and every
other aid which we can look and hope for as His
followers and His members. Unhappy aliens from the
faith, born disinherited, and brought up in ignorance of
what is the true and glorious portion of the children of
God, reproach us for making the gifts of His love and
the rich appanage which His Incarnation, His Passion,
and His Death on the Cross bring in their train, and of
which we are constituted the inheritors by our alliance
with Him, the objects of our hope and of our confidence ; as if we substituted them for Him at whose
hands and through whose merits we receive them. But
it is their ignorance of the true character and the position in the Christian scheme of the Theological Virtues

* Rom. viii. 32.

which makes it possible for them to entertain such
erroneous notions.

These are the terms in which the confessor speaks
of Anna Maria's hope in God :—' Although her life was
one entire and unceasing exercise of works of piety,
nevertheless she founded her hope of eternal salvation
solely on the merits of Jesus Christ, and on the intercession of the Blessed Virgin and of the saints, her
patrons, to whom she had constant recourse for this
object. Her thoughts and prayers, day and night, were
applied to this intention. On her part, she judged
herself unworthy of everything, and her continual exclamation was, " *Peccavi ; Domine, miserere mei* — I
have sinned ; Lord, have mercy on me." ' This detestation of her past sins was always present to her, and she
was continually applying her self-imposed penances and
mortifications, as well as the numerous crosses and
sufferings which were daily sent to her by God, to efface
them. But this deep sense of sin never discouraged or
disheartened her, for her hope was placed, not on herself, but on Him who could never fail her. Her confidence in Him was the counterpart of her non-esteem
and contempt of self. This confidence imparted to her
petitions a holy ardour and a fearless pertinacity, which,
if we may permit ourselves such an expression, God
seems unable to resist. When the Word was made
flesh and dwelt amongst us, He often, as we learn from
the Gospel narrative, encouraged, rewarded, and praised
this audacity and persistency in prayer. Those who
insisted on being heard were heard, and importunity
never failed of success. Thus did He who was the
' Brightness of His Father's Glory and the Figure of
His Substance,' the Only-Begotten Son, revealing in
the acts of His Sacred Humanity what was the true

character of the Invisible and Incomprehensible God, assure us beyond the possibility of error, that a filial and holy violence is acceptable to Him, and that He can refuse nothing to it.

'For Anna Maria,' says Cardinal Pedicini, 'God was the most loving father, the most generous benefactor, the most faithful friend, the most precious treasure, and her only all. She exhorted all whom she loved to place their whole trust in Him in all affairs, however difficult, whether of the spiritual or temporal order. She did not like to see persons pusillanimous and timid, being desirous, on the contrary, that God should be served faithfully and with all the energy of our souls, but at the same time with love and with a perfect confidence in His great goodness and mercy.' She was an enemy to melancholy and down-heartedness, knowing how displeasing these tempers are to God. Mgr. Luquet records some words which our Lord once addressed to her on this subject, indicating the dangers of sadness, and the evil which it works in souls. He manifested to her also the root of pride and insincerity from which it often springs. ' If the cunning serpent,' He said, ' succeeds in casting hearts into profound sadness, be sure that he has laid his nets there, that he is drawing these souls to the brink of a precipice, and that a special grace is needed to deliver them. Dost thou know what My dear Philip' (St. Philip Neri) 'did when a taciturn, proud, and insincere person came to him? He drove him away, and would not hear him. But if a sinner came to him of a cordial, loving disposition, full of frankness, he pressed him to his bosom, and did not leave him till he had placed him in the way of sanctification.' And at another time, 'Take care, My daughter, and be not affrighted. If the devil perceives that

thou givest way to fear, he has obtained the victory.'
Accordingly, Anna Maria, as Cardinal Pedicini observes,
earnestly recommended people 'not to allow themselves
to be cast down by a spirit of fear, which, when carried
too far, leads to discouragement, of which the devil
knows how to profit by besetting the road of virtue and
the service of so good a God, who is so full of love and
kindness to His creatures, with difficulties ever more
and more perplexing.' The Lord was pleased visibly
to recompense the filial confidence which she reposed
in Him, even in the smallest temporal matters. It happened frequently, as both the Cardinal and confessor
testify, that when Anna Maria felt moved to visit the
Seven Basilicas without having a *soldo* at her disposal
to meet the little outlay needed for her companions,
she would beg God to supply what was wanted, and
before the close of the day some one unexpectedly would
bring all that was requisite. Nay more; Anna Maria's
confidence in God almost invariably obtained fair
weather for the little party, a proof, if any were wanting, that our good Lord loves us to have recourse to
Him, like little children, in smaller things as in the
greater.

'How often did it not happen,' writes the Cardinal,
'that the visit of the Seven Basilicas would be commenced in rainy and threatening weather.' (The showers
in Rome, it may be observed, are often like drenching
water-spouts.) 'But Anna Maria, confiding in God,
who is Master of the elements, was not discouraged, and
the day generally proved fine. Her undoubting trust
dispelled the clouds and storms and restored serenity.
Many a time, whether after returning or in the course of
the pilgrimage, and in a thousand similar circumstances,
the goodness of God towards His humble servant, who

hoped in Him for everything, was clearly perceived by others.' But whatever the weather might be, she was still substantially heard, in that the object of her request was the accomplishment of an act of devotion without hindrance or discouragement to any of her companions. 'Rain sometimes fell,' continues the same witness, 'but it was a thing unheard-of that any of the party suffered in health; Anna Maria's hope was in this point never deceived.' So firm was her conviction of the power of this virtue with God, that she was always exhorting others not to place their confidence in men, who turn at every wind, but in God, who is unchangeable in His promises. Indeed, it was a favourite saying of hers that 'man is a weather-cock and God alone stable.' By this filial confidence, we are assured, she almost always got what she asked for, never allowing herself to be cast down by the obstacles which arose or by the delay of God in granting her petitions. 'If,' says the same witness, 'after having prayed, and done all that depended upon herself, to procure for her neighbour the graces she solicited, she did not succeed (and this was rare indeed, for her prayers were almost always heard), then, far from disquieting herself, she adored the designs of God, and humbled herself before Him, and before men, being well persuaded that God disposes all for our good when we have recourse to Him by prayer.'

It was the same in the affair of her own salvation. Knowing that man left to himself, without grace and without supernatural succours, can in this matter only act amiss, and is, indeed, incapable of conceiving the least thought which is truly good or meritorious of eternal life, she was continually imploring divine aid and begging the assistance of her heavenly intercessors. 'To these mediations,' says the Cardinal, 'she solely

attributed the graces she obtained; on all occasions she
acknowledged herself as unworthy of them, and as not
deserving that the earth should support her, as she often
said. She had such low sentiments of herself, that she
was ever praying God to have her in His keeping, and
to grant her perseverance in the midst of her sufferings,
for she dreaded not being able to endure them; at the
same time she hoped all, confiding in the merits of Jesus
Christ and in the assistance of the Blessed Virgin, the
Angels, and the Saints.' Thus it is that hope and reliance on God are invariably proportioned to a true mistrust of ourselves—a *true* mistrust; for there is a false
mistrust, a mere human discouragement, the effect of
timidity or of disappointment from previous failure.
That kind of mistrust Anna Maria, as we have seen,
did not favour or approve.

Her hope, being thus founded on the most solid
principles, partook of their immutable firmness. When
praying for the wants of the Church, of the State, or of
individuals, no obstacles availed to check her fervour
or perseverance; the greatest difficulties could not cause
her to lose heart: for what were difficulties in the way
of God? Her principle was, that when man has done
all he can, it is for God to do the rest—to do all, in
fact; and she used to say that the more arduous an
affair seemed to be, the more was God pledged to take
it in hand, because it became His work, and that obstacles are often removed in ways most unforeseen.
'In the most difficult and complicated affairs, whether
of the Church or of the State,' writes the confessor,
'she prayed, and prayed always with a hope and a
courage which never faltered, and which merited for
her, even in the first years of her fervour, the most
singular promises from God. He promised her, in

effect, to cut the thread of all the sanguinary conspiracies which impious men were plotting against Rome; and this promise was always fulfilled. Unworthy and miserable sinner as she esteemed herself, yet she was confident of obtaining all that she asked by the merits of Jesus Christ : the triumph of the Church and the preservation of the Pope, as well as all the graces and favours she requested in behalf of bishops, cardinals, priests, religious, and all classes of persons, but specially of sinners.

'What did she not obtain,' says the confessor, 'by this lively hope and perfect confidence! How many ecclesiastics, some of high dignity, adopted a line of conduct more conformable to their state! High and low, nobles and common people, rich and poor, all experienced the effects of her lively hope in God. Assassins and criminals sentenced to death felt it also in their turn, inasmuch as her firm confidence discharged the debts they owed to Divine Justice; for she never ceased praying until she had received from her Divine Spouse the assurance that the grace was accorded, although she had to pay for it afterwards in crosses and aggravated sufferings.' Full of the energy inspired by her own invincible hope, she knew also how to encourage sinners. When she had succeeded in shaking and alarming them, and had made them recognise their deplorable condition, straightway she animated them to place their entire confidence in God. Indeed, none did she exhort more strongly to the practice of this virtue than sinners; and no sooner had she happily brought an offender to this state of penitence and hope than, like one who has made a valuable purchase or acquisition, she hastened joyfully to charge herself with the debt he had incurred and pay the penance due for his sins.

While, however, she showed herself an enemy to
that fear which springs from human infirmity and want
of reliance on God, she well knew that there was also
a salutary fear which ought always to go hand in hand
with hope,—seeing that otherwise hope degenerates into
presumption,—a fear lest we should be wanting on our
part ; but this kind of fear animates to exertion, instead
of plunging into despondency. Did she desire to obtain any spiritual favours, all her prayers were preceded
and accompanied with a train of good works and penitential exercises ; and in the case of temporal affairs, she
took care to do besides all that prudence suggested in
order to insure success. 'Although she relied upon
Providence,' says the confessor, 'for the needs of her
family, she did not remain with her hands by her side,
as people say, but worked night and day to earn what
she could. When her work did not suffice, she had recourse to God, with the assurance of obtaining everything, because she had done all that depended on herself.' Her husband bears testimony to the same effect,
that, though full of trust in God and always praying,
she was never idle. ' She did not,' he says in his homely
but forcible way, 'wait for the basket to come down
from Heaven without doing anything herself. . . . She
joined labour to prayer, in order not to tempt God, by
seeming to expect that He should work a miracle for
her. When she found herself in a position of real
necessity, she addressed herself to God with all the
greater confidence, and the Lord helped her so well
that the maintenance of her numerous family without
their ever suffering want was a continual miracle.' And
again, alluding to her perfect tranquillity of mind at the
most critical times, and the marvellous manner in which
the necessities of the family were constantly supplied,

he says, 'What could I have done, with my salary of six scudi a month, if I had not had the servant of God? I had committed to her all the care of the house, I let her do as she chose and go wherever she pleased, because I observed that when she had been performing some devotion Providence came to our aid. On these occasions she would go to the Crucifix of San Paolo, or to that of San Pietro in Carcere, or to Santa Cecilia.'

But this seeking of daily bread was all ordered to a higher end. It was not a mere cry of necessity to the Good Father on whom, as Scripture tells us, even the 'young ravens call,' and the 'lions, seeking their meat from God.'* We, His intelligent creatures, the children of His love, called to sit at the eternal banquet which He is preparing for us in our true home, can never ask, or, at least, ought never to ask, for the supply of our temporal needs with a primary and exclusive eye to them. 'It is needless for me to say,' observes Domenico, 'that her faith and her hope were all for the gaining Paradise; her conversation with me, and with every one in the house, plainly showed that she was enamoured of Heaven, without any pre-occupation concerning the things of earth. She might have made herself comfortably rich, if she had sought this world's goods; but she was contented to labour, in order to maintain the family as well as she could, and did not concern herself in the smallest degree to profit by the persons who frequented her company. The friendship which the late Queen of Etruria felt for her would have alone sufficed to relieve us from our straits.'

We feel bound to give his meed of praise to this honest man. Assuredly Domenico was no saint; he was, indeed, a very ordinary, commonplace sort of Chris-

* Ps. cxlvi. 9, ciii. 21.

I

tian, with his fair quota of faults and imperfections;
he was, moreover, one upon whom the necessities of a
laborious life weighed heavily. He had little rest, scant
leisure, drudging on at a monotonous routine of daily
service in the house of the rich, to return wearied and
jaded to his own humble home, often when the sun
was about to rise to light another day, which was to
set, like the one just closed, on another round of toil.
And then there were his children to provide for upon
extremely small means. Anxiety for their interests
seemed, not merely excusable, but a parental duty;
and meanwhile here were affluent persons, not only
ready, but desirous, to relieve his family and secure them
a competency, if only his wife would hold out her hand
to receive what was offered, or, rather, not draw it back
from accepting what was eagerly pressed upon her. If
she would but consent to act thus, all this solicitude
might be removed, and comfort and ease insured for
life to himself and those who were dependent on him.
Had Domenico, then, been troublesome to his wife on
this point, and taken it ill of her that she would not
agree to do what seemed so reasonable and proper, we
could scarcely have wondered, or even have passed a
very severe censure on one who, not sharing the high
graces and gifts of his partner in life, might well not
understand conduct that sprang from exalted motives
of the supernatural order. Yet he does not appear
either to have been displeased with her, or to have
urged upon her an opposite course with any earnestness
or pertinacity. This unheroic man had, it must be concluded, a faith strong enough to restrain him from in-
terfering with what seemed to be God's will, and from
checking the attractions and aspirations of her who was
spiritually more highly favoured than himself, although

he shared the sacrifice of temporal advantage which
these entailed. Here is what he says on this subject.
'A crowd of distinguished persons used to come to my
house to see her—nobles, prelates, and others. I would
say to her, Why don't you think of mentioning such
and such a thing to this person or that, for the sake of
the family? She would immediately answer me, "O,
let us place our trust in God; let us hope in God;"
with other like expressions, which closed my mouth.
Nevertheless, her faith and confidence in God were so
great, that we never wanted for anything, even at the
most critical periods. God be blessed a thousand times!'

But, it may be said, why did Anna Maria thus de-
cline for husband and children help which they so much
needed, and thus impose on them a poverty which, had
she stood singly, she would have been free to accept or
choose meritoriously for herself alone? It was because
she knew that it was her Lord's will. She knew that
He desired that she should remain poor, and her family
also be dependent on Him day by day for daily bread;
thus offering in the midst of the world an example
of perfect voluntary poverty and disengagement from
earthly possessions all the more striking that, unlike
the irrevocable sacrifice once for all which the Religious
makes, unsurpassed in itself as such a renunciation is,
hers was to have the additional merit of being in a
manner renewed every day, since every day it was open
to her to relieve herself and, what was to her of much
more moment, those belonging to her from these straitened circumstances, without violating any divine precept or breaking any vow. She was to exemplify before the world that which the very words of the 'Pater
Noster' teach, the daily dependence on his Heavenly
Father which the Christian ought to feel. True, all

Christians are not called to act as she did ; they are
not bound to refuse a provision for their family, nor
forbidden, in any other prudent way, to keep future
wants in view or to plan and lay up accordingly ; but
all are forbidden to do this in a spirit which tends to
foster, first, anxiety in the process of acquiring and,
next, a sense of security and independence of God when
competence or affluence has been obtained. It was not
for the fulness of his barns that the rich man was reproved, but for this godless sense of security, expressed
in those words of his : 'Soul, thou hast much goods
laid up for many years :' this was why he was called
'a fool' by the mouth of unerring Wisdom.

Anna Maria, then, was by God's special appointment to support her numerous family always on the
verge of extreme poverty, yet never falling into destitution, and this as by a continual miracle of God's Providence. ' Her Heavenly Guide,' says Cardinal Pedicini,
' who was leading her on to practise heroic virtue of the
highest order ever more and more perfectly, never sent
her abundant resources ; on the contrary, He willed
that she should live on, day by day, like the birds, as
she herself said,' often telling her husband, that she
must have no other granary but that of the Heavenly
Father. Human prudence would have suggested that,
as the family lived thus always on the very border of
want, no margin (so to say) existing, and no superfluity
remaining in the best of times, the assumption of any
fresh charge was not to be contemplated. Yet it was
in the midst of such narrow circumstances that the
whole burden of an additional family was thrown upon
the Taigi. Sofia, as we have already said, returned a
widow to her parents' house, with a train of six little
children, and was more than welcomed. Anna Maria,

herself so utterly dependent on God's Providence for her sustenance day by day, could nevertheless confidently hope to provide subsistence for seven more mouths—like the Israelites gathering manna, who always had enough for their respective needs, enough and no more, however much or little they brought home—and could besides find words of cheerful encouragement for her afflicted daughter.

The following is Sofia's account, as given in her deposition :—'Having lost my husband, I returned to my paternal home weeping. My mother encouraged me, saying, " God must provide ; let us place confidence in Him, for whoever hopes in Him shall not be confounded." In those days of mourning, amongst other thoughts which saddened me, I asked myself how my mother, already so cramped for means, could feed me and my six children. She called me to her, and said, " What are you thinking about? You must know that God never abandons any one ; you will have what you need ; place your trust in God, and give no thought to anything else : as for me, I will never forsake you." Thus it was that she inspired me with confidence, by discovering the secret thoughts of my heart.' Anna Maria not only continued to place unabated trust in God's Providential care of her in seasons of great penury, but she desired to remain thus dependent on Him ; and with a generous contempt, not only of riches, but even of that moderate competence a desire to obtain which is a far more common snare, because disguised under many plausible motives, she declined the means repeatedly proffered to her for its attainment. ' Such was her contempt for earthly things,' says the confessor, ' through her ardent desire of heavenly goods, that, though immersed in poverty, she constantly refused considerable alms from persons desirous of knowing her, or who went to thank her for signal graces obtained by her prayers. She would say on such occasions, " I do not serve God for self-interest ; thank the Blessed Virgin, or such a saint, and not me." ' When these persons would urge her to accept what they offered, if not for herself, yet in order to give to the poor, it made no difference; and she would tell her benefactors that they could very well distribute their alms themselves.

But it was not merely in such instances as these, when a refined delicacy might have prompted refusal of anything that bore the appearance of payment for her charitable offices, and for the benefit of spiritual assistance, that this holy woman was immovable in her determination to refuse all aid ; but in other cases, where the offers made sprang from the purest friendship, love, and respect which she had personally inspired by her eminent virtues, she alike declined them. Maria Luisa, Queen of Etruria and afterwards Duchess of Lucca, was extremely attached to her, and having had occasion to appreciate the value of her counsels, desired greatly to have the advantage of her near neighbourhood. She accordingly offered to take Domenico into her service with a very good salary : it will be remembered that the remuneration he received from the Chigi family was but six scudi monthly. Anna Maria thanked the duchess for her kindness, but declined accepting any offer made with the object of bettering their condition. Many a time would Maria Luisa complain that her friend never asked her for anything ; and one day, when Anna Maria had gone to see her, the princess opened a drawer full of gold, and said, ' Take, take, Nanna mia, what you will.' But Anna Maria, smiling, answered with that simplicity, freedom, and frankness

which distinguished her in speaking to any one, however exalted in rank the person might be, ' How simple
you are, Madam! I serve a Master richer than you; I
trust and hope in Him; and He provides for my daily
necessities.' About a year before her death, knowing
the distressed circumstances in which herself and family
were placed, in consequence of her disabled and afflicted
state, Cardinal Pedicini offered her an apartment attached to his own residence. Here she might have
reckoned on enjoying many advantages in addition to
that of a gratuitous and comfortable abode, but the very
reasons which recommended such a plan to human
prudence, discredited it in the eyes of this waiter on
Providence. She thanked him most courteously, but
would not move. Cardinal Fesch made her a like
offer, but equally without success.

Nevertheless, although there were particular cases
in which she invariably refused help, as we have seen,
and although she always declined to profit by the opportunities afforded her of improving her condition,
still, when it was question of actual want, she did not
reject the necessary aid which God was pleased to send
her; for then she regarded it as the result of His Providential appointment. Sometimes she received a divine
intimation to this effect; as when, on one occasion of
pressing want, she was praying before the Crucifix of
San Paolo, and, having fallen into an ecstasy, a voice
told her to return to her house, where she would find
the assistance she needed; and, in fact, as soon as she
reached her dwelling, a letter was put into her hands
from the Marchese Bandini, written to her from Flo-
rence, and enclosing a small sum of money. At other
times, persons would experience a kind of movement
resembling inspiration, to succour her in her needs;

and this would happen in the case of individuals who
were living at a distance and were very slightly acquainted with her. Her friend, Cardinal Pedicini, after
mentioning this striking fact, as a corroborative testimony to her strong confidence in God, who is wont to
deal thus with those who lean wholly on Him, says
that he was himself several times inwardly moved to
carry her some assistance, although she had never let
him know that she was in peculiar want at that moment. On arriving at her house, he would always find
his anticipations realised.

As we throw fuel on fire in order to feed the flame,
so was Anna Maria in the habit of maintaining hope
and confidence alive within her by frequent ejaculations,
and she recommended a like practice to others, as being
most profitable. ' She frequently excited the virtue of
hope in her heart,' says the confessor, ' by fervent ejaculations : such as, " Jesus, my hope, have pity on me ;
Mother of hope, pray for me;" and she was in the
habit of giving utterance to similar ejaculatory prayers
in the course of the day.' And so the fire was kept
alight, and she was never taken by surprise or cast on
her own resources when the hour of trial came ; and
such hours came to her often, bringing causes for
anxiety far deeper than any which mere penury could
produce : as when her son Camillo was drawn for military service during the French occupation. She had
brought up this son, as she had her other children,
with the utmost care, training him in the holy fear of
God and the hatred of sin, and shielding him from
temptation, so far as lay in her power. But sad times
had now fallen on Italy and on Rome. The ambition of
Napoleon was filling Europe with carnage and ruin and
bringing desolation to the hearths of countless families,

who saw those in whom their best hopes were treasured, the flower of their youth, torn from them to be sacrificed to the greed of power and dominion of one man. He had iniquitously seized the States of the Church, and his troops had taken possession of the city of Peter, from which the Vicar of Jesus Christ had been dragged away captive. The Romans were consequently subjected to that tribute of blood, the terrible conscription. In Camillo's case the cruel enactment was by some fraud, we are told, stretched beyond its legal limits. When Anna Maria heard that her son was taken to be enlisted in the army of the North, then about to be engaged in a fierce struggle 'in distant and barbarous lands,'* her mother's heart was pierced with grief. We may well imagine how great was her tribulation, but anxiety for the soul of her child swallowed up all other considerations, bitter as these must have been ; the thought of the rude and licentious soldiers of whom he was to become the companion, the demoralising and godless life he was about to be compelled to lead, and the scenes of violence and disorder in which he was to be constrained to bear a part—all this arose as a horrible vision before her. She flew to the barracks, that she might at least see her child before they were parted, perhaps for ever, and give him her blessing together with some last fervent words of counsel. But the poor mother met with a repulse : she was not allowed to speak with him or even to see him, and returned all desolate to her home in speechless agony. Still, wrung with anguish as was her soul, she made no outward demonstrations, but retained her self-possession, giving utterance to her woe only at the feet of

* Napoleon was, no doubt, on the eve of his Russian campaign.

Him who could aid her, though all human help had
failed. 'O Jesus,' she exclaimed, 'Thou art my sole
hope; save, save my son, and do not permit, O Redeemer of men, that I should have suffered so much for
him in vain.' Having thus poured out her soul, she
was consoled with a secret assurancee that her son
should be soon restored to her. Here is Domenico's
account :—' I remember when my son Camillo, now
deceased, was taken for the French conscription ; he
was fraudulently carried off; and my poor wife remained for a long time unable to speak. Her grief
assuredly was very great, she felt it keenly ; nevertheless, she continued silent and resigned, without complaining of any one, not even of him who we had good
reason to believe was the cause of this injustice, and
whom she met several times. She encouraged me by
leading me to hope that Camillo would return ; and he
did return as if by miracle.' In all trying circumstances she displayed a similar spirit of confidence and
resignation. 'On the most distressing occasions,' says
her husband, 'she never worried herself, or broke out
in groans and sobs, as so many other women commonly
do ; she kept silence, and contented herself with saying, " May God's will be done !" Besides, she animated
and encouraged me to suffer for the love of God. If
they were things which concerned herself, she remained
silent and prayed : how many crosses,' he added, 'had
not this blessed soul !'

Her confidence in God was manifested not only by
a filial abandonment to His will and by a continual
looking to Him for consolation and help in her sorrows
and necessities, but by an heroic perseverance in the
penitential exercises and other difficult works which she
had undertaken. As she entered on them always in

the strength of divine grace, and not from mere natural impetuosity, she was not discouraged by obstacles which would have caused a change of purpose had she acted only from human impulse or even ordinary fervour, and which, indeed, in common cases would have seemed to justify such change. For often, after having begun a vigorous fast or other penance, she would be attacked with fever, acute internal pains, or excruciating headaches, to which she was liable, but nothing could avail to check her save obedience : the prohibition of him who had spiritual authority over her was followed ever by the most unquestioning acquiescence. In only one other case did she modify the rigour of such of her mortifications as might injure health, and that was when she was about to become a mother, because to act otherwise would have been to tempt God and require a miracle at His hands. Under all other circumstances, her sublime confidence in God made her persevere in spite of illness ; and this trustfulness, after being put to the test, would often be recompensed by a sudden cure.

We have seen that she exhorted all whom she knew to hope and confidence in God ; and when, probably by some inward intimation, she was aware that they were capable of the higher degrees of this virtue, she would strongly urge upon them its more perfect exercise. Two instances may here be given. They occurred in relation with the confidential priest* whom, it will

* Monsignor D. Raffaele Natali, Abate of San Vittore, Chaplain of the Capella Pontificia, Secretary at one time to Mgr. Strambi, and afterwards to Cardinal Barberini. He did not become a Roman Prelate until after the death of Anna Maria. It was as a priest of Macerata that he first became known to Mgr. Strambi, the Bishop of Macerata and Tolentino, who recommended him to the position of confidant of the Venerable

be remembered, Cardinal Pedicini had substituted for
himself in the year 1815. He might have obtained
some considerable ecclesiastical benefice by the help of
powerful recommendations which would have been made
to the Pope in his behalf, had he so desired, but she
earnestly dissuaded him from availing himself of them.
The Emperor of Austria wrote twice to his *chargé
d'affaires* at the court of Leo XII. bidding him use his
interest with the Pontiff to forward this priest's promotion, but Anna Maria was unwilling that the Austrian
minister should even speak to the Dataria in the Emperor's name. But more than this : we find her actually
hindering him from profiting by the successful exertions
of friends. For when two benefices had become vacant
by the death of Cardinal Pallotta, and the relatives of
this priest were in consequence exerting themselves in
his favour, Anna Maria was resolved that their efforts
should not prove successful, and told him plainly that
she was praying God to defeat them. It seems that,
in point of fact, the acceptance ultimately rested with
himself ; but, Cardinal Gregorio having informed him
that the Pope (Gregory XVI.) was desirous of conferring the two benefices, which were at Macerata, on an
ecclesiastic of those parts, the priest, acting by the ad-

Servant of God. 'He is at this day my penitent,' writes P.
Filippo, Anna Maria's last confessor, in his deposition. 'I
charged him to take note of everything, and enjoined the pious
woman to hide nothing from him. She, however, told him
several times, as he has assured me, that she was under an impossibility of manifesting everything to him, but that she would
speak unreservedly to her confessor; for she used great circumspection, above all, in matters of conscience and when it was
question of persons known to this ecclesiastic. Mgr. Natali
appears among the witnesses, and survived until a very recent
period.'

vice of this holy woman, instantly withdrew his claim and gave them up to the Holy Father, who was pleased to express his satisfaction and to promise him a compensation in Rome itself. But this engagement escaped the Pontiff's memory, nor would Anna Maria permit her friend to take any measures, direct or indirect, to recall it to his mind. The promise therefore remained without effect, and Anna Maria used to tell this good priest that he must be content to live on as he was, asking alms* for the love of God in behalf of a poor family, and abide in the way of humiliations for the love of Jesus Christ, in whom he ought to place all his hopes.

The second instance to which we have adverted was the following. A young woman of the name of Ursula Annibali fled, terrified, from her husband, and took refuge in Anna Maria's house. He was a man of low extraction, bad habits, and a ferocious temper; furious at his wife's flight, he was searching for her everywhere. Anna Maria charitably received the poor fugitive and recommended her in prayer to God. After glancing at her mysterious sun, she turned to her companion, the confidential priest, and said, 'Go and seek the husband of this unfortunate woman: you will tell him that his wife is here. I forewarn you, however, that when he sees you he will rush at you with a great knife; but do

---

* The deep poverty of Anna Maria and her family in the latter period of her life, when she was unable to work, reduced her to the necessity of receiving pecuniary assistance. One of her spiritual sons contributed a little, and the confessor collected some alms; but, as this aid was insufficient, the priest Natali had to make a kind of daily quest, which was a source of indescribable pain to this holy woman, although he only asked the alms as for a poor mother of a family, without mentioning her name.

not be alarmed, trust in God, and invoke His Holy
Name in the depth of your heart : He will not allow
you to perish. Nevertheless administer severe reproofs
to this man, coupled with threats, and he will become
gentle as a lamb.' All happened as she had said. The
man rushed at the priest with a knife, and the priest
followed the directions of her who was to him as a
spiritual mother. Instantly this hardened ruffian burst
into tears, and fell upon his knees. Anna Maria had
the satisfaction of seeing the couple happily reconciled.
They breakfasted together at her house, where the re-
pentant husband had come to seek his wife, and, after
addressing to them words of earnest exhortation, she
sent them back to their home in peace. P. Filippo, in
his deposition, mentions that they were still living at
that time in perfect harmony.

One character peculiar to confidence in God, when
it arrives at an heroic degree, must be noticed in conclusion as having distinguished that of Anna Maria;
we mean a certain boldness which, had it not been
authorised by the faith, confidence, and love from
which it sprang, would have worn the appearance of
unpardonable familiarity. Similar behaviour is related
of Saints, and is akin to those paradoxical desires which
are also recorded of them. 'For the conversion of
souls,' says the confessor, 'she employed, if the expression may be excused, a holy boldness. Burning ejaculations, couched in the most energetic language, would
escape her lips, in the midst of her domestic occupations, her pains, crosses, interior sufferings, and maladies. St. Paul desired to be anathema, and Moses to
be erased from the book of life, rather than not obtain
the salvation of their brethren ; and in like manner
this pious woman, making use of affectionate expres-

sions, significant of a perfect confidence, would reproach her Divine Spouse, telling Him He did not love her, and that if He did not grant her such or such a favour, she should be obliged to quarrel with Him.' O unimaginable familiarity with the Eternal, as unimaginable to our poor cold hearts—which have no title to venture on language such as only that perfect love which equalises lovers and, so to say, annihilates distances, even when infinite, could reverently use—as is the condescension which deigns not only to excuse but to be pleased with these follies of love ! 'By her fervour,' adds P. Filippo, 'her penances, her faith, and her lively confidence, she obtained all.'

CHAPTER IX.

ANNA MARIA'S HEROIC CHARITY TOWARDS GOD AND TOWARDS HER NEIGHBOUR.

'Charity,' says a witness of her virtues, 'burned in the heart of the servant of God with so intense a flame, that you might have deemed that her interior was a volcano.' Such, and such-like, is the universal testimony as to the degree in which the heart of this holy woman was inflamed with this greatest of all the Christian virtues. The virtues which have God for their immediate object, that is, the Theological Virtues, faith, hope, and charity, take the highest rank, and amongst these charity, as the Apostle testifies, holds the most exalted place. Moreover, unlike the other two, which will be absorbed in the Beatific Vision, when the obscurity of faith will be exchanged for the

splendours of sight and unveiled knowledge, and the
aspirations of hope will be accomplished in the possession and enjoyment of the Supreme Good, charity
will eternally endure. Charity is the end of the commandment, charity is the goal, charity is union with
God, for God Himself is Charity ; and he who dwells
in Him (as shall the redeemed for endless ages) dwells
even here on earth in God and God in him. Not that
the infused virtue of charity is God Himself, the Holy
Ghost dwelling and loving in the souls of the just,
with whom some have erroneously confounded it,* but
a supernatural gift, created by the Holy Ghost in the
will of man, where, like hope, it resides, enabling it to
make acts of the love of God for His own sake, because
He is infinitely good in Himself. Thus supernatural
charity loves God with the same love wherewith He
loves Himself ; and herein we see its superiority to
hope, sublime and essential as is that virtue, because
hope regards God as our end and supreme good, and as
infinitely good to us, while charity regards Him as
good in Himself, and loves Him because He is so, with
a love which theologians call the love of benevolence :
so that—to use a paradoxical form of speech, by making

* The Master of the Sentences, Peter Lombard, put forth
the opinion that charity was the Holy Spirit Himself; meaning
thereby that our will formed acts of the love of God immediately through the Holy Spirit, and not by the intervention of
an infused quality, which is the theological virtue of charity.
Against this error the Angelic Doctor, St. Thomas, followed by
all eminent theologians, protested; because the act of love is
the most meritorious act of the will, and must accordingly be its
own act. It must therefore be moved thereto by the Holy Ghost
in such wise that it shall be itself the principle of it and act
voluntarily; to render it such, this act of love must be formed
through the means of some quality which the will actually possesses.

an impossible hypothesis—if God did not possess all possible good in Himself we should desire it for Him, but since He is infinitely perfect, infinitely rich, and infinitely blessed in Himself, divine charity rejoices in this His essential Perfection and Blessedness; and, unable to desire any increase to the Infinite, it burns with ardour to add to it in the only way it can, namely, by contributing to His external glory. It also causes the soul to make God its immediate object in all it does, seeking to please Him solely in order to please Him, from the pure motive of love, and because He is infinitely lovable. Nor is this motive in any way repugnant to, nor does it exclude, that which supernatural hope inspires, namely, the love of desire, which must and ever does accompany it because God has proposed Himself to man as his Sovereign Good; and, when he is enlightened by faith to discern Him as such, man would be doing a dishonour to that Sovereign Good, which is alone capable of conferring on him the perfection to which he is called and for which he is destined, if he did not aspire to Its possession. 'This is why nature is elevated above itself to desire its union with God and its repose in its supernatural end, and it is to this aspiration that hope raises it.' But the love of friendship, charity, also seeks this union, for it causes us 'to desire the presence or enjoyment of God, because it is the nature of the love of friendship to make us aspire after the presence of the loved object when it is absent; nevertheless, this desire, proceeding from the love by which we desire God for His own sake, is an act of charity and not of hope, which latter makes us desire God for our own good.'[*] Thus the two, hope and charity, are intimately and

* Bail, tom. iii. med. xii. 2.

K

harmoniously conjoined, and both tend to the same
end, our union with Him who is our Sovereign Good
and also *the* Infinite Good.

'God,' says the confessor, 'was the last end of all
Anna Maria's actions, of her words, of her thoughts,
and of the affections of her heart; Him alone did she
endeavour to please in all things.' Hence she lived
continually in His presence, alike at all times and in
all places. 'Far from having to make an effort to seek
Him,' says the same witness, 'it required a violent
exertion on her part to turn away from Him for an instant. Her heart was ever constrained by the sweet
necessity of abiding every moment with her God.
From this we may estimate the progress of her heart
in divine love. Her Heavenly Spouse, by an extraordinary mark of His goodness, told her in several locutions 'that He was pleased to dwell in a special
manner in her heart, and establish there His chamber
and place of repose; and that consequently He was
always with her, and never left her.' That this was
indeed the case, and that God was most intimately present to her soul, was evident to all who knew her.
The generosity with which, after renouncing all the
joys and interests of life, she bore for years the poignant sufferings, both external and internal, which were
laid upon her, was alone sufficient to prove that she
received supernatural assistance of an extraordinary
character. Without the presence of this supereminent
love in her soul, sustaining and invigorating it, she
neither would nor could have persevered in the hard
penitential life to which she had devoted herself, and
that in spite of the complicated maladies under which
she laboured. This same fervent love of God made her
also endure calumnies, contempt, harshness, and con-

tradictions, not with resignation only, but with heavenly sweetness. 'Without the flame of the most
ardent charity,' says Cardinal Pedicini, 'she never
could have supported the long martyrdom of her life.'
Yet she considered these sufferings (he tells us) as
being quite valueless when compared with the love
which God manifested towards her by His graces and
gifts. Enduring tortures under which most persons
would have succumbed, and the tithe of which might
well have wrung humble complaints from the lips of
the most virtuous and pious, she was overflowing with
gratitude from the one thought of God's love to her.
In the early days of her conversion especially this
gratitude often expressed itself in tears, and she was
continually beseeching God that He would deign to
teach her what she could do to please Him. This inward fervour, however, did not lead her to hold herself dispensed from making those distinct and formal
acts of charity which are enjoined upon all Christians.
Besides repeating them daily with her family before
their little altar, she used vocally to renew this exercise often in the course of the day and nourish the fire
of love within her—might we not rather say, suffer it
to blaze forth in frequent ejaculations and aspirations
of love? For many years, indeed, until the days of interior trial came on, far from its being needful for her
to use efforts to keep up these flames of charity, she
was obliged on the contrary often to restrain the impetuosity of her heart, and even try to distract her attention, in order to be able to acquit herself of her house-
work. 'Then,' says the Cardinal, 'would begin a
combat of love between her and her Heavenly Spouse.
Bound to fulfil her duties as mother towards a family
of which she was the sole support, she would do all in

her power to avoid ecstasies, raptures, and the frequent swoonings which would at times deprive her of the use of her senses for hours together. But as it was not easy to moderate so great a fire, Anna Maria could not by any artifice she might adopt withdraw her soul from this action of Divine love, even when engaged in her domestic avocations. It was truly wonderful to find her fixed in an ecstasy, broom in hand, in different positions. . . . Going to see her of a morning, as I did for many years, it very often happened that I found her in an ecstasy, and I was obliged to wait patiently till she came to herself again. A rapture would seize her sometimes in the midst of the conversation ; then I had to wait again.'

The confessor gives a similar account of those 'marvellous combats of love' between Anna Maria and the Spouse of her soul of which the Cardinal here speaks. ' What a spectacle,' he says, ' it was, to see the pious woman take her broom to sweep the house ; the Divine Spouse would present Himself to her eyes in the mysterious sun ; as she hastened to look away, she would hear the sweet tones of His voice, and, unable to resist these repeated assaults, she would fall into an ecstasy, and remain deprived of the use of her senses, still holding the broom in her hand : thus she would continue for a long time, immovable as a statue, unknown to herself ; when restored to consciousness, she would hasten to repair lost time, and, thanks to God and to her great activity, the work was soon finished. At other times, when engaged in the kitchen, and busy perhaps skimming a saucepan, these raptures of divine love would come upon her ; and then the torrent of spiritual consolations would oblige her to lean against the wall, or to sit down, where she would remain insensible for some time ; she was afraid afterwards lest she should find the fire gone out or the pot upset ; but what was her surprise to see all in perfect order !' These ecstasies and raptures were, indeed, so frequent for several years, that this pious and humble woman, intent on performing her household duties for the love of God with due punctuality and perfection, used sometimes to expostulate affectionately with her Lord on the subject, saying to Him, with that holy liberty which accompanies such love as hers, ' Leave me in peace, Lord ; leave me to my occupation ; I am a poor mother of a family—retire, retire.' But her efforts were all in vain. ' While she was thus struggling,' says P. Filippo, ' she would hear the song of a bird, or catch sight of some simplest object wherein she read the goodness of God, of which all nature spoke to her in a language understood by contemplatives alone : thus, in the midst of her forced distractions, she found herself vanquished on all sides by divine love, the chains of which enveloped and bore her down like a victim.' Similar is the testimony given by the Cardinal, who also says that a breath of air, the note of a bird, the sight of an insect, were quite sufficient to throw her instantaneously into an ecstasy.

This suspension of the senses, caused by those sudden floods of love pouring in upon her soul at the mere sight of the works of God's material creation, made it dangerous for her to walk alone, and it became necessary that she should have some confidential person with her when going about the streets, where some casual object would often produce this effect upon her. In such cases she had to lean on her companion, who would support and lead her into the nearest church. ' I was often,' says P. Filippo, ' the ocular witness of

her supernatural trances, of her ecstasies and absorption
in God, when we visited the Seven Basilicas in company with Cardinal Pedicini. She generally communicated in the chapel of the Holy Crucifix at San Paolo
[he means on these occasions] ; and many and many a
a time have I seen her immediately after Communion
remain entirely deprived of consciousness. The same
thing would happen in other churches, at the sound of
the heavenly voice. As we had to pursue our pilgrimage, I had no other means save that of addressing to
her tacitly a commandment in the name of holy obedience ; instantly she would return to herself, and cut
short all those celestial locutions in which were revealed to her the greatest secrets concerning the Church
and those things which were the subjects of her prayer.'
The extraordinary graces of this kind which she received became, he tells us, a severe trial to her humility,
and even to her charity towards her neighbour. 'Some
spoke favourably of them, others conceived a bad opinion. The pious woman suffered from beholding her
God thus offended. Dreading to have these raptures
in public, she struggled to repress the ardent aspirations of her heart, but without success. Raptures were
to her as common a thing when she betook herself to
her devotions as it is to us to pray vocally. You would
have said her soul was about to take its flight from the
body, particularly at Communion ; and, as it was impossible for her to control herself, she attracted the
attention of all present. Some, admiring her fervour,
would waylay her at the church-door to recommend
themselves to her prayers ; others said that she was
possessed, or was a hypocrite. After having finished
her thanksgiving, she used to glance modestly around
to see if the persons who might have remarked her

were still there ; and then, seizing a favourable moment, she would leave the church quite timid and confused, to get home as fast as she could.' To avoid becoming thus a mark for observation, so distressing to her, Anna Maria began to wander from church to church, communicating first in one, then in another. But God reproached her for so doing, and bade her not disquiet herself on account either of the mockery or the remarks to which she was subjected, and to fear nothing, since He was with her. He told her that if others offended Him, she was not the cause of this ; and that she must return to her usual church, the Madonna della Pietà, in the Piazza Colonna. She promptly obeyed the divine injunction.

That persons who were strangers to her should draw erroneous conclusions from casually noticing demonstrations of a singular and unusual kind is perhaps not matter for much wonder. An ordinary congregation is of a mixed character ; in it there are always many who are quite unfitted to form an opinion on anything of the spiritual, and still more of the mystical order, but who are none the less ready to have and to proclaim one. Whatever the outer world may believe of the supposed credulous welcome given by Catholics to everything bearing a semblance of the miraculous, it is plain that even in a land where faith is peculiarly strong in the bulk of the population, and where the supernatural has not to encounter the same species of timid and cold mistrust which constant association with those who habitually ignore or disbelieve in it, and who, above all things, despise what they term credulity and superstition, is so apt to foster in the believing themselves—even in Catholic Italy itself, and in Rome, the centre of the Catholic world, persons might be found,

and they not a few, to suspect, misinterpret, and even
tax with hypocrisy manifestations surpassing the customary marks of devotion, and wearing an extraordinary
and exceptional character.   To such suspicions, at any
rate, was Anna Maria subjected ; and, when we consider
what the world is everywhere, finding entrance even
into churches, and that it is always substantially the
same, this need not much surprise us.   But in her own
home, amongst the daily witnesses of her eminent holiness, and where every member of the family had frequent opportunities of observing closely the extraordinary trances into which she so constantly fell, it might
be expected that their supernatural character could not
be overlooked or mistaken.   True, no one under her roof
taxed her with hypocrisy or attributed these manifestations to any suspicious cause ; which, indeed, would
have been impossible.   Her virtues were respected and
recognised in her family, and the genuineness and depth
of her piety were unquestioned ; still upon this point a
most unaccountable obtuseness prevailed.   Domenico
was stone-blind with regard to it, and the daughters
were purblind.   Sometimes (the confessor tells us) she
would be seized with an ecstasy when she was standing
and in the act of waiting on the rest at table.   Suddenly she would seem like one struck by lightning, and
remain a considerable time transfixed and immovable,
still holding her knife and fork in her hands, and her
eyes set like those of a statue.   God had drawn a thick
bandage over those of her husband (says P. Filippo), to
hinder him as well as her children from understanding
what they saw.   It is impossible to resist this conclusion, for such seizures assuredly bore as little resemblance to natural sleep or to a stroke of paralysis as
could well be conceived ; yet such were the only ideas

which seemed to suggest themselves to the dull brain of Domenico. 'This stupid man,' continues the Father, 'would at first call to her, and, finding that she made no reply, would be afraid she was taken with a fit; afterwards, observing that these seizures recurred pretty frequently, he attributed them to convulsions or to drowsiness, according to the different forms which the ecstasy assumed.' When the servant of God had regained her consciousness and a sweet and joyous smile spread over her countenance, he was none the wiser, and would say, 'How can you go off to sleep at table? Why, you are quite stupefied with drowsiness!' adding other similar reproaches. Sometimes these ecstasies would take her when sitting, and then Domenico would shake her violently, without her giving the least symptom of consciousness or feeling. Presently she would rise with the same look of joyous contentment, and, according as the good man was persuaded either that she had been asleep or that she was suffering from some attack of indisposition, he would scold her or press her to take some 'soothing infusions.' 'The eldest daughter, Sofia, had a little more penetration, and conceived some suspicions of the truth without knowing all; for she would say that her mother was praying, and Maria would begin to cry, exclaiming, " Mama is dead ! Mama is dead !" because she saw her give no sign of life.' The same kind of thing would happen when the family were at their evening devotions, and saying the Rosary together. When they had finished, and she did not stir, one of them would go up to her and find her in a state of unconsciousness. To arouse her seemed impossible, but by and bye she came to herself. Domenico, whom the Cardinal describes, in language similar to that of the confessor, as an ' ignorant man, who had not the

smallest conception of these heavenly gifts,' did not
know what to make of such behaviour in his wife, of
whose fervent piety at any rate he was fully convinced.
But as these scenes were of frequent occurrence, they
puzzled and annoyed him, and he would take her to
task for her ' doziness ;' in a moderate tone, however, for
he must have secretly felt that it ill became him to attempt to teach one like her reverence for holy things.
Still he did not spare her a few reproaches, saying that
it was a shame for any one to go to sleep at prayers,
when they had all the night for repose. Nothing but
holy obedience had the slightest effect in recalling her
from these supernatural swoons, but to this recourse
was never had without necessity ; and when, in after
years, the confidential priest, Natali, or some other person cognisant of her state, was present, he would endeavour, on observing that she had passed into an
ecstasy, to divert Domenico's attention by starting some
topic of interest to him, in the hope of thus preventing him from noticing what had occurred and giving
time for the servant of God to come out of her rapture
spontaneously.

In the midst of the delights and consolations with
which her heart was flooded, Anna Maria preserved a
holy sobriety, and never abated aught of her spirit of
mortification. We have seen how frequently she endeavoured to interrupt those colloquies with God which
formed the joy and blessedness of her life, in order that
she might continue to discharge uninterruptedly some
homely piece of household work ; so sacred in her eyes
were the duties of her state, humble as they were. They
were sacred to her because she saw in them the will of
God, who had appointed them for her, and her one object was to please Him. ' Her sole intention,' says P.

Filippo, 'was to please God continually; for true love does not consist only in never turning away our thoughts from the beloved object and in using all the means in our power to render it always present to us; in this repect the servant of God had reached a very high point, since in order to be able to work it had become necessary for her to distract herself; but love, above all, consists in the purity and rectitude of our actions.' Such, then, was Anna Maria's one ruling motive and desire— to please God alone, procure His glory, and refer everything to Him.

But the strongest proof of her love for God was undoubtedly her hatred of sin, and that not of mortal sin alone, but of every the most trifling offence against her Beloved. She, in fact, recognised nothing as evil except sin, and was continually beseeching her Heavenly Spouse to cause her to die rather than ever to displease Him. In a letter which she wrote about some affair to her confessor, she said that rather than commit a venial fault she would mount a scaffold and endure all its shame, coupled with the infliction of every conceivable torture. It would be impossible to express what was her zeal for the glory of God, a zeal which made her ready to sacrifice all, even life itself, for Him; and this desire she indeed accomplished by a life-long self-immolation. In the midst of all her sufferings, even of those which from being interior are the hardest to bear, she preserved an unutterable peace, which nothing could disturb. Now this peace was but another evidence of her perfect love of God. She was at peace because she suffered willingly and joyfully whatever it was His will that she should suffer. That which a soul in the lowest circle of bliss is described by Dante as saying, was a true expression of her feelings,

when sunk in the deepest abyss of human woes and
pains :——

'His will is our peace.'*

We shall have to speak more particularly of what she
endured in offering herself continually for the conversion of sinners and for the extirpation of sin in order
that God might be known and loved, when we come to
speak of her as a victim of expiation ; so that, although
it is one of the most remarkable exemplifications of the
power of divine charity in her heart, we will make no
further allusion to it in this place. Neither will we
dwell here on the purity and generosity of love with
which she offered to renounce all her sensible consolations, as well as to undergo all imaginable sufferings,
in order to diminish the evils predominant in the world
and to promote the interests of Holy Church ; even
pressing this offer upon her Spouse until (as we shall
find) He was pleased to grant her petition, and to cast
her into a very furnace of tribulations and pains, in
which she was destined to spend the last years of her
life, even to her dying hour.

We shall here content ourselves, therefore, with a
brief notice of her fulfilment of that second great commandment of the law, which is like unto the first,
charity towards our neighbour, and the absence of
which proves that the love of God is not in us. He
alone who loves God can indeed truly love his neighbour ; that is, with a love deserving of the name, a love
which has no regard to self, or to the personal recommendations of him who is loved; a love which sur-
mounts all natural repugnances, which is universal and

---

* 'La sua voluntate ò nostra pace.'
Paradiso, Canto Terzo.

unwearied, including strangers, enemies, and persecutors
in the same embrace with friends and kindred.   Such
was the love of which Anna Maria's life was constantly
giving the most affecting examples.   Poor as she was,
and scarcely able to support her own family, she man-
aged always to reserve a portion for those who were
still more needy than herself, a portion chiefly taken
out of her own scanty allowance.   But more than this :
she taxed her time also, already so heavily burdened.
Her nights, after subtracting the small portion which
she allowed herself for rest, were divided between working for the poor and the devotions to which she dedicated those solitary hours—if we might not rather class
both under the same name.   For, truly, it was an intense devotion to Jesus Christ in the person of the poor,
and no mere ordinary movement of Christian charity,
which made her thus spend herself for others, and deny
herself even her needful repose after a day of unceasing
toil.

She practised in an equally sublime degree all the
works of mercy.   If she met a poor woman raggedly
dressed, particularly if it was in winter, she would take
her home, feed her, and give her decent articles of
clothing, not only never testifying the smallest repugnance of nature, however dirty or otherwise disgusting
to the senses the poor creature might be, but treating
her with the same respect as she might have evinced
to a person of high distinction.   For, in truth, she saw
only Jesus Christ in the poor and the afflicted.   On one
occasion her Heavenly Spouse deigned to testify His
gratitude to her.   A poor woman was lying by the road-
side foaming at the mouth and seemingly unnoticed.
Anna Maria came that way and, like the Good Samaritan, hastened to assist her, with her own handkerchief

wiping away the foam and the cold perspiration which
stood on her brow. This act of charity drew the attention of the passers-by, who began to stop and gather
round. The poor woman complaining of acute internal
pain, Anna Maria ran to obtain some medicine to as-
suage it; nor did she leave her until she was sufficiently
restored to pursue her way without assistance. Entering a church immediately after, she heard the voice of
our Lord thanking her for this act of charity, as if it
had been done to Himself; then followed an ecstasy, accompanied with inexpressible peace. Many similar instances are related of her charity, in the hospitals and
elsewhere, to the most repulsive objects. She never
refused alms to the poor who came to her door to
beg; and, fearful lest in her absence they might not
be relieved—for there was often poverty sufficient at
home to excuse a denial—she would say to those of
her house, 'Never send the poor away; when you have
nothing else, give them a bit of bread; you know where
it is.'

We subjoin Domenico's testimony to her charity.
'She was ever solicitous for the good of her neighbour,
whom she tenderly loved. I remember also that when
there was to be an execution at Rome, and the culprit
refused to be converted, she was quite upset; and I
remarked that on such occasions she was more ill than
usual: sometimes she was forced to take to her bed by
reason of the excessive pain in her head, from which
she habitually suffered.' There could be no doubt as
to the cause of this accession of suffering, even without
the testimony of her confessor, who says that when
there was to be an execution she prayed indefatigably
for the conversion of the criminal until she had obtained
this grace, enduring great bodily and mental suffer-

ings, which almost always obliged her to take to her bed.
Of this she complained with a holy confidence several
times to her Heavenly Father, who told her, that since
she had made herself a slave through love, He exacted
payment from her for the conversion of these souls. Although she knew by experience what it would cost her,
this consideration never deterred her from praying with
the same ardent charity on all similar occasions.

Her husband proceeds to speak of her charity to the
sick. 'When the servant of God was sent for by sick
people, she went immediately, no matter what the
weather was. I had given her full permission in this
respect. I remember that during the first years she
was not able to eat a piece of bread in peace, because
people were asking for her on this side and on that;
she went everywhere, for she was very active. Towards
the close of her life, the maladies with which she was
afflicted did not permit her to keep this up; she dragged
herself about, however, as much as her strength allowed,
without respect of persons; indeed, the poor had the
preference. Her great trouble was the not being able
to relieve the miseries of others as she would have
wished;' and then he adds what we have already noticed, that, in order to be able to help the wretched
without wronging her family, she worked at night,
during the most critical periods, in order to earn some
trifle more to bestow upon them; and this she did with
his permission. We may notice here a fresh instance
of Domenico's genuine kindness of heart, than which
none can have been more truly valued by her, as well
as of his faith and trust in God. He might be a coarse,
stupid, and ignorant man, as both the Cardinal and
the confessor call him, and doubtless without doing
him the slightest injustice, but, at any rate, he was not

so stupid in respect to divine things as not to remark that a peculiar Providence watched over his family, a blessing which his wife's self-denying charity and wonderful confidence in God were the means of securing to them. For he adds, after making the statement just quoted, 'And God blessed our family, granting it what was needful by an almost continual miracle. Observing this, I accorded her full liberty to do all which she felt herself moved to do.'

He continues to relate how she used also to visit hospitals, particularly that of San Giacomo, and would sometimes take her daughters with her to teach them how to pity and succour the afflicted. A multitude of persons (he says) used to be always having recourse to her at home in their different troubles and afflictions, to whom she administered consolation with the utmost patience and compassion, helping them to the extent of her ability. Cardinal Pedicini says that when she visited the hospitals, she would take biscuits and a little wine for the convalescents; nor while thus administering bodily refreshment, did she neglect their precious souls, but spoke to them of their true end and of the mysteries of the faith, instructing such as were ignorant with much gentleness and kindly affection. 'She had a special gift,' he says, 'for consoling the afflicted. If it was question of spiritual things, in respect of which her gifts and lights rendered her an excellent mistress, whosoever had recourse to her was sure to come away fully comforted. As regards temporal things, she did not content herself with showing a sterile compassion and with administering consolations unaccompanied with results; but she willingly availed herself of the interest she possessed to aid her neighbour, although she was so delicate as to profiting by it herself. If

these people were in a state of utter destitution, and
she had not the means of relieving them, she overcame
her shame, and asked alms for them. She frequently
addressed herself to me for this object, and I readily
satisfied her. In fine, in one affair or another, whether
it were question of law-suits, sicknesses, indigence, or
domestic misfortunes and troubles, of all who applied
to her none left her without having been consoled.'

Thus compassionate to others, she reserved no tenderness for herself, and neither by word nor look complained of her own continual sufferings. Notwithstanding her accumulated maladies, she was ever, as her
husband testifies, 'gay and affable,' and, so far from
being a burden to any one, was herself the consoler of
all, complaisant and patient with each and every one,
a peace-maker, for which office he observes she had a
peculiar talent, and showing a never-failing charity towards those who injured and persecuted her. 'Without a great love of God,' he observes, 'she never could
have borne tribulations and persecutions for such a
length of time, neither could she have loved her persecutors and done good to them.' With his usual
simplicity he adds, 'It is true I could not see into the
bottom of her heart; God only can see that, and the
confessor who directs the soul may know it; but, generally speaking, people cannot help showing by their
acts what they have in their hearts.' He gives some
instances of her behaviour under injurious treatment,
which we shall notice when speaking of her patience.
Her charity for her enemies, and for all who offended
her, was also exercised in constant prayers for them,
not merely in a general way, but for one or the other
by name when they were known to her. But this was
the only petition of the servant of God which was in-

variably unsuccessful, at least so far as regarded their
exemption from temporal chastisement, in consequence
of a very remarkable promise and engagement which it
had pleased God to make with respect to her, and from
which not all her most fervent supplications could prevail upon Him to depart. We refrain from enlarging
here upon her charity in praying for the necessities,
spiritual and temporal, of others, as well as upon the
heroic self-sacrifice which accompanied these prayers,
as these subjects will recur hereafter, and will content
ourselves for the present with referring to a few passages
in the deposition of the confessor, before passing on to
a brief review of her other Christian virtues.

'She prayed,' he says, ' without ceasing for the sick,
for prisoners, for the persecuted and the calumniated,
for persons of all ranks whom she saw in the mysterious sun. Those who applied to her might feel certain
of being soon relieved. For the sick she counselled
remedies proper to heal them, recommending them to
ask the doctor if they could be injurious. To the indigent she gave what she could ; if she was unable to
give, she addressed herself to one of her spiritual sons.
. . . She overcame for their sake the shame of soliciting alms, and more than once she literally took the
bread from her own mouth to succour the destitute
who applied to her.' We must not omit here to allude
also to the manner in which she bestowed another
species of alms, for which large claims were continually
made upon her, and the administration of which is a
far more arduous and delicate matter than the disburse-
ment of temporal relief : we mean the alms of good
advice and fraternal correction. For some are too eager
to give on all occasions, others timidly shrink from ever
offering any counsel or reproof ; some give reticently

and insincerely, others inopportunely and unpleasantly. Charity, and that simple truthfulness which was one of Anna Maria's most beautiful graces, smoothed every difficulty away. 'He that giveth, let it be with simplicity,' says the Apostle ;* and this exhortation is applicable also to spiritual alms. It makes them acceptable and efficacious. As long as she was able to walk, she never employed an intermediary when giving counsels, admonitions, or encouragement to persons who applied to her. Later, when confined to her own house, she used to send the priest Natali with messages of this nature, which often concerned the peace of families, the reconciliation of married persons, or the pardon of injuries. As these messages were not unfrequently addressed to individuals of high rank or station, she used to exhort her confidant to tread under foot human respect and fear, and to act only for the glory of God. Harmony, peace, and charity were what she was continually inculcating and enforcing on her spiritual children ; and there was nothing which she was more earnest in cautioning them to avoid than the habit of criticising and complaining of others. Her own practice was to compassionate the faults of others, and excuse the intention when she could not excuse the act. When persons came to confide their griefs to her, she took care, however, not to check or interrupt them ; she let them have their story out, and listened with patience and kindly sympathy ; thus affording them the opportunity of relieving their minds by the detail of their grievances. Then she would give them some good advice, exhorting them to pity the failings of others, and, instead of losing their time in useless complaints, to employ it in recommending their husband

* Rom. xii. 8.

or brother to God. Sweetness, patience, and prayer, she would tell them, will triumph over everything : she on her part would not fail to pray for them; but in the mean time they must follow these instructions. Then, referring to the sins and offences complained of, she would add, ' If God did not hold us back, we are capable of doing much worse.'

P. Filippo renders the same testimony as we have seen her husband give, to the sweetness and winningness of behaviour which accompanied all those various acts which charity prompted her to perform, and he especially mentions a circumstance of no little importance, though frequently overlooked even by the beneficent, namely, that 'she listened to all with a perfect charity.' Are we not right in thinking that the grace of listening to what is tiresome is far rarer than the grace of giving? The ears weary much sooner than the hands or the tongue. Witness even the man after God's own heart, the royal David, cutting short the explanation and justification of the injured and traduced Miphiboseth with a ' Why speakest thou any more? What I have said is determined : thou and Siba divide the possession ;'* thereby committing a manifest wrong and injustice, and mulcting the innocent for the benefit of the liar and the traitor. Holy Scripture makes no comment, but records the fact, as it does others, for our admonition and instruction. The grace of listening : how sweet is that grace, when even its counterpart in the natural order is a thing so welcome and so soothing! Anna Maria was patient, sympathising, and condescending to all, but she was specially so to the poor and the afflicted, as those who have the strongest claim upon the charity that 'is patient and is kind;' not

* 2 Kings xix. 29.

scrutinising closely in each case the precise claims of
the individual, but acting with a holy simplicity. Yet,
though thus overflowing in charity, so that she may
seem to have been a very prodigal in that respect,
nevertheless the confessor bears witness that she was
ever prudent and circumspect, taking a reasonable and
due account of circumstances. In this we see a marked
distinction between the overflowings of Christian charity
and the heedless and extravagant bountifulness which
has its source only in natural feeling, or is the result
of weakness and of a certain incapacity to refuse, a
liberality which must be classed as a species, however
amiable, of self-indulgence.

Self-indulgence has certainly no inconsiderable
share in acts of kindness performed by that great mass
of persons generically styled amiable. This reflection
renders a circumstance, which otherwise might be esteemed very trifling in Anna Maria's habitual behaviour,
worthy of a passing notice ; we mean her extreme kindness to animals. ' She had so good a heart,' says her
confessor, ' that she extended her care even to little
beasts, whom she loved as the creatures of God. Besides, she said, "These poor beasts have no Paradise
save in this world." ' She did not scruple, as he tells
us, even sometimes to employ the marvellous gift of
healing with which her right hand had been endowed,
in favour of suffering animals, praying the Divine Goodness to heal some wound or restore some fractured limb ;
and elsewhere we find it considered worth recording
that she often left her own dinner to feed her hungry
cat. Now assuredly many will see nothing remarkable
or meritorious in this. Very ordinary persons will put
themselves out of their way in a much greater degree
for the comfort and even indulgence of their pet animals,

but it must be remembered that this holy woman had
no 'pets.' Dearly as she loved husband, children,
grandchildren, she loved even them with a love so holy,
so disengaged, and so thoroughly supernaturalised, as
utterly to exclude the mere human fondness which em-
bodies itself in the familiar idea represented by 'pet-
ting.' Tender as was her love for all belonging to her,
she was not prodigal of caresses to any; still less, then,
could animals engage that kind of coaxing attention on
her part which in so many is a mere form of self-indulgence. When, therefore, we see one who was ever
living on the portals of the invisible and supernatural
world, and ready, as she stood waiting on others, or
eating her own scanty morsel, to be at any moment rapt
into divine contemplation, or to swoon away through
the love of God, turn to minister to the wants of a poor
little animal, we cannot resist the inference that she
who was so divinely illuminated recognised the claim
of these dumb creatures to a place in our regard, for
the love of Him without whom not a sparrow falls on
the ground,* and who, when in His mercy He spared
the guilty Nineve, had a compassionate eye to the
'many beasts'† as well as to the thousands of human
beings, made to His image, who dwelt within the walls
of that great city. Her confessor sees in this act also
a proof of that obedience and submission of heart
which had made her the servant of all. 'This woman,'
he exclaims, 'who had so many lights and so many
gifts that an ambassador who had the opportunity of
becoming acquainted with her acknowledged that she
knew the world better than the deepest politicians—
this woman, I say, submitted herself to every one, whether at home or abroad; she even obeyed animals, as

* Matt. x. 29.   † Jonas iv. 11.

the proverb says' (some Italian proverb, doubtless, of
which we are ignorant), 'and might be seen interrupt-
ing her dinner to feed the cat.' May we not add that
the attitude of mind which in her prompted an otherwise ordinary act, was an imitation of the perfection of
our Heavenly Father, who ministers to all even the
lowest of His creatures in the scale of being, opening
His hand and filling with plenteousness every living
thing ?*

We will conclude this chapter by quoting the words
with which the confessor closes his own deposition on
the subject of Anna Maria's charity for her neighbour,
in which are summed up several of the characteristics
to which we have adverted. 'Far from seeking her
own interests, she sacrificed them willingly, and gave
herself and her own life, without harbouring resentment
for any injuries done her; she forgave these injuries
from the bottom of her heart, rendering to her persecutors all the good in her power; speaking favourably of
all according to the dictates of common prudence; re-
joicing in the good of others, and afflicted at the evil
befalling them as if it had been her own; full of compassion towards all; bearing with all, particularly with
the tiresome persons whom God sent to try the virtue
of her patience when she was suffering from violent
neuralgia; she offered to God all these sufferings in
order to obtain relief for the afflicted who had recourse
to her. The charity of this pious woman, eminently
intelligent, circumspect, generous, and heroic during her
whole life, was strikingly displayed even in her last
moments, when she was seen begging the forgiveness
of those belonging to her house for all the trouble and
distress which her illness had caused them. This is

* Psalm cxliv. 16.

what I attest and depose *in Domino* (in the Lord) as
briefly as I can respecting the virtue of heroic charity
practised towards her neighbour by my penitent, Anna
Maria Taigi. Glory be to the Father, to the Son, and
to the Holy Ghost now and for ever, to everlasting
ages. Amen.'

CHAPTER X.

ANNA MARIA A SHINING EXAMPLE OF ALL THE VIRTUES.

WE cannot follow the same method with Anna
Maria's other virtues as we have with the theological,
which hold so pre-eminent a rank, but, without attempt-
ing any division of a technical kind, or observing any
particular order, we shall advert to them in a practical
and unsystematic way. It belongs to the saintly character not to be deficient in any Christian virtue, and
to possess all, at least potentially, in a perfect manner;*
nevertheless, some saints are remarkable for one, some

* 'Since, for beatification and canonisation, the virtues
ought not to be imperfect, but perfect, hence it is necessary that
inquiry be made concerning their connection, in order to determine whether they were perfect or imperfect. This does not
imply that the servant of God must have actually exhibited
heroicity in all things, since it suffices, if he was a hero in faith,
hope, and charity, and in like manner was a hero in those moral
virtues in which his state of life enabled him to exercise himself, with a readiness of mind to do the like in others, if occasion were given him to put them in practice. Wherefore St.
Jerome, who admitted the connection of virtues, so that whoever has one must be said to have the rest, makes Critobulus
ask, "And how read we, Whoever hath one, seems to have all
the virtues?" To which Atticus replies, "It is by participation,
not special possession; for of necessity each person excels in
some." The same is to be learned also from St. Thomas,

for another virtue in a more special manner, their characters seeming to centre, as it were, in one more prominently developed excellence and to take their tone from this particular grace.   In other cases it would be difficult to select the virtue which most highly characterised the individual; and this is particularly true of the subject of this biography.   Anna Maria may be regarded as a compendium of all the virtues, and to have been called to exercise all in a shining manner.   Doubtless this formed part of the designs of God in her regard, who was pleased to place her before the world as a perfect pattern of Christian holiness.   In setting before us this bright model, He chose one who was poor, obscure, and despised in condition; He did not raise her from that state, but rendered her illustrious in it by her extraordinary perfections and His own corresponding gifts; that very condition itself furnishing more ample scope for the display in all its inartificial and sublime simplicity of every Christian virtue.   The conventionalities of life in the superior classes of society serve to veil and conceal in many points some of these virtues, even when possessed : not that the practice of any virtue is less obligatory in higher stations or its actual requirements in any degree modified by position, but there are some the exhibition of which cannot in many cases be so patent, while there are others which derive adventitious splendour from the very circumstances under which they are practised.   Nothing of this sort could occur in respect to the servant of God, whose ex-

---

where he explains the connection of the virtues, and shows that it is to be understood, not in reference to acts, but to dispositions of mind.' Benedict XIV., *On Heroic Virtue* (Oratorian Edition), vol. i. pp. 39, 40.

ample, accordingly, is as generally applicable and complete as it is striking.

Nevertheless, when we consider the various perfections combined to adorn the soul of Anna Maria, nothing perhaps attracts our notice more constantly than her patience; nor is this surprising when we consider the large part which patience plays in the formation of the perfect Christian character. In Scripture, indeed, it is sometimes spoken of as if it summed up in a manner all moral perfection; as where St. James says, 'Patience hath a perfect work.'* The same Apostle also says, 'You have heard of the patience of Job, and you have seen the end of the Lord, that the Lord is merciful and compassionate;'† hereby marking how many other virtues are implied in the Christian virtue of patience. The 'end of the Lord,' moreover, was His Passion, in which He suffered rather than acted; and thus also the Christian who treads in his Lord's footsteps is much more often called to suffer and to endure than to do. It is his special work, in a sense that applies to no other in which he may be accidentally by God's appointment engaged; neither is its office suspended by such other accidental work. Moreover, it holds a special position of its own in the secular life: 'What obedience,' says Father Faber, 'is to Religious (not all that it is, but the functions it performs), that patience is to seculars. Independently of its directly supernatural virtue, obedience sanctifies the Religious for four reasons principally : because it comes from without, because the Religious has no control over its requirements, because he must be ready at all moments, and because it involves the giving up of his own will and way. Now all these four offices patience discharges in its measure to the secular. The

* i. 4. † v. 11.

circumstances which exact its exercise come upon us
from without; we have nó control over them; they
may come upon us at all moments; and they always
involve the sacrifice or the mortification of our own will
and way. I do not say that patience equals religious
obedience; but that it is itself the obedience of seculars.'*

Certainly if there was no virtue more conspicuous
in Anna Maria than patience, there was none in which
it pleased God more severely to try her; and this very
thing may serve to confirm the opinion here given by
so great a master of spiritual things; for if this holy
woman was to be set forth as a shining example of sublime perfection in the world, we can well understand
why she was so peculiarly exercised in that which is
its appointed school. And how many other virtues are
there which are either implied in or acquired by the
exercise of patience; such as humility, mortification,
silence, forbearance, fortitude, temperance, charity ! 'It
is,' as Father Faber observes, 'a short road to unselfish-
ness; for nothing is left to self. All that seems to belong most intimately to self, to be self's private property, such as time, home, and rest, is invaded by
these continual trials of patience. The family is full
of such opportunities, and the sanctity of marriage
abounds with them.'† We have seen that such was
the case with Anna Maria. Her house was a Christian house, regulated on the highest Christian principles; her family were all good people, desirous of pleasing God and saving their souls; yet we have seen how
continual an exercise for her patience she found under
her own roof.

* *Growth in Holiness*, chap. ix. pp. 136, 137.
† Ibid. p. 137.

Her rough and irascible husband, who took his
share in thus trying her, was, however, extremely angry
when he saw her injured or insulted by others.   Anna
Maria, as may be well conceived, never stood up for her
rights, a spirit which the eminent writer just quoted
assures us 'is fatal to perfection.'   But Domenico was
well disposed upon occasion to do this for her, and we
cannot blame him.   He himself is our authority.   'Although she endeavoured to do good to every one,' he says,
'there were bad tongues which would not leave her in
peace, whether from jealousy at seeing so many persons
of distinction at the house, or through the suggestion
of the devil.   I remember, amongst others, that a wicked
woman had the audacity to calumniate her in the matter of her honour.   I had this wretched creature impri-
soned, but this pained my wife, who did all she could
to get her out again; and as soon as she was out she
began again worse than ever.   If I perceived any one
molesting her, he had to pay dear for it, but I could
not follow her everywhere, on account of my occupations at the Chigi palace.   Observing afterwards that
the servant of God was distressed when I interfered
about these things, I ended by saying to her, "Well,
do what you please and in the way you please; if you
like people to throw stones at you, and if besides you
choose to give them the stones yourself, you are free to
do so."'

Domenico mentions another instance in his deposition of a woman who persecuted and insulted his wife
at the time they lived on the Corso, whither they removed when the family became too numerous for their
first abode.   She inhabited the same house, and was an
impudent, coarse, and perfidious creature.   She took a
mortal aversion to Anna Maria, and for several years

missed no opportunity of heaping on her every manner of abuse, contempt, and calumny, and injuring her in every way she could.   Domenico says that she must have been either insane or possessed, for the accusations she brought against his wife could not have naturally suggested themselves to any mind.   Yet Anna Maria continued to salute her on the staircase when they met, and would even go up and speak to her, very courteously ; making her moreover, from time to time, some little present.   But the unhappy woman seemed to have (as he says) the heart of a viper, and was not in the least degree touched by this kindness ; on the contrary, her hatred and insolence appeared daily to increase.   Domenico's patience was nearly exhausted, but Anna Maria employed the influence she possessed over him, to restrain him from taking any rigorous measure and persuade him to exercise forbearance. Meanwhile she relaxed not one whit in her own active charity towards this malevolent woman.   She besought God not to punish her, but the reply she received was that this proud woman would one day come to beg alms at her door.   As Anna Maria persevered in imploring the Lord to spare her enemy this chastisement, she heard the following words : ' Be satisfied that I should punish her in this life, instead of chastising her more severely in the next.'   This woman was at that time a laundress in easy circumstances, but some years afterwards she lost everything, and was reduced to solicit alms.   Many a time might she be seen knocking at Anna Maria's door, who, by the money she gave her and the relief she obtained for her, became her chief benefactress.

And yet, notwithstanding the meekness which she thus manifested on the most trying occasions, Anna

Maria was not by any means constitutionally patient.
'Like all persons of a sensitive and lively temperament,'
says her confessor, 'she was naturally disposed to anger;
she checked and tamed it by silence and meekness, and
thus attained to that heroic patience which distinguished
her in so marked a manner, and which was the result
of her deep humility. And again, when alluding to
her possesion of the cardinal virtue of temperance, which
serves to regulate all the actions and passions, he mentions by what great struggles she had obtained the complete mastery over herself, and acquired the virtues most
opposed to those vices to which by nature she was
prone. 'By repressing with all her might her passionate
temper, and by submitting to every one, she acquired
that tranquillity, cheerfulness, and amiability, accompanied by a deep humility of heart and conduct, which she
retained until death.' 'It would be impossible,' he says,
'to describe what patience she exercised towards the
members of her family, with all their different dispositions, towards her spiritual sons, towards her persecutors (and she had many), towards sinners whom she
reclaimed to the right path, as well as in a thousand
other cases, in all her spiritual and bodily sufferings,
under privations, calumnies, domestic afflictions, &c.
To the envy of which she was the object, she opposed
her desire to do good to all and particularly to those
who harboured a spiritual envy against her, for she
prayed constantly for them, and upon occasion humbled
herself before them, although she was aware that she
thereby sometimes incurred their contempt.'

In the Church of the Madonna della Pietà, which
she frequented, she was often exposed, not to censorious
remarks alone, but to the grossest insults. A well-
dressed elderly man used at one time to come and kneel

next her at Communion, and snatch away the cloth violently out of her hands; upon which Anna Maria, without betraying any disturbance or displeasure, would wait patiently until she had the opportunity of communicating at the following Mass. Then the devil, who was doubtless the prompter of this insane piece of malice, instigated the priest who generally said the Mass at which she communicated to conceive some suspicion against her, and to pass her by when she knelt at the altar rails. Again she kept silence, and she had been for some time the object of this double insult, before the priest, her companion, accidentally observed what took place. Full of indignation, he first intercepted at the church door the man who had carried his animosity against this pious woman even to the very altar of the Lord, and severely rebuked him for his scandalous behaviour. The gentleman, imagining, from the priest's indignation, that the woman he had thus insulted was his sister, hastened with much confusion to make his humble excuses, and Natali then hurried back to the sacristy, and, taking the priest aside who had just said Mass, required an account from him of this public refusal of Communion, at the same time threatening to inform his superiors of so unwarrantable a proceeding. Surprised at finding an ecclesiastic who was so honourably distinguished at Rome as was Don Raffaele Natali interesting himself about a poor unknown woman, the priest apologised for what he had done; and henceforward she was left free to receive Communion in peace.

Don Raffaele naturally believed that he had done what must be very agreeable to the servant of God by thus delivering her from so peculiarly distressing a persecution, but the fact was just the reverse; and his in-

terference was no more acceptable to her than had been
her husband's in the case related above.   When he rejoined her outside the church he found her very sad,
and she gently reproached him as if he had robbed her
of a treasure, saying, 'What have you done ! What have
you done ?' Already in an impatient state of mind from
what had just occurred, this lamentation quite provoked
him, and he answered with some sharpness, 'If you
take a pleasure in being insulted, it is all very well;
for God's sake take it; but as for me, I must not permit such things when I see them. Follow your own
way, I must follow mine: this is a matter on which we
cannot agree.'

We may sum up this subject in a few words by
adding the testimony of Cardinal Pedicini :—'She
bore,' he says, 'during her whole life calumnies, out-
rages, insults, for the love of God, with a marvellous
patience, resignation, tranquillity of mind, and a generous affection for those who persisted in persecuting and
assailing her. Assuredly, without a deep foundation
of humility she could not have arrived at so lofty a degree of perfection; but it cost her much, on account of
her naturally quick and passionate disposition.' It was
by a series of secret victories over self that she attained
to the state in which she comes before us, performing
heroic acts of patience, humility, and charity with a
facility which is one of the characteristics of exalted
sanctity, and which is apt to make us feel as if saints
were a class apart from other Christians, endowed with
excellences derived from some extraordinary source un-
attainable to the great body of the faithful. 'Yet,'
observes Father Faber, speaking of the merit and glory
obtained by our victories over self in little things, 'it
was not what we read of in the saints that made them

saints: it was what we do not read of them that enabled them to be what we wonder at while we read. Words cannot tell the abhorrence nature has of the piece-meal captivity of little constraints.'* And it is the unflagging perseverance in this petty captivity of nature which makes the saint, or, we might rather say, which allows the new man, the saint within us, to grow and attain to maturity, 'the measure of the age of the fulness of Christ.'†

The bodily maladies of a most acute and complicated kind from which Anna Maria suffered for years also made large calls upon the exercise of a most sublime patience as well as fortitude. To read a mere list of these complaints would lead us to believe that she endured almost all 'the ills which flesh is heir to.' Her head was the seat of continual pains; she had constant sick-headaches, which were terribly aggravated on the Fridays; to these were added neuralgia and rheumatism, which attacked her ears so acutely that she was obliged to have her head almost always swathed up. The light of the sun, to which she had necessarily to expose herself in following her domestic avocations, occasioned sharp pains in her eyes, the sight of one of which was all-but gone; nevertheless it was with that eye that she contemplated 'the sun of eternal wisdom,' but natural light had little effect on it except to cause the acutest suffering. Her palate suffered, not only through her voluntary mortifications, and also because all food, even in the smallest quantity, at last became repulsive to her, but from an exceeding bitterness, from which her mouth was never free. She seemed, indeed, to have lost all appreciative taste except for what was

* *Growth in Holiness*, chap. xvi. p. 297.
† Ephes. iv. 13.

M

bitter and disagreeable ; for we find it recorded that she
had a particular repugnance to an infusion of poppies,
which she nevertheless submitted—or rather, we should
say, for that very reason rejoiced—to take, three times a
day, during her last lingering illness. Her sense of smell
was afflicted in a peculiar and supernatural manner.
For her, the atmosphere was physically tainted with
the sins of the world : she could literally smell sin.
This was an intolerable torment.   Her sense of touch
had also its share of suffering, particularly the gifted
right hand.   Every sense, in short, was an avenue of
torture.   Besides all this, she was afflicted with gout,
asthma, and other painful maladies, external and internal, the bare enumeration of which makes one shudder.   The rheumatic pains from which she especially
suffered in her arms and legs during the closing years
of her life, and in spite of which she still endeavoured
to work even during her last mortal illness, out of her
great abhorrence of idleness and an easy life, would
have been alone sufficient to force complaints from one
who had had nothing else to bear.

Anna Maria, however, never complained, either by
word or look : this was part of the secret of her victory.
We may be silent under suffering, it is true, from many
motives ; from a mixture of discretion and of kindness, in
order not to become wearisome ; from a natural reserve,
difficult sometimes to account for, but apparently connected in some way with a secret sense of our own dignity ; or, again, from a kind of natural fortitude and
generosity of spirit, which makes us reckon it an unworthy and childish indulgence to lament ourselves.
Yet none of these motives, not even what is a far
higher one, a sense of the duty of Christian resignation,
suffice to achieve the present victory of which we are

speaking, although even those of the natural order
which have been enumerated may, by repressing the
manifestations of impatience or of sadness, more or less
serve to check them, and thus to form a habit of self-
control.   But Anna Maria's motive was the highest of
all, the love of God and conformity to His will, by
which she made His will hers.   Sufferings which came
to her by His appointment became thus voluntary sufferings, combining all, and more than, the merit of what
is self-elected with the characteristics that belong to
voluntary mortifications.   Hence her silence ; for who
is there who does not feel the inconsistency of complaining of voluntary sufferings?   From their nature
these demand concealment.   And this very exterior
silence re-acted again upon her inwardly, to silence the
rebellion of the interior senses.   The inward revolt dies
for want of air and exercise.   The garrison is starved
when it can make no sortie.   But the blockade, in
order to be effectual, must be real and complete ;
otherwise we shall be all the while admitting supplies
underhand, thereby feeding and irritating the very vice
which we outwardly control.   Nay, we shall get to
fancy that we had best pacify it by a little indulgence,
and we seem temporarily to succeed by so doing.   From
this circumstance proceeds the very common delusion
that evil feelings and passions are damped and weakened
by allowing them the relief of some moderate expression.   Father Faber, treating of temptations, alludes to
this delusion, ' with which the devil tries to possess us,
that if we give way in some of the circumstances of the
temptation, or to the temptation itself, short of sin, we
shall weaken it. . . . It is strange that so gross a snare
should succeed ; yet it does so in many cases.   We
must remember, therefore, that to yield is to weaken

ourselves, not the temptation.'* It is because we are
so prone to play this losing game, that we make such
slow progress against our old Adam and always remain
clambering and struggling near the base of the hill,
whose summit is the perfection we aim at, but shall
never thus reach. Anna Maria had struggled after
another fashion and come off victorious. Even when
'crucified on her bed of suffering,' to use her confessor's
emphatic terms, she suffered without uttering a single
complaint, and with so serene and cheerful a countenance that she filled all who saw and spoke to her with
joy and consolation, and inspired the afflicted who applied to her with fresh courage to bear their own trials.
Instead of craving sympathy for herself, as is the custom
with great sufferers, she was as much as ever all sympathy for others; forgetting her own pains, she interested herself affectionately in the troubles of every
one with a sweetness and tenderness of manner which
was inexpressibly soothing; and, no matter what she
might be called to endure, it was ever the same. She
was always placid, cheerful, courageous, always abandoned in all things to the will of her Lord.

'In order to prolong her painful existence,' says the
confessor, 'God vouchsafed, for the interests of her
neighbour, to indicate to her minutely what remedies
she ought to take; and this favour certainly deserves
to be counted among supernatural graces.' Yet we shall
find her spirit of obedience causing her to submit to the
fallible and, as she knew to a certainty, the erroneous
opinion of doctors, when they prescribed what was in
contradiction with her divine lights.

Humility and patience are kindred virtues, nay,
they are so closely connected as to be inseparable. No

* *Growth in Holiness*, chap. xvi. p. 292.

one can be perfectly humble without being patient, or
perfectly patient without being humble. Patience implies humility, and humility works and produces patience. Hence humility may be regarded as the main
root and principle of patience. Humility, again, has
an intimate connection with obedience; these three
virtues being so closely interwoven as to become almost
identified with each other. It is true that humility lies
at the basis of the whole Christian character, so that in
its absence the entire superstructure rests on an unsound
foundation; and where humility is deficient not a single
virtue can be practised with any excellence, however
little connection it may appear to have with it. It will
be either quite vitiated or more or less alloyed, as the
case may be; but, as we have just said, the two virtues
of patience and obedience are so obviously conjoined
with humility that they may be almost viewed as being,
not its fruits merely, not simply as deriving their perfection from it, but another aspect of itself; in short,
humility in exercise. 'Without an extraordinary foundation of humility,' observes the Cardinal, 'Anna Maria
would never have practised continually this tranquil
and imperturbable resignation to the Divine will on the
most painful occasions. Without an extraordinary fund
of humility she could never have arrived at the perfect
obedience which she practised constantly and in the
most heroic manner, whether towards her confessor or
towards her husband, and that in spite of his trying
temper, and generally towards all the members of her
household, renouncing her own judgment in all things,
notwithstanding the supernatural lights with which she
was endowed.' Anna Maria was profoundly convinced
that the creature of itself has nothing but an inheritance
of miseries and evils caused by sin; hence she referred

all good, whether spiritual or temporal, to God, and was most solicitous to direct others to do the same. Accordingly, it troubled her much to be thanked when she had effected a miraculous cure, and she would instantly bid the grateful person thank God, who had healed the sick through the intercession of the Blessed Virgin or of such and such a saint.

She watched also with a jealous fear over this ownership of God as regarded herself, trembling lest she should ever defraud Him, and never ceased imploring the Lord with tears and sighs to sustain her in her battles. This was one of the ends for which she mortified herself; and, intimately convinced of her own nothingness, weakness, and misery, she avoided most carefully even the smallest occasion of offending God, using as much caution as if she had been a mere novice in the paths of virtue. She so dreaded the dangers attending human praise and distinction, apprehending therein some snare of the devil to work her perdition, that in the early days of her conversion, when persons began to flock in crowds to her for advice or to beg her help for the sick, their esteem and admiration were a positive torment to her, of which she complained to God, telling Him in her simplicity that she saw well that He did not love her; otherwise He would lead her by the path of abjection and obloquy, which He Himself had trodden. Her prayers were heard in the end, and she obtained her full share, as we have noticed, of opprobrium and contempt. Meanwhile her prudence came to the assistance of her humility to enable her to keep herself as much as possible concealed; and the Cardinal records it as one of the proofs of the heroic degree in which she possessed that virtue; for, urged and animated as she was by a burning zeal to do as much good, private and public, as lay in her power, it was assuredly a difficult task, requiring a consummate discretion, to reconcile such a vocation with a hidden and obscure life. 'Certainly,' says the Cardinal, 'it needed ability of a supernatural kind to let light shine in the midst of darkness, and yet keep the focus whence it proceeded concealed. What profound humility,' he continues, 'what detachment, what heroic prudence did it not require to keep herself in the shade, while she was giving counsels to sovereigns, ecclesiastics, princes, and persons of every class who sought her advice ! She did not swerve from this rule save in cases of most obvious necessity, and she was able to meet every demand upon her by the most admirable regulation of her time.' Yet, notwithstanding all her efforts, the splendour of her supernatural gifts, of which she made use for the glory of God and the benefit of her neighbour, would not always permit of her eclipsing herself as she desired. 'She earnestly recommended silence,' he tells us, 'to those who received extraordinary graces through her means, and by a holy artifice strove to convince them that she was the most miserable creature in the world. Still, as people naturally are disposed to point out to others the remedy which has been successful in effecting a cure in their own case, the reputation of Anna Maria, particularly in these first times, spread so widely, that she was perpetually besieged both at home and in the churches by persons who sought her aid. Her poor little house at the bottom of a lane was frequented by persons of rank, who trod under foot human respect to enjoy the advantage of consulting so privileged a soul. Prelates who were afterwards raised to the Cardinalate, princes, distinguished ladies, were often to be seen there. The Cardinal Ercolani, the Cardinal Riganti, the Cardinal Cesari, Monsignor Mastai, and others were acquainted with her. Foreign bishops visiting Rome consulted her on the most important concerns of their dioceses; amongst others, Mgr. Strambi* used to recommend affairs of consequence to her prayers, and wait for her answer before proceeding to act. Pope Pius VII., of holy memory, was wont to ask me news of Anna Maria every time I sought an audience of him; he used to charge me to give her his blessing and re-

---

* Vincenzo Maria Strambi was born at Civitâ Vecchia in the year 1745, and, after being ordained priest, became one of the earliest associates of St. Paul of the Cross, the Founder of the Passionists. Strambi devoted himself to missions, catechetical instruction, and the other exercises of the Evangelical ministry. In 1801 he was made Bishop of Macerata and Tolentino by Pope Pius VII., and soon acquired general esteem and respect by his charity and the wisdom of his administration. Deported by the French usurping government, in consequence of his fidelity to the Pope, he bore his sufferings and privations with heroic constancy; and to whatever place he was taken he won the love and favour of the inhabitants, so that he was enabled to collect abundant alms for the poor of his own diocese. On his return he devoted himself energetically to repair the evil that had been done, and to restore and increase the institutions of piety. From the hour that he was made Bishop to his most advanced years he never ceased to discharge with zeal one of the special offices of the Episcopal office—preaching the Word. He would even go and help his colleagues in neighbouring dioceses; but so strict an observer was he of ecclesiastical discipline, that he always on these occasions procured a Papal dispensation on account of the obligation of residence. His humility was as remarkable as his other virtues, and it led him to make frequent applications for permission to resign his see. In 1823 Leo XII. consented to his resignation, and caused him to take up his abode with him in the Quirinal, that he might have the benefit of his counsels. He died of apoplexy Jan. 2, 1825. The cause of his beatification and canonization was introduced in the month of June, 1843. He left several religious works written in Italian, chiefly relating to the Passion. One work of Mgr. Strambi is well known in England, his Life of St. Paul of the Cross, forming part of the Oratorian series.

commend himself to her prayers. Leo XII. also conceived a great esteem of the servant of God in consequence of what Mgr. Strambi told him; Mgr. Menocchio,*
Brother Felice of Montefiascone, a Capuchin, and a
number of other personages who have died in the odour
of sanctity, kept up continued relations with Anna Maria
on account of the high esteem in which they held her.'

Considering the great lights vouchsafed to her, and
her connection and interest with so many influential
individuals, she might easily, the Cardinal is of opinion,
have made herself illustrious in the ways of God by
founding some pious institute. Other holy souls have
been moved to do so, but this was not her vocation,
and to her vocation she strictly adhered. More than
this, in the absence of any such divine call, she was extremely averse to everything of the sort, owing to her
fear of all novelties and especially from her dread of
self-love. 'On several occasions,' says the same witness, 'she advised certain persons who consulted her
to improve and develop the many excellent institutions
already existing in Rome, instead of creating fresh ones.
"Thus," she said, "good is done, and the devil is played
a trick, finding no means of introducing himself through
self-love, ambition, and the glory of propagating the
name of a new institution."' Maria Luisa, Queen of

* The Venerable Bartolomeo Menocchio of the Hermits of
St. Augustine. He was made Prefect of the Apostolic Sacristy
and Bishop of Porfirio by Pius VII. in 1800. He was also the
Pope's confessor. He accompanied him to Paris when he went
to crown Napoleon in 1804. When that Pontiff was carried away
prisoner in 1809, Mgr. Menocchio was the only Bishop allowed
to remain in Rome, notwithstanding his refusal to take the oath
of allegiance to the French Government. On the return of
Pius VII. in 1814, Mgr. Menocchio resumed his office of Apostolic Sacristan and confessor to the Pope. He died in 1822, or
1823. His cause was introduced 22d April, 1871.

Etruria, and afterwards Duchess of Lucca, had a special
veneration and affection for Anna Maria. So high was
the opinion she entertained of her great lights and consummate prudence, that she abstained from taking a
single step in either public or private affairs without
consulting the servant of God. When this princess
happened to meet Anna Maria in the streets of Rome,
she would, although accompanied by her court, eagerly
kiss her hands to her and salute her most affectionately
and familiarly. But the holy woman did all in her
power to avoid having such an honour paid to her, and,
if she espied the duchess's equipage in the distance, she
would slip under an archway, to hide herself till the
train had passed. She would not have taken this
trouble to shun contempt; nay, she would have gone
cheerfully to meet and welcome it. The same humility
which made her shun honour made her pay due honour
to all. She treated every one with unaffected respect,
a respect proportioned in its degree and in its forms to
the claims and position of the individual. Priests, on
account of their sublime office and the consecration they
have received, had the first claim on her regard; after
them, she honoured those upon whom God had been
pleased to confer secular rank or dignity; 'she saw in
them,' says the Cardinal, 'a providential order, and
humbled herself with the deference to which they are
entitled.' In the poor she saw the favourites of Jesus
Christ, and this gave them a title in her eyes to special
reverence and affection. For if in the great ones of the
earth she respected and honoured the delegated authority
which they had received from Him, in these little ones she
venerated and loved His person, which they represented.

Another genuine evidence of humility noticed by
the Cardinal may here be adduced, and this was that

if she perceived she had committed some fault, albeit
an involuntary one, she never laid it to anything or
anybody. How rare such abstention is, it requires but
a little observation or, indeed, self-examination to convince us. Many who will refrain from shifting the
blame upon others in order to exonerate themselves
can seldom forego the alleviation to mortified self-love
of a mild species of excuse, which takes the form of
merely mentioning what caused or occasioned a fault
which otherwise would not have been committed. But
Anna Maria not only never accused creatures of being
in any way the occasion of her shortcomings, but she
did not even relieve herself by throwing the responsi-
bility on the devil, whose temptations (as the Cardinal
observes) so many persons are in the habit of urging
in extenuation of their faults. 'It breaks the shame
of our faults,' says Father Faber, 'to believe that in
every instance we have wrestled and been thrown by
an evil angel of tremendous power, and not that through
cowardice, effeminacy, and self-love we have simply
given in to the suggestions of our own irresolute will.'*
But Anna Maria acted very differently; she accepted
for herself the whole shame and blame of her slight
and infrequent faults or imperfections—in her eyes
always great, because defects in the service of Him who
is Infinite Majesty and Infinite Goodness, and who had
made her so rich by the abundance of His favours—and
turned with a holy indignation against herself, saying
that she was a proud and foolish creature, fit only to
do wrong; and then followed redoubled mortifications.
And all this was done without petulance or vexation,
for she was thoroughly convinced in her heart that she
was the most miserable and contemptible of beings;

* *Growth in Holiness*, p. 186.

the sublime gifts she had received serving but to humble
her the more, from her view of her own unworthiness.
So far from being tempted therefore to parade them,
she would gladly have altogether concealed them, had
that been compatible with the purpose for which they
had been conferred on her, or with submission to those
who had the spiritual direction of her soul.   When
forced by obedience to manifest her heavenly gifts, her
humility took refuge in the most modest forms it could
adopt : for instance, she would never say, 'The Lord
spoke to me,' or, 'The Blessed Virgin said so and so
to me,' but she would use some such phrase as,
' While I was praying to God, or the Holy Virgin, or
such a saint, I heard this or that.'   To conclude in the
words of Cardinal Pedicini, who had so long and intimate a knowledge of her : ' she was humble in heart,
humble in demeanour, humble and simple in her dress,
humble in her conversation, in all things keeping herself as low as she could ; and this gift of profound
humility was a special grace.'

Her humility in her behaviour to those above her
in station, was never tainted with the least obsequious-
ness.   She was as true and frank as she was humble.
' Respectful by education and from humility,' says her
confessor, ' but at the same time sincere and frank
when it was question of speaking the truth for the
glory of God and the good of her neighbour, she never
knew what it was to practise adulation towards the
great.'   Her letters to the Duchess of Lucca as well as
those to the Princess Vittoria Barberini are alone a
proof of this.   A Cardinal* who desired to see her and
make her acquainted with his sister, sent to request her

* Monsignor Luquet says that this Cardinal was Cardinal
Fesch, Napoleon's uncle and his sister Mdme. Letitia Buona-
parte, the Emperor's mother.

prayers, begging her to inform him of the lights she
might receive. The servant of God replied by bidding
the Cardinal tell his sister to meditate in the mean time
on these three points : what she had been, what she
was, and what she would soon be ; and prepare for
death. To persons of all ranks, indeed, who presented
themselves to her for advice, she kindly but without
reserve pointed out their faults, for she had an instant
and unerring knowledge of them by means of the mysterious sun. 'A thousand instances might be cited,'
says the confessor, 'which testify to her frankness and
to her love of truth ; she could not endure those pre-
tences, disguises, and flatteries which are so common
in our day. "He who serves God," she used to say,
"ought to be respectful and humble, but at the same
time frank and simple." '

We shall not attempt to follow any farther the
enumeration of Anna Maria's virtues. To do so would
detain us too long ; besides, they will incidentally come
before us when treating of other subjects. We have
chosen patience and humility for particular consideration, as in a former chapter we selected mortification,
not only because so many other virtues are included in
their eminent practice, but because, if any were more
especially characteristic of one who was called to exhibit so perfect an example of all Christian excellences,
assuredly these three must be named : mortification,
humility, patience. Hers was a penitential life, and
her greatest penance was the continual and unceasing
contradiction of her will in all things. She was nailed
to the cross all her days. By humility she accepted
the cross, by mortification she crucified herself, and by
patience she allowed herself to be crucified, and thus
performed her part in accomplishing the work to which
she had been called and fulfilling her vocation.

CHAPTER XI.

ANNA MARIA'S DEVOTION TO THE MYSTERIES OF THE INFANCY AND PASSION, AND TO THE BLESSED SACRAMENT.

ANNA MARIA had the tenderest devotion to the Sacred Infancy. Hence, when Christmas was approaching, she always made a very fervent preparation, especially during the nine preceding days. For this end she used to assist at a very early hour at the Novena in the Church of San Bartolomeo in the Piazza Colonna, taking no account of the cold of the dark winter mornings or of her many bodily infirmities; and God rewarded her by according her very special graces during those nine days. She used also at that season to place a little image of the Infant Jesus on her own domestic altar, before which, in prolonged contemplation on a God thus abasing Himself and becoming poor and little for our sakes, she daily studied the lessons of the Crib. Several times, when thus engaged, she heard a divine voice exhorting her to a generous imitation of the poverty of the Infant Saviour. Bethlehem and Calvary were Anna Maria's two abodes. The Sacrifice of the Lamb of God was ever present to her mind: she saw it begun in the Manger and consummated on the Cross; and it was this sight continually before her spiritual eye which animated her courage, furnished ever fresh aliment to her love, and filled her with a generous spirit of perseverance. The Cross received special honours in her family sanctuary; she had a particle of the wood of that sacred tree, '*in quo pependit Salus Mundi*,' and every day, with her children, she adored and kissed it with profound veneration. 'It was the continual occupation of her life,' writes the Cardinal, 'to contemplate the inexplicable sufferings of our dear and gracious Jesus; after His example, and in order to resemble Him in suffering, she endeavoured to crucify herself entirely in flesh and spirit for the love of Him.' Hence her mortifications, her fasts, her disciplines were redoubled on the Fridays, but all, as we have said, subject to obedience to her confessor; for well she knew that 'obedience is better than sacrifice.' She had no greater desire than to be despised for the love of God, and to drink with Him of the chalice of His Passion—if we might not rather say that it was her one predominant desire; and God abundantly satisfied this longing of her soul.

She would seek in preference the least frequented or most solitary places, there to indulge her devotion freely and meditate undisturbed on the Passion of our Lord. She often went to the Cemetery of the Santo Spirito, or that of St. John Lateran, and to the Crucifix of San Paolo without the walls, particularly on Fridays; and yet Friday was a day of great bodily suffering to her, the habitual pains in her head being then aggravated, as we have already noticed, and this most of all during the three hours of our Lord's agony, forcing streams of tears from her eyes if she attempted to occupy herself or encountered the light. Regardless of these sufferings, which, however, were sometimes so excessive as to confine her to her bed, she would walk barefooted to the above-mentioned places, and there remain speechless for hours, all absorbed in the contemplation of the Dolorous Mysteries. She would also visit in the evening the Mamertine Prison for forty consecutive days in the same manner. The devotion of the Way of the Cross was peculiarly dear to her, her

Lord having made known to her that it was very agreeable to Him. Accordingly, she had herself inscribed
in the Confraternity of the Coliseum, and never, if
possible, omitted to assist publicly at this exercise.
During the unhappy times of the military occupation
of Rome by the French, when the holy pontiff Pius VII.
had been carried away into captivity, she multiplied
her visits to the Seven Basilicas. It was her custom
to take off her stockings at the gate of San Paolo, and
thus make her whole pilgrimage of six or seven hours
barefooted.* She would undertake these same pilgrimages, notwithstanding the heavy cross which her
own physical sufferings and the ever pressing needs of
her family laid upon her, whenever she perceived that
any one who had injured, calumniated, or persecuted
her was undergoing chastisement from God, and this
with the sole object of obtaining pardon and grace for
her enemies, after the example of Jesus, who prayed on
the Cross for His murderers.

These acts of virtue were the more meritorious because, as Cardinal Pedicini, who mentions them, states,
the vivacity of her character inclined her naturally to
resentment. They show how deeply she must have
learned the lessons of the Cross and drunk of the spirit
of the Crucified. It is not the absence of resentful
feelings which makes the true Christian. Resentment
in itself, as appertaining to our nature, and apart from
any accidental disproportion to its cause, and from any
evil interior tempers of mind or exterior acts offensive
to charity to which it may lead, is not sin; neither is

---

* In the last years of her life, when she was assailed by so
many infirmities, she contented herself, out of obedience to her
confessor, with going barefoot only from the gate of the city to
the Basilica of S. Paolo.

there any merit in the want of it. It is the sense of
wrong and injustice, combined with the natural love
of self as their object, which excites it. Persons of
refined sensibility, of lively consciousness of what is
right and wrong, and of high-strung nervous organisa-
tion, will feel keenly where duller and more obtuse and
unexcitable natures will be comparatively unmoved.
As is the case with all the human passions, it is in its
indulgence that sin is to be found, and in its rebellion
against the supremacy of reason. But the true Christian aspires to something much higher than the due
regulation of his passions and their reduction to the
obedience of reason. He does not aim simply at returning to the state of the first Adam and regaining his
lost advantages. Glorious as were the gifts and the
beauty of the state of innocence, which included the
integrity of nature along with the possession of supernatural grace, the redeemed state surpasses and excels
it in dignity by reason of the superior dignity of the
Second Adam, the Lord from Heaven. By virtue of
his union with the crucified God-Man, the true Christian adopts all the sentiments, all the desires, all the
predilections of his Divine Head. He loves what He
loved, hates what He hated, chooses what He chose.
Christ alone now lives in him; and when that divine
life is thus allowed its full and perfect development—
as alas! it so seldom is—then we have a saint in the
degree and measure of sanctity to which his soul was
called. All former things have passed away, everything within has received a new bent and direction, no
matter what the old disposition may have been; and
if the old nature had some leaning more excessive than
another, it was only that the triumph of grace in the
formation of the new man might be more splendidly

N

manifested. And so it was with Anna Maria : she had
no resentments now according to flesh and blood ; she
hated only sin, but she loved the sinner, for whom the
Precious Blood was shed and the Sacred Heart was
pierced ; while for those who had injured her personally she had only a tenderer compassion, loving them
with a special charity as the instruments of rendering
her more perfectly conformable to the Passion of her
Lord. So penetrated was she with this compassion
that, in recommending any one to God in prayer, her
heart seemed as it were dissolved. Tears, of which she
had the gift, poured from her eyes ; and it was the
same the moment her thoughts dwelt on the Passion of
the Saviour, or on the Dolours of His Blessed Mother.
To the Precious Blood the price of our redemption and
the ransom of sinners, and to the Sacred Heart of Jesus,
opened for the love of us, which gave forth Its last
drops, she was most tenderly devout. The Heart of
Jesus was her refuge at all times, to which she fled for
the supply of every necessity, for fortitude and consolation under every sorrow. Each day she fervently
invoked that Divine Heart when kneeling with her
family before the domestic altar, committing to It their
wants and desires, the conversion of sinners, and all
the needs and interests of Holy Church, in accents of
filial confidence and love which testified to the close
bond which joined her heart to the Heart of her Lord
and to the likeness which love had created between
them. 'Her heart,' says the Cardinal, 'was of wax for
God and for her neighbour.'

Words fail to describe her devotion to the Blessed
Sacrament. By the order of her confessors she communicated daily, a practice which she began in the early
times of her conversion and was enabled to maintain

until the last day of her life.   We have seen how this
holy woman would pass into an ecstasy at the mere sight
or sound of some object of God's material creation.
His power, His goodness, and His love therein displayed
ravished her soul with delight : what, then, it may be
imagined, were her sentiments in regarding that Miracle
of Infinite Love, the Adorable Eucharist, and still more
in partaking of It !   The Cardinal Pedicini, so long the
confidant of the most secret thoughts of Anna Maria,
avers that the transports of her heart towards this great
Mystery are as difficult to believe as to narrate, and that
language is utterly inadequate to express the joy which
filled and inebriated her soul when she was kneeling
before the Tabernacle, or the divine favours of which
she was the recipient at those times.   She had no sooner
knelt down before the altar than her countenance would
become like that of an adoring seraph, in which we
picture to ourselves love and veneration as blended in
an ineffable manner.   Her whole figure assumed the
immobility of a statue, and you might have believed
her to be inanimate but for the tears which coursed
down her cheeks and the irrepressible sighs which from
time to time arose from the depths of her bosom.

These sighs and tears must not be confounded with
the demonstrations in which ordinary pious souls will
sometimes indulge, and with which an excitable nature
has not seldom as much to do as sensible devotion.
We seem to know this instinctively, since we may
venture to say that few persons will be found who are
not more teased and disturbed than edified by having a
neighbour of this class at church.   But it was otherwise in the case we are describing.   Anna Maria's tears
and sighs had a supernatural source, and people loved
to draw near and observe her reverentially, feeling their

own faith and love renewed at the spectacle. Her
spiritual sons in particular loved to be near her when
she communicated. While in this ecstatic state, her
senses would be so completely dead to all external impressions that no noise whatsoever was capable of recalling her to herself, although even a tacit command
from one who had spiritual authority over her, and even
from any priest, would have an instantaneous effect.
Cardinal Pedicini says that frequently, after giving her
Communion, he secretly transmitted to her from the
altar the command to repress the movements of her
heart. This was in order to avoid attracting attention,
particularly in a church of moderate dimensions like the
Madonna della Pietà. When these emotions occurred
in distant and thinly frequented churches, such as San
Paolo fuori le Mura and others, where he happened to
say Mass for her, he did not interfere with the effects
of her fervour. And indeed it was most painful to
witness the efforts which obedience cost her when she
was enjoined to repress them, manifested, as the Cardinal says, by the streams of perspiration which poured
from her face, and this even in winter. In these efforts
she was generally successful, God permitting her to prevail, and she would then fall into a calm and delightful
ecstasy, unconscious of anything around her. If the
ecstasy began before Communion, she came to herself
when the priest approached with the Sacred Host, received It with great devotion, and returned to her state
of contemplation.

A striking instance of the complete suspension of
her external senses, when in the ecstatic state, occurred at the time of the French Republic. There was
a call to arms on the Piazza Colonna, where all the
troops mustered. The beating of drums and the loud

vociferations of the mob, which had also gathered there, alarmed the quiet congregation in the Madonna della Pietà, who all hastily left the church.   In a moment the sacred edifice was cleared, and the sacristan was about to close the door as a precautionary measure, when he perceived one worshipper still remaining, fixed and immovable.   It was Anna Maria.   She had heard nothing of the uproar without, and had noticed nothing of the disturbance within and the sudden departure of the congregation.   She continued equally deaf to the sacristan's voice, and his repeated requests that she would leave the church.   In fact, she had just received Communion, and had fallen into an ecstasy. The sacristan, finding himself unable to rouse her, finished by locking her up in the church ; and great was her surprise, when at last she was restored to consciousness, to find herself alone in the sacred building !

These raptures, indeed, were so frequent after Communion that they might almost be said to be habitual. As soon as she had received her Lord she would commonly hear His voice internally, and its first accents would plunge her into an ecstasy, which usually lasted a considerable time.   Occasionally, however, surprised by the flame of divine love, she would fall to the ground after receiving the Sacred Host, like one in a death swoon.   Cardinal Pedicini relates one instance when, many persons being present and remarking the occurrence, Anna Maria, on coming to herself, was overwhelmed with confusion.   She lovingly remonstrated with her Heavenly Spouse, but received only this reply : ' You will have to suffer these things yet many times.'   The Cardinal was himself to be the frequent witness of these occurrences.   ' Often,' he says, ' have I seen her fall, after receiving Communion, as if struck

by lightning, and thus remain a long time in the sweet
expansions of divine love. Whoever drew near to her
on such occasions felt an impression of heavenly tranquillity. Sometimes persons would experience in their
hearts a deep sentiment of the love of God, accompanied with humility and compunction; sometimes a
celestial perfume was perceptible; and the same phenomena would occur during her visits to the Blessed
Sacrament, when exposed during the devotion of the
Quarant' Ore.'

She knew by a kind of heavenly instinct where the
Blessed Sacrament was, and would at once go up to
the chapel in which It was reserved, when for some
reason It had been removed. She had also the gift of
discerning It by a delicious sweetness in her mouth as
soon as she had received Communion. A priest in the
church of San Ignazio, whether to prove her or for
whatever other motive, one day committed the very
reprehensible act of giving her an unconsecrated particle. Anna Maria discovered the fraud at once through
this special gift with which she was favoured; she was
at the same time inwardly directed by the heavenly
voice to apprise her confessor; and it is from him we
learn these facts. The priest on being taxed with the
deception acknowledged his fault.

Many other marvels might be mentioned of this
holy woman in connection with the Blessed Sacrament;
such, for instance, as occurred in the Church of San
Carlino, the same where she had so fervently assumed
the habit of the Third Order of the Trinitarians. An
Irish priest was saying Mass, and Anna Maria was
waiting to receive Communion, when behold! upon
his turning round to the congregation holding aloft the
Sacred Host and pronouncing the words : ' *Ecce Agnus*

Dei ; ecce qui tollit peccata mundi,' the consecrated particle flew from his hands and rested on the lips of the servant of God.   Several persons present in the church were witnesses of this prodigy.   And again, our Lord appeared to her in the Blessed Sacrament, when exposed in the Church of Sant' Andrea' della Valle, surrounded with light and glory and arrayed in kingly majesty ; and upon another occasion of Exposition, in Santa Maria della Consolazione, she beheld in the Sacred Host a lily of dazzling whiteness and beauty, from which a voice issued, which she distinctly heard to say these words : ' I am the flower of the fields and the lily of the valleys.'   The confessor, on whose authority we relate these manifestations, says that he selects these two instances from others of a similar kind.

CHAPTER XII.

ANNA MARIA'S DEVOTION TO THE MOTHER OF GOD, AND TO
THE SAINTS AND ANGELS. HER CHARITY TO THE HOLY
SOULS IN PURGATORY.

WE have several times alluded to Anna Maria's tender devotion to the Blessed Mother of God ; and, had we not noticed it, it might well have been inferred. What good Catholic but loves and is devout to Mary ? what saint but has excelled in this love and devotion ? We might say that the love of Mary is the test and the measure of the love of Jesus ; and therefore it is but natural to expect that those who have abounded in love to the Son should have had a corresponding love for the Mother.   They have also had a corresponding

veneration for her and appreciation of her high position in the scheme of redemption; for the more the
mind ponders on the great mystery of the Incarnation,
which ranks next to that of the Adorable Trinity, the
clearer becomes its insight into the sublime dignity of
the Divine Maternity,—into all that is included therein,
and all that flows therefrom.

But such souls not only grow in love and veneration for the Mother of the Divine Redeemer, because
she is His Mother, but they also attain to a fuller perception of her relation to themselves, as their mother
also. That she is our mother by adoption we all know,
and how that adoption took place in the person of St.
John at the foot of the Cross; but when souls obtain
a deeper view of their own adoption in Christ, and of
all that is meant by that filiation which enables us to
cry 'Abba, Father' to Him who is by nature the Father
also of our Lord Jesus Christ,—an adoption not merely
nominal, like human adoptions, but true and real,
through a new and spiritual birth,—then also do they
come to have a more intimate and tender realisation of
the motherhood of Mary in their regard, and they perceive that she was given by her Son to us, not only to
exercise a mother's care in our behalf, great as such a
boon alone would have been, but to be in a real sense
also the mother of our souls, as she became by her
fruitful compassion and dolours at the foot of the
Cross. Anna Maria was so deeply penetrated with
this truth, she loved her with so child-like an affection,
that she could not name her without manifesting the
tenderness of her feelings. '*Mia cara madre*—my
dear mother,' she would commonly call her, or '*mia
cara mamma*,' by a tender familiarity of affection so
beautiful in Italian, but which we shrink from using in

our uncatholised language and uncatholised land ; thus
appropriating her to herself as her own special mother,
and no less so because she is also the mother of all
who are brethren in Christ. Her whole soul kindled
with love at the thought of Mary ; and thus, when
any occasion presented itself to speak of her, she became eloquent with that eloquence of the heart which
has the gift of communicating to others something of
the fire with which it is itself consumed.

We have seen how she fasted every Saturday in
her honour ; she also prepared herself to celebrate her
different feasts by novenas and other fervent exercises
of piety, fasting on the vigils. She addressed her frequently during the day in fervent ejaculations, never
failing to kneel down and say the 'Angelus' when the
bell rang, and affectionately saluting her images at the
corners of the streets. The sight of Mary at the foot of
the Cross on Calvary always moved her deeply, and
drew the tears from her eyes ; and she was often ravished in ecstasy when meditating before the images of
Our Lady of Dolours or of Pity. To the mystery of the
Dolours, indeed, she felt herself particularly attracted,
the other of our Lady's mysteries which shared her
special devotion being that of her Immaculate Conception. She also prayed frequently before the Madonna in her own oratory ; and, besides wearing the
scapular, she had constantly next her heart a little
image of the Mother of God, which was also the instrument of working many miracles. For as Anna Maria's
confidence in her 'dear mother' was unbounded, and
she never undertook anything without recommending
it to her patronage—attributing all happy results to her
intervention, and never ceasing to exalt the greatness
and goodness of this incomparable Virgin—so did the

Queen of Heaven repay the filial tenderness of her devoted child by the most signal and singular favours.

These marks of predilection were especially bestowed in seasons of sorrow and suffering, when this pious woman never failed to run to Mary for help and protection. They were given sometimes in the form of consolation, sometimes in that of warning, advice, and instruction. A few instances of these heavenly locutions may here be noticed. Amongst the most remarkable, was the following. Having seen in the mysterious sun the loss of many souls, Anna Maria had been interceding fervently with the Blessed Virgin for their salvation, when the Mother of God was pleased to dictate to her this prayer: ‘Prostrate at thy holy feet, great Queen of Heaven, I venerate thee with profoundest reverence, and acknowledge thee as the Daughter of God the Father, the Mother of the Divine Word, and the Spouse of the Holy Ghost. Thou art the treasurer and the distributor of Their mercies. It is because of thy most pure heart, so full of charity, sweetness, and tenderness for sinners, that I call thee mother of divine compassion. Wherefore I present myself to thee with great confidence, my most loving mother; I am in affliction and filled with anguish, and I pray thee to make me taste the truth of thy love by granting me the grace I ask of thee, if it be conformable to the Divine Will and good for my soul. I entreat thee to turn thy most pure eyes upon me and all belonging to me, especially those who have recommended themselves to my prayers. Behold the terrible war which the devil, the world, and the flesh wage against our souls, and how many of these souls perish. Remember, O most tender mother that we are all thy children, bought by the Precious Blood of thine only Son. Deign most ardently to pray the Blessed Trinity to grant me the grace always to vanquish the devil, the world, and all my bad passions, that grace by which the just are sanctified yet more, sinners reclaimed, heresies destroyed, infidels enlightened, Jews converted.

'Ask, O most loving mother, this grace through the infinite goodness of the Most High God, by the merits of thy Most Holy Son, by the milk with which thou didst nourish Him, by the devotedness with which thou didst serve Him, by the love wherewith thou didst love Him, by the tears which thou didst shed, by the sorrow thou didst experience in His most Sacred Passion. Obtain for me this great gift, that the whole world may form one only people and one only Church, which may render glory, honour, and thanksgiving to the Blessed Trinity and to thee who art the mediatrix. May this grace be accorded to me by the power of the Father, the wisdom of the Son, and the virtue of the Holy Ghost. Amen.

'Mother, behold the extreme peril of thy children. Mother, who canst do all things, have pity on us.

'Virgo potens, ora pro nobis. Three Ave Marias.

'Eternal Father, increase ever more in the hearts of the faithful devotion to Mary Thy Daughter.

'Eternal Son, increase ever more in the hearts of the faithful devotion to Mary Thy Mother.

'Eternal Spirit, increase ever more in the hearts of the faithful devotion to Mary Thy Spouse.

'Gloria Patri.'

Cardinal Pedicini himself took this prayer to the Sovereign Pontiff, Pius VII., who, by a rescript of the 6th March, 1809, granted an indulgence of a hundred days, to be gained for every recital, with a plenary indulgence once a month on the usual conditions. It

was printed in the names of some pious persons, Anna
Maria not wishing to be mentioned in connection
with it.

One day, when she was praying in the Church of
Ara Cœli, she heard a sweet and gracious voice issuing
from a figure of our Lady painted on a column. The
voice said, ' My daughter, fear nothing; I watch over
thee amid the troublous sea which thou art traversing.
Tell Father —— that I am here without a light, and
that I wish to be particularly honoured in this place. If
the Fathers should not do what I direct, I shall oblige
them to do so by miracles.' Anna Maria faithfully
transmitted the message with which she was charged,
but it met with no attention, and her request was not
granted. Then graces and prodigies speedily began to
be manifested amongst those who honoured the sacred
picture; the piety and ardour of the faithful were re-
vived; and soon ex-votos and gifts concurred to attest
the benefits received and the gratitude of Mary's devoted clients. All honour was now paid to the sacred
picture, which is known to this day as the Madonna
of Fra Petronio, that being the name of the holy Religious who undertook its special care.

Besides what she beheld in the mysterious sun,
Anna Maria had other visions, and to one of these we
will here allude, on account of its connection with our
Blessed Lady and the office of Mediatrix of Intercession
which she fills for the whole world; an office to which
Anna Maria was so peculiarly drawn to unite herself.
Cardinal Pedicini received the account of this apparition from her own lips. It took place when she was
kneeling before her little domestic altar, and occurred
on the night of the 21st March, 1812. The evils with
which the world was afflicted in those days of trouble

and calamity, and especially the sufferings which the
Church was undergoing, were the subject of her fervent
prayer, when suddenly she beheld aloft a globe like
to the earth, and entirely surrounded with flames, which
threatened to consume it. On one side was Jesus Crucified, torrents of blood pouring from His Sacred Wounds,
and at His Feet was the Blessed Virgin, who, with her
mantle spread out on the ground, was earnestly beseeching the Saviour, by the merits of this Blood, which
she offered for sinners, to turn away the scourge which
menaced the world. Anna Maria united herself in
spirit to this petition of Mary, and after awhile the
vision vanished. Her confessor wished Luigi Antonini
to execute a drawing representing what she had seen.
He complied ; and when the Cardinal wrote his deposition he informs us that this spiritual son of the Venerable Servant of God, still preserved it as a memorial of
the apparition.

Anna Maria also received instructions and heavenly
locutions from the holy Apostles, as the Cardinal tells
us. 'She profoundly venerated,' he says, 'in St. Peter
and St. Paul the promulgators of the holy faith in this
city of Rome.' Among the martyrs, confessors, and
virgins she had also many patrons. To St. Joseph, the
spouse of our Lady, she was tenderly devout, and used
to fast on Wednesdays in his honour. St. Philip Neri,
St. Francis of Paula, St. Aloysius Gonzaga, St. John
of Matha and St. Felix of Valois, the founders of the
Order of the Most Holy Trinity, were also objects of
her special devotion. We must not omit to notice in
particular the glorious martyr, St. Filomena, through
whose intercession Anna Maria performed some miraculous cures, and to whom, when dying, she bequeathed
the care of her family. 'To all the angels,' says Car-

dinal Pedicini, 'and, above all, to St. Michael, St.
Gabriel, and St. Raphael, she was singularly devout.'
Her guardian angel, he tells us, guided and directed
her continually in a supernatural and sensible manner;
and this, not only in the paths of virtue and holiness,
but even in her common domestic work, teaching her
how to do certain things and aiding her by his instructions to rule and govern her household. So familiar
and sensible, indeed, were these communications, that
we are told by her confessor that, when engaged in
sweeping the house or in some other ordinary work,
she would sometimes stop to ask her good angel why
he did not answer her at once; then, smiling, she would
resume her occupation, having probably received her
reply.

Assistance of the character here described, we cannot doubt, would be, if not sensibly, yet substantially
given much more frequently if it was sought in the
manner in which Anna Maria sought it; for she not
only begged for help and light from her heavenly guide,
but she listened and attended internally for his reply.
The absence of listening in prayer all spiritual writers
agree in signalising as a great mistake, into which even
the devout often habitually fall.* Not that they would
have us look out for supernatural manifestations, interior

* Speaking of 'Docility to the Holy Ghost,' Father Faber
says, 'A habit of listening to Him is an essential part of the
spiritual life; without it, prayer can never be supernatural, or
more than a pious habit; not a real familiarity, or union of the
soul with God.' He specifies three consequences which result
from not listening to divine inspirations. '1. Our own spiritual
life and God's designs upon us are nothing but mist, confusion,
and unmeaning generalities. 2. So we come in outward things
to work on impulse, or from natural activity, without consulting or listening for the Holy Ghost. 3. Hence neither our works
nor ourselves have the secret of success, or the root of perse-

words, and the like : this would be the height of presumption ; but they tell us that we may, and, indeed,
ought humbly to expect to be influenced divinely, at
least through the workings of our own mind or in some
way proportioned to our state and needs.*   Such constant application to him who is ever beside us for the
one purpose of helping us, and who (without intending
thereby to disparage the love of any of God's saints or
angels whom we may particularly honour and invoke)
may be said to have for us that species of love which
the human heart so covets, an exclusive love—seeing
that we are the objects of the exclusive care of this
dear heavenly friend—cannot ever fail to be rich in re-

---

verance.' *Notes on Doctrinal and Spiritual Subjects*, vol. i.
p. 123.   These remarks are equally cogent whether applied to
the movements of the Holy Spirit or to the inspirations of our
heavenly monitor, who speaks to us in the name of God.

* ' To perfect souls the divine voice and light is in a manner a continual guide, and they have a continual correspondence
with it, even in their most ordinary smallest actions.' F. Baker,
Sancta Sophia, chap. vi.   The whole chapter, ' How God communicates Internal Light,' is well worth a careful perusal, as
also is the following chapter, ' How to obtain Light in Doubtful
Cases,' in which we meet with the following remarks bearing on
the present subject. ' Now there are two ordinary ways by which
God intimates His will to His servants, that with humble and
resigned prayers address themselves unto Him. The first is by
clearing of the understanding, thereto adding a supernatural
light, by which natural reason comes to see something that it
saw not before, or at least did not esteem before so considerable. For, by this new light of supernatural discretion, such
obscurities as did before hinder reason from discerning truth
are removed. . . . The second way by which God doth immediately signify His will to the intellective soul in virtue of
prayer, is by imprinting a blind, reasonless motion into the
superior will, giving it a weight and propension to one side of
the doubt rather than to the other, without representing actually and at the present to the understanding any special motive
or reason to determine the will.'

sults. But to insure the continuance of such favours, gratitude and an affectionate return on our part are, as we need scarcely observe, essential conditions. Accordingly, Anna Maria, besides hearkening internally for her angel's voice, which such habitual listening, apart from all special and supernatural cases, tends to render clearer and clearer, took care also to thank him gratefully and affectionately for the assistance he gave her.

One of the devotions most remarkable in Anna Maria was her tender love and solicitude for the relief of the suffering souls in Purgatory. This devotion came to her with the force of a threefold appeal: First, because to help the souls in Purgatory ranks among the highest acts, if it be not itself, as some hold, the very highest act, of mercy. Now the tenderness and devotedness of Anna Maria's charity shone, one may say, like some choice brilliant amongst her other splendid virtues. In the second place, she was specially called to intercede for the whole Church, as we shall more abundantly see when we come to speak of the mysterious sun; and this being so, how should not that province of the Church, so dear to Jesus and to Mary, peopled with souls confirmed in the grace and in the love of God, yet suffering untold torments by their separation from Him, and unable to help themselves, have had a large share in her intercessory prayer? In the third place, her vocation was to be a victim of expiation, and in this capacity she was to be continually offering herself to pay the debts of others. Hence the incapability of performing the least meritorious act of their own gave the holy souls in Purgatory a peculiar claim upon her charity. The prayers which she offered, and the penances and expiatory works which she performed for their relief, were unceasing, and, as Cardinal Pedicini forcibly remarks, 'to effect their deliverance Anna Maria doomed herself to a continual Purgatory.' She often followed the Way of the Cross for them in the Cemetery of the Santo Spirito and in that of St. John Lateran, knowing, as we have already said, that this exercise was specially pleasing to our Lord. For this reason she constantly resorted to it, as in all her own greatest needs, spiritual and temporal, so also in behalf of these His suffering spouses; and our Lord often permitted the souls that had been freed through her assistance to come and thank her before taking their flight to Heaven. One instance in particular is recorded, when she was purposing to receive Communion at St. John Lateran's for a departed soul. During the first Mass, which was said by her own confessor, she suffered much both in body and soul ; nevertheless she did not cease praying, offering what she endured to the Divine Justice. Mgr. Pedicini said a second Mass, and when he began the ' Gloria' Anna Maria felt herself inundated with a flood of joy, and the soul, which just at that moment had been released from Purgatory, approached and said, 'I thank you, my good sister, for your charity. I will remember you before the throne of God in Heaven, where, thanks to your prayers, I am going to be happy for all eternity.' One of her daughters was in the habit of accompanying Anna Maria when she went to the Cemetery of San Spirito to pray for the dead. She says in her deposition that these visits would be made for forty consecutive days, and in all weathers, yet always barefoot, in spite of rain or mud. She would say three Requiems and a prayer on each of the three hundred tombs. ' While my mother was praying,' she says, ' I used to walk about the cemetery, perform the

Way of the Cross, and then go and wait for her in the Chapel of the Rosary.'

Anna Maria used strongly to urge others to be devout to the souls in Purgatory, particularly the souls of priests, and to have Masses offered for them. 'Accustom yourself,' she would say to her spiritual children, 'to recite a hundred Requiems for them daily; and in assisting at holy Mass, offer it in their behalf. This devotion will preserve both you and your families from many misfortunes.' She herself, in saying her hundred Requiems, was accustomed to add two prayers. After the first fifty she would say, 'O holy Wounds of my Lord, which from love have given forth so much blood, have pity on the souls in Purgatory, and on me, a poor sinner.' After the second fifty she said, 'Holy souls, who from this world have passed into Purgatory, and whom the blessed in Paradise are expecting, you will ask graces for me when you appear before God.'

We may remark in conclusion that Anna Maria's great devotion to the souls in Purgatory, whose relief by her own penitential exercises and sufferings was to form part of her special mission, had doubtless acted as an attraction in drawing her towards the Trinitarians. For that Order, which was instituted for the redemption of captives suffering bondage on earth from the cruelty of man, had always taken a peculiar interest likewise in those prisoners of divine justice detained amongst purgatorial flames until they have paid the last farthing. The Trinitarians, in fact, have, as P. Calixte observes, never omitted to labour efficaciously for the souls in Purgatory, their rule even obliging each member to pray for the dead several times in the course of the day; and indeed the devotion has received among them a still greater development in modern times.

CHAPTER XIII.

ANNA MARIA A VICTIM OF EXPIATION.

Anna Maria lived at one of those critical epochs
in the world's history of which the present through
which we are passing offers another similar phase:
times of disorder and confusion, of blasphemy, of revolt against God, persecution of His Church, and of
her august head, denial of Christian principles, and the
substitution of such as are false and ungodly, which
issued, as we see them issuing also in our day, in the
disregard of all justice and right, in the contempt of
lawful authority and in the worship of brute force,
as also in the destruction of morality, public and private, threatening thus the utter dissolution of human
society. True, the contest between good and evil, between the Church and the world, never ceases; but
at periods like these it assumes a more terrible character, when the flood-gates of wickedness seem to be
thrown open, and the nations deluged with impiety.
At such times the Church is exposed to trials so
fearful, and passes through an ordeal so appalling,
that, to look at things under a mere human aspect, it
would appear as if her overthrow were inevitable. It
is from this point of view that her enemies regard
her, and thus, in these days of rebuke, they begin to
sing insulting pæans over her destruction. But the
Church has her Lord's promise of victory, and she
must prevail and triumph in the end; meanwhile He
provides her with defensive weapons of the potency
of which her foes know nothing, and which even many
Catholics whose faith is weakened by the surrounding
worldly atmosphere which they imbibe, do not suffici-

ently value. The arm of flesh and a worldly policy are
patent and intelligible things, but the weapons of the
Church are, not carnal, but spiritual. They seem to
the eyes of men altogether out of proportion with the
greatness of the struggle which is going forward—not
only inadequate but utterly vain and powerless for
effecting their purpose. Just as if one had gone and
proclaimed to the hosts of Madian and Amalec, who
'lay in the valley as a multitude of locusts'* for their
number, that Gedeon with his three hundred men, each
with a trumpet in one hand and a pitcher containing a
lamp in the other, would utterly discomfit their whole
host, and that they should fall by each others' swords,
those men would have scoffed at such an announcement as the raving of a madman, so it is ever with the
world. Although it has a secret presentiment of ultimate defeat, as had the inhabitants of proud and popu-
lous Canaan when they heard of the approach of the
Israelites, and dread of the God-protected people fell
upon them, nevertheless this presentiment serves only
to embitter its animosity and does not diminish one
whit the supreme scorn with which it regards the
soldiers of the Church, armed only with the folly of
the Cross, and combating only with patience in the
support of injuries, with prayer and with sufferings.
No wonder the world should mock at these defences,
which in its eyes are but symbols of weakness. 'Let ·
Him come down from the Cross, and we will believe
Him,' cried the Jews, but Christ continued to hang
upon the Cross, and triumphed there and thereby; and
the Church triumphs after His pattern. The world, it
is true, feels that a strength lies hidden somewhere,
which, as a rock of adamant, is resisting all its efforts, yet

* Judges vii. 12.

it suspects not wherein this strength consists, and refers it to everything, real or imaginary, which it conceives of the Church rather than to its true supernatural source.

God has chosen the weak things of the world to confound the strong, in order that no flesh may glory in His sight, and that the victory may be acknowledged to come from Him alone. He Himself is the strength of His Church; she knows that He is so, and in her need has recourse to the omnipotent weapons which He has placed in her hands. Moreover, in times of special trial He is used to send special graces of intercession to souls unknown to the world or, if known, despised by it. These souls are called to be the chief instruments in the supernatural work which God is carrying on in His Church. Others may seem more actively engaged in the strife, and to be doing more effectual battle for God's cause, like the Israelites fighting hand to hand with Amalec in the plain; but, even as it was Moses's upraised arms on the mount which were bringing victory to the host below, and, when he lowered them, not all their valour could enable them to stand against the enemy, so is it in the Church militant: the victory is mainly due to those who are lifting up their hands to God in prayer on the mount of perfection. Again, days of trial to the Church are also days of great offence against God, such as would call down upon a guilty world the most terrible scourges of His wrath if His vengeance were not stayed. Now these chosen souls generously present themselves as victims to receive in their own persons the chastisements due to God's offended justice: sickness, sufferings, and every manner of tribulation; and God accepts a sacrifice which He Himself in His ingenious mercy has inspired them to make.

Such was the mission of Anna Maria Taigi. She was not left in ignorance of her calling, even in the very first days of her conversion, as we have seen; and upon the occasion of her assuming the habit of the Trinitarians she had an interior revelation of a very peculiar character, to which some allusion has already been made. After Communion she heard a voice which said these words to her: 'My beloved daughter, approach, and I will make thee experience My sweetness, and how pleasing to Me are those who love Me. Tell thy spiritual father that I choose thee this day to go forth into the world to convert souls and to console persons of all ranks: priests, religious, nuns, prelates, cardinals, and even My Vicar; and thou wilt have to contend against a host of weak creatures subject to many passions. To all those who shall hearken to thy words with a sincere and generous heart, and shall put them in practice, I will grant signal graces; and they shall enjoy happiness in the depths of their hearts. Listen also, My daughter, to this: Thou shalt meet with many false and perfidious souls; thou shalt be turned into derision, insulted, despised, calumniated; but thou shalt bear all for the love of Me, and I assure thee, great God as I am, that thy persecutors shall render an account to Me of such conduct, and I will punish them either in this world or in the other.' So fully was this promise accomplished, that even the slightest contempt shown to the servant of God never went without chastisement; and her spiritual sons all bore witness to the remarkable fact, that if they so much as interpreted disadvantageously any simple action of hers, they were sure to pay dear for it in the course of the day.

When the ecstasy in which Anna Maria heard these

words was passed, she said to her Divine Spouse, 'Great God, whom dost Thou choose for such a work? I am a miserable creature, unworthy to tread the earth.' So deep was her humility and her sense of her own nothingness, that she began to pour forth her soul in tears and sighs before her Lord, when the voice again addressed her. 'My beloved daughter,' it said, 'such is My will. I will guide thee Myself by the hand, like a lamb, and all that I have said will be verified. Its accomplishment will be one day manifest.' Reassured by the Saviour's voice, and the sweet words He spoke to her, Anna Maria now renewed and ratified her previous acts of self-oblation, again devoting herself without reserve to endure every species of suffering, that all men might come to know and love their God. How pleasing to the Lord were these sacrifices is proved by various locutions with which she was favoured in these early times, and by the spiritual delights with which He inebriated her soul. It seemed also as if God could absolutely refuse her nothing, and He Himself was pleased to confirm this stupendous idea by what He said to her on more than one occasion : namely, that as He could deny her nothing which she asked, and as on the other hand the ingratitude of men was so great that He was resolved to chastise them, He would take away from her the fervour of prayer, and set her soul as it were to sleep.* Anna Maria no sooner heard

* This divine incapability, if we may use such a term, of resisting the prayer of His faithful servants is indicated in several passages of the Old Testament, and especially where God uses those remarkable expressions : 'Let Me alone, that I may destroy them' (Deut. ix. 14), when speaking to His servant Moses, as if prayer constrained the very liberty of the Almighty ; and again when bidding Jeremias (vii. 16) not to pray for the people.

this announcement than she set herself with redoubled courage and generosity to obtain the graces which she might later be precluded from soliciting, and especially the conversion of the world and the salvation of sinners.

We have already, when speaking of the mortifications of the servant of God, alluded to her acts of self-denial as regarded spiritual sweetnesses and consolations : how she tore herself away even from the foot of the altar and the happiness she was enjoying through the close union of her soul with God in prayer, lest self should be seeking some secret gratification. But here it may be well for us to pause a moment to consider this question of the refusal of spiritual consolations and sweetnesses. Is such refusal proposed for general imitation? Of course there is such a thing as spiritual greediness; and, short of such a fault as may deserve this name, there is always danger lest the soul, when receiving an abundance of consolations, should rest in them too much. On this point all are agreed, and that we cannot be too watchful in order to guard ourselves from the possibility of delusion. But this is not the question. The question is whether it is in every individual an act of more perfect virtue to refuse sweetnesses and consolations than to accept them. Would all do well, when favoured with them, like Anna Maria, to shorten their period of prayer? Passages certainly may be often met with in spiritual writers which seem to recommend the practice of always drawing back when God extends His Hand to give, while others seem to speak of such sweetnesses almost in an undervaluing tone, regarding them as sugar-plums given to children —an opinion which Father Faber, whom we are about to quote, qualifies as 'strange.'

This eminent writer tells us that these spiritual

favours are sent to perform a great work in our souls, and to make work easy to us which otherwise we should not have the strength to accomplish. So far, then, from its being advisable to refuse them, it is even right and desirable to pray for them.* 'Well,' he observes, ' may Alvarez de Paz say, " they err, then, who do not magnify this spiritual sweetness, and do not thirst for it in prayer, and are not saddened if it withdraws. They show that they have never learned by experience its manifold utility. For if they had once tasted it, and seen how by its impulse they rather ran than walked, yea, and even flew to perfection, they would indeed have esteemed that to be precious which brings with it so great an increase of virtues and purity. . . . It is not the sign of a soft-living man, and an effeminate heart or over-delicate spirit, to sigh after this sweetness ; but it is the work of a wise and strong man, who, recognising his inborn infirmity, desires that which will enable him to run to God with more speed and with greater agility, and to do greater and more heroic deeds. He whose judgment is otherwise neither knows himself, nor has any ardent desire after perfection, nor comprehends the true and solid riches of this sweetness." '

In farther confirmation of this view, Father Faber also quotes Da Ponte and St. Teresa. Nevertheless, as he says, we must not run into the other extreme on the subject of these sweetnesses and consolations. For it is undeniable that saints have spoken of the way of

* It need scarcely be observed that Father Faber is not alluding to favours of a different and extraordinary order often vouchsafed to the Saints. To pray for or to aspire to these would be presumption, as he clearly states, and therefore he expressly excludes them from his consideration when entering on the subject of spiritual favours.

pure faith and the absence of sensible consolations as the best road to the summit of the mount of perfection, and St. John of the Cross opines that it is the only one that leads to the *topmost peak* of his Carmel. The saint allows, however, that there is another road which leads upward, on which he writes the words, 'Science, Counsel, Sweetness, Security, Glory:' from all which the obvious conclusion we are led to draw is 'that the highest perfection is in the renunciation of these gifts, but that there is also a perfection which seeks them, and a perfection, too, by which the tops of Carmel may be scaled.'* Here, then, we think is a practical answer to the question asked. Granted that the refusal of spiritual consolations is the most excellent way, it is evident that it is only the most excellent and the highest to those who are called to choose it. All are not called to scale the very topmost peak of Carmel, nor would they attain any nearer to it, but the reverse, by declining the help needful to carry them to the height which is their allotted spiritual goal. In the absence, therefore, of an express movement of the Holy Spirit, it seems well thankfully to accept, and even ardently to desire, the aid and consolation which God is willing to afford us. He Himself is pleased often to withdraw this help for the soul's probation and purification; but to seek and desire and offer ourselves to such abandonments cannot be safely or prudently done of our own impulse and choice.

The whole resolves itself, in short, into the question of our vocation. Holy souls which have voluntarily embraced austerities appalling to flesh and blood and offered themselves to spiritual derelictions, even to that

* See a very valuable chapter on the 'Right Use of Spiritual Favours' in Father Faber's *Growth in Holiness.*

of dying alone, abandoned, and without the sacraments, have done so from an inspiration of the Holy Ghost. In one sense, therefore, it was not their own voluntary election, inasmuch as it was not done from the spontaneous choice of their own will, although by freely accepting what the Holy Ghost suggested, without commanding, they had the merit of an heroic voluntary act. Yet to these exalted souls the promptings of the Holy Spirit, to whom they have yielded themselves as docile instruments, come inwardly as a kind of Providential law, just as the events and contingencies of outward life are a Providential law to other men. The decrees of Providence subject us all, whether we will or no, to sorrows, pains, privations, and other trials; and it is in the power of every devout Christian, by a willing and joyful acceptance of sufferings as they arise, to convert them into so many voluntary acts of penance and self-sacrifice: this is a deeply consoling reflection. Thus at each step of his way, he accepts his vocation and says, 'Lord, I come to do Thy will,' after the pattern of his Divine Head. In the notes preparatory to a work which Father Faber unhappily did not live to write, we find the following among the considerations suggested on the doctrine of the Passion: 'It is remarkable that our Lord's satisfactions were not in voluntary penances, but in things which came on Him through His Father's will—this is a characteristic of His sanctity—the consolation of it to us.'*

To return to Anna Maria. She felt that her abode was not to be on Tabor. 'I have a baptism wherewith I am to be baptised,' said our Divine Redeemer; 'and how am I straitened until it be accomplished!'† To

* *Notes on Doctrinal and Spiritual Subjects*, vol. i. p. 192.
† Luke xii. 50.

chosen souls, called, like Anna Maria, to a special life
of self-sacrifice, He often imparts a participation in this
supernatural thirst for His Passion, to which He desires
to associate them.   An interior magnet accordingly
drew her constantly to Calvary, and to a life of expiation, internal as well as external; and she again and
again offered to her Heavenly Spouse the sacrifice of
her spiritual consolations, generously renouncing them
in order to diminish the evils in the world and in the
Church, through the acceptance of every kind of suffering.   Seeing that her sacrifice was not accepted, she
strove to supply by her own external penances.   Nevertheless she continued to persevere in the magnanimous
offer she had so often made, and which, indeed, she
was continually making by the preparation and attitude of her soul; for this offer was not the mere out-
burst of fervour, however frequent; it was a never-
ceasing tendency of her heart producing an abiding
oblation of self as its fruit.   'God,' says Cardinal Pedicini, 'satisfying at last her ardent desire, was pleased
to accept the offerings of her generous heart.   After
the lapse of several years the heavenly consolations
vanished like lightning, and left in their place dryness,
suffering, toil.   To the tears of compunction succeeded
the most afflicting aridity; to celestial joys, torment;
to sweetness, sadness; to tender devotion, the most
overwhelming weariness.   Her soul passed rapidly from
noontide splendours to the shades of night; from the
heavenly cabinet, the most brilliant court, she was precipitated into the darkest prison.   She was expelled
from delicious gardens, and cast upon the most barren
and desert sands.   It is true that God did not deprive
her of the other heavenly gifts, but they only served to
increase her martyrdom, as they also served to increase

her merits, because the knowledge of the perfections of
the object of her love augmented her grief at being deprived of it and her fear of losing it.'

To this privation, in itself so real a martyrdom to
one who has tasted of the choicest favours of God, were
added temptations of the devil, persecutions, calumnies,
insults, to some of which we have alluded and which
are to be referred chiefly to this season. It was then
also that she began to suffer more peculiarly from the
unpleasant tempers of different members of her family,
whose jars and dissensions were continually exercising
her patience, and which she was so often occupied in
the ungrateful task of calming, as we have related.
Then also her own bodily ailments were greatly aggravated and became well-nigh incessant, while it was
during the same period that the poverty and straits of
the family were, from the circumstances of those unhappy times, much increased. 'She lived through long
years,' says the Cardinal, 'with this accompanying train
of sufferings, save during rare moments when it pleased
our Lord to give her some flashing gleams of divine consolation, without which she could not have borne up
under the struggle.' He tells us also that her pains
continually increased up to her very last moments; for,
as we shall find, the hour of death formed no exception
to this unsparing rule ; and even in that supreme hour
of her life her assimilation to the Passion of Jesus was
as complete as it had been ever since He had begun to
make her partake of His chalice.

We have the following description, from the pen of
the Cardinal, of some of her spiritual sufferings and of
her behaviour under them. 'Who could describe,' he
says, ' the terrible nights which she passed alone in her
little room? In prayer she met only with the most de-

solating aridity.   Although turned towards heaven for
hours, sighing after her Beloved, seeking Him on all
sides and everywhere, that He might console her heart
and fill its void, the heavens were as bronze to her.
Tears might have served to soften her painful exile, but
tears were denied her ; and she was fain to resign herself to the Divine Will, drinking by slow draughts the
chalice of sharpest bitterness without either alleviation
or support.   How were it possible to reckon up the assaults of the infernal spirits, who tempted her under the
most seductive forms and by the most humiliating suggestions !   Terrified by these temptations, she opposed
to them the buckler of patience and prayer, although
she did this without any sentiment of compunction,
with difficulty formulating prayer in the depth of her
heart, where she humbled herself before God.   How
relate all the dolorous exclamations she made to her
God, whom she desired more and more ardently to
possess !   It seemed as if every creature were saying to
her, " *Ubi est Deus tuus ?*—Where is thy God ?'   Her
heart being unable to find the satisfaction which it desired, the devils endeavoured to excite it to anger and
hatred of God; and so powerful were these assaults that
she could not repress them without enduring mortal
agonies.'   It is difficult so much as to form a conception of the dreadful nature of this trial.   It seems a
kind of figure of what reprobate souls are described as
enduring in Hell, where they know God to be the
supreme good, while they are themselves eternally de-
barred from attaining it.   Indeed she herself told Cardinal Pedicini that she felt as if she were in a corner of
Hell.

The violence of these frightful trials not only greatly
aggravated the maladies which already afflicted her, but

was the occasion of fresh bodily ailments, which tormented her until death. During all this period of her desolations, Anna Maria nevertheless faithfully allotted the same time to her preparation for Communion and to her thanksgiving after it. 'Formerly,' says the Cardinal, ' she remained immovable because divine consolations inundated her soul; during her trials she strove to remain firm and intrepid in her interior martyrdom. Human nature suffered much; the devils besides used all their efforts to distract and torment her, but, without dwelling either on her mental pains or on her bodily sufferings, she continued motionless as a statue in the presence of her God whenever she went to the church in order to communicate or to visit the Blessed Sacrament, as well as when performing her domestic devotions.' What this effort must have cost her is proved by what he adds, that ' after whole hours of immobility she would be all bathed in a most painful perspiration.' She persevered with constancy in her accustomed exercises; she even multiplied her acts of piety and mortification with a courage truly heroic amidst her trials and anguish of soul, and in spite of an unspeakable weariness, inward agitation, and repugnance of the senses which was the chief cause of the extraordinary cold perspiration, like that of death, to which the Cardinal alludes.

Unable to gain the smallest advantage over her, the spirits of evil, who, from their confirmed opposition to God, delight in mischief for its own sake, and who hate with peculiar bitterness the souls which have given themselves wholly to Him and devoted themselves to the salvation of sinners, revenged themselves upon her by tormenting her in every possible way, either themselves appearing to her in visible and horrible shapes or

employing the instrumentality of creatures. It is related in particular how in the summer they would send
swarms of flies and other insects to assail her, which
would enter eyes, nose, ears, hoping perhaps thereby to
cause a momentary distraction or movement of impatience, or, failing this, at least to afflict and plague.
Again, in winter they would cause a great accession of
the pain which she habitually endured at that season,
from rheumatism, asthma, chilblains, and numerous
other complaints. The very number and variety of her
sufferings is, indeed, one of the most striking features
of her trial. No part of her seemed to be free from
the crucifixion of soul and body to which she was subjected.

'It is true,' says the Cardinal, 'that her Heavenly
Spouse would aid her from time to time, and the voice
of God encourage her for a moment, in order that she
might continue her march along the dolorous way of
Calvary; but these heavenly consolations, which disappeared like lightning, only increased the longing of
her heart continually to possess her Infinite Good. A
mouthful of bread cast to a famished dog sharpens instead of satisfying his hunger; besides, there is no
possible comparison between the natural instinct and
that devouring hunger which a soul wounded with
divine love experiences for its God. True, she continually had celestial locutions, particularly at the time
of Communion, but, instead of the spiritual delights
which heretofore she used to enjoy, she was rapt in the
most painful contemplations, by means of which God
discovered to her the evils of the world, the scourges
prepared, the sins of the people, especially those of
ecclesiastics, &c. This is why the locutions and raptures brought no solace to her heart; on the contrary,

charity urged her to renew her prayers to the Lord that
He would suspend His wrath and His just vengeance,
and to reiterate her acts of self-oblation; and then God,
accepting the offer, avenged upon her the claims of His
justice.'

Amongst the other sufferings and trials which Anna
Maria underwent, and which were to her most excruciating, were temptations against faith, on the part both
of men and of devils. We have seen in what a sublime
and heroic degree she possessed this virtue : to hear a
word spoken against any truth of the faith was unut-
terably painful to her, so that what she endured in this
way can only be compared to being scorched with a hot
iron. She was often brought into contact with hardened
sinners whom she had undertaken the task of convert-
ing, and the devil would instigate these miserable men
to broach maxims contrary to faith and morals, suggesting to their minds the most specious arguments
which had been ever framed by the subtle intellects of
heresiarchs. Three individuals in particular thus exercised the faith and patience of the servant of God. One
was a priest, who, having travelled much, and made a
prolonged residence in Protestant countries and at
several foreign courts, had become corrupted in his
faith, though not in his morals. She ultimately obtained this man's conversion, who made a retreat in a
convent, and died soon after. The second was a layman with whom she had been acquainted for many
years. He was a good-hearted man, and tolerably,
though not thoroughly, well-conducted. The devil took
occasion to tempt this indifferent Christian when assailed by temporal troubles. Among men of his stamp
some are drawn to God by worldly disappointments,
others seem thrust farther off from Him; they quarrel

P

with God and His Providence, and are easily led to
arraign His justice when He no longer ministers to their
earthly comfort and prosperity. So it was with this
unhappy man : he cast off his faith altogether, and,
having done so, he hated it. He became a heretic and
a blasphemer. Nevertheless, Anna Maria did not cast
him off, although, when he came to see her, he would
utter the most fearful impieties, and propound heresies
black enough, as the confessor expresses it, 'to eclipse
the sun ;' and then he would go into paroxyms of rage,
testifying thus to the appalling dominion which Satan
had obtained over him. It is difficult to imagine what
attraction drew him to the house and to the company
of a pious woman such as Anna Maria ; but, whatever
it might be, God was overruling it for the wretched
man's salvation. For more than twenty years he continued thus to try her forbearance and her charity.
These never failed her ; she gave him good advice, exhorted him kindly to patience, and, through the influence she had obtained over him, often held him back
when he was on the very edge of the precipice, and
strongly urged by Satan to commit suicide. The miserable man used to come and hold long conferences with
her, which lasted nearly to the close of her life, and
therefore mostly took place when she was suffering
under cruel bodily tortures and spiritual trials ; nevertheless, she would never send him away when he came.
'For the love of God and of souls,' says her confessor,
'she had constituted herself their slave, and had offered
herself under that title to her Divine Spouse.' And
God at last accepted her sacrifice in behalf of this in-
veterate sinner against His grace. He was converted ;
and at the time P. Filippo wrote, he was still leading
a good and Christian life.

The third individual who severely tried this holy woman was a young man who, in spite of the good Christian education he had received, had led a scandalous life from his earliest years. He filled some high situations under the French Government, but ruined his fortunes by his luxurious and profligate living. When the Pontifical Government was restored, affairs took him to Rome: the servant of God had already been praying for his conversion, as she told the person who brought him to her. In the midst of all his corruption, and in spite of the hardening effect of sensual indulgence, this young man had preserved one soft spot in his heart: he had a tender charity for the poor. This at least was a hopeful sign. Yet he seemed impervious alike to the representations of those who laboured to bring him back to God and to the shafts of divine grace; for many signal mercies were vouchsafed to him. That holy man, Mgr. Strambi, spared no exertions to move him to repentance, but at last even this saintly prelate was discouraged: he lost all hope, and to one who would have persuaded him to make some fresh attempt, he replied that this young man was already in the power of the devil, and quite abandoned by Providence; and so indeed it seemed, for he no longer so much as believed in the existence of God, and was leading a very dissolute life. He belonged, besides, to the secret sect of the Carbonari, and we well know what hold Satan obtains over those who have bound themselves by Masonic oaths. Anna Maria foresaw that if he persevered in his evil courses he would in the end be condemned to death and executed. Nevertheless, her prayers and penances were destined to obtain his conversion; divine grace seizing him, as she expressed it, by the hair of his head. 'The fox changes

his skin,' she said, 'without quitting his vices; by a
triumph of divine mercy, which has already decreed to
save this man, he will be struck down with a long illness, at the end of which he will be converted ; but he
will lose consciousness as soon as he has made his confession, and will not be able to receive Communion :
otherwise the devils would send him temptations under
which he would succumb.' All this was literally accomplished three years later. 'I informed myself of
the circumstances of his death,' says Natali, 'from his
family and from his confessor, the Canon Ambrogio
Campano of Macerata, who, when he was at Rome,
assured me that all the details given by the servant of
God were verified.'

But how dear had this grace cost her ! Not to
speak of the severe fasts, penances, and a series of devotions, such as we have already described, amongst
which must be reckoned the frequent ascent on her
knees of the Scala Santa, which she at once undertook
in his behalf, nor of the additional bodily sufferings
then laid upon her, or of a thousand persecutions of
which she became the object, what she endured on the
part of the devils and of their miserable slave was alone
most appalling. There was, indeed, a heavy price to pay
for this soul, and God exercised the outraged rights of
His justice upon her, as he apprised her in several
locutions with reference to this conversion. The very
first day this man set foot in Anna Maria's dwelling
Hell seemed moved to its centre ; and, dreading the
escape of their victim, the infernal spirits, after overwhelming her with abuse, endeavoured during the night
to strangle her. Their impotent rage was also directed
against the priest who had introduced him to her, and
who passed that night in mortal terrors, his ears being

assailed by the most frightful diabolical noises. Anna
Maria, besides ceaselessly offering prayers and penances
for this sinner, used every argument in her power to
turn him to God. The evil one then suggested to the
wretched man the idea of perverting the faith and even
corrupting the morals of his benefactress; but not all
his malice and ingratitude could weary her patience or
quench the charity which had its source in the love of
Him who prayed for His murderers on the Cross. The
conversion of this notorious and obstinate sinner must,
without doubt, be regarded as one of the most signal
recorded instances of God's mercy, and also as one of
the most remarkable proofs of the power of intercessory
prayer. That we have good reason for this conclusion
appears from our Lord having Himself told the servant
of God that He wished all the world to know of the
conversion of this famous Carbonaro.

Her faith was also violently assailed by the devils
during the time of great interior pains, when her soul
was left without conscious support or aid, without sensible love of God, and apparently adhering to Him only
by a dry act of the will. These spirits of darkness
would cry aloud in her ears, taunting and ridiculing
her for believing that there was any judgment to come,
any hell for sinners, or that the Son of God had died
upon a cross for men; telling her that it was only
silly women and the ignorant common people who really
believed such things, with more of the same nature,
couched in the most artful and insidious language.
Anna Maria never answered them, but cast herself on
God, imploring His grace, and making firm protesta-
tions of her faith and love. The enemy, seeing that
he gained nothing in this way, then betook himself to
addressing her under some assumed visible form; at

one time under that of a venerable Religious, at another
of the head of an Order, or some prelate. Availing
himself of this respectable disguise, he would give bad
advice, recommend her to abandon her mode of life,
and proceed to put forward evil maxims supported by
the most captious reasoning. Then, throwing off all
reserve, he would begin to assail some of the most vital
articles of the faith.* 'I have often seen her weep,'
said D. Raffaele Natali, 'on account of the violence of
these temptations and her dread of succumbing to
them.'

But the devils did not confine themselves to artful
and dangerous solicitations; they endeavoured at other
times to intimidate and subdue her by ill-treatment,
and thus weary out her courage and resistance. They
often scared her by horrible nocturnal apparitions, and
dealt her most terrible blows; and then, despairing of
obtaining the victory over her, they endeavoured more
than once (as before related) to kill her, because they
saw that all who fell into her hands were lost to them.
Alone at night in her room, for Domenico (as has been

---

* Sister Maria Crocefissa, a Franciscan nun, who passed
through a most terrible ordeal of passive mystical purgation,
suffered much in the same way. 'A devil in the form of an
angel suggested to her the most perfidious heresies that were
ever promulgated by the sectaries, and, internally instigating
her to give consent to them, set before her the grounds and
arguments by which these innovators were in the habit of popularly accrediting their errors. He then singled out one by one
all the precepts of the Decalogue, and by the help of plausible
and most subtle reasoning presented to her what he advanced
in so very striking a manner, that her director, to whom she
reported all, was quite astonished; seeing that she could not
have better explained these diabolical maxims if she had been
brought up in the school of the most impious heretics, although
she had never read such things, nor heard them spoken of.'
Scaramelli's *Direttorio Mistico*, vol. ii. p. 238.

said) often came home very late, she would see it filled with filthy demons, and hear them taking counsel together and declaring that they must make an end of her. Then would they all rush upon her, some clutching her by the throat to strangle her, others beating her furiously, or torturing her in divers other ways.[*] By and bye they would all vanish, and the evil one would re-appear to his exhausted victim under some beautiful human form, and strive by every manner of suggestion to obtain at least some momentary consent to sin. In these battles, Anna Maria's weapons were humility, patience, contrition, prayer, and the holy names of Jesus and Mary. Sometimes at night, the usual season for these infernal assaults, she endeavoured to turn away and distract her mind by manual work; at other times, when the devils appeared to her, she had recourse to holy water, or, spitting in their faces, would turn with all her heart to God. Although her confidence in Him never wavered, yet on occasions she felt great fears for herself; trembling and weeping she

[*] The Lives of the Saints are full of similar details of what these servants of God suffered from the infernal spirits, while passing through this trial, which has been characterised as a 'siege,' in contradistinction to 'possession,' which is a state altogether different. St. Mary Magdalen of Pazzi was thrown down-stairs by devils more than once; and others have been also precipitated from heights, or their heads dashed violently against walls; or they have been dragged along the ground over rough stones. But all seems little as compared with what Sister Maria Crocefissa was subjected to. Scaramelli observes that in such cases the protection which God affords these persons is clearly manifested; 'for their heads are never fractured, nor are their limbs dislocated, as ought naturally to result from such serious falls and desperate blows, but they only feel the pain, with some slight remaining contusion and discolourment. . . . And, in fact, St. Mary Magdalen of Pazzi, after these precipitate falls from the top to the bottom of long flights of steps, used to get up able to pursue her usual avocations.' *Ib.* p. 233.

would call on our Blessed Lady, the holy angels, and particularly St. Michael, whom she honoured especially as the protector of the holy faith and her defender against the evil spirits, to come to her aid. So lively was the confidence with which she would pronounce the names of Jesus and Mary, that the devils were often put to flight thereby, and she would see them retreat precipitately, gnawing their fingers and foaming with rage.

Before leaving this subject of the temptations which she endured from the evil spirits, we must record one which took place, we are told, on the 28th August, 1821. It was of a peculiarly terrible kind, the devil repeating to her with confidence and pertinacity that she would not be saved; and it is the more remarkable as having been the occasion of a divine locution of a very extraordinary character, even amongst such extraordinary communications, since it would seem to have amounted to an assurance of salvation. About five o'clock in the afternoon, while she was oppressed by this temptation and engaged in prayer, the Lord was pleased to dispel it by the following gracious words: 'Thou rememberest well what I told thee one day; My promise has been fulfilled, and will be yet fulfilled. I have never granted such graces to those who live out of My favour. As I am the beginning and the end of man, I do not thus manifest My secrets to those who are to make a bad end. It is true that there are many who having begun well have finished ill, but I had never given them similar illuminations. I have gone so far as to cause thee to know one by one the different persons whom thou wast to endure for the love of Me; and wilt thou still say that I do not love thee? Have I not made thee like to Myself upon the

Cross? Instead of complaining, thou oughtest to rejoice. At this point thou hast to arrive, . . . and soon
afterwards thou shalt come to be happy with Me.' And
in fact, although Anna Maria's sufferings never ceased,
she attained at the close of her life to a state of peace-
ful union with God and to a tranquillity of mind which
nothing could interrupt or disturb.

We have already, when speaking of her patience,
sufficiently alluded to her bodily sufferings of a natural
kind, some of which took their rise, while others were
severely aggravated, after her entry on the life of expiation. As each sense seemed to enjoy some supernatural gift or endowment, so each seemed subjected
to the fiery purification of maladies ; for, no doubt, the
pains, both external and internal, which she had generously taken upon herself in the spirit of sacrifice, all
served to accomplish a double object, and helped on the
work of her sanctification while they were paying the
debts of others and impetrating grace for sinners. With
the exception of those saints who have completed their
course briefly, and have been gathered like flowers in
their early bloom, or those who have won their crowns
by a martyrdom of blood, few of great eminence, with
whose interior life we have become acquainted, seem
to have been exempted from these purifying pains ;
and, in particular, those who have been called to the
sublimer grades of contemplation and union with God,
and to the supernatural heights of the mystical life,
have not attained thereto without passing through this
night of the soul and undergoing, in a greater or lesser
degree and for a longer or shorter season, the interior
pains and spiritual privations which ordinarily succeed
the first fervours. For these pains and privations have
a far more searching and purifying effect than any

penitential mortification which we may embrace of our
own choice; not only because self cannot find any
entrance, as in the latter case is always possible, the
creature having here no share except that of passive
abandonment, and blind conformity to the Divine Will,
but because, God Himself being the operator, the purifying process extends far deeper than we ever think of
or could succeed in applying it ourselves; thus dislodg-
ing self-love from its last and most hidden recesses.
Yet the length and severity of this trial, which may be
called a kind of meritorious earthly Purgatory, has
differed greatly even in saints of seemingly equal
eminence; some being led by this way more than
others, for reasons known only to Him who is the
author of both nature and grace; and also because, as
in Anna Maria's case, some have had a special mission
of expiation and of that peculiar conformity to their
suffering Lord which consists in being charged with
the sins of others.

That the sufferings of this holy woman were exceptional for their variety, intensity, and duration, we
may indeed infer from the testimony which our Lord
Himself vouchsafed one day to give her for her encouragement and consolation. 'Thy sufferings,' He
said, 'are beyond expression; I desire that they should
be recorded in writing; but, in spite of all that shall
be read, never will any one be able to comprehend the
torture of thy soul. As for Me, I write all in letters of
gold, and it is in Heaven alone that the greatness of
thy suffering love shall be understood; it is there that
it shall be rewarded, it is there that the patience of thy
long and voluntary agony shall be crowned. Also have
I more than once told thee that I have chosen thee to
be of the number of the martyrs, and that thy life was

to be nothing but a long and painful martyrdom.' These assurances comforted and strengthened her soul and infused into it fresh ardour to make renewed oblations of herself even in the very midst of her most excruciating pains, and when it would have appeared impossible for nature, without a miracle, to endure more. It was the '*Sitio*' of the Cross.

But Anna Maria was not called simply to offer herself for the conversion of sinners in general, and to devote herself in a special way to the conversion of individuals whose state became known to her. Her vocation embraced a much wider field, as we have already indicated; and to this end God conferred upon her singular supernatural gifts, of which the most remarkable was the permanent vision of a sun, to which we have before alluded, and of which it is time now to speak more particularly on account of its intimate connection with her peculiar mission of expiation and intercession.

CHAPTER XIV.

ANNA MARIA'S VISION OF THE MYSTERIOUS SUN.

It is a truth of undoubted certainty that when God chooses a soul for a sublime mission, He provides it with the means for carrying it out. The mission for which He had chosen this poor, obscure, and uninstructed woman was, so to say, a universal mission. 'The world,' writes P. Bouffier, 'was traversing one of those crises, deep and radical, which upon the ruins they are heaping up seem to be accumulating for the present disorders without issue and for the future in-

terminable tempests. After a half-century passed amid
the frenzies of crime and the debaucheries of science,
those who had constituted themselves the chiefs and
guides of the people were given up to a spirit of error
and impiety. Apostles of a singular genus, they professed to preach the Gospel of a new era ; and soon,
their desolating doctrines producing bitter fruits, men
saw God driven from His temples, His altars profaned,
His sanctuaries demolished, the head of the Church
persecuted, the priesthood degraded, decimated, all principles and all rights trampled under foot, and the whole
of Europe ravaged by war and filled with blood and
ruins. It was the hour for tears, prayer, and expiation.' It was the hour for the lovers of the Cross, souls
inflamed with divine love, to unite themselves to the
Passion of their Lord and complete in their persons
His sufferings for His mystical body, the Church, even
as the Apostle, speaking of his own tribulations, says,*
' who now rejoice in my sufferings for you, and fill up
those things that are wanting of the sufferings of Christ
in my flesh for His body, which is the Church.' Anna
Maria was called to take a share in this the highest
and most honourable work to which the creature can
be called, and of which, through its divinisation by its
union with the God-Man, it has been rendered capable.†

* Col. i. 24.
† The following passage extracted from the Preface to the
Life of Anne Catherine Emmerich by Father Schmœger refers
to this mission of expiation, to a share in which the shepherdess
of Flamske, we have every reason to believe, was called. ' God
in all times has chosen certain souls, which, whether in a retreat hidden from view, or publicly and under the eyes of the
world, have served Him as instruments destined to suffer and to
combat for His Church and for the holy Catholic faith. The
circumstances of the exterior life of these persons are sometimes
extremely dissimilar, and their very sufferings have a character

The Holy Spirit had moved her, as we have related, to offer herself as a victim of penance for the sins of the world and the evils which afflicted the Church; and God accepted the generous sacrifice which He Himself had prompted. But it was also part of the Divine design to confound a proud and self-sufficient age, an

---

which makes them differ completely the one from the other. Thus, for example, Lidwine of Schiedam and, in our days, Domenica Lazzari (the Addolorata of the Tyrol) manifest themselves chiefly as purely corporal victims, like to the ancient virgin martyrs, while others, like St. Mary Magdalen of Pazzi or B. Colomba of Rieti, fight and suffer for the Church in a spiritual manner. But all resemble each other in this point, that their life is a continual sacrifice, an uninterrupted state of suffering, in which everything is abandoned without reserve to the leading and to the designs of God. By their sufferings they are to expiate or do penance, in the place of the guilty, for shortcomings in the Church and the damage she has sustained though the fault of the different classes of persons composing her. By their prayers and supplications, or, rather, by an extraordinary gift of grace, which renders their prayer an action, they have to turn away the tribulations and dangers which menace the Church, her head, &c.; to obtain for sinners the grace of conversion, for the wandering and the feeble, purity and firmness in the faith, for pastors and guardians of the faith, intrepidity and indefatigable zeal; finally, they have to struggle for those souls which would be lost through the negligence of pastors. Besides the task of prayer and expiation, there is also the militant task which souls favoured with extraordinary gifts have to accomplish. This consists in taking on them personally the dangers menacing soul and body, the ills, the temptations, the strong allurements to certain sins : here, then, it is no longer simply a suffering or a sacrifice, the fruits of which are to profit another ; it is a question of exposing themselves personally to a definite danger menacing body or soul ; it is a question of taking entirely on themselves an evil, a malady, an assault, or a temptation, which necessitates on the part of those who act as substitutes a real combat and a complete victory for the profit of the souls from whom they have thus averted the danger or evil.' Anna Maria seems to have fulfilled all these several offices as a victim of expiation.

age in love with its own progress in science and in the
penetration of nature's secrets, and which thought itself
wise enough to do without God, by imparting to this
poor woman a knowledge, a science, and a penetration
into things both human and divine, an acquaintance
with events past, present, and future, by comparison
with which all the boasted wisdom of the world's phi-
losophers, statesmen, diplomatists, men of genius, should
be as sheer ignorance. She was not simply to love,
to pray, to do penance in secret : ' If,' says P. Bouffier,
' Heaven had only desired a victim, her mission, like
that of so many others, might have been accomplished
and finished in obscurity. The victim being laid upon
the altar, the perfume of its prayers, of its tears, and
of its expiation ascending daily before the Lord, silence
would have shrouded the holocaust and its immola-
tions, and the justice of God, being satisfied, would
have given place to mercy without revealing the secrets of a hidden life whose merits Heaven reserved to
itself to crown. But the Venerable Servant of God
had yet another mission. In choosing her for a victim,
God had at the same time chosen her to manifest His
glory : she was to be, under the guidance of His grace,
an instrument of that power which confounds and
abases pride.' It was eminently a sceptical age, a ma-
terialistic age, which boldly denied the supernatural.
God was denied the power, so to say, of intervening in
His own creation even by those who condescendingly
admitted the existence of a Supreme Being. Be it that
He had created the world, it was constituted according
to laws which its maker or framer Himself could not
infringe. Miracles were therefore not only improbable,
they were essentially impossible. ' Before these bold
contemners of all Divine intervention God intervened,'

says P. Bouffier; 'and Anna Maria was one amongst
those chosen souls in whom He affirmed with an invincible force the existence of the supernatural. In
this humble woman the supernatural displayed itself
in all its splendour, and that, too, all of a sudden and
without preparation. While human events appeared, in
the humiliations of the Papacy, to justify proud science
and the criminal calculations of anti-religious and anti-
social conspiracies, an obscure woman arose who possessed the secrets of the future, and gave consoling
assurances of the triumph of justice and of truth. In
the depth of the night which envelops civil and religious society, we behold Anna Maria set as a lighted
candle upon a pedestal of ignorance and poverty, causing the supernatural to shine forth with an evidence
which confounds the most incredulous.' She was to
know, to see, and to foresee what unilluminated mortal
sight can neither behold nor penetrate, and that with
a clearness, a comprehensiveness, and an unfailing certainty, unparalleled hitherto in the lives of the most
eminent contemplatives.

But it was not merely for the purpose of confound-
ing the pride and false wisdom of the age that God
was thus pleased to enlighten this favoured soul; it
was in order to enable her to exercise the special Apos-
tleship for which He designed her, and to accomplish
the sacrifice to which she had devoted herself. She
must know the divers needs of the souls whom she
was to aid, the deplorable state of sinners; she must
be aware of the snares which Satan was spreading, of
the perils of the Church, everything, in fine, which
God had called her to remedy. For this end the abiding possession of that divine mirror to which we have
often alluded was the appointed means; while the

sights and secrets it revealed were to conduce to her own sanctification, nourishing and intensifying in her the virtue of divine charity, and keeping alive the spirit of self-oblation.

We propose to devote this chapter to a description of the mysterious sun and to some observations upon the nature of this gift. And first we must premise that her possession of this extraordinary favour was established by thousands of facts of which the principal are recorded in the depositions made by the witnesses in the juridical inquest. Its divine origin is equally well established. The tree is known by its fruits, and the eminent virtues of this great servant of God, especially her humility and obedience, would be alone sufficient to prove that she was under heavenly guidance and not the victim of any illusion. The numerous conversions obtained in consequence of the light she derived from this 'sun' equally attest its supernatural character. No fact, indeed, can be considered as ever having been more abundantly and satisfactorily demonstrated.

This luminous disc was of the apparent magnitude of the visible sun in the heavens, surrounded by its rays. According to what Anna Maria told those to whom obedience constrained her to describe this wonder, the sun appeared to be at about four feet distance from her, and the height of one foot above her head. It always maintained the same position. At the extremity of the upper rays was a large crown of interwoven thorns, co-extensive with the dimensions of the sun. From each extremity of the crown issued a long and thick thorn, curved downwards, so that the two finally crossed each other under the solar disc, their points emerging on each side from the rays. In the centre of the sun was a beautiful woman, majestically

seated on the right side, her face raised towards heaven
in ecstatic contemplation, and her garments resplendent
with the most vivid light ; two rays of great splendour
issued vertically from her forehead, as Moses is represented when he came down from the Mount. The feet
of the figure touched the lower extremity of the left
side of the solar orb, which shone with the most intense brightness ; it was inaccessible to the shadows
and figures which arose from beneath ; when they approached it they seemed to be dispelled, as if an invisible force had impetuously repulsed them, and they
vanished and were extinguished at the foot of the disc.
But they commonly passed to the right or left of the
rays, and above or beneath the disc. With the solitary exception of the souls of the blessed, everything
which entered the luminous centre was dissipated and
lost. The figures were described by Anna Maria as
passing in the sun's rays as in a magic lantern. 'She
assured me many times,' says the Cardinal, 'that the
brilliancy of the mysterious sun would have dazzled
the strongest sight ; and yet she beheld it with her
afflicted eye, of which she had almost entirely lost the
use, and with which she could not clearly distinguish
other objects. In this mysterious sun,' he elsewhere
says, 'she not only saw things of the natural and moral
orders belonging to this lower world, but she penetrated the abysses and the heights of heaven. She
knew the state of the departed with an assurance beyond expression. She saw objects at the greatest distance, the physiognomy of persons whom she did not
know, and who might be at the extremities of the
earth ; she had a knowledge of the profoundest mysteries of nature and of grace. She discerned the secret
thoughts of persons who were present, and even of

Q

such as were far off. The state of consciences was
manifested to her with the greatest certainty. The
order of time did not exist for her; the events and the
men of the past and of the future were before her at
will, with all the circumstances appertaining, both natural and moral, in the fullest detail. It sufficed for
her to cast a glance on the mysterious sun : instantly
the thing to which her thoughts were directed became
present to her, with an immediate perception and a
complete knowledge of all she desired to know, in all
its particulars.'

Cardinal Pedicini, moreover, thus expresses his
opinion upon the sublime character of this gift. ' There
is not the slightest doubt but that the Divinity resided
in a special manner in the mysterious sun. Thanks to
this extraordinary and truly unexampled favour, Anna
Maria possessed and enjoyed the knowledge of all things
in God, so far as it may be had in this life. It was a
gift of Paradise ; the blessed alone possess it in its
fullest extent in beatific glory; but it is certain that
the servant of God had a continual and permanent
participation of it at her pleasure. The knowledge of
all things in God was always at her disposal, so far as
the intelligence of a soul still in the condition of this
present life is capable of such knowledge. Also we are
assured that the Heavenly Spouse said to her, at several
different times, that for her He had done what He had
never done for others ; and that if the persons who
came to see her had known what was with her, they
would have fallen upon their knees, not on account of
her, who was a poor and miserable creature, but on
account of Him who abode always with her ; and other
like affectionate expressions did He use. He told her
also that He had established His seat in her heart, and

that He made known to her His heavenly decrees, His divine appointments, His greatest secrets, admitting her into the privacy of His chamber. We may apply literally to the mysterious sun of which we are speaking those words of the Prophet-king : "*In sole posuit tabernaculum suum*--He hath set His tabernacle in the sun."* One† who was deeply experienced in mystical things has explained the symbolic sign as representing the Divine Incarnate Wisdom, who resided therein after a special manner. This interpretation seems well founded. The luminous sun represented the Divinity ; the crown of thorns and the two long thorns which formed a cross indicated the passible Human Nature, with its chief dolorous mysteries, and represented the Son of God made Man for our salvation. Wisdom is specially attributed to the Second Person of the Blessed Trinity. The majestic female figure seen, in the mysterious sun, seated in the attitude of contemplation confirms this interpretation.' Moreover, the Venerable Servant of God admitted that this explanation was substantially correct, and said that the Omnipotence of the Divine Incarnate Wisdom resided in the sun. God, we know, is present everywhere. Nevertheless we learn from Revelation that He has at different times and in different places been present in a special manner. We need but instance the Ark of the Covenant, the mysterious cloud in the Temple, the burning bush, and, again, the thunders and lightnings which accompanied the giving of the Law to Moses on Mount Sinai. If

* Psalm xviii. 6.
† The Cardinal here alludes to P. Poggiarelli, an Augustinian, who had the opportunity of being fully acquainted with the spirit of Anna Maria, as he directed her in the absence of her confessor.

such was the case under the Old Law, before the Second Person of the Blessed Trinity had become incarnate and taken human flesh, how much more might we expect to find analogous favours under the New Covenant of grace, when God has come so marvellously near to us that, after the Unity of the Three Persons in the Godhead, there is no unity so marvellous or so close as that existing in virtue of the Hypostatic Union of the Divine and Human Natures in Christ.

Before proceeding to any details, we will say a few words with reference to the Cardinal's express assertion, confirmed by the assurance given by our Lord Himself to the servant of God, that this favour shown to Anna Maria was unexampled, and respecting its nature as a permanent gift; availing ourselves chiefly of some observations extracted from the apologetic memoranda of the postulators and inserted in the *Analecta Juris Pontificii.**

This supernatural gift, then, was certainly new and unprecedented in its form, but it was not altogether unexampled in its substantial nature. St. Frances of Rome, for instance, enjoyed during twenty-seven years the permanent vision of an archangel, who fulfilled towards her an office very similar to that of which the sun was the instrument in Anna Maria's case. St. Frances was twenty-nine years of age, and engaged in the married state, when the archangel appeared to her for the first time. He was replaced by a spirit belonging to an order superior to that of the Archangels, namely, one of the Powers, at the period when the holy widow entered a convent. The permanent vision of this angel, which is attested by the Roman Breviary, exercised a marvellous influence on the sanctification

* Vol. iv. part i. pp. 421-4.

of Frances, while it was at the same time a source
of precious graces to her neighbour. The presence of
so pure and glorious a spirit produced a profound sentiment of humility in the soul, which clearly perceived
its own vileness and unworthiness. If Frances committed a slight involuntary fault the angel disappeared,
and only manifested himself again after she had recognised her failing and besought God's pardon. By the
assistance of the angel she saw near things and distant
things, present and future, as also the secret thoughts
of others, with a certainty which made persons believe
that she could read hearts. The sun afforded the same
kind of light to Anna Maria, and she exercised by its
means a continual control over her dispositions and
behaviour; she saw her involuntary defects, in this
luminary, in the form of shades, or specks, like flies;
and when the servant of God humbled herself, imploring forgiveness, the sun immediately resumed its
cloudless lustre.

Perhaps amongst the analogous gifts with which
saints have been favoured, none bears so much resemblance to that vouchsafed to her as the gift which was
accorded to the great seer and prophetess of the twelfth
century, St. Hildegarde, Abbess of the Benedictines of
Rupertsberg, near Bingen on the Rhine.* 'This pious
woman' (we quote from the *Voix Prophétiques*† of
the Abbé Curicque) 'was not naturally what is called
a great genius nor of superior intellect. But the Holy
Spirit blows where He willeth, and ordinarily reveals
to the humble and the little the most hidden secrets

* The heart of this Saint has remained incorrupt, and is
preserved, with her other relics, in the church of Elbingen, on
the right bank of the Rhine.
† Vol. ii. p. 12.

of Divine Wisdom; and, it is worthy of remark that, in distributing His gifts, He has most frequently chosen simple women to whom to communicate His light, because He found them humble and docile.' Here is the account which St. Hildegarde herself gives of the divine light which she enjoyed : 'From my childhood to this present time, when I am more than seventy years of age, I have always beheld this divine light in my soul; and I perceive it neither by the eyes of the body, nor by the thoughts of the heart,* nor by any action of my exterior senses, my eyes nevertheless remaining open, and the other corporal senses preserving their activity. This light which I perceive is not local, but it is infinitely more brilliant than that of the sun, and I could not scan either its height, or length, or breadth. Its name I am told' (she means inwardly) 'is " the shadow of the living light;" and even as the sun, the moon, and the stars are reflected in the water, so the writings, discourses, virtues, and works of man are manifested to me in this light. Of all that I see or learn in this manner I retain the memory a long time. I see, I hear, and I know all together, and what I know I learn as in a moment of time; but I remain ignorant of what I do not see, for I am almost entirely illiterate; and as for what I write about this vision, I do not set down any other words but those I hear, employing Latin words *undeclined*' (such seems to be the meaning of the expression she uses, which clearly refers to her own ungrammatical use of the Latin tongue). 'I do not understand these words after the manner of sounds

---

* It appears from this account that St. Hildegarde's vision was intellectual. In this characteristic it differs from that of Anna Maria, who permanently beheld the mysterious sun with her bodily eye.

formed by a human mouth, but like a sparkling flame, or a cloud gliding in a clear sky. I cannot at all understand the form of this light, any more than I can gaze directly at the sphere of the sun. Nevertheless, I occasionally perceive in this light' (*lumen*) 'another light' (*lux*), 'but I do not see it often, and I should be still less able to state its form than I am that of the first. When I contemplate it I lose the memory of all sadness and of all pain; then I have the simplicity of a child, and not the sentiments of an already aged woman. My soul enjoys uninterruptedly the sight of the "shadow of the light." It appears to me like a firmament without stars in a bright cloud, and it is in this that I see what I have stated of this splendour of the living light. From my childhood to my fortieth year I had not ceased to behold this vision, and at that time it was the means of my recovering the fulness of my strength, of which numerous maladies with which I was afflicted from my youth up had deprived me. Then, constrained by the Spirit, I revealed all to a Religious whom I had taken for my guide, and who, much surprised, bade me secretly commit to writing what I had seen, or might hereafter see, in order that he himself, after having examined this writing, might form a judgment or, at least, a conjecture concerning it.'[*] So far the saintly Abbess. The author of the *Voix Prophétiques*, referring subsequently to the 'mysterious sun' of Anna Maria Taigi, and recording our Lord's assertion that He had done for her what He had never hitherto done for any of His servants, conferring upon her an unprecedented gift, adds, 'This must be understood only as regards the form and mode of operation. Let the reader revert to what we have already said of

[*] *Voix Prophétiques*, vol. ii. p. 15.

the " light" and " the shadow of the light" of which St.
Hildegarde never lost sight, and he will be struck with
the similarity of these two kinds of prophetic vision.'*

The providential mission of Anna Maria Taigi offers
many analogous features to that which St. Catherine
of Siena filled heretofore, as also to that of St. Rose of
Viterbo and St. Margaret of Cortona. Compare the
account of the vocation of St. Catherine of Siena, for
instance, with what has been narrated in the case of
the Venerable Anna Maria when received as a Tertiary
of the Trinitarians. God said to Catherine, 'Thou must
fulfil all justice; and this will be when I shall render
thee by My grace useful and full of fruits, not only for
thyself, but also for thy neighbour. . . . I will send thee,
although thou art devoid of knowledge and without
education, to confound the presumption and pride of
the wise of this world.' Catherine humbled herself, exclaiming, 'How can it be possible that a mean and weak
woman such as I am should be useful for the salvation
of souls?' God replied, 'Fear not that I should ever
abandon thee; far from it, I shall be ever with thee in
all which thou shalt have to do.' But Anna Maria was
not as free with respect to her movements as were St.
Catherine of Siena and other saints chosen to similar
missions. Her poverty and her married state alike contributed to deprive her of the free command and disposal of her time or of her actions. She therefore
specially needed supernatural illumination, and could
not have adequately fulfilled her mission without such
aid, which made her acquainted with the needs of souls
and with the condition of the world and of the Church.
The mysterious sun, by continually revealing to her
the state of consciences and the sins whereby God was

* *Voix Prophétiques*, p. 144.

offended, excited her, moreover, to prayer, expiation, and those generous oblations of self which resulted in a martyrdom of multiplied and continual sufferings.

This gift, which was one of the *gratis data*, was, as we have said, permanent. Not only was the orb of light always before her eye, not only was she continually seeing visions and receiving revelations therein, but she had practically the entire command of it, so to say. It was a mirror in which she could at any time see whatever she desired, and obtain an answer to any question she asked; and although, as we shall find, she was very temperate in her use of this power, it was none the less at her disposal every day, every hour, and every minute of the forty-seven years that elapsed from the moment at which she first beheld this mysterious luminary. Yet the gift, though permanent, was not *habitual*, in the theological sense of the term. Grace, as we know, is distinguished into habitual and actual. By a habit we understand a quality inherent in the soul: such is sanctifying grace, which, given us in baptism, abides so long as sin does not deprive us of it. Actual grace is an operation by which God enlightens our minds, or stirs our hearts, to aid us in the performance of a good action, in resistance to temptation, in endurance of suffering, and to prompt us to generous acts of sacrifice. The grace ceases with the occasion for which it was bestowed. Does, however, the same kind of division into habitual and actual exist in the case of the gifts *gratis data?* Do any of these gifts belong to the class of habitual graces?* Theo-

---

* To this question Sylvius thus replies:—' Quædam sunt habituales, eæ scilicet quæ permanenter insunt, sapientia, scientia, fides (excellens nimirum), donum linguarum, donum interpretandi sermones: aliæ vero sunt actuales, hoc est, cou-

logians tell us that such as reside in the soul, as the
gift of wisdom, science, eminent faith, that of tongues,
and of the interpretation of tongues, &c., are of this
character; while those which cease with the action of
God producing them, as the gift of healing and of
miracles, the gift of the discernment of spirits, that of
prophecy, &c., must be classed as actual graces.

Of a grace which is habitual, and is therefore inherent as a supernatural quality in the soul, the soul
can make use at will; not so as respects actual grace,
which is an impulse, or a light, or a help, imparted by
God according to His will with reference to some particular object. The sun was external to Anna Maria's
soul, and independent of her will; and she was enabled
to behold it by a supernatural virtue communicated to
her eyes, a virtue renewed every time she beheld it,
and with respect to which she was purely passive. All
this differs essentially from a habit inherent in the soul,
which has no need of an external object to accomplish
its act. Since the corporal vision of the sun was actual,
so also necessarily were the lights resulting from it.
They could not possibly constitute an habitual gift,
founded on an interior principle inherent in the soul.
Therefore no *habit*, in the theological sense of the word,
existed. There is, however, no contradiction in terms
when we say that this gift was permanent. There is
nothing in the nature of an actual grace to hinder it
from being so, when God so wills it. We may instance
the gift of miracles, one of those gifts which are not
habitual, yet which some saints have possessed in a

---

sistentes in actu, in actuali scilicet Dei motione, quæ simul
cum tali gratiarum exercitio finitur et transit, ut sunt opera
virtutum seu miraculorum, gratia sanationum, prophetia, dis-
cretio spirituum (C. i. 2, Quæst. 171, Art. 1).

permanent manner.   Witness what we are told of St.
Vincent Ferrer.   Teoli, his biographer, observes, ' The
saint possessed the gift of miracles in so marvellous a
manner that, although it was not a *habit*, seeing that
God does not communicate to the saints the power of
working miracles as a habit, nevertheless the saint
wrought them so frequently and so freely that a mind
little versed in theological principles might suppose
that the gift was habitual.   For just as we use habits
at our will, so the saint fixed the hour and the moment, and even caused a bell to be rung to assemble the
persons who were desirous to have a miracle wrought ;
and when his superiors forbade his performing any, he
delegated to others the power of working them.'   Of
St. Francis of Paula it is narrated that he worked no
less than three hundred miraculous cures in the course
of a few days.

It is possible, then, for the exercise of a gift to be
so frequent and, indeed, so constant, as to wear the
semblance of an habitual gift, although it is not really
so.   Anna Maria herself declared that she was purely
passive with reference to the astonishing gift which she
had received.   She saw in the sun only what God willed
to manifest to her.   It is true that practically she may
be said to have had the use of it at will, for God accomplished all her desires by manifesting to her what
she desired to see or know.   Nor need this surprise us
when we remember the great circumspection with which
she invariably acted in this matter ; never directing her
attention to the sun from curiosity or any mere human
motive, but solely when the glory of God or the spiritual good of souls was concerned, or by obedience, or
in consequence of a divine movement or impulsion.
But, strictly speaking, she had not the command of

the gift. So independent of her was it, that often things were presented to her in the sun which she was not seeking to see, and which she could not possibly have been seeking; things which frequently she did not understand, and the explanation of which she even abstained from asking. All this fully proves that the gift was in no way derived from an interior principle, which would have conferred upon her its free and voluntary exercise.

The gift, then, although permanent, was not habitual; neither was it in continual exercise: for such a continuous act would be impossible under our present conditions of existence. The permanence of the gift consisted in this—that she always possessed the power of using it in conformity with the end for which God vouchsafed it; according to need, and according to the impulse of divine grace. It was thus with the Apostles: they received special gifts, particularly after the coming of the Holy Ghost; the exercise of those gifts was not continual; but the gifts themselves were permanent, and they possessed the uninterrupted power of employing them for the glory of God.

God granted to His people during their forty years' sojourn in the desert a cloud which shaded them from the heats of the day, and a column of fire to guide their march during the night towards the promised land; these two signs succeeded each other uninterruptedly; and, in spite of the ingratitude of the people, the gift was not withdrawn. We can therefore feel no surprise if now, under the New Law, when God bestows His benefits with a far greater profusion, He should confer an abiding gift on a highly privileged soul, at once to aid its own advance on the spiritual path and to contribute to the salvation of a multitude of others. Anna

Maria many times assured the Cardinal Pedicini, as also her own confessor and the confidential priest, that she possessed the gift of the sun in a permanent and uninterrupted manner, and that it was ever before her by night as well as by day. God gave to Moses the extraordinary gift of miracles attached to a rod, as a necessary means to the accomplishment of his mission, which was to deliver the people of God from Egyptian bondage; and the same God was pleased to bestow on the Venerable Anna Maria Taigi the extraordinary gift of the knowledge of supernatural things by means of a mysterious light, wherein she saw the spiritual needs of a multitude of souls whom she was called to aid in freeing them from spiritual enslavement. As the gift of Moses was permanent, even as was his mission of lawgiver, why should not that of Anna Maria have been permanent likewise, seeing that her mission lasted wellnigh half a century? Another, and a conclusive, reason for its permanence was that God had granted it to her, before all things, for her own personal sanctification, as already stated : to make her cognisant of her faults, and to excite her to the practice of all virtues, especially to those generous acts of expiatory self-sacrifice which were to procure the conversion of sinners, a mission which formed the ceaseless occupation of her life.

CHAPTER XV.

WHAT ANNA MARIA SAW IN THE MYSTERIOUS SUN, AND
HOW SHE DISCERNED THE INTERIOR STATE OF SOULS.

WE have mentioned in a general way what Anna
Maria saw in the mysterious sun, as summed up by
Cardinal Pedicini. We must now descend to a few
illustrative details.

There was, in fact, nothing which Anna Maria did
not behold, or might not behold, if she sought to do
so, in this luminary. During the first hours of the
night, when, in the solitude of her chamber, she betook
herself to her customary devotions, she would from
time to time cast a glance at the sun in order to kindle
her fervour. There she would behold various figures,
which, indeed, it would appear were continually passing
within its rays, but which during those hours seem to
have been peculiarly multiplied. Sometimes she would
see pictures, or representations, of natural objects; such
as storms, flashes of lightning, torrents of rain, pesti-
lences, revolutions, battles, massacres, &c. At other
times she saw allegorical figures; such as daggers, nets,
bullets, incendiary bombs, or crowns, necklaces of gold,
precious stones, golden showers, and the like. These
beautiful symbols, the confessor tells us, her Lord caused
to appear in the sun, often explaining their meaning,
to recompense her for the mortification of all curiosity
in regarding it, and to encourage her more and more in
the practice of perfection. Often she saw the rays part
asunder and torrents of blood issue from the aperture;
at other times, and that frequently, she beheld black
globes flying in the air, which suddenly took fire and
covered the earth with a dense smoke. For several

successive days, she would see an extremely thick fog, followed by the falling of walls and beams, as if a great building had crumbled into ruins. This vision she beheld many times. And again, she would see heaps of warlike arms piled up, and fireworks discharged. Sometimes it pleased God to explain the signification of these different symbols; on other occasions, He left her in ignorance; nevertheless, He desired her to record them, because their explanation would be seen in events hereafter to take place. But all these images and representations, whether natural or allegorical, would vanish the moment she looked at the sun with a definite object in her mind; and at once what she sought appeared, and that with perfect clearness. She used, however, as we have observed, great reserve in fixing her eye on the sun; for she said that when she contemplated it she was penetrated to the very marrow of her bones with a sentiment of awe and reverence, resembling the fear with which the Israelites were seized at the sight of the two rays of light issuing from Moses's brow. So intense was this thrilling awe, that she told her confessor it sometimes constrained her to cast her eyes down to the ground. The mortification of all mere natural feelings and the respect which she exercised in the use she made of this gift were, as we have said, very pleasing to her Lord, who several times testified to her His satisfaction thereat. Further, she had received a divine assurance from the very first that nothing which she should behold in this sun would be subject to the least illusion or misapprehension; and Mgr. Natali attested that there never was the smallest error or the least uncertainty in any of the answers which Anna Maria gave.

But it was not only particular and individual things

which she beheld in this mysterious mirror ; she was
acquainted generally with the good and evil going on
throughout the world.   She saw the scourges decreed
for each nation and kingdom, the causes of these chastisements, and the remedies which might have been
applied.   She saw the disorders of all ranks of society,
the dissolution of morals, and the insubordination of
the people, the crimes of the rich, the propagation of
erroneous doctrines.   She saw the whole world in all
its minutest details, as we see the face of a wall before
which we are standing ; except that we are obliged to
scan successively every separate part, if we would have
an exact knowledge of what we otherwise see only
in the general, whereas we are assured that she took in
all at a single glance.   It is quite impossible to explain
how this could be; for it is a thing beyond our ordinary understanding and the comprehension of our natural powers : these must be supernaturally raised and
sublimated in order to render them capable of such a
mode of vision, and, in the absence of such capability,
explanation is obviously out of the question. Nay, the
very recipient of such a favour finds no words in human
language to express its nature.   We meet with instances, however, in the lives of Saints which fully
prove that it has pleased God at times to enable souls
on whom He has bestowed eminent gifts of the mystical
order, to see things in a similar manner, which would
have seemed to be the exclusive privilege of the blessed
already in the enjoyment of the beatific vision.   We
are told, for instance, by St. Gregory that St. Benedict
saw the whole world in a single ray of the sun.   This
offers a striking resemblance to the mode in which
Anna Maria saw all things in her mysterious luminary.

By the help of her sun Anna Maria became a theologian, a seer, a prophetess ; and accordingly we find that she was held in the highest veneration by persons of the most eminent sanctity ; such as the Venerable Monsignor Strambi, the Venerable Monsignor Menocchio, the Venerable Gaspar del Bufalo,* and other servants of God who had attained to the highest perfection, such as D. Vincenzo Pallotti, P. Bernardo Clausi, Monsignor Basilici, Bishop of Sutri and Nepi, Signor Roberti of the Congregation of the Missions, the Capuchin Fra Felice of Montefiascone, and Fra Petronio of Bologna. To these we could add the names of many more, illustrious for their virtue, their learning, or their

* Gaspar del Bufalo was born 6th January, 1786, at Rome, and died there in the same year as Anna Maria, on the Feast of the Holy Innocents, Dec. 28th, 1837. His parents were respectable pious people, and from his earliest childhood he took no pleasure in anything which did not regard the service of God. He loved to make little altars (a favourite amusement with Catholic children, but his sole recreation), and to imitate holy ceremonies, surrounded by other children, to whom he endeavoured to teach the fear of God and reverence for their parents. His after course was in every way in accordance with these beginnings. He applied himself to the practice of every virtue, and the study of theology, and entered the priesthood. He ever manifested a singular zeal and address in the instruction of the poor and of the young. Pius VII., on his restoration, specially selected him to confide to him the direction of the missions which he had established throughout the Pontifical States. To perpetuate their salutary fruits, this holy man, in concert with that great Pontiff, instituted a congregation of missionaries under the title of the Most Precious Blood of the Divine Redeemer Jesus. He founded more than twelve missions during his life, which was entirely devoted to apostolic labours, and which was illustrated by miracles. On the 15th January 1852, on the report of the Sacred Congregation of Rites, Pius IX. declared him Venerable, The Ordinary and Apostolic Processes were pronounced valid in September 1865, and in March 1870 his writings were declared to be no hindrance to his cause, which is progressing.

R

rank and station, often for all combined, who might be
seen from time to time ascending the staircase of her
poor abode and conversing with her in her little room
with all and more than the respect they might have
shown in the presence of royalty. Cardinal Pedicini,
we are informed, never failed to go and see the servant
of God when he was about to visit his diocese of
Palestrina, in order to receive her instructions; she acquainted him with the disorders reigning there, whether
amongst clergy or people, and told him what remedies
ought to be applied; she also apprised him of things
which would befall himself. And all invariably turned
out precisely as she said. What wonder that this prelate should have held her in the highest esteem, so that,
as the priest Natali says, ' he would not so much as
move a straw without her advice !' Here is the Cardinal's own testimony on this subject:—' How many
times have I not consulted her about the affairs appertaining to the charges I held under Government; and
what wise counsels and what lights have I not received
from her ! The instructions and advice which she gave,
and the lights which she communicated, proceeded
indubitably from the Divine Wisdom; it was quite
impossible that a poor ignorant woman should possess
a knowledge so encyclopedic and exact that the study
and experience of a whole life would not have sufficed
to acquire it. She also revealed to me things far above
the reach of human intelligence. If I was uneasy from
not receiving expected family news, she would cast a
look on the mysterious sun, and tell me the cause of
the delay; this was enough to tranquillise me. Experience had taught me never to doubt these indications.
She frequently warned me of things about to occur to
myself, in order that they might not take me by sur-

prise. Affectionate and grateful, she interested herself
in the least circumstances which concerned me.   Her
generous heart moved her to console every one.   On
leaving her, you felt, not only instructed and enlightened, but touched, encouraged, comforted ; she related
to each person his whole life in its every detail, she
discovered his most secret thoughts ; she announced
what would happen to him, and gave the best advice.
After all this, it was impossible to doubt but that she
was divinely illuminated, and that the measures which
she suggested must be truly efficacious to attain their
proposed end, particularly where it was question of the
spiritual good of souls.   And all this she did with the
greatest facility, in a natural and unaffected manner,
under the form of a friendly conversation; for her,
indeed, it was easier to know minutely at a glance the
state of a soul, the situation of an affair, or anything
else, no matter what, than it is for another to read
what is written in a book ; for this is a process which
takes some time, in order to master a subject and the
way in which it is treated.'

To all questions of the theological order she replied
with the simplicity of a child, but with a promptness
and a certainty surpassing that of the most consummate
master of spiritual science.   For she had no need to
pause a moment for consideration, or to betake herself to study and examination ; she had only to look at
her sun.   Her confessor tells us that, if questioned on
some dogmatic point, such, for instance, as the concilia-
tion of predestination with the goodness of God, or if
asked how the Humanity united to the Divinity could
suffer, she would at once reply with a precision and a
theological accuracy at which the most deeply versed
in the science of divine things were amazed.   It was a

pleasure, he says, to hear her speak on such subjects as
the Incarnation of the Word or the Maternity and Vir-
ginity of Mary.   Neither, he adds, did she require any
book to help her to meditate on the mysteries of religion.   The moment she turned her mind to the consideration of any one of them, she at once saw it reflected and represented in the sun.   If she thought of
the Garden of Olives, for example, she beheld the whole
scene: the treachery of Judas, every detail of the Agony,
the flight of the Apostles, and all the indescribable
sufferings of Jesus.   'What a delight,' writes the confessor, 'was it for pious souls to hear Anna Maria talk
of the Journey into Egypt, of the Last Supper, and the
other mysteries of the Saviour's life ! She saw and described in its minutest particulars the House of Naza-
reth, the simple furniture of the Holy Family, the place
where the Blessed Virgin took her repose, or, rather,
where she contemplated ; for, said this pious woman,
the repose (moreover, very short) which the Holy Virgin gave to her body was a continual contemplation.
She also saw all the details of the life that Mary lived
in the house of St. John the Evangelist after the As-
cension of her Divine Son.   If she desired to witness
the martyrdom of St. John the Baptist, she saw at a
glance the horrors of his prison, the humility and resignation of the Precursor bowing his head under the
sword of the executioner, and at the same time she beheld the sumptuous banquet of Herod and all the
abominations which were there perpetrated ; and the
like took place with regard to the martyrdom of other
saints.   Again, if she wished to see the countenance of
any one of the blessed, one look sufficed to satisfy her
desire.   As she had a great devotion for St. Joseph,
she felt a holy curiosity' (natural curiosity, we have

seen, she never admitted as a motive) ' to see him in the sun.   Accordingly, she beheld him there as very beautiful and young, although of a more advanced age than Mary, such as became one who was to be the guardian of that incomparable Virgin.   It was solely from a motive of respect, she affirmed, that the Church had given him the features of an aged man.   She, however, did not speak of these things except with such of her spiritual sons as were admitted to her closest confidence, and by the permission of her confessor.'   Indeed, if she had followed her own bent, she would have been silent altogether concerning these extraordinary revelations. Obedience, charity, and the movement of God's Spirit alone caused her to open her lips.   This was because, in her humility and her love of simplicity and of the hidden life, she avoided all extraordinary things.   Hence she who was so marvellously and undoubtingly illuminated was, as we have seen, respectful and compliant with all about her, renouncing, whenever this was possible, not only her own will, but her own views and judgment, in deference to those of others.   She who had at her disposal the mirror of Divine Wisdom, who was raised to the loftiest grades of contemplation, and to whom heavenly locutions were being constantly addressed, might be often seen quietly saying her prayers out of a little book, like any good devout soul who can aim at nothing higher, and has no experience of anything better.

We have already alluded more than once to her spiritual sons, of whom it may be well to say something further.   Very soon after her conversion, and when she entered on her mission of charity to her neighbour, which first caused her to become known to a more extended circle, a certain number of persons placed them-

selves under her direction. These were regarded by
her as a kind of second family, and they continued to
pay her the respect and deference of children as long
as she lived; among them were young men who attained to the priesthood, and whose hands, now rever-
encing them as her fathers, she would humbly kiss
when she met them in the street, yet who never ceased
to regard her as their spiritual mother. Nothing could
exceed the indefatigable solicitude and care with which
she watched over this family of hers. Amongst the
different counsels which she gave them, we are told
that she was continually urging on them the value of
force and resolution of character, that force which
springs from utter distrust of ourselves and entire confidence in God. She considered it a virtue most essential to the perfection of a Christian, and, as has
been seen, she was herself remarkable for it. Her
supernatural insight into the state of consciences quali-
fied her eminently for this office of director. Her confessor tells us that she distinctly saw all the temptations
of her spiritual sons; and it often happened that when
they visited her, she would affectionately reproach them
with having parleyed with the devil, it might be, that
morning or the previous evening. She used to advise
them to cut the matter short with him, and to dread
his stratagems, which inflict such direful injury on un-
wary souls. These youths, whom the pious woman was
wont with truth to call the sons of her soul, had so
constantly had experience of the divine lights she possessed, that often, before receiving Communion, they
would ask her whether they might do so without fear;
whereupon she would just cast a look at her sun, and
say to them, 'Do not distress yourself,' or, 'Make an
act of contrition for such or such a careless fault, which

you forgot to confess, or which you have committed since your confession.'

The confessor, speaking of Luigi Antonini, the young man who used to help the servant of God, in the matter of her household expenses, says, ' Being well aware of the great gift she possessed of knowing in an instant and with the minutest particularity the state of consciences, he would often ask her whether he had made a good confession. Anna Maria did not answer immediately, but, if he insisted, she would glance for an instant at the mysterious sun, and, taking him aside, would say, " In accusing yourself of such a fault you forgot this or that circumstance." Then he would reflect a moment, and reply, " Ah, yes, it is very true!"'
' Hear,' says the priest, her confidant, ' what happened to myself, and that many times. When I returned to the house' (it will be remembered he was an inmate) ' she used to tell me what temptations I had had, and instructed me how to behave in such cases. Sometimes, observing me thoughtful and ill at ease before saying holy Mass, she would disclose to me my secret thoughts, and the inward disquietude of my heart, and would then console me.'

The following incident, related also by the same priest, will exhibit Anna Maria's maternal tenderness for her spiritual children, and at the same time her jealous fear lest she should give entrance to any mere natural tenderness. It will also illustrate the simple and affectionate terms which our Lord employed in addressing this favoured soul. One of her spiritual sons had particularly pleased her by a faithful correspondence to her counsels. He was obliged to leave home for a time; this distressed Anna Maria, and, fearing that too human an affection might have some share in this sorrow of hers, she one day knelt down with this dear son before her little altar, and addressed the following fervent prayer to the Lord : ' God of all goodness, behold me prostrate at Thy feet, with my child. I sacrifice him to Thee willingly; only give him Thy holy love. Thou knowest my secret dispositions; if, then, Thou seest that my heart is too weak in his regard, take away my life, but do me the charity of granting me all that I ask in his favour, not because I ask it, but because Thou art great.' She had scarcely uttered these words when she was transported in spirit to the Cœnaculum, and received this tender reply from the mouth of the Redeemer : ' See, My daughter, what great love I had for My Apostles; how I treated them, how I loved them, and all I did for them. Three of them failed Me in the Garden of Olives, and although My sufferings were so excessive as to make Me sweat blood, yet, seeing them asleep, I rose and went to waken them. They took fright, fled, and abandoned Me. See, My daughter, all I did for Judas; how I embraced and caressed him; but his ears were deaf to Me, and he was bent on his own destruction. Thus no one can reckon for long upon the good-will of creatures. See, again, how notwithstanding the great love which I bore My mother, I was fain to leave her with complete disengagement and detachment; and wilt thou not, for the love of Me, make this sacrifice of being separated from thy child, and that only for some short time ?'

The discernment of consciences was as easy to Anna Maria, as it is to us to read a book in our native tongue. Nothing escaped her; she clearly perceived the faults, the natural and moral dispositions, of each person, and even his secret intentions. It was by this means that

she converted so many sinners ; for, besides the charity,
zeal, and cordiality with which she received them, besides the penances which she imposed upon herself in
their behalf, she made their examination of conscience
for them with an accuracy which perfectly astounded
them, often revealing to them sins of which they had
not been themselves aware. She was visited one day
by a young lady of good family. Anna Maria had
never seen her before, but she read her interior at a
glance, and frankly told her the state of her soul. The
surprise of this lady was very great, and equally so was
the beneficial change that was wrought in her. She
at once prepared herself to make a good confession, and
devoted herself henceforward to the service of God.
She kept up a frequent communication with her benefactress, who was the means of consoling her in a reverse of fortune caused by her husband's refusal to
serve the usurping government in obedience to the
commands of Pius VII., then a prisoner in France.
He lost thereby a high employment he had held under
the Pontifical administration. His wife was in great
dread of falling into want, but Anna Maria told her to
have no fear. 'Your husband,' she said, 'has lost his
office through conscientious fidelity to duty. God will
provide the needful.' And, in fact, her husband obtained without any compromise of principle a situation
which placed him in as easy and even better circumstances than before. Another instance is related of a
young lady, who was converted from a life, not merely
of carelessness, but of sin. She came to Anna Maria,
and implored her with tears to obtain a particular favour for her. The pious woman received her with
much affection, but unfolded to her the deplorable condition of her soul, exhorting her to reconcile herself to

God by a good confession, and a firm resolution to
change her life. Anna Maria addressed the most fervent petitions to God for the conversion of this soul,
and received the assurance, by a heavenly voice, that
her prayers were granted. The lady made her confession, and, this done, the favour she had solicited was
accorded. The sincerity of her conversion was proved
by her thorough amendment; the accomplice of her
guilt was also converted.

D. Raffaele Natali, who lived with her, was not
the only priest who was indebted to her for relief when
suffering from inward perturbation of spirit. An archbishop, Mgr. Guerrieri, was giving the Benediction of
the Blessed Sacrament in the Church of San Bartolomeo on the Piazza Colonna. The servant of God was
present, and beheld in the mysterious sun the mental
distress and disturbance with which this good prelate
was harassed. After Benediction she sent him word,
probably by means of D. Raffaele, that she desired to
speak with him. He willingly consented; she then
manifested to him the interior pains from which he
had suffered during the function, and gave him some
excellent advice. So surprised and consoled was he
by this communication, that from that hour he conceived the highest regard for her, and remained in
confidential relations with her until death. P. Bernard Clausi, a Religious of the order of St. Francis of
Paula, whom we have already named among the holy
persons who held her in high estimation, also received
(Mgr. Luquet tells us) great assistance, when suffering
interior pains, from the light and counsels communicated to him by her through the medium of another;
probably (as in the last-mentioned case) the same who
was her confidential agent in all affairs of this kind.

But many persons, amongst whom were numbered not
a few of high rank, received counsels and warnings
from her without so much as knowing to whom they
were indebted. 'Meeting any one in the street,' says
her confessor, 'she discovered in an instant the interior
of his conscience and the divine decrees concerning him
in regard both to death and eternity. If she met a
corpse being carried to the grave, she had at once before
her the whole life of the deceased, his punishment or
his reward, and the grounds of the sentence. Persons
who happened to be accompanying the pious woman,
seeing sadness or joy reflected in her countenance,
would inquire the cause, and then, if she felt it to be
allowable, she would tell them.' Soon after the birth
of one of her own children, she knew that if he continued to live, he would one day forfeit his life on a
scaffold, albeit for a crime of no very great magnitude.
She had recourse to the Divine goodness, and obtained
that the infant should die a few months afterwards.

If any one who was affiliated to the secret societies
presented himself before her, immediately a dark veil
would pass over the mysterious sun, and she beheld
instantaneously all his plots and designs ; but, on the
other hand, if a virtuous person came to see her the
solar disc immediately bore witness to his merits   'I
remember,' says D. Raffaele, ' that on one occasion
Don Vincenzo Pallotti,* coming to visit me, spoke for

* Vincenzo Pallotti was an ecclesiastic of remarkable holiness. He died in 1850, after having devoted his life to the
practice of the most heroic charity ; the influence he thus acquired was so great that the very sight of him and the mere
sound of his voice would draw tears from the most hardened
sinner. His self-denial and mortification were extreme For
many years his daily food consisted only of roots and herbs, and,
except when ill, he never lay down. It was his practice to pass

a minute to Anna Maria. When he was gone, I inquired of the pious woman what she had seen in her sun during the visit. She replied that it shone with unusual brilliancy. This holy man received particular consolation from the servant of God, at a time when he was much distressed about one of his cousins, who, having fallen into a state of great mental depression on account of the disorder of his affairs, had fled the country. Nothing could be discovered concerning him notwithstanding the most diligent inquiries, so that his friends feared that he had put an end to himself. Don Vincenzo begged the priest to ask the prayers of Anna Maria. She immediately raised her eyes to the sun, and saw the place where Don Vincenzo's relative had concealed himself, of which he was informed, to his great relief. The sequel proved the truth of her assertion.'

Her knowledge of secret intentions was the means sometimes of preventing great misfortunes and great crimes. An instance occurred in the case of a gentleman for whose salvation she was particularly interesting herself: 'While thinking of him,' says the same witness, 'she cast her eyes upon the sun, and, calling suddenly

---

whole nights in some church, kneeling, on the bare stone, in adoration before the Blessed Sacrament. Public opinion attributed to his intercession a number of cures and other favours reputed to be supernatural. Like another holy man, P. Bernardo Clausi, he foretold that great calamities were about to fall upon the Church, and on the city of Rome; but he comforted those who were saddened by these predictions with the assurance of a great triumph of religion through the all-powerful mediation of Mary, to whom both these holy persons were most devout. We shall see how perfectly these prophecies coincide with those of Anna Maria Taigi. An English Life of this holy man has been published by Dr. Raphael Melia (Burns & Oates, 1871).

to me, bade me run to this man's house, because he was on the point of committing suicide; that he had been seized with melancholy owing to the derangement of his affairs, and the devil was tempting him violently. I ran and found him alone in his room and much agitated. I only spoke a few words to him on the part of the servant of God, and strove to tranquillise his mind; he then acknowledged to me that, had I delayed but another minute, he would have discharged a pistol at himself, and I should have found him dead.' Anna Maria was likewise instrumental in preserving persons from Satanic deceits and impostures on various occasions. 'P. Settimio Poggiarelli,' says the same priest, 'an Augustine Religious, of great repute for piety, told me one day in confidence that, while praying for an affair which deeply interested him, he had, during the night, an apparition of two angels, who assured him of its success. However, as he had a high esteem for Anna Maria, he commissioned me to consult her in the matter. The pious woman, after casting a look at her sun, gave the following reply : " These two pretended angels were two devils, who had assumed this form in order to deceive him ;" she added that the affair would turn out in direct contradiction to what they had announced ; and so in fact it did.'

The same witness observes that her knowledge of consciences and discernment of spirits were unerring. 'I was in the habit at one time,' he says, ' of frequenting the society of P. di Capistrano, General of the Observantines Minor. One day he told me that he had under his guidance a holy nun of Monte Castrillo, whose gifts and virtues he highly extolled. I spoke to him of the entire confidence I placed in our servant of God; upon which he begged me to consult her, and ascertain what she thought of this Religious. Accordingly I spoke of her to Anna Maria; and at first she made me no reply, for she was very delicate in the matter of charity. As I insisted, she said to me, "It is useless for you to go and take an answer; do not lose your time in all these visits." I understood that there must be something reprehensible concealed under all this; so I left off visiting the Father. Very shortly afterwards, he was summoned before the Holy Office with his nun, and they were punished.' 'Cardinal Franzoni,' he also tells us, 'received a letter from a worthy person containing certain prophecies; he made me acquainted with them in confidence, and bade me consult Anna Maria. She replied that no value was to be attached to these predictions, for that the confessor had exaggerated things and made too much of them.' 'There was a time,' he says, 'when some of the most learned and eminent ecclesiastics were agreed in their admiration of the piety and supposed supernatural gifts of a Poor Clare who was establishing a reform of the Third Order of St. Francis. Anna Maria, aware of the way of perdition along which she was going, and the abyss towards which she was hurrying, seeing that she was persuading people that she and a companion of hers were favoured with supernatural gifts, went to her for the express purpose of manifesting to her the unhappy state of her soul. She asked to see her, but could not speak to her freely, because the foundress came accompanied by another Sister. Anna Maria, however, gave her some significant looks, which made her understand that she and her accomplice were detected. The servant of God went a second time, but to no purpose, because the foundress was not sent into the parlour. She related these circumstances to me by

order of her confessor. It is needless to add that her
previsions were always justified.'

The following instance of her spiritual discernment
and prophetic spirit is recorded by the same priest.
Cardinal Cristaldi, who at that time was an eminent
prelate under Leo XII. but not yet raised to the purple,
was about to repair to Naples. Meeting him accidentally one day in the antechamber of the Pope, Natali
observed that he was unusually thoughtful and out of
spirits. The two were well acquainted, so that he
ventured to inquire the reason; when Mgr. Cristaldi
confided to him that he was a little uneasy about his
projected journey. 'That would be a trifle,' he said;
' but the misfortune is that a Passionist has told me not
to go, for that I should die there; and the worst of it
is,' he added, smiling, 'that the Passionist is a holy
man. Do you know any one who possesses supernatural lights, and who would consult God in prayer for
me? I know not what to do. Although I am little
of a believer in modern prophecies, yet I am sad, I confess, because the matter concerns my life.' The priest
promised to recommend the affair to a holy soul, and
report the answer. On speaking to Anna Maria on the
subject, she raised her eyes to the sun, and, laughing,
said, ' Tell him to go without fear. His journey will
be a happy one, and his return still more so, and, as
a proof, tell him that for such and such reasons'—(' I
have forgotten,' says the witness, 'what these were,
but I know they related to some financial complication.')—' the thought which occupies him will not be
realised, for it is impossible of execution. When at
Naples, let him go to a certain convent, where they
will inform him of two nuns, one of whom is reputed
to be a saint; let him avoid her, for she is under an

illusion ; the other is reckoned to be out of her mind, and is despised accordingly, but she is a true saint; let him try and speak to her, if they will allow him to see her, which is doubtful.' When Mgr. Cristaldi was informed of all this, stupefied at the revelation of his profound secret, he struck his brow and said, 'Rest assured that this idea had never had access to my brain, if I may so express myself; so true is it that I kept it in the very depth of my heart. I never communicated it to any one ; and, whenever it occurred to my mind, I drove it back into my heart. Now I set off satisfied.' He wished to give D. Raffaele a sum of money for the poor woman who had been his informant, but he positively declined to take it, knowing that Anna Maria would refuse to accept of anything. Neither would he tell him who she was, notwithstanding the prelate's great desire to know. 'He publicly related the fact,' says the witness, ' at a dinner which he gave his friends before his departure, and his guests were as desirous as himself to discover the servant of God who was endowed with a gift of insight so remarkable. The only clue they possessed was the knowledge they had acquired, that Mgr. Strambi had been in intimate relations with her ; but so closely at that time was the secret kept by those who knew her, that all their efforts failed. Amongst the guests at the prelate's table that day,' adds Natali, 'were his nephew, the Canon Antonio Muccioli, now dead, and Pietro Sterbini, also dead. All was fulfilled to the letter, of which Pietro Sterbini gave me a written attestation, but I-lost it during the last revolution.'

Some time later the same prelate, then a cardinal, had several attacks of illness; and, finally, one which at first gave no symptoms of any serious character, the

Cardinal, indeed, expected to get well again speedily;
but Anna Maria had seen his death in the sun, and, desirous that he should set his affairs in order while he
was in a favourable state for doing so, she sent him a
warning.   He resigned himself, followed her advice,
and died a few days afterwards.   Anna Maria never
availed herself of the interest she had with him save
for the purpose of recommending a poor father of a
family who had come to her bewailing his destitution.
She could not help him, for, indeed, she was herself
poorer than he was ; but she caused him to be recommended in her name to Cardinal Cristaldi, who allowed
him a monthly stipend as long as he lived.

The following instance of her acquaintance with
the state of souls in the case of persons whom she had
never seen is related by the priest Natali. ' I knew,' he
says, ' the Irish family of Redington ; they lodged in
an hotel in the Piazza del Popolo. The lady was pious,
but of a stiff and haughty temper ; she recommended
herself to my prayers. I informed Anna Maria, who
was confined to her bed. She consulted the sun, and
told me things which revealed the secret thoughts of
this noble lady. I saw her afterwards just as she was
going out to an evening party. When she had heard
what I said, she was struck with astonishment, and fell
at my feet exclaiming " You are a saint ; all you have
told me is perfectly true." I replied that I was no
saint, but only the echo of a pious soul, who desired to
remain unknown.'. Dr. Cullen,* now Bishop, entered
at that moment, and so the conversation ended. The
warning consisted in putting her on her guard against
some suspicions which she harboured in her mind,
and against a temptation to judge ill of her neighbour,

* The present Cardinal Archbishop of Dublin.

s

258 V. ANNA MARIA TAIGI.

a temptation which she was energetically to repel, instead of fostering. From that moment this lady conceived a great esteem for the servant of God, whom, however, she never personally knew. Anna Maria stood god-mother at Confirmation to one of her nieces.'

We have yet to notice many recorded instances of her knowledge of distant or future events. Hitherto we have chiefly related those which manifest more particularly her acquaintance with the state of souls, but it is difficult, and not very essential, to divide these subjects with any degree of accuracy.

CHAPTER XVI.

ANNA MARIA'S KNOWLEDGE OF THE STATE OF THE DEAD
AND OF THE APPROACH OF DEATH.

WE have already alluded to Anna Maria's knowledge of the state of the departed, as revealed to her in the mysterious sun. When praying for a deceased person, she immediately saw his eternal destiny. If the soul was in Purgatory, it appeared, below the rays, symbolically represented by a heart that was soiled, or by a diamond that was deprived of its lustre ; and she perceived, with the utmost clearness, its sufferings, the reasons for which it suffered, and what would be the period of their duration ; her charity would then address itself to abridge the time by prayer and penance. The image remained sufficiently long to enable her to comprehend the exact condition of the soul, and then gently sank and disappeared. But if the soul was already in possession of glory, it appeared under the figure of a shining heart, or a sparkling diamond; it remained for a moment, during which the servant of God clearly understood, by a single look, the reward which it had received and the virtues which it had specially practised. The figure would then move a little, give forth a vivid splendour, and lose itself in the luminous disc. No other figures, as we have said, were ever seen to enter this centre of light, but seemed to be forcibly repelled when they approached it. Finally, if the deceased were a lost soul, the rays of the sun parted asunder on the left side, and discovered a horrible cavern beneath, in which Anna Maria beheld the wretched soul, the reasons of its sentence, and the terrible pains it endured; then in an instant, the dreadful vision would disappear amidst an awful shock of thunderings and lightnings, and the rays of the sun would close again. But she invariably refrained from specifying the persons whom she saw in this condition. Observing her silence on this point, the priest, her companion, said to her one day that the damned being deprived of charity, we could not offend charity by mentioning them; to which she replied that if the damned have no longer any claim upon our charity, their surviving relatives and friends are entitled to it, and to make such a revelation would be to cause them the deepest pain.

'She constantly saw numbers of souls,' says the confessor, 'that were lost—persons of all stations, ecclesiastical dignitaries of the highest rank, religious, nuns—all of whom, according to appearances, might have been believed to be in a state of salvation; but the servant of God was very reserved on this point, and never named any one. One might conceive suspicions on observing her emotion or from some other symptom,

but none carried their curiosity so far as to question
her with regard to the judgment of God in the case of
condemned souls.' This same witness notices that she
evidently thought it a bad sign, in such an epoch as
that through which they were passing, when any one
died possessed of large sums of money, particularly if
he were an ecclesiastic. She also said that salvation
was very difficult for those speculators who furnish the
necessary articles of food, and who so often starve the
people in order to enrich themselves. 'O, how displeased,' he exclaims, 'was the servant of God with
men of this class, she, whose heart was so filled with
charity, especially towards the poor !' Her revelations
respecting the state of different individual souls go
strongly to prove this point (which, moreover, harmo-
nises fully with the criterion of judgment which is
alone mentioned by our Lord where He describes all
nations as summoned before Him for their final sentence), namely, that nothing has more influence on our
future condition than the exercise or non-exercise of
fraternal charity and pity, and that charity truly avails
to cover a multitude of sins : not, we need scarcely say,
that acts of kindness and liberality atone for unrepented
sin or avail to purchase Heaven, but because there is
something in them which specially moves God to show
mercy and grant more grace, and that effectual grace,
while, in regard to those who are already in a state of
acceptance, there is no fruit of grace dearer and more
pleasing to the Heart of Him who is Essential Love.

We will subjoin an instance or two in confirmation.
Anna Maria was apprised of the salvation of a certain
count, a man well known in his day. His life had
been one of much self-indulgence, and he had dissipated
his mind by a restless love of travelling ; in short,

there had been little externally to mark his being a
Christian.   Nevertheless he was saved, and she saw
that the reason was that he had not only forgiven an
enemy but had bestowed some benefit upon him.   He
was, however, to remain in Purgatory for as many
years of suffering as he had passed useless ones on
earth.   A priest with whom she had been acquainted
having died, she saw that he owed his salvation to
having on one occasion done violence to himself and
given a trifle to an importunate beggar; this act of
virtue (for an act of virtue it was, not a mere concession
to importunity) had been to him the principle of many
other graces, which excited him to the performance of
meritorious works.   She saw his sufferings, and knew
the time they were to last.   She also beheld the soul
of the Duke Giovanni Torlonia, and knew that he was
saved on account of the great works of beneficence
which he had performed during his life.   Being present
at a solemn *Requiem* for an ecclesiastical dignitary, she
saw, and also heard (for these visions were often accompanied by audible locutions), that he received no
benefit whatsoever from all that was being done for
him, either in that church or elsewhere, but that the
prayers and Masses were applied to poor beggars left in
Purgatory without succour.   It was revealed to her,
however, that the soul of this great personage would
be somewhat assisted when another Mass was offered
for him; and that she herself would have to expiate
for a long period certain faults of which he had been
guilty.

It seems clear that in the case of this ecclesiastic
what hindered the application of the first suffrages
offered for his soul was a certain hardness towards
paupers: a fact which it is well to notice, as a cau-

tion to ourselves, for, in the present day, mendicancy
and the manner in which it ought to be met is a very
perplexing question.   Impostors abound, and street
beggars are, to say the least, not the most deserving of
their class, nor the greatest sufferers from want, who
are ever to be found amongst the bashful and retiring
poor.   There lack not therefore good reasons for turning a deaf ear to importunate requests for relief, and
certainly discretion and well-ordered charity alike for-
bid indiscriminate almsgiving; yet if, under the shadow
of these reasons, or pretexts, for refusal, a hard spirit
of unconcern is being fostered in our bosoms,—if we
find that we are contracting a cold dislike to the voice
appealing to us for pity, and a disposition to pass a
sweeping judgment on all beggars and vagrants, as
though by a kind of necessary consequence they belonged to the class of thieves and impostors, or, at any
rate, had no title to commiseration, as having probably
brought misery on themselves by their vices, so that
rags and wretchedness are becoming offensive in our
eyes,—it is to be feared that we are beginning to fall
into great danger of a prolonged Purgatory, to say no
more : a danger compared with which the risk of inju-
diciously giving a few coins to some unworthy object
is a matter of little consequence.

    The following are examples of other faults which
Anna Maria saw punished in Purgatory.   She saw an
ecclesiastic who had enjoyed a high reputation, while
living, for his activity, his zeal, and his eloquent preaching cruelly tormented in Purgatory because, instead of
seeking purely the glory of God, he had been ambitious
of being reckoned a great orator, and had not divested
himself of self-love.   A layman, who was a friend of
her own and who died with the credit of being an ex-

cellent Christian, she saw condemned to great sufferings for having cultivated too assiduously the friendship of influential persons, and for having on the other hand never deliberately faced the contempt of the world. These revelations (we may observe by the way) throw a strong light upon our incapacity to form any correct judgment either of a person's spiritual state or of the degree of merit that attaches to acts externally good. Along with an inclination to rash judgments in the way of censure, nothing perhaps is more common than a readiness to canonise or, at any rate, send straight to Heaven the souls of those whose Christian virtues we have had near occasions of appreciating and admiring. Yet Anna Maria saw in Purgatory the soul of one of her friends who had enjoyed supernatural lights, because she had not kept silence as she ought, and because she had not faithfully used the gifts she had received. She also saw two Religious of her acquaintance sentenced to Purgatory. The first, who had died in the odour of sanctity, had been too much attached to his own judgment. The second, who had left behind him a high reputation as a spiritual director, had during his latter years associated too freely with the world, under the pretext, and, indeed, from the motive, of exercising his ministry with greater efficiency : a condescension, doubtless, regarded by his admirers as a proof of zeal and active charity rather than a fault. Had he observed more strictly the requirements of community life, Anna Maria said he would not have died so soon. Amongst other instances of her knowledge of the causes which detained souls in Purgatory Natali mentions that P. Giovanni of the Visitation, Superior General of the Discalced Trinitarians, had told him more than once that, having heard of the death of his father, he apprised Anna Maria, with the view of obtaining the benefit of her prayers for him. She informed P. Giovanni that his father was in Purgatory, and specified the reasons for which he was there detained; describing exactly the employment he had held while living, and the nature of his occupations in minutest detail. And yet P. Giovanni had never so much as told her what was his father's condition in life; and anyhow it was quite impossible that she could by natural means have become cognisant of all the particulars which she mentioned.

She had also visions of souls which passed straight to glory. She saw a Capuchin Brother whom she knew well, Fra Felice of Montefiascone, transported from his bed of death to Heaven, and beheld his blessed soul, all resplendent with the most ardent charity, occupying one of the highest thrones among the Seraphim. A priest named Roberti, Superior of the Congregation of the Mission, was taken ill, and earnestly desired to depart, that he might be united to God. Whenever Cardinal Pedicini visited him, the sick man would beg him to inquire of the servant of God how much more time he had to spend on earth. He believed his death to be imminent, and hoped it would occur on a particular day which he specified; but Anna Maria commissioned the Cardinal to tell him that his time was not yet come. When the day so much longed for at last arrived, she beheld in the mysterious sun the soul of this holy priest fly direct to Heaven. She also heard the praises of his hidden virtues, which God manifested to her. She had previously seen a young priest named Folchi, also a Lazarist Father, pass likewise straight from this present life to a high place in glory,—as well as a lay brother of the Observantines Minor, whom she beheld assisted in his passage by the Blessed Virgin. P. Rossini, of the Company of Jesus, a prefect of novices, caused one of their number named Valori, lately deceased, to be recommended to the prayers of the servant of God. Anna Maria replied that the beautiful soul of this youth had gone straight to Paradise; an announcement at which P. Rossini, who was well acquainted with the young novice's virtues, was by no means surprised.

We may here allude to the manner in which Anna Maria became first known to this Jesuit Father. At one time she was in the habit of frequenting San Andrea, the church of the Jesuit noviciate, where the prefect noticed her modest behaviour and deep recollection. Probably he made inquiries which led to his speaking of her to the priest who accompanied her, whom he begged to recommend to her prayers a sick brother, named Marcelli, who was much depressed in mind, in consequence, it was supposed, of a distressing malady with which he was afflicted. Anna Maria readily consented, and soon informed the priest that it was not his bodily malady which was the chief cause of the Brother's suffering, but interior spiritual pains; and, in fact, Brother Marcelli confessed that so it was, and was much relieved by the message which she sent him. This incident had the effect of increasing P. Rossini's esteem for the servant of God, and, being very devout to St. Joseph, a few days before the Feast of his Patronage he asked Natali to beg this pious woman to recommend the interests of the Company to that great saint. Anna Maria accordingly offered some special devotions for that intention; and on the evening of the Feast of the Patronage of St. Joseph she saw the entire Company at one glance in the mysterious sun, in

such a manner that she could have described its several
members scattered over all countries, their houses, their
condition, the progress they were making, and whatever concerned the Order, as regarded both the present
and the future. 'I remember,' says D. Raffaele, 'that
on this occasion she again saw (for she had had previous revelations of a similar character) the persecutions, as unjust as they are violent, to which in these
latter times the Company has been subjected.'

One day Anna Maria, having gone to confession to a
Trinitarian Religious, P. Fernando of San Luigi, told him
that the General of the Trinitarians who was in Spain,
at that time invaded by the French armies under Mas-
sena, had been surprised by the enemy in New Castile,
when on his road accompanied by one of the brethren,
and, after much ill-usage, had been put to death by
them along with his companion. She also described
minutely the street in the neighbouring city to which
they had been led, and where their martyrdom was
completed. She added that, having borne all their
sufferings, and death itself, for the love of God, their
souls had flown straight to Heaven. The Father was
much surprised at this piece of information, and acquainted his brethren with it. A month later, letters
from Spain confirmed what Anna Maria had told him
respecting the massacre, and the Community, seeing
the full accomplishment of the first portion of her
announcement, entertained no doubt as to the truth of
the second; namely, that the souls of these two Religious were in glory.

She saw the state after death of several exalted
personages who had played a conspicuous part on the
world's stage in her time; amongst others the Czar of
Russia, Alexander I. Count Alexander Michaud, a

native of Nice, and aide-de-camp to the Russian Emperor, to whom he was warmly attached, having gone
to Rome for a Jubilee granted by Leo XII., heard during his residence a vague report of the death of the
Czar, founded probably on his then ill state of health.
He hastened to the Russian embassy, where he was
assured that the news was utterly false, and had probably been put about by the 'liberals,' for that late
dispatches did not even allude to any such rumour.
Michaud, still uneasy, went to see Queen Maria Teresa
of Sardinia, the widow of King Victor Emmanuel I.
From her he received the like assurances.   Her recent
letters from Vienna made no reference to th: matter.
All this seemed thoroughly satisfactory, but the Count
was apparently possessed by a kind of sad presentiment,
and, speaking of the report to a friend, he was advised
by him to go and consult a poor woman who had a
great reputation for sanctity. This was Anna Maria.
Michaud had no sooner stated his apprehension to her
than she told him that the news was too true. He
urged that the dispatches at the Russian embassy, and
recent letters from Vienna received by the Queen of
Sardinia, contained nothing which lent any support to
the rumour afloat; but she added, without hesitation,
'To-morrow the Russian embassy will receive the official communication of the Emperor's death.' Inquiries at the embassy the next morning proved that
her prediction was true : Alexander was dead. Michaud was an excellent Catholic, and Anna Maria consoled him much by telling him that the Emperor had
died in the true faith, and had been reconciled to the
Church ; and that she had seen his soul in Purgatory.
She had also seen the causes of his death, and said that
he owed his salvation to having shown mercy to his

neighbour, reverenced the Sovereign Pontiff, the Vicar
of Jesus Christ, and protected the Catholic Church;
in reward for which God had given him grace and
light to discern and embrace the truth.   The Count,
speaking in after years of this revelation, averred that
he had heard on good authority that a Cardinal, in
celebrating Mass, had mentioned the Emperor Alexander by name in his 'memento' for the dead.   His
chaplain overheard him, and, attributing it to a distraction, delicately reminded him, on his descending from
the altar, that that prince was a schismatic; but the
Cardinal replied that he knew very well what he was
about.   Michaud did not say who this Cardinal was,
but, if the anecdote be authentic, we may conclude that
the prelate had derived his information from the same
source.   Circumstances have in late years become known
which have confirmed the truth of Anna Maria's assertion that Alexander became a Catholic before his death.
It was an event sure to be sedulously concealed, and
the Emperor's complete seclusion,* at a distance from
the capital, in the closing days of his life would at
once facilitate his secret reception into the Church and
enable those about him to withhold the fact from public
knowledge.

     In addition to his grief at the loss of his sovereign
Count Michaud felt considerable solicitude respecting
his own prospects.   He had many enemies at Court,

---

     * The circumstance of this singular seclusion is related by
Von Grimm in his *Life of Alexandra Feodorowna, Empress of
Russia*.   The Russian correspondent of the *Tablet*, May 3d,
1873, says, that the holy woman certainly spoke the truth about
Alexander I.; and he also mentions a prediction attributed to
her (we know not on what authority) as widely known and believed among the people, although coming from a Catholic, viz.
that Russia is to play a great part in Italy at an early date.

and had reason to dread the effects of their intrigues in
damaging his position under a new reign. On the
other hand, being a sufferer from gout, he hesitated to
undertake a journey to Petersburg in the depth of
winter. Anna Maria assured him that he had nothing
to fear; that his journey would be prosperous; that
he would be well received by the Emperor; and that,
instead of afflicting and disquieting himself, he had
reason to regard his future with hope and satisfaction.
Observing the poverty of the family, Michaud was anxious to relieve their distress, but he at once perceived
that any offer of the kind would only cause her pain
and would certainly be declined. He then betook himself to her confidant, and pressed him to accept some
alms for the poor of Rome, with whom, as he significantly said, he must be well acquainted. This device
also failed; so at last he begged him to say six Masses
for his intention, at the same time giving him the sum
of six scudi. 'It was I,' says the confessor, 'who celebrated these Masses, and the servant of God directed
the money to be bestowed on a poor father of a family.'
The grateful officer, on reaching Nice, sent a barrel of
excellent oil to the pious woman, who he knew kept
wellnigh a perpetual fast. All turned out on his return
to Russia precisely as she had predicted. The Czar received him most kindly, and at once conferred on him
the rank of Lieutenant General, a promotion far above
his expectations, coupled with a good stipend. The
General wrote to D. Raffaele requesting him to thank
the servant of God, to whose prayers he attributed his
unlooked-for good fortune. His letter has been preserved.* He was also desirous of placing her in com-

* The facts we have related above were told by General
Michaud to the Bishop of Aqui, who met him in the year 1825

munication with one of his friends, a person of exalted rank, but this she declined on the plea of ill-health.

The state of the soul of Leo XII. was also made known to Anna Maria. At the time of that Pope's last sickness, early one morning she saw in her sun the catafalque prepared for him, and heard the voice of her Divine Spouse saying, 'Arise and pray: My Vicar is on the point of coming to render an account to Me.' Some years later, while speaking of him, she saw his soul appear beneath the sun, at the edge of its rays, under the form of a magnificent ruby, which as yet lacked in part its full lustre: as she gazed, it sank slowly and disappeared.

She was frequently apprised of the approaching death of persons. As we have already remarked, she could always know by means of her sun everything she desired to know; but, although this knowledge was always at her disposal, she acted entirely by the divine movement. God, however, would make things known to her when He pleased, and when she was not seeking to know them. We will here give a few examples of her prescience of coming death. One day, meeting a lawyer near the Chigi palace, she betrayed signs of emotion; and on her companion, Don Raffaele, asking her the cause, she answered with sadness that this man would die that very night of a fit of apoplexy; as

---

or 1826, in the Capuchin Convent of St. Bartholomew at Nice, as he states in his deposition. They were also well known to the confidential priest. The Bishop of Aqui's account is given in the *Analecta Juris Pontificii*, vol. ii. part ii. p. 1977. The prelate there states that it was not till later that he ascertained, from seeing a letter (unquestionably the one alluded to above), that the pious woman to whom Michaud referred was Anna Maria Taigi.

in fact he did. We have just alluded to her knowledge of the imminent death of Leo XII. ; and we have a parallel instance in the case of Pius VIII. She saw in the mysterious sun the catafalque prepared for his obsequies, surmounted by the tiara. He had been indisposed for some time, and Anna Maria, who had already foreseen his death, had been praying for him during several months. At the time she saw this vision, he seemed, however, to be recovering from a recent illness, and his state inspired no apprehensions. That very evening the priest, her confidant, went to see the Marchese Carlo Bandini, who was acquainted with Anna Maria's great gifts, and was then residing at the Quirinal, where he held an office of trust. He apprised that nobleman of what she had told him, and Bandini informed Cardinal Pedicini, who expressed much surprise ; but, as he knew well from experience that Anna Maria's communications were always verified, he felt no doubt but that the event would justify her prescience on this occasion also. Pius VIII. died a few days afterwards. She had also foretold the coming death of Pius VII. under somewhat similar circumstances ; that is, when no one about him believed his departure to be immediate. While praying for him, she had perceived that his malady was incurable, and that he was hurrying rapidly into eternity. She was thus the means of securing for him the reception of the Last Sacraments; for through her usual envoy she conveyed an intimation of his danger to the Quirinal, which was promptly attended to, for we have already seen in what high estimation the servant of God was held by Pius VII., as she was also by his successors.

One day, when Natali and the servant of God were walking together, they met Cardinal Marazzani going

in state to St. Peter's after his promotion, according to
custom. 'I told Anna Maria,' he says, 'to look at the
procession; she cast an eye on her sun, and replied,
"To-day great pomp; in a month the tomb."' And, in
fact, the Cardinal was buried a month afterwards. She
also announced the death of Mgr. Strambi. Leo XII.
had fallen seriously ill after his election. Rome was
full of anxiety on his account, fearing to lose a Pontiff
who had so lately seated himself on the throne of Peter.
Those about him shared the general apprehension,
which was greatly increased towards the close of the
year 1824, for the end seemed too plainly at hand.
When Leo's time on earth might to all appearance be
reckoned by hours, not days, Mgr. Strambi sent some
one to Anna Maria with a request that she would pray
fervently for the dying Pope. She was engaged in the
kitchen when the prelate's messenger arrived; and
after glancing at her sun she answered, smiling, 'No,
no, the Pope is not going; he has still time left to
labour for the good of the Church; but you may tell
Monsignore that it is he who ought to prepare to die.'
Mgr. Strambi's envoy replied that the prelate was quite
well. Then she gravely said, 'I assure you that a few
days hence Monsignore will lie exposed in the church.'
The Christmas festivals were at that time being celebrated, and the body of Mgr. Strambi was actually exposed in the church of the Passionists early in January,
he having expired on the second of that month by an
apoplectic stroke. His sudden illness had deprived
him of speech and of the use of his faculties, to the
great distress of the good Fathers, who were thus unable to administer the sacraments to him. They were
anxiously on the watch for an interval of returning
consciousness, but had begun to lose all hope, as they

saw their sick brother sinking, and death rapidly approaching. 'I frequently entered his room,' says D. Raffaele, 'and, beholding him in this state, I felt myself moved to go and beg Anna Maria to entreat the Divine Goodness to grant him the favour of being able to receive Communion.' The priest found her sitting before her table in the act of knitting a stocking, and remembered well how that, upon hearing his request, she laid down her work, rested her elbows on the table, and, burying her face in her hands, prayed for a few moments; then, after looking upwards, she turned her eyes towards him, and bade him warn the assistant priest to begin Mass for him at dawn; for that, although he would leave him in a state of unconsciousness, yet at the Introit the dying man would revive, with his mind perfectly clear, so that he would be able to receive the Viaticum, and would even have sufficient time to make his thanksgiving, but that he would then relapse into his lethargy, from which he would pass to eternal rest. The priest hastened back to the house of the Passionists, and all was literally accomplished as she had predicted. Thus departed this holy man, whom the Church has pronounced Venerable; nevertheless the confessor tells us that Anna Maria saw his soul in Purgatory and knew the reasons of his detention; she also beheld him afterwards ascend to glory.

There is a very interesting circumstance attending Mgr. Strambi's death which must not be omitted. Leo XII. had permitted him, in 1823, to resign his bishopric, as had long been the object of his desire, and wished him to come and live at the Quirinal, where the Pope himself resided. When the illness of Leo XII. had become so serious as to threaten his immediate death, Mgr. Strambi, while celebrating Mass, offered his own life to prolong that of the Pontiff. Full of faith, the prelate afterwards told those who assisted at his Mass that God had accepted his offer; and, in fact, it was immediately upon this that the Pope, who seemed about to enter on his agony, rallied in a wonderful manner, while his generous friend was shortly struck down, as we have related, by an apoplectic stroke.

We will add a few more instances of Anna Maria's prevision of death. 'While I was Secretary to the Maestro di Camera of his Holiness,' says D. Raffaele, 'a Russian consul, named Ponteves, came to see me, with his wife and a little boy, whose name was Alexander. He had some business in hand, and had come to beg an audience of Leo XII. in reference to it. Anna Maria, who had observed them, said to me, " This poor family will be entirely destroyed in an instant of time;"' and, in fact, they all perished shortly afterwards by shipwreck on the coast of Italy. Again, the son of a large farmer in the neighbourhood of Rome, belonging to a class known as 'mercanti di campagna,' was attacked by a dangerous illness, and his two aunts came to recommend him to Anna Maria. She was silent for a moment, then, looking at her sun, she said, ' You need not fear this time ; but bear in mind that five years hence this young man will have a fall from his horse, and will be borne to his house half-dead and unable to speak. Then invoke with faith the Holy Name of Jesus, and he will recover the use of his tongue, but you must see that he makes his confession without delay and procure the Last Sacraments for him, for he will die shortly after; the inward complaint under which he labours will render his recovery impossible.' Five years afterwards the young man fell

from his horse; one of his aunts was already dead, but
the survivor had never forgotten the warning she had
received. She promptly invoked the Holy Name,—
and her nephew instantly recovered his speech; he
made his confession, received the Viaticum and Extreme Unction, and then passed into eternity. A medical examination of the body proved the existence of
an internal complaint such as Anna Maria had specified.

Maria Luisa, Queen of Etruria, but at the time of
which we are speaking Duchess of Lucca, fell ill at
Rome. Mgr. Strambi and Mgr. Sala interested themselves greatly for her cure. They proposed a *triduo* to
St. John and St. Paul, and exhorted the patient to beg
the special intercession of the Venerable (now Saint)
Paul of the Cross, founder of the Passionists. The
triduo was accordingly celebrated with much solemnity,
and the two prelates were full of hope, which some
little improvement in the queen's condition seemed also
to warrant. At the commencement of the *triduo* Mgr.
Strambi charged Anna Maria's confidant to obtain her
prayers and inquire what opinion she had formed and
what lights she had received with regard to this illness. She answered with frankness and simplicity
that Monsignore ought not to bestir himself so much in
the matter, for that both he and his founder would
'make but a sorry figure.' But Mgr. Strambi was not
easily discouraged. 'I went to see him for several
consecutive days,' says Natali. 'The accounts of the
queen being pretty good, he would say to me, smiling,
"Maria Luisa is better still to-day, you see; tell Anna
Maria so." I replied, "I am very glad to hear it, and wish
she may obtain this cure." Suddenly the patient had
a relapse, and danger of death became imminent. Her
attendants did not venture to tell her that she must

make ready for her passage to eternity; but as they
knew the great esteem in which the queen held Anna
Maria, they sent a carriage for her, entreating her to
come at once.' Anna Maria went immediately to the
sick princess, and, using all kind discretion, told her
she must prepare for death, at the same time exhorting
her to submit to the will of God and to place all her
confidence in Him. She also reminded her to set her
temporal affairs in order. All this came unexpectedly
on the queen; she had been buoyed up with the hopes
of recovery, and it cost her something to resign herself
to die. She did, however, resign herself, and had also
time to make her will. When Mgr. Strambi heard of
the queen's imminent danger,' adds D. Raffaele, ' he
exclaimed in my presence, "Ah, if I had but hearkened
to Anna Maria !" '

The same witness relates what took place in the
case of Lady Clifford's illness and death. Her father
and husband, as also Cardinal Weld, were making the
most strenuous efforts to save her life by obtaining the
prayers of holy persons in her behalf. D. Raffaele was
acquainted with them, and recommended the sick lady
to the prayers of Anna Maria. She looked at her sun,
and told him that God willed to take her to Himself,
because in her youth she had made a vow (of which
her father, mother, and confessor alone were cognisant),
and this vow He had accepted. D. Raffaele was himself the bearer of this reply to the Cardinal, who was
exceedingly struck by it, and begged his permission to
communicate it to Lord Clifford. Nothing could exceed the astonishment of the latter at the manifestation of a thing so secret, and he acknowledged that
God alone could have revealed it. He begged D. Raffaele to make him acquainted with the servant of God,

coupling his request with the most generous pecuniary
offers.   Undiscouraged by a first refusal, he sought
another interview with Anna Maria's confidant, accompanied by his own confessor, when he again urged his
desire to assist this holy woman, on whom he wished
to settle a regular allowance.   When Natali communicated this message to her she said, ' I need not his
.oney ; let us place our trust in God.'   It so happened
that at this very time Anna Maria was suffering from
extreme indigence, but, in spite of all the steps that
were taken by the relatives of Lady Clifford, and all
their entreaties, she adhered to her determination of
keeping herself concealed.   Lady Clifford died, as she
had predicted, and Lord Clifford subsequently appeared
among the witnesses and gave his testimony to the
facts we have related.

Cardinal Galeffi and Cardinal Weld both fell ill at
the same time, and were recommended to the prayers
of the pious woman.   Cardinal Galeffi's illness was very
serious, while that of the other Cardinal appeared to be
of a slighter character.   But Anna Maria, after giving
a look at her sun, immediately said that Cardinal Weld
would die, but that Cardinal Galeffi might recover, if
he would be very careful of his diet during his con-
valescence, and if he would for the future give up
visiting convents for the purpose of direction.   She
foretold that this fatigue, if renewed, would cause a
relapse, and that his malady would then be incurable.
When Cardinal Galeffi was made acquainted with this
reply, he abstained from inquiring the name of the
person from whom it came, but he was desirous, at
least, of knowing if she was poor, in order that he
might send her some alms.   This offer was declined,
as it always was on such occasions.   He did not profit,

however, by the caution given him, and had very
shortly a serious relapse, which in the course of a
few days terminated in death.   As for Cardinal Weld,
Anna Maria had never seen him ; she was at this
time confined permanently to her bed ; she, however,
accurately described his features, complexion, and manners, adding to the person with whom she was speaking, and who purposed proceeding to inquire after him,
'Go, you will find him at the point of death ; he is
dying without being assisted by his Jesuit father.'
This proved to be perfectly correct, and the Cardinal
shortly expired.

One of the highest among the Pope's Camerieri,
who at that time was very rich and advantageously
connected, desired to know the servant of God.   He
began by saying that many good persons, of acknowledged sanctity, had announced to him that he, in
concert with the Holy Father, would do great
things for the Church.   It may be presumed that this
individual was seeking a confirmation of these flattering vaticinations ; but Anna Maria remained silent.
Pressed to speak, she answered, with her usual sincerity, 'I know that God wills to chastise some families severely, because they have not been faithful in
acquitting themselves of their functions and fulfilling
the obligations of their state.'   She then warned her
visitor to prepare soon to die, together with his wife,
and predicted that his family would be entirely destroyed before the end of the calamities, alluding to
the military occupation of Rome by the French.   The
wife sank first, and the husband followed, after becoming bankrupt and witnessing the ruin of his whole
family.

Anna Maria's confessor said to her one day, 'Pray

much for Spain; my father is at the Court, and I fear
that he may fall into great troubles.' She complied,
but her answer was far from consoling. She told P.
Filippo that his father would die during the troubles;
that all Spain would revolt, and that he himself would
see what would be the end of the head of that nation.
Shortly after, the confessor's father died, the Revolution broke out in Spain, and the dethroned monarch
came to finish his days at Rome.

Upon another occasion, her confessor asked her
prayers in favour of a noble family; but she told him
that her Lord had made her this reply: ' My dear
daughter, this family must suffer. It will be destroyed,
and its head will die a terrible death.' Much distressed,
the confessor bade her pray anew with great fervour,
but all was in vain, for again the Lord renewed His
declaration in her hearing. 'It is useless,' He said;
' they must be extirpated on account of their sins, and
you will see the death of their head, as you have been
told.' The unhappy man did, indeed, endure death,
as it were twice over. Condemned to be shot, he was
taken to the place of execution, which his companion,
standing by his side, underwent. His sentence was
then and there commuted into perpetual imprisonment; and he died soon after. ' I should never finish,'
says the confessor, after recording many of the wonderful revelations made to her, ' if I were to relate all
that concerns this mysterious sun. Who could remember and state all that has taken place during half
a century? Yet a glance sufficed her to see a thing,
discern all its circumstances, foresee all its results and
final issue. And, in fact, whether it were living persons she met, or corpses being borne to the church,
you might see her sometimes mournful, sometimes

joyous, sometimes restraining her tears, according to
what she beheld concerning them in her sun.'

We conclude these instances of her prevision of
death with a case in which, it is to be feared, she saw
something worse than the death of the body; but, as
we have said, she was silent on such occasions, and
nothing could be known with certainty, although her
sadness might suggest a painful suspicion. Her prayers
were requested for a poor man who had been struck
the previous day with apoplexy; he had entirely
lost his speech, and it was hoped that she might be
able to obtain by her prayers and penances that he
should at least recover the power of utterance, in
order that he might set his affairs in order and receive the sacraments. This man was one who had
treated Anna Maria with contempt; which with her
was only an additional reason for prayer in his behalf.
His wife begged her to send the little Madonna which,
as we have said, the servant of God wore round her
neck, and which had worked many miracles. But the
heavenly voice said to her, 'He who despised thee
during life cannot have thee at his death; and he
who does not approach the sacraments, and cares not
for them during life, shall be deprived of them at
death.' Before hearing this locution, she had, indeed,
seen all in the mysterious sun; and what she saw had
evidently saddened her, for she replied, 'It is useless
for me to send the little Madonna.' The man died
that very evening; and Anna Maria knew the moment
of his soul's departure and, no doubt, had learned his
eternal destiny.

CHAPTER XVII.

ANNA MARIA'S KNOWLEDGE OF THINGS IN THE NATURAL ORDER AND OF FUTURE EVENTS.

ANNA MARIA in her mysterious sun possessed a mirror in which she beheld, not only all the secrets of the moral and religious order, but of the natural and physical also. She was sparing, however, in her use of this knowledge, profiting by it only when occasion arose. Yet she might have cleared up, we are assured, every intricate or obscure point in history, whether sacred or profane, ancient or modern; for the past, with all its multitudinous events, was to her as the present; time and space seemed annihilated in her regard. She saw the bottom of seas and lakes, and of the fathomless ocean; she penetrated the heights of heaven, and saw into the abysses of the earth, as clearly as she discerned the four walls of her room. As an example of her possession of this kind of knowledge, we may mention that when some speculators had undertaken to explore the bed of Lake Nemi, having, as they believed, reason to hope that antique treasures of art would be discovered therein, on the subject being mentioned before Anna Maria, she glanced at her sun and saw at once that they were wasting their money and their efforts in a fruitless search. 'They will find nothing there,' she said; and in point of fact the explorers found absolutely nothing at the bottom of the lake. Often, when she beheld in her sun inundations, earthquakes, conflagrations, and other calamities menacing Rome, she succeeded by her prayers and penitential acts in averting these scourges; but sometimes the divine decrees were irreversible on account of

special sins. She saw the burning of the Basilica of
San Paolo several months before it took place, while
praying before the Holy Crucifix; and she knew by
revelation that God permitted this disaster in punishment for profanations that had been committed there.
The voice said, 'I will make of this place a heap of
ruins;' and in this instance her fervent prayers were
unavailing. She was continually beholding in her sun
conflagrations, storms, earthquakes, and other convulsions of nature, as well as thousands of symbolical figures,
to which she gave no particular heed, unless our Lord
vouchsafed her an explanation, or she was divinely
moved to inquire. 'The conversion of sinners was
what interested her,' says her confessor. Whatever
had reference thereto, or to the general good of the
Church and of Christendom, never failed to arrest her
attention. It was with these subjects that her vocation was concerned, and to these she was therefore
especially drawn. Yet it was marvellous to see how
her compassionate charity would lead her to place her
supernatural knowledge at the disposal of persons who
came to inquire about what might be regarded as
trifling things, though they were not trifling in their
estimation. The following passage from the confessor's
deposition sets this in a conspicuous light.

'Notwithstanding her desire,' he says, 'to remain
in obscurity, she was generally unable to abstain from
taking a part or interesting herself in affairs of high
importance which were recommended to her through
the medium of one of her spiritual sons, or by some
other person who had succeeded in ascertaining something about her. Nevertheless the fly and the camel,
the flea and the elephant, were alike to her. I mean
that she occupied herself indifferently with great af-

fairs or small, for she saw them all with equal clearness in the mysterious sun. . . . It was truly wonderful to hear and see her comforting some poor woman who was complaining of want because the trade she carried on with her poultry was not prospering, and who was unable to make her livelihood because her hens would not lay as usual ; with the greatest kindness and particularity she would instruct the poor woman how to manage her hens, and a moment after, would turn her attention to some serious affair, some delicate and complicated business, which, however, was of no greater moment in her eyes than the poor woman's hens.   To both she addressed herself with the same facility and promptness.'   Both were, indeed, equally easy to her, but to her charitable and sympathetic heart the troubles of the poor and the lowly made the tenderest appeal.   In cases of sickness, for instance, P. Filippo tells us, ' she prayed equally for the fruit-seller, the carter's wife, and the princess, but her fervour and charity were greatest where the sufferers were the poor of Christ.'

In praying for a sick person, she immediately saw in her sun the nature of the complaint, the possibilities of cure, the remedies which ought to be used, as well as the reasons for which God had sent the malady. Her friends, and particularly her spiritual children, were always running to consult her when they were suffering from indisposition.   Her prudence and humility would lead her on such occasions to advise the applicant to see a doctor ; if she afterwards found that the doctor had understood the complaint she said no more, but if he was mistaken in his opinion or the advice he gave, then she would say, ' My child, just try such or such a remedy ; your complaint is so and

so;' and she would explain naturally and simply the
treatment which ought to be followed. But although
she might advise recurrence to further medical aid, her
spiritual sons had such implicit confidence in her discernment, that when once they had got her to prescribe
for them they were certain to desire nothing further.
She might in all cases have cured them instantaneously by the touch of her hand, but she was wont to
say that we must be content with ordinary remedies
when they are procurable, and have recourse to what is
miraculous only in cases of necessity. By these ordinary remedies, which, however, she knew, by a supernatural science, she effected many cures. Her son-in-
law brought a youth to her who had long suffered from
a troublesome and exhausting complaint. The doctors
could do nothing for him. Anna Maria looked at her
sun, and knew in a moment what was the proper medicine ; she insisted on preparing it herself, and gave
it to the poor boy, who took it for three days and returned to her on the fourth to announce his perfect
recovery. An only child, who had fallen dangerously
ill, and whose parents, in addition to their grief at his
death, would have had to regret the loss of a valuable
succession, was recommended to her prayers. She
immediately knew the nature of his malady, and indicated a remedy of a very simple nature, but she saw at
the same time that the doctors, who did not understand
the case, would refuse to try her prescription, and that
the child would in consequence die. The confessor,
who relates this circumstance, adds, 'And this actually
occurred, although the doctors were very clever men
and eminent in their profession.' If the doctors allowed
this child to die by rejecting, in their ignorance, an
effectual remedy, we have in the following instance a

case in which they shortened the days of one who preferred to follow their mistaken advice to abiding by the recommendation of the servant of God. Duke Vincenzo Lanti was suffering from the stone; and the confessor of Anna Maria commended him to her prayers. She sent the following reply : ' Let the duke beware of allowing the operation to be performed, for he will die of it; but if he does not undergo it, he will live for some time longer.' But the duke, choosing to attend to his medical advisers, submitted to the operation, and died the following day.

Although Anna Maria often effected a cure by her knowledge of the natural properties of things, we do not reckon these among her miracles of healing, of which we shall speak elsewhere. For these cures seem to have been in themselves natural, although her knowledge was acquired supernaturally. Her spiritual sons were well aware to what a treasure they had access, and regarded her as a divine oracle, which in truth she was. Encouraged by her unwearied kindness and willingness to interest herself in every matter, whether small or great, which was a subject of anxiety to her neighbour, they would sometimes refer to her very small matters indeed, which, besides, were of a merely temporal character. Their good mother would listen, however, with her customary charity and patience, and never refused to reply to their questions or to afford them the benefit of her counsels. For example, one would come and ask if he should find a person whom he was desirous to see on some business that morning. Anna Maria, after looking at her sun, would tell her inquirer whether the person he wanted was at home ; and inform him, moreover, what the individual would say, and how the matter would end.

Another, uneasy at receiving no letter from his absent
family, would want to know the reason, and then
Anna Maria would tell him if his relatives were in
good health, if they had written, if their letters had
been lost or were detained by the post, and would
even acquaint him with their contents. Another
would complain of some one having received him very
ill, and she would enlighten him as to the reason.
Nay, a lost key or snuff-box was considered a matter
of sufficient importance to be referred to her. In short,
they treated her as little children do their mother,
running to her for comfort or help in every little
grievance or trouble, and she on her part treated them
as a loving mother treats her little children, neither
rebuking them, nor driving them away, nor showing
any contempt for their miniature misfortunes. 'Why
don't you search for it?' she would gaily reply to one
of these bewailers of lost articles; 'is God obliged to
look after careless people?' Then, if all searchings
proved fruitless, she would say, smiling, 'Go to such a
place; you have left it there;' or, 'Such a person has
found it; make him give it you back; but be more
careful another time.'

A person had taken it into his head that his father,
when dying, had committed a large sum to the care of
some third party, to be conveyed to him, his eldest
son. This idea was continually tormenting him, and
at last he consulted Anna Maria, who bade him think
no more about the matter. 'In the first place,' she
said, 'the sum was not so considerable as you imagine;
it was only so much' (and she stated the amount).
'Besides, some time before your father's illness, some
of his servants plotted together to rob him of it; they
are dead, and are undergoing their punishment in the

other life ; trouble yourself therefore no farther, all inquiry would be useless.'

It will be noticed that the subjects on which she was consulted had often no reference to spiritual interests, yet she did not refuse her sympathy or help on that account ; thus furnishing an example of the exercise of kindness, taken in its simple and general sense, a virtue which, even when unsupernaturalised, is perhaps the most like to a fruit of grace of any of the mere natural virtues. Anna Maria was eminently kind, and this is worthy to be noted as something over and above her charity. This kindness we see exemplified, in this her readiness to reply to questions, however trifling the subject-matter might be, if only they regarded matters of interest or anxiety to the inquirers. But if she had reason to doubt whether there might not be some impropriety in the inquiry, she would demur, as not knowing the will of God. For instance, when one of her spiritual sons, who was in great indigence, came to beg his good mother to look in her sun and tell him the numbers which would be drawn for prizes in the coming lottery, so that he might select three which would free him from his straits, Anna Maria desired first to ascertain whether God would permit of such inquiry, and received for answer, ' Beware of looking into the mirror with the view of choosing lottery tickets ; that is not right'—('questo non è la buona via'). Nevertheless, towards evening, when looking into the sun for other objects, she several times saw certain numbers, which she mentioned, without, however, indicating their value.

She was the means of warning persons more than once of dangers to which they were about to be exposed, but which they were free to avoid. Nothing

appears more clearly, it may be remarked, from
these revelations in the sun than the fact that, while
some disclosed the irreversible decrees of God, others
referred to decrees which would not have been changed
but for the intervention of her prayers and penances;
and others, again, simply manifested dangers which
could be avoided by a particular line of action, as in
the case of certain maladies to which we have alluded.
We subjoin an instance of this latter class. A distinguished Cardinal was intending to take his evening
walk in a certain quarter of the city. Anna Maria
beheld in the sun a plot of the sectaries to waylay
him, and lost no time in commissioning the priest, her
companion, to go and warn his Eminence not to walk
in the direction he had proposed to himself, but to
take another road. This communication extremely
surprised the Cardinal, as he had not mentioned his
purpose to any one.

Sometimes she simply announced a coming peril,
from which, however, the person threatened escaped,
no doubt by the help of her powerful prayers. The
following incident is extracted from the deposition of
the Marchese Carlo Bandini, who appears among the
witnesses. 'The fame of the surprising gifts and extraordinary lights enjoyed by the virtuous servant of
God, Anna Maria Taigi, having reached our country
(Maccrata), my father, who loved to place himself in
connection with persons of this kind, recommended
me to go and see her. On my arrival at Rome, I was
taken up by other business, and neglected my commission. I returned home, but affairs obliged me to
repair again to Rome, and then my father repeated his
injunction that I should visit Anna Maria. Accordingly I went to her immediately on my arrival at

Rome. She told me of the repugnance I had felt to seeking her, and other things regarding my own interior which she could have known only by revelation; all which greatly astonished me. My surprise, however, was increased when one day, shortly before my return to Macerata, she came to see me in order to warn me of a great danger which I should encounter on my journey. "The postillion," she said, "will leave the old road at such a place, in order to follow the one newly made. You will perceive the danger and cry out to him, but he will not listen to you." ' All happened as Anna Maria had foretold. Whether Bandini forgot the caution he had received or did not observe the road which the postillion was taking, so it was that the latter diverged from the safe track at the spot she had indicated. When the vehicle had proceeded some way, Bandini recollected her words, and called to the postillion to moderate his speed. But the man either would not heed or could not stop his horses (probably the latter, for Bandini even menaced him with his pistols), he kept rapidly on, and, on arriving at the dangerous point of the road, the carriage was upset with such a shock that Bandini's servant received a blow on the head which caused his death. ' I myself,' he adds, ' escaped quite miraculously.'

We will here relate a few miscellaneous instances of her knowledge of persons, and of events both distant and future. The Queen of Etruria was at one time extremely uneasy respecting her brother, the King of Spain, as rumour had asserted that he had fallen into the snares of his enemies. She sent for Anna Maria, who fully tranquillised her. She indicated the place where the king was at that time, and described the appearance of many persons belonging to his Court,

U

and the queen subsequently ascertained that all the information given her was perfectly accurate.

At the time that Camillo, Anna Maria's son, was drawn for the conscription, and before his return to his family, she was seen to leave her house weeping, and hasten to the Madonna della Pietà. Her neigh-bours inquired what was the cause of her trouble, and she replied that her son was on the point of being drowned. By and bye she returned home, her face beaming with joy, and to the sympathising persons who had questioned her she said that the Madonna had saved her Camillo. In fact, at that very time the ship in which he and other conscripts were sailing was exposed to all the fury of a violent tempest, and the captain had already announced to both crew and pas-sengers that all hope of saving the vessel was gone; he afterwards declared that their escape from ship-wreck was quite miraculous.

Don Raffaele states that when he was Secretary to the Pope's Maestro di Camera, Mgr. Barberini, he allowed himself to be guided in everything by the servant of God. In the evening he used to read her the list of the persons who had requested an audience of the Pope for the morrow. After consulting her sun, she would tell him if there was any one to whom he should deny entrance. She would occasionally, for instance, point out certain foreigners as suspicious characters, and direct him to make inquiries concern-ing them at their respective embassies, before ad-mitting them. On one occasion he remembered that she bade him beware of an individual whose name appeared among the applicants, for he belonged to the secret societies, and came with the worst in-tentions. Further investigation invariably justified the

prudence of her advice. Leo XII. accordingly reposed
so much confidence in D. Raffaele for the direction of
his audiences, that when Mgr. Barberini was disabled
from attendance through sickness, he retained the Secretary of the Maestro di Camera at his post, contrary to
all precedent, as the office of regulating the audiences
devolved in such cases on the Camerieri Segreti for
the week. Leo XII., as we have said, was already
well acquainted with Anna Maria's extraordinary gifts,
of which Mgr. Strambi had spoken to him ; and so
high was the esteem which he entertained for the
servant of God that on more than one occasion he
sent his own physician to her when she was ill.

The following instance of her supernatural knowledge is also related by D. Raffaele. Mgr. Strambi
was extremely anxious to give up his bishopric, desiring
to exonerate himself from the charge of souls and pass
the remainder of his days in retirement ; and after the
return of Pius VII. to Rome, in 1815, he requested
him to accept his resignation. The ground was so well
prepared that the suit seemed likely to prosper. Cardinal Pacca, Secretary of State, had spoken to his
Holiness on the subject, and the Pope seemed well
disposed to accede to Mgr. Strambi's desire, who accordingly flattered himself that he had all but obtained
the solicited favour. 'Nevertheless,' says Natali,
'such was the confidence he placed in Anna Maria,
that on the eve of the day when he was to go and see
the Pope, he commissioned me, who happened to be at
the Passionist convent, to go and tell the servant of
God in his name that he was about to offer his resignation to the Holy Father, and to beg the help of her
prayers.' Anna Maria, on receiving this message,
raised her eyes to Heaven, and, after a moment of

recollection, replied that the Pope had, indeed, been in
the first instance disposed to grant Mgr. Strambi's request, but that he would have thought the matter over
in the night and have altered his mind; that upon seeing
him in the morning his countenance would be changed;
he would receive him roughly, and command him to
depart immediately to his diocese. 'I carried back her
answer,' proceeds the witness, 'to Monsignore, who smiled
and said, " This time our holy chirper (cicala) has made
a great mistake; know, my son, that I have arranged
all with his Eminence, Cardinal Pacca, the Secretary
of State, who has prepared his Holiness, and I am
rather going to return thanks than to prefer a request."
It pleased God,' continues Natali, 'that I should
accompany Mgr. Strambi to his audience, and be
present at his reception by the Pope.' Passing through
the antichamber, which was not yet opened for the
morning audience, but where Monsignore was already
in waiting, the Pope on his way to his own private
apartment perceived him. His countenance immediately betrayed displeasure, and with an impressive
severity of manner he said these words : 'We already
know the purpose for which your lordship has come.
Every one is pleading health; we also are infirm at our
advanced age, and yet we support the weight of the
whole world. Whom are we to send as bishops? Are
we to send the scavengers? All want to resign. Let
your lordship set off, and that immediately, for your
diocese—Lei parta, e parta subito, per la sua diocesi—
mò' (a frequent interjection of Pius VII.'s), and with
that he abruptly left him. The disappointed prelate
waited some time longer, and then requested through
Mgr. Doria a private audience for the affairs of his diocese. When that was over, he entered a carriage, with

D. Raffaele, to return to the house of the Passionists.
' Not a word passed between us,' observes the latter,
' until we reached the Arch of Titus, when Monsignore
broke silence, and said, " You have heard, my son.   I
resign myself, and think no more of the matter."   I
repeated this to Anna Maria, and she assured me that
Monsignore would come and pass his last days at
Rome, as he desired, but it would be only to lay his
bones there ; that is, for only a brief period.   Some
time later, his infirmities increasing, the good prelate
made another attempt to give up his bishopric, but
without avail, and he therefore lost all hope of ending
his days in Rome.   He wrote to me begging me to
speak on the subject to Anna Maria, and she again
affirmed what she had formerly declared.'   And, in fact,
after the death of Pius VII. his successor, Leo XII.,
called Mgr. Strambi to Rome, and made him his own
private counsellor and confessor.

Mgr. Strambi then left his diocese, and came to live
near the Pope at the Quirinal.   Leo XII. was at that
time engaged in organising certain reforms in his
States, and was every day in conference with Mgr.
Strambi on the subject.   The latter requested D. Raffaele to come and see him every evening, when he used
to inform him, with due circumspection, of the principal matters which had been discussed in the private
conference which he had held that day with the Holy
Father, in order that he might communicate them to
Anna Maria, whose counsels had so high a value in his
eyes.   Sometimes this holy woman's opinion differed
altogether from that which Mgr. Strambi had formed ;
nevertheless he reported it to the Pope, along with the
prudent reasons she had alleged, reasons which won
the approval and admiration of his Holiness.   Mgr.

Strambi honestly abstained from appropriating anything to himself, but confided to the Holy Father the source from which he derived the counsels he gave. The high idea which that Pontiff already entertained of Anna Maria's supernatural wisdom was thus greatly enhanced, and he continued to avail himself of her advice, so that it may be said of her with truth that she became the intimate counsellor of the Sovereign Pontiff in the highest matters of state, as she already was of the Queen of Etruria.

Nor was Leo XII., as we have said, the first Pope who valued the lights of this holy woman. Pius VII. had heard of her great gifts from Cardinal Pedicini (then only a Monsignore), and his esteem had not been founded on that prelate's report alone, but on a revelation which she had made respecting himself. He had charged Mgr. Pedicini to tell her to write something for him. Her humility was much alarmed at this request, and she trembled at the thought of writing to the Vicar of Christ; but she felt that she was acting under obedience, so she took up her pen and chose a very simple subject, a circumstance relating to the childhood of Pius VII., which she described in its minutest particulars. The Pope was surprised, and said that it was all perfectly true.

A young person acquainted with Anna Maria had begged her prayers that she might be enabled to realise her desire of embracing the religious life. She was poor and could bring no dower, and Mgr. Menocchio, whom she consulted, did not think she had a vocation. She returned quite discouraged to Anna Maria, who bade her not fear but wait patiently, for she would certainly be a religious. A short time after, a benefactor supplied the necessary dower, and she entered a Capuchin convent, where she afterwards became abbess and, after living a holy life, made an edifying death.

Anna Maria not only saw all things, past, present, and future, in her sun, but she was able to receive directions from a distance given in the name of holy obedience, and to execute them, even when her obedience also necessitated a miracle. We have already seen exemplifications of the extraordinary power which the tacit command of a priest officiating at the altar would have over her, as also in recalling her from the ecstatic state. Similar instances have not been unfrequent in the lives of saints; but the following case is remarkable enough to deserve notice, as it goes to prove her supernatural knowledge. The Duke of Altempo, who was about to be united in marriage to the Countess Caradori, went to make a preparatory retreat in the Convent of St. Bonaventura. He begged D. Raffaele to accompany him. 'I remained, then, in the convent,' says the latter, 'without myself going into retreat, and I used to go out every day towards evening to see Anna Maria. I found her one day in bed, to my great sorrow, suffering much pain in her legs, which were exceedingly swollen, and left her in this state, worse, indeed, than I found her. The following morning I experienced great disturbance in my mind, and did not dare to celebrate the holy Mass. I had recourse to God, and commanded Anna Maria, in the name of obedience, to cure herself at once by the merit of this virtue, and get up and come and see me at St. Bonaventura's. Less than an hour afterwards, hearing the convent bell ring, I ran to the door, and found Anna Maria there, quite heated from her rapid walk. She said to me with a smile, "Do not play me any more tricks of this sort, because I am the mother of a family; I cannot waste my time,

and come so far." She quieted my mind, and hastened
home again.'

This incident might be recorded amongst her miracles, since she evidently healed herself, as well as among
the examples of her supernatural knowledge. The extracts that follow from the Princess Vittoria Barberini's
testimony* contain a circumstance which in like manner exhibits an exercise of these two supernatural
powers; only that the glory of the miracle seems in this
case to be shared with St. Philip Neri. The lady in
question had been in the habit before her marriage of
frequenting the Church of San Ignazio, and there her attention was attracted to Anna Maria, then in her youth.
She used to see her going to confession to the Abate Salvatori, and was struck by the evident fervour of her
piety and her profound recollection. After her marriage with the Prince of Palestrina, she frequented the
Church of Santa Maria della Vittoria on account of its
greater vicinity to her palace, and took for her confessor P. Filippo Luigi of San Nicola, with whom we
are already acquainted as the director of Anna Maria.
'By a disposition of Divine Providence,' says the princess, ' the pious woman, whose name was Anna Maria
Taigi, came also to confession to the same priest for
many years, and until the period when she fell ill.
This furnished me with the opportunity of knowing
her better, of speaking to her, and of establishing relations with her which enabled me to appreciate her great
piety, her uncommon virtues, and, above all, the extraordinary lights which God had communicated to her.

* The Princess Barberini (born Colonna), fearing that she
might not live long enough to appear as a witness, made her
attestation, which appears in the Processes, previously to her
death.

Accordingly I took great pleasure in conferring with her whenever a favourable opportunity presented itself; and I remarked in the course of these conversations how deeply penetrated she was with the maxims of our holy religion and with a reverential attachment to the Holy Catholic, Apostolic, and Roman Church.   When I could not see her I wrote to her, or sent some one who enjoyed our respective confidence. She used to pray God for me, on one affair or another, and the result was always such as she had foretold.   Whether speaking or writing, she was respectful and discreet, and at the same time frank and cordial. If my children were ill, I had recourse to her, because I had good reasons to confide in her prayers, having had experience of their happy effects in cases concerning both my family and my own individual needs.'   She proceeds to relate how her brother-in-law, Monsignore Barberini, Maestro di Camera to the Pope, having fallen dangerously ill a little while before his promotion to the Cardinalate, she sent word to Anna Maria, who took her accustomed charitable interest in the matter. Although the malady increased in violence, and at length reached such a point that the utmost apprehensions were entertained for the life of the patient, nevertheless Anna Maria reassured the princess, bidding her fear nothing, and recommending her to have recourse to the Madonna of San Agostino and send thither six young girls, barefoot, to pray, together with a little offering of candles. 'This I did,' continues the Princess Vittoria; 'she also bade me seek the intercession of St. Philip Neri, the special patron of my family, and discard all uneasiness. And, in fact, when people were talking of Extreme Unction being administered to him, he had a sudden crisis, which saved him. The physicians marvelled, and

were fain to acknowledge that this change could only
be attributed to a true miracle of St. Philip Neri. The
above-mentioned Taigi had sent me a relic of the saint,
bidding me make the sign of the cross with it on the
sick man's forehead, and then hang it round his neck;
all which we did.' The princess adds, in the solemn
attestation which she made, that upon many other
occasions which she had not thought needful to specify
she had personal experience of the wonderful preroga-
tives and supernatural gifts of the servant of God.

CHAPTER XVIII.

ANNA MARIA'S KNOWLEDGE OF EVENTS, POLITICAL, ECCLESIASTICAL, AND RELIGIOUS.

ANNA MARIA was quite illiterate. She had not acquired in her early schooling anything beyond the
merest rudiments of secular knowledge. She was intended to earn her livelihood in a humble class of
society, and her education was directed to fitting her
for that object. Of history, geography, physical science,
politics, and the like, she knew nothing. In those
days such subjects formed no part of the programme of
primary instruction for the lower orders; and certainly
the 'Maestre Pie' had not imparted any knowledge of
them to their scholar. Neither had Anna Maria made
any attempt since to supply this deficiency. Her whole
attention had been concentrated on the duties of her
state, and she had laboured to advance in no kind of
knowledge save that of God. Whatever else she knew

besides, came of divine, not human, teaching. About
the affairs of the world, its politics, and its news, she
never interested herself, at least of her own movement.
If she knew them, it was because it was God's will to
manifest them to her, and, in fact, she knew all. Anna
Maria, D. Raffaele tells us, saw in her sun the massacres of Spain, the war in Greece, the 'three glorious
days' of Paris, describing minutely everything as it
occurred, just as if she had been on the spot. The revolution at Brussels, the war in Poland, and all its
miseries, she saw with the like distinctness both before
the events and while they were in progress. They came
before her at her will. She saw the localities, the physiognomies of the combatants, as in a mirror. In like
manner, many years before, she had seen the defeat of
the French army before Moscow at the very time it
took place. 'She described to me,' says Natali, 'the
defeat of Napoleon, and gave all its details, long before
the news arrived or could arrive. She also beheld his
death at St. Helena, his bed, all his testamentary arrangements, his tomb, the ceremonial of his funeral,
and knew, moreover, what was the destiny of that
prince in time and in eternity.' 'I remember very
well,' says the same witness, 'that while the last war
in Poland was going on, the Marchese Carlo Bandini
used to be in the habit of visiting the servant of God
in order to recommend his own special needs to her.
Knowing his disposition and his discretion, I did not
refuse to communicate to him the visions of which I
have just spoken, according as Anna Maria imparted
them to me, for her confessor had ordered me to take
notes of everything. I described, then, to him the
places and physiognomies which the servant of God had

seen in her visions.* The Marchese, who read the
papers, was conversant with geography, and also knew
the principal actors in the war, used to take a pleasure
in mentioning in society, without stating the source of
his knowledge, events which could not be known before
the lapse of a good many days; and as the truth of
what he announced was always confirmed, the world,
as may be imagined, was greatly astonished. Accordingly the Prince Gagarin, the Russian ambassador at
Rome, came frequently for the purpose of questioning
the Marchese, whose information was always so won-
derfully accurate and more rapid in its transmission
than could be supplied by the modern telegraph. Moreover, he was what the telegraph is not, a prophet, for
he could give the future as well as the present news.

Circumstances occurred which obliged Anna Maria
on one occasion to receive a visit from an eminent
diplomatist, then ambassador from France to the Court
of Turin. After answering with precision all his questions, she proceeded to unfold before him his whole
past career; she described the incidents of his youth,
the persons whom he had known during the Great
Revolution, the circumstances connected with his sudden arrest at night, together with other particulars of
his life, pointing out at the same time the faults he
had committed. The ambassador listened in astonishment. He then led her to the sphere of politics; she
immediately drew out an abstract of the general situation of affairs, so that his wonder increased every
moment. She clearly described the state of things at

---

* From the Marchese Carlo Bandini's attestation it would
appear that he learnt all these revelations immediately from
Anna Maria. We have given Natali's account. In substance
it is precisely identical with that of the Marchese.

the various European courts, and in the other nations
throughout the world; she unveiled the policy of the
different cabinets, the objects to which they were
directing the measures they adopted, their several
projects and covert designs, most of which were to
be dissipated like smoke; she pointed out how such
or such an intrigue of some European power had been
defeated by Providence, and she went on to show what
ought to be the end at which sovereigns should aim
and with what fidelity and circumspection ministers
ought to acquit themselves of their trust.   She also
entered into details concerning the Turkish Government and its policy with regard to a court which she
specified (doubtless Russia), as well as the policy of
that court in regard to the former government.   In
short, this poor illiterate woman described the whole
state of the political world, the character of its govern-
ments, its diplomacy, its negotiations, its secret intrigues, its false principles, and the consequences to
which they would infallibly lead.   Of all this she
delivered herself with great energy and force, for when
speaking under the impression of the mysterious light
she appeared quite another person.   The ambassador
was perfectly astounded.   He remained with her for
above an hour, and when he left the room it was with
tears in his eyes.   Turning to the person who had introduced him, he exclaimed, 'What a prodigy! how
marvellous!   How is it possible for a woman to know
all these things?   She seems to embrace the whole
world in her ken, as I hold my snuff-box' (raising his
hand as he spoke), 'while we old politicians do not
even know all the secrets of the courts to which we
belong.'   He could not recover from his astonishment;
and he confessed, moreover, that all she had told him

of the most secret incidents of his life and his most
hidden thoughts was perfectly true.

While engaged in prayer, whether for Italy or for
other lands, she used to see before her all the miseries
and sufferings of which those countries were the scene.
She saw prisoners in their dungeons, sailors exposed to
shipwreck, slaves groaning in bondage, in fine, all the
necessities, temporal as well as spiritual, of those for
whom she prayed. Her soul was, as it were, in perpetual motion, continually interceding with her Lord
for them, but more especially for their salvation, since
that is the highest of all goods.' The nations which
have been separated from the unity of the Church had
a large share in her prayers, as well as Jews, Infidels,
and Turks. 'One may say,' writes Cardinal Pedicini,
'that her life was a laborious Apostolate, exercised
throughout the whole world in a manner as surprising
as it was novel and secret.' In beholding the idola-
trous superstitions of Pagan nations, he tells us, and
the profound ignorance of the true God in which they
are immersed, she used to entreat her dearest Lord
in the most simple and affectionate terms to show His
face and make Himself known to them. And if she
thus ardently poured forth her soul for the conversion
of those who as yet knew Him not, and therefore had
not abused His greatest gifts, with what fervour did
she not pray for those sinners who had done terrible
despite to the Spirit of grace, and particularly for those
who were enduring a slavery far worse than any which the
cruelty of man could impose—we mean those wretched
men who were affiliated to the secret societies and
banded together to do the work of Satan ! She prayed
for them, and she also prayed against them. She used
to see in her sun, as the Cardinal tells us, 'their secret

assemblies, their impure conventions, in the farthest parts of the world, as well as their sanguinary conspiracies against the good; and the sight animated her to fervent prayers and generous self-oblations to her Heavenly Spouse, that He might not permit the accomplishment of their impious designs. What did she not obtain of this kind, especially for Italy and, above all, for Rome? God overturned the projects of the sectaries by the all-powerful breath of His mouth, and with His hand cut short the dark plots they had woven, when they had just reached their completion. But He never failed afterwards to exercise the rights of His justice on His beloved Anna Maria by augmenting her sufferings in proportion to the graces she obtained; of which she received the assurance from His own lips when she had made her generous offers.'

Her prayers for the Church, for the Sovereign Pontiff, for the Cardinals and Bishops, were unceasing, and, in particular, she offered the most fervent petitions for the tranquillity of the States of the Church. We have already noticed how during the captivity of Pius VII. in France she used to be continually going barefoot to the Crucifix of San Paolo, a devotion which she practised frequently at all times; but to these penitential exercises she added many bodily mortifications, in order to appease the anger of God and obtain the restoration of peace to the Church, and the return of the Roman Pontiff to his See. By her perseverance, says the Cardinal, in these works, which were all animated by the most ardent charity, she merited to be assured by our Lord Himself of the very day when His Vicar would return to Rome, and how he would solemnise the first Pontifical Mass at St. Peter's on the Feast of Pentecost. This revelation was made long before

the Pope's restoration, and at a time when, humanly
speaking, not a ray of hope of such a blessed event had
as yet beamed on the Christian world.   She beheld in
her sun the departure of the French, and the festal reception of the Pope all along his journey through Italy
and especially in Rome itself. Of these predictions notes
were taken at the time. She also saw all that followed
on his restoration, the governmental measures adopted,
as well as the renewed plots of impious men. She saw
the election of all the succeeding Pontiffs, down to that
of our present holy Pontiff Pius IX., whose accession
she did not live to behold on earth ; and she foretold
the acts and events of their successive Pontificates.
She beheld in the fullest detail the conspiracies of the
secret societies, particularly as directed against the head
of the Church and the superior ranks of the clergy.
To avert the accomplishment of their nefarious designs
was at this period one of the main incentives to her
generous and repeated acts of self-oblation, and to the
increased severity of her penitential life.   Her prayers
and penances, offered so perseveringly for this end,
were at last successful, and she received a promise from
our Lord that during her life the machinations of the
wicked should not succeed in Rome, but that He would
always frustrate their designs when they seemed to be
on the very eve of triumph.   It was on a day when
she was walking barefoot to the Basilica of San Paolo
that she heard our Lord give her this assurance, but the
condition was attached that she should offer herself to
satisfy the divine justice.   Gladly did she renew an
oblation which she had already repeatedly made, and
return the most fervent thanks to God for the boon
which He had granted her, a boon which was to convert the remainder of her days into one protracted

martyrdom. She may, indeed, be justly styled a martyr for the salvation of her country. Our Lord also
promised, but probably many years later (for this
scourge as yet had not menaced Europe), that the
cholera should not attack Rome during her lifetime,
and in fact its appearance and her death were contem-
poraneous.

But although our Lord had engaged to protect
Rome against the enemies of His Church so long as
she remained on earth, on the condition of her suffering for His offended justice, this compact by no means
precluded the necessity of continued prayer for the
same end. Accordingly, Anna Maria, who in the light
of her sun saw all that was going on in the dens of
darkness, where men instigated by Satan were hatch-
ing their diabolical plots, never ceased raising up her
hands to God and reminding Him of His promise ; and
He as often granted her petitions, but invariably with
an aggravation of her sufferings. Scarcely, for instance,
had she recovered from a mortal illness which assailed
her under the Pontificate of Pius VII., when God revealed to her new projects, more menacing than those
which had preceded them, which were on the point of
being executed. Indeed, the secret societies never
wearied of conspiring during his reign, as also during
the reigns of his successors, Leo XII., Pius VIII., and
Gregory XVI., and were as often defeated of their
infernal purpose in some unforeseen manner.

God revealed to Anna Maria that her sufferings
were necessary for divers ends with which she was
acquainted, and for others which she must be content
not to know. These sufferings used to be announced
by repeated blows which she distinctly heard in her
heart, and which were more or less violent according

x

to the magnitude of her coming trials. She resigned
herself with tranquillity, but nature felt the whole bitterness of all which she endured and of all which she
foresaw; and God willed that so it should be, in order
to add to her merits. How would the world scoff at
the bare notion of the prayers and sufferings of a few
holy souls, such as Anna Maria and other hidden saints
associated in the same sublime work, availing to change
the whole course of events in its history, and to arrest
for years the destruction which was threatening it!
But these souls were the friends, nay, the spouses of
the Most High God, and He could refuse them nothing.
He would have spared Sodom if ten just men could
have been found within it, and it may be that even
fewer would have sufficed to avert its doom if he who
was the 'friend of God' had ventured to ask Him.
And this was before 'the goodness and kindness of
God our Saviour' had 'appeared,' and human nature
had been assumed by the Person of the Word.

Anna Maria, however, knew well, through the revelations made to her, that days of great and terrible
persecution were impending over the Church, and often
spoke on this subject to D. Raffaele. Numbers of persons who had previously been held in high esteem
would, she said, be unmasked and appear in their real
characters during those unhappy days. It would seem
that it was also signified to her that pride was to be
the cause of these defections and apostasies; for when
she begged the Lord to tell her who were they who
should be able to stand firm and resist in this time of
trial, He replied, 'They to whom I shall grant the
spirit of humility.' It was in consequence of this revelation that Anna Maria established in her family the
custom of saying every evening, after the Rosary, three

Paters, Aves, and Glorias to the Blessed Trinity to obtain from the mercy and goodness of God that He would mitigate the scourges with which the world was threatened. God also revealed to her that the Church, after passing through many trials, would obtain a triumph so splendid, that men would be struck with amazement; entire nations would return to the unity of the Church; and the whole face of the earth would be changed.*

Although this holy woman abstained from ever passing a word of censure on superiors, and especially ecclesiastical superiors, and discouraged any such observations in her presence, yet she beheld clearly in her sun the sins, abuses, relaxations, and shortcomings of every class; and zeal for the house of God may be said to have consumed her. The sanctification of all orders of the clergy had the first place in her prayers, as these ministers of the altar also held the first place in her heart. At the time of the Church's deepest affliction, during the captivity of Pius VII., while praying that the enemies of God might be humbled by His all-powerful arm, she would add the most fervent supplications that when the Vicar of Christ should be restored to Rome, the cardinals, bishops, and other ecclesiastics might be filled with the Spirit of God, and that the religious orders, when reëstablished, might edify all by the strict observance of

---

* Anna Maria's prophecies concerning events yet future, although registered in the Processes, have, from obvious motives of discretion, not been published on authority in any detail. Many of them have become commonly known, however, in whole or in part, in consequence of their being mentioned by persons who enjoyed her confidence, or who gathered them from the lips of those who had been thus favoured. We shall speak of these predictions in the following chapter.

their rule and by their holy lives. During the con-
claves she used to offer prayers and penances with
special devotion for the election of the new Pope;
and, moreover, she knew well on whom the election
would fall. Thus we learn that at the death of
Leo XII., while the Cardinals were in conclave, she
predicted that the new Pope would be elected in eight
days, and that the Pontificate of Pius VIII. would be
short. In like manner, she foresaw the choice of his
successor.

D. Raffaele gives the following account of a circumstance which took place some time before the
death of Pius VIII. ' I went,' he says, ' with the
servant of God to visit the Holy Crucifix at San Paolo
fuori le mura. The Cardinal Cappellari came on foot
from San Gregorio. Anna Maria was occupying the
only prie-dieu which the chapel contained. I tried, by
shaking her, to make her vacate it for the Cardinal;
but she was unconscious, and perceived nothing. The
good Cardinal signed to me to leave her in quiet, and
he knelt down at the balustrade. Anna Maria after a
while came out of her ecstatic slumber, gazed upwards
for a moment, and then fixed her eyes on the Cardinal.
On our way back to Rome, I asked her why she had
looked so long and earnestly at the Cardinal. As she
was bound by obedience to manifest everything to me,
she frankly said, "That is the future Pope." She then
described to me the allegorical signs which she had
remarked in her sun. She had seen a little dove, surrounded with golden rays, which rested upon him;
the bird was veiled with clouds, which indicated the
troubles of his Pontificate. At the time that Anna
Maria foretold the election of Cardinal Cappellari,
Pius VIII. was not very well in health; and she

forthwith redoubled the fervour of her prayers in his behalf. He died some months afterwards. The conclave having met, Anna Maria again beheld in the sun signs of the election of Cardinal Cappellari. She saw a little dove bearing a cross, another with the keys, and another carrying the tiara, while two more were drinking from a chalice which had the arms of the Camalduli engraven upon it. Cardinal Cappellari always showed me much kindness; he used to offer me snuff out of his box, as well as to Mgr. Barberini; a practice which originated in a witty remark made to him by the latter in the antichamber of Leo XII. at the time of his elevation to the Cardinalate; he then declared that Mgr. Barberini and myself should always have a pinch out of his snuff-box. I met him at Santa Maria della Vittoria a little while before he entered the conclave, and he called me to take my snuff; as I took it I said, " I should not like this to be the last time; but who would venture to put his hand into the Pope's snuff-box ?" He smilingly answered, " Nay, I have no thoughts of that," and stepped into his carriage.

'The conclave had lasted many days, when, in consequence of what Anna Maria had told me, I repaired to one of the *ruote*,* at which Mgr. Spada presided, and asked for Cardinal Barberini. After making inquiries concerning his health, and whether there was anything he needed, I said, "Take seventeen or eighteen pinches of snuff from our friend's box, and tell him from me that I shall not be able to have any more." This

---

* The 'ruote,' or 'tambours' (as the French call them), are the apertures by which alone the Cardinals in conclave are allowed to communicate with persons outside, and by which letters and the like are passed in to them   They are carefully guarded within and without, and are open only at certain hours of the day.

was clearly to foretell the Papacy. Cardinal Barberini did as I had said; he took seventeen pinches out of Cardinal Cappellari's box, but, as he could not make use of them all, he kept throwing them on the ground The Cardinal, surprised at this, said, "What are you about? You are throwing away my snuff." "I will tell you later," replied Cardinal Barberini; and he continued to count out his seventeen pinches. Cappellari smiled at the message I had sent him through Cardinal Barberini. In fact, he was elected seventeen or eighteen days afterwards. The doors having been opened, he saw me standing in the great hall with the ambassador of Portugal, and cast a significant glance at me; later I went to pay my homage to him along with my colleagues, the Pontifical chaplains; he bade me remain after the others, and offered me some snuff, which he continued to do whenever I attended his audiences. After Anna Maria's death I caused a lithographed portrait of her to be presented to him through his first Ajutante di Camera, the Cavaliere Gaetano Morini, and acquainted him with the whole of the above-mentioned prophecy relating to his august person, as it had been communicated to me by the Servant of God.'

CHAPTER XIX.

PROPHECIES CONCERNING PIUS IX. AND HIS REIGN.

ANNA MARIA survived the election of Gregory XVI. only six years; dying in 1837, nine years before Pius IX. was chosen to fill the See of Peter. She had seen, however, all the events of his Pontificate in the myste-

rious sun, but for the present these details, though
recorded in the Processes, are not given to the public;
it becomes necessary, therefore, to test the evidence of
those which are currently reported. Subjected to this
test, many of them will be found to rest upon satisfactory authority. We shall devote this chapter to
recording what has transpired of most interest concerning this, to us, the most interesting portion of her prophecies, limiting ourselves to those which can be referred with most certainty to the Venerable Servant of
God.*

Mgr. Luquet gives the following particulars as communicated to him, during the early days of the reign
of Pius IX., by an estimable priest† in whom Anna
Maria had the greatest confidence, and who also attested the same in writing. ‘She spoke,’ says Mgr.
Luquet, ‘one day to this same priest of the persecution
which the Church was to undergo. She foretold what
impious men would do at Rome, as we have unhappily
seen verified; and she particularised what he who conducted the bark of Peter would then have to suffer.‡
Wishing to know who this Pontiff would be, the priest
asked her if he was then among the Cardinals; she
replied that he was not, but that he was a humble
priest not at that time in the Pontifical States, but in
a very distant country. And, in fact, the Abate Mastai
was a simple priest attached at that period to the
Nunciatura in Chili. Anna Maria described the future
Pontiff: she said that he would be elected in an extraordinary manner; that he would introduce reforms;

* Others which are respectably attested, but which we have
not been ourselves able to verify, will be found in the Appendix.
† Unquestionably Mgr. Natali.
‡ Mgr. Luquet alludes to the troubles of 1848-9.

that, if men were grateful for them, the Lord would
load them with blessings; but that, if they abused
them, His all-powerful arm would inflict heavy chastisements upon them. She said that this Pontiff, chosen
according to the Heart of God, would be assisted by
Him with very special lights; that his name would be
famous throughout the world, and applauded by the
people; that the Turk himself would venerate him, and
send to compliment him. She said that he was the
holy Pontiff destined to bear the rage of the tempest
which was to be let loose against the bark of Peter;
that the arm of God would sustain him, and defend
him against the impious, who should be humbled and
confounded; that in the end he would have the gift of
miracles,* and that the Church, after painful vicissi-

---

* A confirmation of the truth of this prophecy is confidently
believed to have taken place some years ago. P. Calixte quotes
an account of it from a letter received from Rome and inserted
in one of the French leading religious journals, the substance
of which is as follows. The Princess Odescalchi, who was distinguished for her piety and good works, had been keeping her
bed for eight months, afflicted with a cancerous disease which
placed her in danger of death. She was every day getting worse,
and for about three weeks had been almost unable to swallow,
so that it was a question whether it would be possible to administer to her the Holy Viaticum. On Wednesday, the 15th of
February, the Holy Father sent her by Mgr. Franchi his blessing *in articulo mortis.* He also sent his own physician the
Doctor Viale Prela, in order to have the earliest and most accurate information of her state. She had no sooner received
the Holy Father's blessing than she was able to take a cup of
broth; two days passed, and on the Saturday she again relapsed
into danger of immediate death, which was expected every moment. The princess then received for the second time the
Pope's blessing; and on the following day two carriages of
the house of Odescalchi drew up at the Vatican, and it was
announced to the Holy Father that the princess had arrived to
receive his benediction. It would be impossible to describe the
surprise of all present when they saw her alight from her car-

tudes, would obtain so glorious a triumph, that the world would be astounded.' So far Mgr. Luquet, writing above twenty years ago.

We have already referred, on the authority of extracts from the Processes, to the signal triumph which she predicted would follow the persecutions of the Church. Cardinal Pedicini records a divine communication on this subject which the servant of God received, but, as quoted in the *Analecta*,* many gaps have been left unfilled. She was at the time praying fervently and shedding abundant tears, offering her pains and sufferings for the conversion of sinners, that sin might be banished from the world, and God become known and loved. 'The Lord,' he writes, 'was pleased to

---

riage and kneel down to receive the Papal benediction, which the Pope bestowed from one of the windows of his palace. Her recovery was complete.

Early in June 1871, Rome was to witness a prodigy connected with the circumstance we have related. The grateful princess had built a hospice attached to the Trinitarian Convent of San Crisogono in Trastevere, in memory of her cure, and had placed an image of our Lady over the door, on either side the B John Baptist of the Conception, a Trinitarian, whom she had invoked, and Pius IX., who sent her his blessing, were represented in the attitude of prayer. The people called this image the Madonna del Papa. One day a poor mother whose son had been carried off for the conscription, coming out of the church, cast her eyes on Mary and exclaimed, 'O Mother most powerful, when wilt thou deliver us from these robbers, who tear away our children to pervert them?' Immediately she uttered a loud cry and cast herself on her knees. Those who were passing by, attracted to the spot, saw the same marvel which she had witnessed. The Madonna del Papa was alternately opening and closing her eyes Many times the police endeavoured to disperse the crowd, who were continually gathering in front of it, and removed the lights which they brought and always perseveringly replaced. At last the Fathers took the precaution of removing the image into their convent.

* Vol. iv part i. p. 401.

manifest to her the dreadful sins of persons of all classes, and how highly He was offended by them. At this sight she felt a poignant sorrow, and said, sighing, " O my Beloved, how can so great a disaster be remedied ?" Then it was said to her in reply, " My daughter, My spouse, My Father and I will remedy all. After the chastisement . . . the survivors will act thus." . . . .' This omission is naturally supplied by what is elsewhere asserted, that she saw crowds of heretics returning to the bosom of the Church, and beheld their edifying behaviour as well as that of all the faithful. It will be seen that the nature of the chastisement which is to precede this happy time is not specified, at least in so much of the revelation as it has been considered fitting for the present to lay before the public. All will be fully known when the cause has proceeded to its completion, and the honours of beatification have been awarded to her whom our holy Pontiff has already declared Venerable. But, although the nature of the judgment and punishment which she foretold was to overtake the persecutors and oppressors of the Church is not precisely defined in any authoritative document, yet private individuals have spoken of it, and, in particular, one whose testimony is unquestionable, namely, her confidant, D. Raffaele Natali, to whom, under obedience, she made known all her revelations, and who God willed should survive her so many years. This scourge, he told many persons, was to be a supernatural darkness, which was to prevail for three days,* during which blessed candles would alone give light.

* The present writer is enabled to add the testimony of an Italian ecclesiastic, formerly parish priest of San Marcello, but now in England, who was personally acquainted with D. Raffaele Natali. The latter, he says, called upon him in order to

It will already have been observed, in the passages which we have quoted from the *Analecta*,* that during several consecutive days Anna Maria saw the world enveloped in a dense and awful darkness, accompanied by the falling of walls and timber, as if a great edifice were crumbling into fragments.   As, however, the servant of God saw many allegorical figures and representations in her sun, the question would still remain whether moral or physical darkness were signified. But if this vision be identical with the one mentioned by D. Raffaele, there is every reason for concluding that the latter is the correct reading of the prophecy. Her confidant must have had the best opportunities of knowing her mind and hearing her explanations, and, indeed, the mention of blessed candles alone giving light seems to show that the darkness foretold is to be real and sensible, not figurative.   We may consider it therefore as certain that Anna Maria foretold a judgment of three days' darkness, and that, not only because we have the testimony of persons to whom D. Raffaele confided the fact, but also because P. Calixte's Life of the servant of God, in which this prediction is confidently attributed to her, has (as he himself declares in connection with this subject) been carefully examined at Rome and pronounced to be the most exact and con-

---

ascertain from the register the date of Anna Maria Taigi's marriage, which had been misstated in Mgr. Luquet's Life.   This, he believes, was in 1863.   D. Raffaele confided to him at that time Anna Maria's prophecy concerning the three days' darkness, when only blessed candles would give light.   He told him, however, that she had assigned no date to this event, but had said that it would come to pass when every human hope for the persecuted Church shall have vanished.

* Supra, p. 239.   Comp. *Analecta Juris Pontificii*, vol. iv. part i. p. 717.

formable to the Apostolical processes of any hitherto
published.* This favourable judgment, one may naturally conclude, would certainly not have been expressed
had he ventured on an assertion not borne out by her
recorded and attested prophecies, which are reserved
under the seals of the Sacred Congregation of Rites.
We may add that P. Calixte's work was approved by
his own Superior, the General of the Trinitarians and
Postulator of her cause.

If, however, it might be deemed rash positively to
decide that the predicted darkness will be physical, it
would be something more than rash to ridicule the
idea of such an occurrence as being preposterous and
absurd. The very state of men's minds, so prone to
regard any intervention of God in His material creation
as a thing out of date, if not a species of impossibility,
renders it perhaps the more likely that God has reserved such a judgment as a lesson to the present sceptical generation. Some remarks to this effect made by
M. Amédée Nicolas, a French *avocat*, in a late publication,† appear to be much to the point. 'True it is,'
he says, 'that men everywhere laugh at the idea of
such an event occurring, and regard it as a dream : so
they laughed about the deluge during the hundred
years that Noe was employed in constructing the ark.
As for me, I do not affirm that the darkness foretold
will be physical darkness ; but it does seem to me that

* 'Nous pourrions nous contenter de répondre que notre
seconde édition, qui déjà les [ténèbres et autres événements
extraordinaires] citait, a été examinée attentivement à Rome,
et trouvée conforme en tout aux procès Apostoliques, plus com-
plète et plus exacte que nulle autre des Vies de la Vénérable
données jusqu'à ce jour au public.' (3me éd. note, p. 239.)

† *Les Prédictions Modernes devant un Savant Théologien*,
p. 92. Marseilles, 1871.

the subject is sufficiently serious for men to abstain
from scoffing at it; and both history and Scripture
prophecy, as well as the state of minds at the present
epoch, may well justify apprehensions on this subject.
Seeing that three days of physical darkness occurred in
Egypt, it follows that we may have the same again in
our time; for if a thing has once been, we must conclude that it can be.   The Apocalypse, at the opening
of the sixth seal, seems to me to predict darkness,
when it says* that suddenly there shall be a great
earthquake, and that "the sun shall become black as
sackcloth of hair;" and if we have arrived at this
period in the duration of the world, how shall we be
able to see when the sun gives no light?' (We shall be
in darkness.)   'The errors and corruption of men are
at the present time deeper than were those of Egypt in
Pharaoh's days; atheism and materialism reign supreme
among the masses.   An event patently divine is needed,
in order that people should return to a belief in the
existence of God and of the spiritual world.   Now this
darkness would be an irrefragable proof, to which
there could be no reply; and therefore it is more
opportune and more necessary than was that of Egypt.
The same 6th chapter of the Apocalypse, renewing a
prediction already uttered by the prophet Isaias,†
announces that "the kings of the earth, and the princes,
and tribunes, and the rich, and the strong, and every
bondman, and every freeman" shall be seized with such
dread on witnessing this cataclysm of nature, that they
will hide themselves "in the dens and in the rocks of
mountains," and say to the mountains and the rocks,
"Fall upon us, and hide us from the face of Him that

* vi. 12.   † ii. 21.

sitteth upon the throne, and from the wrath of the
Lamb ; for the great day of their wrath is come, and
who shall be able to stand?"* This horrible scene
does not belong to the convulsions at the end of
the world, for it is followed by a great religious renewal; it does not refer to the judgment of the dead,
but to a sort of judgment of the living, which may be
signified by those words of David :† "*Judicabit in
nationibus, implebit ruinas.*" And what fact could
occur which would strike such great terror? The
darkness which some fear and others turn into derision,
would it not be well calculated to produce it? And if
its result should be the conversion of the world to Jesus
Christ, would it not be a great blessing for our human
race, so widely gone astray, and ought it not to be
desired and earnestly begged of God by those who
desire that His Name should be hallowed, His kingdom come, and His will be done on earth as it is in
heaven?'

But whatever may be the precise nature of the
judgment impending over a guilty world which Anna
Maria and many other holy souls, not only in modern
times but in past ages have combined to predict, one
thing seems to be unquestionable, that it will be both
sudden and terrible, and such as shall force men to
confess the power and hand of the Almighty. Our
Holy Father himself very recently used some remarkable expressions with reference to the future triumph
of the Church and the nature of the Divine intervention in her behalf which we have reason to expect. It
is contained in a letter which he addressed on the 6th
of February, 1863, to the Director of the *Unità Catto-*

* vi. 15-17.   † Ps. cix. 6.

*lica,** then engaged in collecting an offering for his
Holiness on occasion of the late centenary of St. Gregory VII. After speaking of the successful vindication
of the Church's usurped rights by that holy Pontiff,
although he himself breathed forth his soul in exile,
and alluding to the still fiercer battle now being waged,
not against certain of the rights of the Church alone,
but against her very authority and constitution, nay,
against the Catholic religion itself, and that, not by
one prince alone, but by well-nigh all the powerful of
the earth, the Holy Father proceeds to say, ' Seeing
that we know for certain that the gates of Hell shall
not prevail against the Church, these many and great
difficulties ought not to depress the mind of him who
considers them, but ought to animate him to greater
hope.   For, relying on the incontrovertible oracle of
God, the very atrocity of a war so vast and manifold,
waged by Divine permission against the Church, is
sufficient to convince the believer that such a triumph
is prepared for her as for fulness and splendour shall
surpass all that have preceded.   And whereas God in
lighter and less perilous struggles prepared for her an
efficient aid in the arms of princes, or in the marvellous energy and authority of holy persons, and whereas in the present far greater trial He withholds all succour, this again proves that He has reserved to Himself
the victory over His enemies.   And this will be more
manifest if we consider that the root of present evils is
chiefly to be found in this,—that men, having turned
themselves with their whole mind and strength to
earthly things, not only have forsaken God, but have
altogether rejected Him, in such wise that it would
seem that they could in no other way be recalled

* See the number for the 15th of March, 1873, pp. 739-40.

to Him save by *some fact which cannot easily be attributed to a second cause,* but is of such a nature as to constrain every one to look up and exclaim, " This is the work of God, and it is marvellous in our eyes." '

The Pope expressed himself in similar terms to an Eastern prelate who, writing to the Bishop of Angoulême, thus described what passed :—' The Holy Father said to me, " The world is immersed in evil ; it cannot thus continue ; a human hand is powerless to save it, the hand of God must manifest itself visibly, and, I tell you, we shall see this divine hand with our bodily eyes." These words he pronounced with an air of inspiration, raising his two fore-fingers significantly to his eyes as he spoke.'*

As a peculiar interest attaches to all the utterances of Pius IX., especially with reference to the present crisis, we record the following words, pronounced by him in public on the 16th July, 1871, and addressed to the Collectors of the Archconfraternity of St. Peter : —' There was a good old priest,' said the Holy Father, ' Mgr. D. Raffaele Natali, a zealous promoter of the cause of the Venerable Anna Maria Taigi, who related to us mavellous things of this servant of the Lord and, amongst others, various predictions regarding these present times. We do not place too much reliance upon reported prophecies ; these, however, are recorded in the Processes, and the Holy See will judge of them. We have not read them, but this good priest repeated several times that the Venerable, foretelling the trials we now behold, said that a time would come during which the Holy See would be obliged to live upon the alms of the entire world ; but that the money would

* See *Le Grand Pape et le Grand Roi,* p. 153.

never be wanting. Truly,' added the Holy Father, 'it would be difficult not to recognise the accuracy of such a prediction.'*

Anna Maria never declared the precise time at which the impending judgment was to take place, although we may be led to infer that the period is not far distant, on account of its connection with other events which she foretold, and of which we seem to be now beholding the progressive fulfilment; viz. the violent persecution of the Church and the despoilment of the Vicar of Christ, a despoilment which, she said, would be so complete that 'the Pope, shut up in the Vatican, would find himself hemmed in as by an iron circle.' All human hope, she added, would have failed, and it would be then that God would cause His mercy suddenly to shine forth.   The same conclusion may be drawn, as we have said, from the prophecies of other holy persons who have enjoyed the possession of super-natural lights in our times; and they have been far more numerous than is commonly imagined. Amongst these was P. Bernardo Clausi, a Religious of the Order of the Minims, who often foretold the coming of a ter-rible judgment on the wicked and the subsequent glo-rious triumph of the Church, and who always spoke of it as near at hand.   He told Sister Maria Margherita Laudi, a Religious of San Filippo and his penitent, who has now attained her eighty-third year and who will appear, or, more probably, has already appeared, to make her deposition as a witness in the process for

* *Discorsi del S. Pontifice Pio IX.* p. 194, Roma, 1872.

St. Hildegarde, at the close of the twelfth century, prophesy-ing the fall of the Holy Roman Empire, a prediction the accom-plishment of which was witnessed at the beginning of the nine-teenth, also foretold the successive dismemberment of the pa-trimony of St. Peter.

Y

the introduction of his cause, that she would behold
the coming chastisement which he himself would not
live to see, and also the general reorganisation and triumph of the Church which were to follow. 'Blessed,'
he added, 'are they who will live in those happy days,
for it will be a reign of true fraternal charity. The joy
you will feel will be so great that it will cause you to
forget all past sufferings. But before these things come
to pass, evil will have made such progress in the world
that it will seem as if all the devils had issued from
hell, so great will be the persecution raised by the
wicked against the just, who will have to endure a
very martyrdom.' He also told her that the scourge
which God would bring upon the earth would be something new and unparalleled, and directed solely against
the wicked. 'Heaven and earth,' he said, 'will be
united, and great sinners will be converted, because
they will then know God. This scourge will be felt
throughout the world, and will be so terrible that survivors will imagine they are the only persons spared.
All will be good and penitent.' He spoke in a similar
manner to others, who have also attested the same on
oath, saying that when things are come to the worst,
and when all will seem lost, then God will set to His
hand and rectify all, as it were, in the twinkling of an
eye, so that the impious themselves will be constrained
to confess that it is the work of God. If persons of so
advanced an age as this nun are indeed to behold these
things, it must be concluded that the time is not far
removed.*

If the very general hope entertained by the faithful,

* The Italian priest already mentioned was intimately acquainted with P. Clausi, and often heard the same predictions
from his lips.

and amounting almost to an expectation, that Pius IX. will witness the beginning of the Church's triumph be well grounded, this again would give us reason to expect this terrible event very shortly, for a well-attested prophecy of Anna Maria's, which has perhaps become more generally known than that of the days of darkness, assigned to Pius IX. a reign of twenty-seven years, and something more. It is also very confidently asserted, and the assertion certainly seems to rest on good authority, that she declared that Pius IX. would witness the beginning of the Church's triumph. If, then, this 'something more' signify but a portion of another year, then, indeed, brief would be the time remaining which separates us from this awful judgment and the subsequent triumph. Prophecies, however, are not designed for the purpose of satisfying curiosity, even though it may be a holy curiosity, but for higher ends, and purposes more profitable to our souls. At present, however, the predictions of this favoured soul concerning events yet future — predictions to which naturally much importance is attached owing to the fulfilment of so many that she uttered concerning events now past—have reached us but in fragments, those fragments also having been only orally transmitted. But, supposing it to be proved beyond a doubt that she promised that Pius IX. should witness the beginning of the Church's triumph, it would still be impossible for us to decide in what sense the promise is be understood. It is well, therefore, while sharing the general hope and, above all, while joining in the fervent prayers which the whole Church is unceasingly offering to God for his deliverance, not to be led away to entertain a conviction which might only prepare for us a sharp disappointment, a disappoint-

ment which would result, not from the failure of the
prophecy itself, but from our own premature and rash
interpretations.

Leaving, then, this deeply interesting question for
the future to decide, we are perhaps not wrong in concluding that the close of the reign of Pius IX. is at
least closely connected with the period of the predicted
deliverance. P. Calixte, writing evidently some time
in the latter half of the year 1870, and considering as
he does that Anna Maria's prophecies imply that he
will witness the commencement of the triumph, observes, 'We may therefore conclude that the present
uneasy state of things will yet last nearly three years;
and it is precisely during a period of three years that
the secret of La Salette, now partially disclosed, averred
that God would seem to have forgotten France the born
' protectress of the Holy See.' These three years are
now approaching their completion. 'Marie Lataste on
her part,' continues P. Calixte, 'speaking of Rome, declared that the Saviour Himself said to her, "Oppres-
sion will reign in the city that I love, and where I
have left my Heart. It will seem to succumb during
three years and a little longer." It would appear,
then,' adds P. Calixte, 'that we must date the beginning of this trial from the entrance of the Piedmontese
into Rome.' Marie Lataste also declared that our Lord,
after announcing these three years of captivity to the
city of Rome, during which time she was to be 'in
sadness and desolation, surrounded on all sides like a
bird taken in a net,' said, 'But my Mother shall descend into the city; she will take the hands of the old
man seated on a throne, and will say to him, "Behold
the hour, arise, look at thy enemies: I cause them to
disappear one after another, and they disappear for

ever. Thou hast rendered glory to me in heaven and
upon earth, and I will render glory to thee on earth
and in heaven.* Look at men—how they venerate thy
name, thy courage, thy power. Thou shalt live, and I
will abide with thee. Old man, dry thy tears ; I bless
thee."' These are doubtless encouraging words, but
they cannot be said to specify with unmistakable
clearness the nature of the glory which Pius IX. is to
receive in this world. Heaven has a different measure
from that of earth. Yet one thing we know. If God
has His absolute decrees, which not even saints can
move Him to reverse, all that He has revealed to us in
Scripture, and all that the testimony of such chosen
souls as that of Anna Maria makes known to us, of
His adorable goodness and His readiness to hearken to
prayer, serve to prove that He can be turned from His
conditional purposes, and that He will prolong seasons
of grace or of life at the cry of His children. To Pius
IX. has been promised a reign of twenty-seven years,
and something more. He has now completed the
twenty-seven years. The *more* remains. What that
more imports Anna Maria did not say. Perhaps its
length, which is thus left indefinite, may depend upon
our own fervent and united prayers.

In respect to the great calamities which Anna Maria
announced as impending over mankind, as well as the
splendid triumph which will follow for the Pope and

---

* The glory to which Mary here alludes as having been procured for her by Pius IX. was the definition of the Immaculate
Conception, which Marie Lataste foretold, as did also Anna
Maria, and, before her, St. Leonard of Port Maurice. The *Life
and Writings* of Marie Lataste have been before the public ever
since the year 1862. In the year 1844 she entered as lay-sister
a convent of the Sacré Cœur, and died before attaining her
twenty-sixth year.

the Church, together with the renovation of the entire
world, one may say that such is the general object and
the common end of all the prophecies, whether ancient
or modern, which bear upon these latter times. Each
seer, it is true, has added or dwelt more at large on some
special circumstances, but they all agree in two leading
features. First, they all point to some terrible convul-
sion, to a revolution springing from the most deep-rooted
impiety, consisting in formal opposition to God and His
truth, and resulting in the most formidable persecution
to which the Church has ever been subjected; and,
secondly, they all promise for this same Church a victory more splendid and complete than she has ever
achieved here below. We may add another point upon
which there is a remarkable agreement in the catena of
modern prophecies, and that is the peculiar connection
between the fortunes of France and those of the Church
and the Holy See, as also the large part which that country has still to play in the history of the Church and of
the world, and will continue to play to the end of time.
Pius IX., indeed, is reported to have addressed these
encouraging words to the Bishop of Poitiers, when
speaking of the calamities which the French were enduring:—'Let them console themselves, and hope in
the midst of their terrible trials, for France shall not
perish. God has great designs in her regard, and she
will be more than ever the firm support of the Church.'
And Mgr. Dreux Brézé, Bishop of Moulins, in an allo-
cution which he delivered after his return to his diocese,
declared that the Holy Father had said to him, 'No,
no, France will not perish; if France were to perish, it
would be a sign that those evil days which are to precede the end of time had arrived.'

The Revolution first attacked France, which we

have seen bruised and lacerated by its fangs, and from thence it has extended, and has yet to extend, its ravages to other lands, but everything leads us to expect renovation to spring from the same quarter whence the evil arose. 'France,' says P. Calixte, 'the first to be punished for her excesses, will also be the first to arise, by a sudden and, as it were, miraculous restoration under a wise and good monarch. She will then aid the other nations to stifle in their bosoms that revolution which they have received from her.' These anticipations may be said to express the hopes and confident expectation of Catholics, as they are also supported by the general voice of modern prophecy reckoning from the first formation of Christendom.'

We need scarcely add that in recording any as yet unfulfilled prophecies either of Anna Maria Taigi or of others, however well attested, we are not presuming to pass any confident judgment respecting them. We know that the gift of prophecy, like the gift of miracles, is possessed by the Church of God, but, apart from and previous to any pronouncement of the Holy See, we have no title to do more than express with all submission an opinion in regard to any particular prophecy as in regard also to any alleged miracle. One of the errors of which we are specially bound to beware, is that of fixing the precise time for the accomplishment of this or that prediction. 'Many of the faithful,' says P. Curicque, 'strike upon this rock of dates;' and he proceeds to quote a very apposite remark of the Curé de Malétable (who is said himself to have received supernatural lights). 'We must be very reserved,' says the Curé, 'in our applications and, above all, in fixing epochs. I have myself often been deceived by judging of things after the manner in which we commonly judge

of the distance of objects which we view against the
horizon.   If, for instance, you look at several summits
of mountains in the same direction, you may perhaps
be able to calculate with tolerable accuracy the distance
which separates you from the nearest, but, as the wide
valleys which are on the opposite side are hidden from
your sight, you readily believe, and are often mistaken
in this belief, that the second peak is very near the
first; nay, you sometimes fancy that both rest on the
same base.   He for whom the Lord vouchsafes to lift
up a little the veil which conceals the future, is liable
to fall into this error when the epoch of certain future
events remains concealed : he judges that these latter
facts follow close upon their precursors, and this often
is not the case.'   'If the seer himself may thus be deceived,' adds P. Curicque, 'what of us short-sighted
ones ?'   Precipitation in fixing the date for the fulfilment of prophecies is the parent of subsequent incre-
dulity.   Persons who have suffered this disappointment
come to despise all prophecy save that which they are
bound by faith to believe, as being contained in the inspired record.   But surely this attitude of mind is an
unfortunate one, to say the least.   One who thus puts
aside almost with contempt all modern prophecy suffers
a loss, since assuredly, if God has bestowed this gift
upon His Church, it was intended for our consolation,
encouragement, and support, as well as to maintain fresh
in our minds what is so easily lost, the remembrance
that we have no abiding-place amongst these gross,
material, and transitory things which go to build up
our present earthly state, but that we seek 'a city which
hath foundations, whose builder and maker is God,'
looking for the setting up of that spiritual kingdom
which shall finally break in pieces and supplant all the

empires of the world. 'Despise not prophecies,' says the Apostle;* 'but prove all things: hold fast that which is good.' In these few words we have both a command and a caution, summing up all that we need for our direction and guidance.

CHAPTER XX.

ANNA MARIA'S GIFT OF HEALING.

WE have more than once alluded to the gift of healing which Anna Maria had received from our Lord. This power was communicated to her in a vision not long after her conversion, at the time she inhabited the house in the little Strada Sdrucciolo, near the Chigi palace. We possess the account put on accord by Cardinal Pedicini, to whom she frequently related all the particulars. She was seriously ill at the time, and during one night great fears were entertained of her life, when, towards the dawn of day, the Lord Jesus appeared to her. His demeanour, as she described it, was that of affectionate confidence. He was arrayed in a violet-coloured garment, over which He wore a magnificent blue mantle, the wide folds of which He spread over her bed. 'She told me,' says the Cardinal, 'that His beauty and grace were marvellous to behold. He took her hand, and kept it pressed closely in His own, while He held a long conversation with her. It was then that He told her that He chose her for His spouse, and that He communicated to her the gift of

* Thess. v. 20, 21.

healing the sick by the touch of that hand which He
held clasped in His own. He also cured her instantaneously of all her own maladies.' So intense had
been the joy of that interview that, when Jesus left
her, she felt a pang of sorrow so poignant that it extracted from her a loud cry of anguish, which was heard
all over the house and speedily brought all the terrified
inmates to her bedside. She reassured them as best
she might, for she did not tell them of the vision, saying only that she was perfectly cured ; and, in fact,
shortly afterwards she arose as usual, and went to Communion at the Madonna della Pietà, no vestige remaining of her late illness.

The witnesses who made their depositions in the
canonical process testified to a very great number of
miraculous cures which had been wrought by her and
duly attested. Cardinal Pedicini alone had taken notes
of hundreds of which he had cognisance at the time they
were performed ; and thousands more, he added, have
never been recorded. Indeed amongst the different
supernatural gifts which she received there seems to
have been none which she more liberally used for the
benefit of her neighbour. We have seen her exert it
even in favour of animals. The greater number of her
cures were operated during the first years which followed her conversion, when, as we have related, her
services were continually requested in behalf of the
sick ; and it may be added that, in devoting so much of
her time to this external work of charity, she acted in
strict obedience to her confessor. Her miraculous cures,
however, were not all performed by the immediate touch
of her hand ; commonly, when called to the bedside of
sick persons, she used to invoke the Blessed Trinity,
then make the sign of the Cross devoutly over them,

and give them her little image of the Blessed Virgin to kiss. Several cases are recorded of her having healed persons afflicted with that most dreadful of all maladies, cancer, which may be regarded as well-nigh incurable by human remedies; the means she commonly employed being the application of oil from the lamp which she kept ever burning before her Madonna. One of these cases was that of a gentlewoman belonging to the house of Albani, who could not resolve to submit to a medical examination. Her confessor went to beg Anna Maria's assistance, who gave him some of the said oil, at the same time bidding him exhort the sufferer to have faith. Its application removed the tumour that very night without the least pain. In the first fervour of her gratitude the gentlewoman expressed a strong desire to be made personally acquainted with her benefactress, and engaged to furnish as long as she lived the oil for her Madonna's lamp. As time went on, however, she failed to keep her promise, and God punished her avarice by sending her various troubles and maladies, which entailed great expenses upon her. Mother Doria, of the Convent of S. Domenico e Sisto, from similar motives of modesty had concealed at its commencement the same terrible disease with which she was afflicted. Growing worse, she sent for the servant of God, and disclosed to her the nature of her malady; adding, 'You must set about curing me; I will not permit any doctor to examine me, and no one must know of my complaint.' It had now become extremely serious, for a wound had already formed. 'My mother,' replied Anna Maria, 'you apply to a very bad person; I am quite frightened at your speaking in this way. Do not you know that I am a poor sinner?' 'No matter,' rejoined the nun, 'you must cure me. I feel myself

moved to ask this.' Then Anna Maria bade her make
the sign of the cross with the oil of her Madonna which
she brought her, and the cancer disappeared miraculously. Another Religious of the Convent of the Bambin
Gesù was to have an operation performed for the removal
of a cancer. Anna Maria's prayers were requested. She
replied, ' If the Religious has a great deal of faith the
operation will not take place, but confidence is needed.'
Unfortunately the nun as yet had very little. Her confessor laboured to inspire her with the requisite sentiments, in which, if he was not entirely successful, the
firm faith of the servant of God and the ardent charity
of her prayers supplied what was deficient, for again
the Madonna's oil worked a perfect and instantaneous
cure. One day, as the Cardinal tells us, when Anna
Maria was on her way to confession, she was surprised
by a heavy shower of rain, and called at the house of
an acquaintance to borrow an umbrella. The mistress,
before fetching one, said, ' We have some one dying
here.' The sick person was, in fact, at that very moment about to breathe her last; she had received Extreme Unction, and the priest's stole was laid on the
bed. Anna Maria, entering the room, placed her hand
upon the head of the dying woman, and made the sign
of the cross, invoking the Most Holy Trinity. ' Be at
peace,' she then said; ' the grace is granted;' and went
her way. Some hours passed, and then the woman
spoke, partook of some food, and arose in perfect health.
Visiting one day a youth afflicted from his childhood
with the falling-sickness, and suffering at that moment
from an attack, she simply bade him animate his faith
and arise. He arose, and his cure was perfect and lasting. Thus, like her Divine Lord, from whom she had
received this miraculous gift, she healed the sick some-

times merely by laying her hand upon them, sometimes by virtue of an application coupled with an exhortation to faith.

Cardinal Barberini and Maria Luisa, the Queen of Etruria, were both indebted to Anna Maria for an unexpected restoration to health. The former, to whose illness we have already alluded, was in a very dangerous state, and the doctors with good reason feared a fatal termination. Anna Maria knew the peril he was in with a higher kind of certainty, for she read it in her sun, and moreover saw that this prelate's death had been decreed in the counsels of God. The decree, however, as the result proved, was conditional, not absolute. He would have died had not Anna Maria prayed for him, and prayed perseveringly. Far from being discouraged, she besieged the throne of grace night and day, although the only answer she received for some time was that all must submit themselves to the will of God. But her faith was to triumph, as heretofore that of the Syrophenician, when similarly tried and apparently repulsed by our Blessed Lord. Anna Maria insisted, and obtained her request. But, before granting it, God told her that this cure would not be attributed to her, but to the physicians and to the prayers of other persons. She replied that she was well content to remain unknown to creatures, only she implored the Divine Goodness to heal the sick man. All hope of the Cardinal's life had been abandoned, when an unlooked-for crisis took place; he rallied and recovered. Whatever others may have thought, there was one, as we have seen, who recognised Anna Maria's share in obtaining this favour, and that was the Cardinal's sister-in-law, the Princess of Palestrina, whose name appears among the witnesses in the process, and the

substance of whose deposition we have given elsewhere.
The queen's cure took place at the time when General
Miollis, then occupying Rome with the French Imperial
troops, had confined that princess in the Convent of S.
Domenico e Sisto along with her young family. Maria
Luisa was subject to occasional epileptic seizures, which
used to throw her into frightful convulsions. Accordingly, it was necessary to have her rooms doubly car-
peted, for she would suddenly fall to the ground, where
she would struggle and knock herself violently about,
howling fearfully and foaming at the mouth, until at
length she lay exhausted and as one dead, like the possessed youth in the Gospel. As it may be supposed,
no medical advice had been spared in the case of a
person of her rank. She had consulted Italian doctors,
she had consulted foreign doctors, and they had consulted each other. Every remedy which art could de-
vise had been adopted without success. The princess
was at this time going through one of these fearful
paroxysms. Anna Maria was sent for. She touched
her with her little Madonna, and assured her that she
would never more suffer from this frightful complaint.
The convulsions, in fact, entirely disappeared, and never
returned. It may readily be imagined how much this
miraculous cure, experienced in her own person, contributed to enhance the love and confidence with which
Maria Luisa regarded her holy benefactress.

Anna Maria worked several cures in her own family.
One of these was performed in the case of little Peppina, her grand-daughter,* and is thus related by Domenico, who was certainly neither enthusiastic nor
over-credulous. Indeed, while competent to observe

* Giuseppa Micali, the same who appeared among the witnesses in the Processes.

and accurately to report a fact, he seemed to have a certain strange incompetence to discern its supernatural character, however patent this might be, until it was pointed out by others. 'I remember,'. says this good man, 'that Peppina, Sofia's daughter, hurt her eye ; the surgeons said that the pupil was lacerated, and despaired of her cure, on account of the inflammation which must necessarily ensue, which besides endangered the sight of the other eye. The servant of God made the sign of the cross with the oil of St. Philomena, laid her hand upon the child's head, and sent her to bed. Peppina slept very well, without feeling any pain, and the next morning the eye was so thoroughly cured that she was able to go to school at the Maestre Pie of the Gesù. The surgeon could not believe it, and wished to make several experiments to ascertain if she could see. This miraculous cure, which was a radical one, took place in winter, when the rigour of the season would have rendered it more difficult.'

Another miracle of healing performed by Anna Maria in her own family was in the case of her husband. Domenico is again the narrator. 'I also recollect being taken very ill,' he says, 'in the Church of San Marcello. I had scarcely reached home when I lost all consciousness, and they told me afterwards that it was (God preserve us from the same) an apoplectic seizure, not to say stroke, which I had. When I came to myself, with no recollection of what had occurred, I saw at my bedside the priest and my wife, who had laid her hand on my forehead, and was praying to the Blessed Virgin for me. It was a true miracle to get the better of such an attack without its leaving any bad result, especially in the head ; and I have no doubt but that the servant of God obtained for me this marvellous and instantaneous cure. I was told that the priest who perceived my pulse cease beating, had given me absolution.'

It must not be concluded, because Domenico, when giving his evidence, uses the word 'miracle' in both these cases, and although at the time he no doubt was persuaded that a great '*grazia*,' as the Italians say, had been obtained in answer to his wife's fervent prayers, that therefore he then realised the fact that his wife had a supernatural gift of healing, which she exercised on these occasions, or that she literally performed a miracle. On the contrary, his simple statement as to his enlightenment after her death, through the instrumentality of others, bespeaks his entire failure to discern while she lived the wonders which he was almost daily called to witness. He says, it is true, 'I believe that the servant of God was favoured with many supernatural gifts,' but he was expressing his acquired conviction upon a retrospect of the past, not that which he entertained at the time. Had he believed that she was the recipient of such exalted divine favours, how could he possibly, for instance, have remained so blind in the case of her raptures and ecstasies? With respect to these latter he makes this singular and candid avowal: 'As for the ecstasies, I never could much perceive them;' after which he proceeds nevertheless to describe the outward appearance they presented. No sooner, however, had Anna Maria expired, than he began to open his eyes. Many persons who had known her stopped him in the streets to inquire all the particulars of her death. 'Some,' he says, 'spoke of the special gifts she had received from God; others told of the graces they had obtained through her means; every one had some good to say of her, every one lauded her, regarding her as one who was replenished with merits and virtues; many went to visit her tomb in the cemetery of San Lorenzo notwithstanding the prevailing epidemic' (the cholera). 'As for me, I always esteemed her, and I say that the Lord took from me this good servant of His because I was not worthy to possess her. I repeat that I had always esteemed her as a soul of very high virtue, but I neither knew nor suspected a host of things which I have learned from one person or another since her death. I believe that the Lord placed her immediately on her decease in Paradise for her great goodness and eminent virtues, and I hope that she prays for me and for all her family.'

Thus it was that it pleased God that this plain and simple man should have his eyes kept from discerning the brightness of his wife's supernatural endowments, that he might be all the more impartial and unbiassed a witness to her perfect possession of those humble Christian virtues which, after all, and not her sublimer gifts, went to form the title of her heavenly crown and her claim to the veneration of the faithful on earth. No one can have the slightest ground for suspecting that his mental eye was dazzled or his judgment influenced in the estimate he formed of her character. Each word, each act of hers, he had viewed with the coolness with which we regard the ordinary behaviour of our friends and relatives: he had not seen her conduct in the light of her supposed sanctity, but had to learn her sanctity afterwards from the sum of her acts when she had run her course, and from the train of glory which she left behind.

CHAPTER XXI.

ANNA MARIA'S CLOSING DAYS AND DEATH.

ANNA MARIA walked all her days in what the author of the *Imitation of Christ* calls the royal road of the Cross. ' O my dear daughter,' Jesus said to her in a vision with which He one day favoured her, ' I am the flower of the fields ; I am all thine, as also in like manner I give Myself to all who courageously take up their cross and walk in My steps. The children of the Cross are My beloved ones, and their sufferings constrain Me to love them more and more. He who would win Heaven must lead here below a life of penance; he who would follow Me must suffer, and whosoever suffers is not subject to illusion, but advances securely in the way of salvation.' In this way Anna Maria never halted, and was advancing at an ever-accelerated pace during those declining years when a dispensation from rigour and a relaxation in the matter of mortification and penance seem so allowable. For she was now entered on that evening of life of which we say and think such sad things. Looking only at what is external, we see nothing in this unwelcome season but gradual decay, the failure of strength, the fading away of all that adorned and embellished life, the departure of pleasures and, what is generally still more bewailed, the loss of all power to relish the little that remains. Such are the outward accompaniments of advanced age : joy and sunshine left behind, ever-deepening shades gathering in front ; while in Anna Maria's case there was an accumulation of the most painful maladies incident to our mortal nature. But if such be the aspect presented to the eyes of flesh by suffering humanity, the eye of faith has other prospects, on which its gaze is ever fixed. For there is an inner man which is being renewed in everlasting youth day by day as the outward man decays.* He is walking in another region, which has other skies and is lighted by other suns. 'The path of the just,' says Solomon,† 'as a shining light, goeth forwards and increaseth even to perfect day.' Such was the path of the holy woman whose life we are now accompanying to its blessed close.

Besides the sun of grace, which illuminates the path of every true Christian, the brightness of which is proportioned to his own fidelity to its light, Anna Maria had her supernatural sun, the splendour of which, as we have said, increased with her own increasing perfection, till it attained a seven-fold lustre. Every day she beheld its brilliance become more dazzling, as does that of the orb of day when nearing its summer solstice —the same, but O, how different from the veiled luminary of the winter season ! How could this gifted soul pause or think of rest with such an horizon around her, illuminated by so divine a light? Walking in the still dearer presence of the invisible God and in close union of soul with her Beloved, Anna Maria pressed on, not knowing what it was to seek a dispensation from any pain or penance which her mortal frame could bear or which holy obedience would permit her to lay upon it. She hastened on towards the goal, never pausing or reposing, as if she had attained to perfection ; for, like the great Apostle,‡ she also counted not herself to have apprehended, but was ever following after to apprehend

---

* 'But though our outward man is corrupted, yet the inward man is renewed day by day.' 2 Cor. iv. 16.

† Prov. iv. 18.

‡ Phil. iii. 12, 13.

that wherein she had been apprehended by Christ Jesus, pressing forward to the prize of her supernal vocation.   No worthier object of ambition can there be for
any soul, none so worthy as this apprehending and perfect fulfilling of its vocation ; and, blessed be God, it
is attainable by all with the help of His grace, which
He gives liberally in proportion to the work allotted
by Him to each.   Anna Maria's vocation was indeed a
lofty and exceptional one, and for its accomplishment
she received immense graces, but she nobly and faith،
fully corresponded therewith.   Hers were the ten pounds
but she had so traded with those ten pounds as not only
to deserve more than those who have received a lesser
deposit, but proportionately more than do by far the
greater number, on account of her rare correspondence
to grace ; for such perfect correspondence to grace as
she exhibited is quite as rare, we may say, as were her
exceptional graces.   'Take the pound away from him,'
said the Lord in the parable, speaking of the slothful
and wicked servant, ' and give it to him that hath the
ten pounds.'   And they said to him, 'Lord, he hath
ten pounds.'   Then the Lord replied, 'But I say to
you, that to every one that hath shall be given, and he
shall abound; and from him that hath not, even that
which he hath shall be taken from him.'*   Memorable
words these.   Anna Maria, then, abounded ; poor, despoiled, and suffering externally, within she was overflowing with riches and with the joy which no man can
take away.   She abounded in grace, she was full of
merits, and she was now going home with joyfulness,
like the labourer described by the royal Psalmist,†
  carrying her sheaves.'
    Towards the close of her life the demonstrations of

----

* Luke xix. 24-26.   † cxxv. 7.

respect which she received became more marked than
ever. If it was a striking spectacle to witness the honour
paid to her by the great, the learned, and the noble, far
more touching was it to note the love and veneration
with which she was regarded by the poor. 'Anna
Maria la santa' was the name by which she was familiarly called by the common people, who have the true
instinct of real goodness, and when they are a Catholic
people are the first to recognise sanctity. It is the people who canonise by their devotion before the Church
canonises by her authoritative and infallible judgment.
Of these poor people, who besieged her in the streets,
the sick, the suffering, and the unfortunate formed a
large proportion. They thronged around her to beg
relief either for their spiritual or their temporal needs ;
often to tell her long stories about their domestic
troubles and to seek her advice ; even in church one
or another would approach her softly, and respectfully
whisper a request for her prayers.

As she grew in holiness, Anna Maria grew also in
her longing desire for solitude, silence, retirement, obscurity. She wished to be forgotten, to be alone with
her Beloved and with her sufferings, which were, one
might say, an integral portion of her love and were to
be its expression so long as she remained in the exile
of earth,—the bundle of myrrh which day and night
was to lie in her bosom. For the joy, be it remembered, was only in the supreme summit of her soul ; the
sensible joy never returned, save in temporary flashes,
from the day on which God accepted her sacrifice and
gave her the crown of thorns in the place of that of
roses. We are told, indeed, that the choice between
the thorny and the flowery path was once, as heretofore
to St. Catharine, made to her in vision, and, though

her answer is not recorded, we know with equal certainty what it must have been; for not only did Anna
Maria joyfully accept the cross, but it had been the
object of her most ardent aspirations and constant
prayers long before she obtained it. But though she
so ardently desired to be hidden from the eyes and the
very knowledge of the world, yet she never withheld
her hand from any work which charity towards her
neighbour demanded of her, any more than from her
household duties. These latter, indeed, continued to
receive from her an attention as close and assiduous as
is wont to be bestowed upon them by any good and
careful mother of a family, who knows of nothing
higher than the discharge of these humble duties; nay,
with far more, for, all with her being done for God, inferior motives never being allowed to inspire her simplest acts, all was done with a perfection to which mere
nature never attains. God, however, had hearkened to
the longing of her heart and designed to accord her a
season of concealment and seclusion before He took her
to Himself. The time was approaching when Anna
Maria was no more to be seen in streets and in churches;
she was to retire from the public view, which is all one
with being forgotten by the world at large; she was to
be nailed to a bed of suffering in the secrecy of her own
little chamber, for suffering was to be her close companion to the last. As usual, she was not left in ignorance of the Divine purpose, for God treated her as a
friend, not as a servant; the favour which, when on
earth, He promised to those who should do the things
which He commanded. 'I will not now call you servants,' said our Lord to His Apostles at that last supper
when He disclosed to them all the tenderness of His
Adorable Heart; 'for the servant knoweth not what his

Lord doth. But I have called you friends.'* He who thus abides in God's love by the keeping of His commandments shall never be taken by surprise, although few indeed may be those who have specific revelations such as were vouchsafed to Anna Maria.

On the 20th May, in the year·1836, she was on her way to San Paolo fuori le mura. This accustomed pilgrimage she was performing that day by the order of her confessor; the priest, her habitual companion, joining in it. As they walked along, she told him that this was the last time she should perform this devotion. We have seen how often her naked feet had trodden that path. Well did the Fathers at the Basilica know her, having so often beheld her, for years past, coming to kneel before the sacred image of the Crucified, and remaining rapt in ecstatic contemplation for hours together. They held her in high veneration, and as soon as they saw her approaching would at once hasten to uncover the Crucifix, which was ordinarily veiled. So great, indeed, was their persuasion of her sanctity that, when she died, these good Fathers were desirous of possessing her body; a boon, however, not reserved for them. After hearing Mass, which was said by Natali, and receiving Communion, she remained kneeling before the Holy Crucifix. Her heart was in a state of profound humility and great peace, the peace which Jesus left as His legacy. Presently she heard the voice of her Lord, who spoke these words to her :—' Live in peace, My daughter, and disquiet not thyself about what is exterior. Thou hast not spoken this thing at random. Farewell, My daughter; thou wilt see Me in Paradise; and for the act of obedience which thou hast this day performed, I have granted thee a grace, as also

* John xv. 15.

to thy companion; and before long you will both behold it. Yes, my daughter, I bid thee adieu; we will
converse together at thy house, and thou shalt be with
Me in My kingdom. Hasten to go whithersoever thou
willest, for anon all will be over.' In short, the time
was come when she was to be totally separated from
the world, and was no longer to be able to visit Jesus
in the Tabernacle, or in His holy images, which abound
in the Sacred City; but He would keep His loving
promise, and come to visit her in her own dwelling,
where she was to abide as the prisoner of His love,
drinking the dregs of that bitter chalice of which all
His great lovers have partaken. The dregs of a bitter
draught are always bitterest, and bitter indeed were
those which Anna Maria had still to drain; but she
thirsted for its last drops, and then to go and be with
Him for ever.

On the following 24th October, Anna Maria became so ill that she was forced to take to her bed,
from which she was never more to rise. Here she was
to lie for near eight months. But it was no bed of
repose on which she was to recline; it might rather
be likened to a rack, upon which she was laid out for
torture. No part of her frame enjoyed a moment's
ease, but every member seemed to have its special disorder appointed for its torment. To these were added
cold perspirations, like those of death, and the most
appalling inward spasms. She was passing now through
the crowning trials of that patience which we have seen
distinguishing her during forty-seven long years of toil,
trouble, and suffering, and which was to have its perfect work. The sublimity of that patience it would be
difficult worthily to describe, as it was difficult also
fully to appreciate it; for, as patience is one of those

virtues whose province lies in endurance, not in action, much disappears from the sight of all but God; and the more perfect it is the more it becomes hidden, because the sufferer bears not only with resignation, but with joy, and seeks not to make known his pains, as one desiring sympathy must needs do, but rather endeavours to hide them for the love of God and from his own charitable sympathy with the feelings of those around him. But whoever hides his sufferings, hides his patience likewise, more or less. Anna Maria's maladies, however, were too marked in their character and in their external symptoms for it to be question whether or not she suffered most acutely. Yet not only did not a single lamentation ever escape her lips, but her countenance exhibited the most perfect serenity; and, when able, she conversed with her children and friends with even more than her accustomed cheerfulness. It was she who supported and comforted and encouraged *them.* For herself she asked nothing by either word or look. She had none of those thousand little exigencies which the sick so often manifest; desires after some alleviation, some possible or impossible relief, which the most patient cannot sometimes refrain from expressing. On the contrary, it was necessary to urge her to mention anything which she would wish to have, or which she thought might afford her some solace. But, in fact, she desired nothing but those very sufferings, and the God of her heart, who was so lovingly sending them to her.

The only solace she valued, and that was never denied her, was to receive Him in His Adorable Sacrament. Every day the priest who lived in her house celebrated Mass at her little altar, and gave her Communion. This Bread of Life was her food and her medicine ; she wished for no other. But a difficulty as to her daily reception might now have presented itself. Anna Maria, who certainly put no faith in physicians, and who moreover knew more by a glance at her sun than all their science could teach them, always paid them respect; and when they were called in by others to attend her she' obeyed them submissively, though she often knew that they were mistaken, and at all times could have done far better without them. Now, as her maladies increased, and her state became more and more alarming, medical advice was sought by her family, and in proportion as she grew worse, they became more active with their prescriptions. They had their medicines, which must be given at stated intervals, and Anna Maria, who was a pattern of obedience, as she also was of patience, invariably submitted without remonstrance to their directions. At this juncture, Cardinal Pedicini requested Gregory XVI. to grant her a very unusual permission—that of communicating daily even when medicine had been administered to her after midnight. This dispensation is itself sufficient to prove the high opinion which the Sovereign Pontiff entertained of her holiness.

While thus liberally fed with that Bread of Heaven, the Flesh of the Son of Man, which is 'meat indeed,' she scarcely partook of any other nutriment. To so small a quantity indeed was the portion she occasionally swallowed reduced, that it is wonderful, considering her exhausting sufferings and excessive perspirations, which seemed as if they must waste away her frame in a few days, that she should have lingered on so many months. The complaint of which she is reckoned to have died was an inflammation of the chest; which, at first chronic, subsequently became acute in consequence of wrong treatment. Among the many other maladies with which it was combined, one of the chief and most excruciating was a species of rheumatic gout, which ended by depriving her of all power in her limbs. Up to that time she still plied her needle industriously, notwithstanding her torturing pains; and she continued to direct the concerns of her little household in all its homely details until about three days before her departure. But who could tell what she underwent during these seven months, which were the climax of what our Lord Himself had called 'a long martyrdom'? As difficult would it be to calculate what are the capacities for suffering of our passible humanity. Who can fathom them? A thought which to nature is appalling and to the wicked and impenitent most terrible, but sweetened to the true Christian by the remembrance of his Saviour's Passion; while to the ardent lovers of a Crucified God it is a thought full of joy, since to be able to suffer, and even to suffer much, is to be capable of conformity to their Lord, such as angels, who cannot suffer, might even envy them. Amongst these great lovers of the Cross, we need scarcely say at the conclusion of such a life as we have here recorded, Anna Maria was conspicuous; and so, while thirsting to go and be united to her God, she did not cease to thirst also for sufferings.

This conformity to the Passion of Jesus, so remarkable in saintly souls, was to be enhanced in Anna Maria by an act of obedience which gave a peculiar character to her death. *Facta est obediens usque ad mortem.* Some few days previous, it was revealed to her that her complaint needed a soothing and calming treatment; that by the aid of medicines of this nature she might recover, as she had at other times; but that if strong and violent measures were adopted, they would irritate and excite her whole system, and she would certainly die. Nevertheless, if those about her insisted, she was to obey, and her obedience would be recompensed in Heaven. All this she told to the priest who was the confidant of her supernatural lights, and to whom obedience bound her to make them known. He in consequence combated the opinion of the doctors, who were bent on vigorous appliances for the purpose of subduing the inflammation. They were not, however, to be shaken in their views; doubtless they thought that if D. Raffaele knew more of theology than they did, and was a good physician of souls, they understood their own business best, and the doctoring of the body was their province. There is nothing to surprise us in the pertinacious reliance of these good men on their own professional skill; but, strange to say, Domenico and the rest of the family sided with them. Truly, one would have imagined that after the many instances they must have witnessed of Anna Maria's marvellous penetration and knowledge, as well as of her success in healing the sick, they would have given more weight to her own expressed desire, fortified and supported as it was by the opinion of him whom they knew to possess her full confidence. But so it was to be. Anna Maria submitted, and said no more, though she was aware of all she would have to suffer, and the doctors had their way, with their blisters and issues, and their other torturing appliances. The pain which she endured besides, from the exasperation of all her maladies which ensued, was indeed excessive; but the end was approaching, and she knew it.

On Friday, the 2nd June, she had a slight accession of fever, but the family, who had seen her recover from far worse attacks of that kind, did not take the alarm, and the doctor attending her assured them that there was no cause for apprehension. She smiled sweetly at their confidence, for she knew that her hour was come. On the Sunday night the fever returned with increased violence ; and on Monday morning, after communicating, she fell into a long swoon, which bore so much the appearance of the immediate approach of death that her whole family believed that its last agonies had begun. Nevertheless, the swoon was of a supernatural character, and during its continuance she received a divine intimation that she would die on the following Friday.

When she came to herself, she asked for D. Raffaele, and, with a joy ineffable illuminating her whole countenance, she communicated to him the happy summons home which she had received. Never in all the twenty-one years during which he had known her had he seen her look so joyous as when she told him that she was about to die. It was a look which, he said, it was impossible to describe. Death to her, indeed, was the entrance into life and bliss eternal. She also announced her approaching departure to her family, speaking of it to them with a radiant cheerfulness, as of one about to make a short and pleasant journey. Then she called Domenico, and thanked him with the tenderest affection for all the care he had taken of her and all the kindness he had shown her. The worthy man's heart was ready to break. If he was not aware of all she was in the sight of God and in the esteem of many on earth, whose eyes were opened to discern what had remained hidden from his own, yet he knew what she had always been to him—the light, the joy, the consolation of his poor toilsome existence, the support of himself and of their family in every trouble, in every

difficulty, in every strait. He knew her virtues, and
felt that in her he was losing his best treasure. What
more she said we do not know; but she had a long and
private conversation with him. Doubtless she spoke
to him words of consolation, with affectionate encour-
agements to live for God and for eternity which he
must have treasured up and often recalled to mind
during the remaining years of his pilgrimage. Then
she called her children to her bedside, and gave to each
her parting counsels. To them all collectively she
made a touching exhortation to the practice of virtue,
fidelity to God and to their duties, and to assiduous
prayer; begging them in particular never to give up
their custom of saying the Rosary together. ' My children,' she said, ' have Jesus Christ always before you;
let His Precious Blood be ever the object of your veneration. You will have to suffer much, but sooner or later
the Lord will console you. Keep His commandments,
cherish devotion to the most holy Virgin, who will be
your mother in my place. I entreat you never to let
harmony and peace be broken amongst you; it is one
of the greatest treasures which a family can possess.'
Anna Maria had no earthly goods to bequeath to her
children, but she placed them solemnly under the care
and protection of the glorious martyr, St. Philomena,
and declared her to be their guardian.

Poor she had ever been, but poorer still she was in
these last days of her life, when the whole family sub-
sisted only on scanty alms collected by D. Raffaele;
the very sheets on the bed in which she died having
been supplied by the charity of her confessor.* Her

* This may seem strange, considering how many rich
friends she had who esteemed and even venerated her, but it
must be remembered that she never suffered them to be made

affectionate mother's heart had experienced some natural feelings of regret at leaving them in such an utter
state of destitution and dependence, but she speedily
stifled them, casting this care, as she had ever done all her
other cares, into the bosom of her God. Yet uneasiness
might seem to have been reasonably justified by the
extreme penury in which she knew they were involved.
Had the matter been concealed from her, or had it been
possible to conceal it, she would have learnt it from an
unjust summons which she received on her very death-
bed for the payment of a small debt which her daughter
had incurred, and had probably delayed discharging
through utter inability to meet it. The hard-hearted
creditor, who thus summoned the dying saint into court,
enjoyed robust health at that time, but before a few
months had elapsed he died of a sudden and violent
illness, and went to render his own account before another tribunal. Her confidence in God never failed
her; and, though she knew that she was leaving her
family in complete destitution, when by the slightest
word or act she might have procured for them ease,
comfort, and independence, she was consoled by the
remembrance of the many assurances she had received
from her Divine Spouse that He had them under His
special protection, and that she need not fear to leave
them in poverty for the love of Him. All, He had
often said, to whatsoever land they might belong, who

---

acquainted with her necessities. D. Raffaele, it is true, asked
alms for her, but he never mentioned the name of the person
for whom he applied. They were scanty therefore, as alms
thus gathered are apt to be. And besides, God so willed it.
She was never to have anything beyond what was strictly
necessary. We shall by and by see that what is here suggested
of the ignorance of her friends is no mere hypothesis.

should show kindness to her or to her family should be rewarded, while He would withdraw His mercies from such as should withhold their alms.

It remained for her now to take the last farewell of these dear ones. All were clustered kneeling and weeping at her bedside. Her face alone beamed with joy, and with a peace inexpressible, which had never left it since the vision in which she had received the summons of her Lord. She bestowed her last maternal blessing on her children, and then tenderly took leave of her husband. These adieus, it may be observed, are in Italy and other Catholic lands usually taken before the end arrives, in order that the soul of the dying person may be freed from the thoughts and cares and affections of earth and able to occupy all his remaining time in preparing to meet his God.

On the following day (Tuesday), she became much worse, and then the doctors had recourse to their most energetic measures, which they had kept in reserve, and which were in fact the immediate cause of her death by driving the inflammation to a vital organ, her lungs. She had foreseen the fatal effects, and the additional torture which their treatment would inflict upon her, but she submitted without an observation. On Wednesday she asked to· receive Communion in the way of Viaticum, in order thus publicly to honour her Lord. The Blessed Sacrament was accordingly brought to her from the neighbouring parish church with the usual ceremonies, and she received It with a fervour and a tenderness which drew tears from all who assisted. A Trinitarian Father had been sent for to administer to her the absolution *in articulo mortis*, with the indulgences attached to the Third Order, to which she was affiliated. After this she entered into her long and painful agony; but, ever thoughtful of others, she begged her family to go and recruit themselves with a little rest.

The priest who had been her companion for so many years, had been in constant attendance on her since the beginning of her mortal sickness, and she had exercised her gift of healing for the last time in his behalf. We have seen that she did not avail herself of it usually for such illnesses as were removable by natural means; in this case, however, she departed from her rule, and, seeing him suffering from a bad cold on the chest, occasioned by a chill after violent exercise, she called him to her, and, on his approaching her bedside, 'Come near,' she said, smiling. He complied, and, raising her hand, she touched him, and then made the sign of the cross in the name of the Most Holy Trinity. 'Go now,' she said, 'and lie down on your bed for about half an hour.' He did so, and at the end of that time his breathing had become perfectly free and his strength fully restored, so that he was enabled to bear the fatigues and anxieties of these last days.

Perhaps no one needed consolation and strength more than did this good priest, for no one knew the value of her who was departing better than he did; and, moreover, a spiritual tie of a very remarkable character had bound these two souls together. What a signification lies hid in that name of 'confidant,' so generally applied to him in the extracts from the Processes! Who was ever the confidant of so astonishing a secret as was D. Raffaele Natali; a secret which must have burned in his bosom for those twenty-one years, and of which, even until long after her death, he was not permitted freely and publicly to speak? What wonder that, even in the feeble days of extreme old

A A

age to which it was given him to remain on earth, he could scarcely speak of any other subject than the Venerable Servant of God, Anna Maria Taigi! And now he was beholding this holy associate entering on her last earthly conflict, her mortal agony. Her internal peace seems never to have been troubled; the enemy of souls was never suffered to afflict her, for the victory was won: all that remained was suffering the most intense, under which she was, it is true, inwardly supported by that joy and peace which occupied the supreme region of her soul, but of which she did not enjoy the sensible realisation. She had none of that consolation which has been accorded not seldom to martyrs amidst their flames and on their racks in such abundance and with such sweetness as to overpower their pains and render them almost unconscious of them; accordingly, when the priest asked her once during those bitter hours what she now felt, she replied, 'Pains of death.' He, desiring to fortify her resignation, repeated those words: '*Fiat voluntas tua;*' and then, in slow and broken accents, but with a heavenly smile on her faltering lips, she murmured softly, '*Sicut in cœlo et in terra.*'

On the Thursday evening she received the sacrament of Extreme Unction, and after its reception her pains, great as they had been, seemed to be redoubled, but she had been strengthened by that wondrous rite to bear the aggravation. Her sufferings, however, deprived her of the power of speech, although she retained her perfect consciousness. The family were now desired to remove into another apartment. We have said that the parting with friends and relatives is not in Italy delayed until the closing hours, so neither is it common for them to remain by the bedside until life has flown. The idea of dying in the arms of those they love, an aspiration which we so commonly hear, gives place to another amongst this Catholic people— that of dying amidst the ministries of their Holy Mother, the Church ; aided, indeed, by the prayers of those who have been dearest to them, but not distracted by the spectacle of their sorrow from the one thought which ought solely to occupy their minds. But though the presence of those who recall earthly ties and affections is thus withdrawn, the dying man has in its place the close attendance of those who can substantially aid and comfort him. It was so ordained, however, that Anna Maria should have neither consolation ; not the sympathy and love of her surrounding family, so soothing to many in their last moments, and the absence of which, if not replaced by something higher in kind, must be a simple pain and deprivation, nor yet that peculiar support and comfort which the minister of God, the priest, is able to impart. She was to have a crowning conformity to her Lord, and to the dereliction of soul which He endured when hanging on the Cross, by a three hours' abandonment at her death. That she should be thus forsaken she had predicted twenty years before to D. Raffaele, but at the same time she had told him that he would be with her when she died. In this there seemed to him to be an inexplicable contradiction, but, as had invariably happened, the event verified her words.

This complete neglect at such an awful time, which makes the most solemn appeal to the ministrations of charity, was owing partly to a mistake. It was supposed that her end was not so near as it really was ; but, whether her intense agony accelerated it, or whether the placidity with which she bore it, great as

all knew her patience to be, helped to deceive them as
to the proximity of death, it is impossible to judge.
The confessor says that in fact she would have lived a
few hours longer had she not undergone the fatigue of
having her bed made—a thing never done when a person is in the last extremity, yet both the doctor and the
Father Ministers of the Maddalena,* whose constant
attendance on death-beds must needs have given them
ample experience, agreed in allowing and, indeed, in
ordering that this daily arrangement should proceed as
usual. How distressing and exhausting such a process,
involving necessarily much disturbance, must have
proved to one in her last agony we need scarcely say.
As her misery was thus to be shortened by a brief span,
P. Filippo was of opinion that God compensated for
this abbreviation by the additional suffering entailed
upon her. Be this as it may, these good Father
Ministers were so blind, or so blinded, to her state
that they thought they might return to their convent
for the night ; and the Vice-Parroco, who was in the
house, being equally persuaded that the end was not at
hand, retired into another room to say his office.   D.

* St. Camillus of Lellis founded the Order of the Clerks
Regular, Ministers of the Sick. It had been his original design
that his congregation should minister only to the sick in hospitals,
but it was the will of God that it should embrace a wider field.
' Camillus,' as we read in his Life, ' had never thought of assisting the dying in private houses ; but God, who saw the numbers
and numbers of souls whom the devil won by waiting to make
his final attack upon them in that terrible moment, not only
inspired him, but, we may even say, forced him, to undertake
this office, as most important of all for the Catholic world.'
Oratorian Series, vol. i. p. 53. This being the saint's special
object, it is the more remarkable that the Fathers of the Maddalena should have left Anna Maria at such a moment, and
serves to demonstrate still more evidently that the error was a
Providential dispensation.

Raffaele, who had sat up the whole of the previous
night with her, had at the urgent request of the family
been persuaded to go and take a little rest. Consequently no one remained with her except the two servants; but had these kept good watch, this would have
sufficed, for, on noting any change, one of them could
have called the priests; yet not only did they share
the common delusion, but they were negligent in their
duty, for they ceased to attend to her and went off to
the farthest corner of the apartment, where, engaged in
gossiping talk, these women saw and heard nothing.
Indeed there was nothing to hear; for Anna Maria
never uttered plaint or groan during those agonising
three hours, any more than she had done from the commencement of her illness.

Just at midnight, D. Raffaele felt so strong a movement to rise and repair to her that he could not but
believe it to be an inspiration. He accordingly got
up, and went down to her room, when he found her at
the very last extremity, having indeed but a few more
minutes to live. He immediately sent for the Vice-
Parroco, and together they recited the Church's recommendation of a departing soul. He then gave her the
last absolution; and, while he was sprinkling her with
holy water, and invoking for her the Precious Blood of
Jesus, to which she had been through life so devout,
Anna Maria heaved one long deep sigh, and with that
sigh she breathed forth her spirit to God. P. Calixto
sees in the strength of this last expiring breath a sign
and testimony of the heroic fortitude of her great soul,
and a further conformity to her dying Lord, who, when
He yielded up His spirit to His Father, 'cried with a
loud voice.' She died about half an hour after mid-

night on Friday morning,* having just completed sixty-eight years† and a few days of life.

No sooner had the servant of God breathed her last than he who had been her friend and companion for so many years hastened to inform Cardinal Pedicini, who immediately addressed the following letter to Cardinal Odescalchi, the Pope's Vicar :—

'Your Most Reverend Eminence,—It having pleased our Lord to call to eternal rest the soul of Anna Maria Taigi, domiciliated in the Via Santi Apostoli, No. 7, whom the undersigned Cardinal Vice-Chancellor has had the happiness of knowing and visiting for above thirty years, admiring her singular virtues, no less than her extraordinary gifts and the special divine lights with which she was as abundantly enriched as have been the greatest saints; whereof he has had thousands of proofs, both in his own particular person and also in regard to public events of the Church and the world, indicated with such precision, long previously to their occurrence, and so minutely verified, that it was impossible to attribute the same to anything but extraordinary illuminations received from God; the undersigned

* P. Calixte inadvertently says ' quatre heures du matin—four o'clock of the morning,' without adding that he is giving the Italian time, which is reckoned from sunset, not midnight. To those who may not be aware of this circumstance the assertion is puzzling, coupled with the fact, which he states, of D. Raffaele rising at midnight and being only just in time to render assistance to the dying woman in her last moments.

† All the biographies, as well as the *Analecta Juris Pontificii*, assign the 29th of May as her birthday, but the inscription on her tomb gives the 30th. As she was baptised on the day after her birth, this circumstance may account for the discrepancy.

Cardinal therefore has thought good to acquaint your
Most Reverend Eminence, in order that your religious
piety may provide that the mortal remains of this
happy soul, which was its companion in the exercise of
so many virtues, may receive that particular respect and
care which is paid in similar cases of rare occurrence.

'If it has pleased God, for His secret purposes, to
keep hidden from the world during life a soul so highly
favoured by Him, albeit she was not only known but
esteemed by persons of high distinction in their time,
as Pius VII. of holy memory, who conversed with her
more than once,* and Leo XII. in consequence of what
Mgr. Strambi had told him concerning her, as well as
various persons of note in this city, not to speak of
foreigners, as lately Mgr. Flaget, who visited her during
her illness with much satisfaction before quitting Rome
—who can tell the secrets of God, and whether He may
not design later to manifest in this favoured creature His
mercies, as we have most just reason to believe He will?

'The undersigned Cardinal profits by this opportunity to assure your Most Reverend Eminence of the
profound respect with which he humbly kisses your
hands.

'Your Most Reverend Eminence's
'Most humble and truly devoted servant,
'CARLO MARIA CARDINAL PEDICINI.'

We subjoin the letter of P. Filippo, the confessor
of Anna Maria, addressed to the same Cardinal on the
following day.

* The Cardinal would here seem to imply that Pius VII.
had actually seen Anna Maria, and that several times. Of this
circumstance, if true, no note appears in the extracts made
from his deposition and laid before the public.

'It is very just and proper seasonably to reveal the works of God, for His greater glory and for the edification of the faithful. Yesterday, Friday, the 9th of the current month, passed to eternal rest the soul of Anna Maria Taigi, who lived in the parish of Santa Maria in Via Lata. I know that the Secretary of his Eminence Cardinal Barberini, D. Raffaele Natali, who has lived with her nearly twenty years,* has addressed, in conjunction with other persons, a petition to your Eminence, to the intent that regard should be had to the body of this holy woman, which merits all respect. As for me, who have been her confessor for more than thirty years, until the day before yesterday, when she received the last sacraments, I believe myself to be bound in conscience to make known to your Eminence that not only did she exercise the Christian virtues in an heroic degree, but that God favoured her also with special graces and extraordinary gifts, which will excite admiration, should it please God to publish them authentically before the whole Church, as I hope. I should have much to say on this head. I content myself with testifying to the charity of this holy soul, which constituted itself as a victim before God, and which obtained signal graces for Rome; I hope that God will cause this to be recognised later. The mortal remains, therefore, of so virtuous a soul, and one so highly esteemed by Pius VII. and Leo XII., by Mgr. Strambi, Mgr. Menocchio, and a crowd of persons of every rank and every country who obtained extraordinary graces through her intervention, seem to merit special regard, in accordance with the constant practice of the Church.

---

* In fact, twenty-one years, since he was appointed in 1816; but it may be that he did not at first inhabit the same house.

' Respectfully kissing the hem of your Eminence's purple, I have the honour to subscribe myself, with the most profound obedience,

' P. FILIPPO LUIGI DI SAN NICOLA,
' Discalced Carmelite.

' From the Convent of Santa Maria
della Vittoria, 10th June, 1837.'

These letters from two out of the three persons who knew her most intimately (of the opinion of the third, her confidant, we need not speak) are sufficient to show the undoubting opinion entertained by them of Anna Maria's extraordinary sanctity and high gifts, an opinion which they had no hesitation in thus solemnly recording from the very first. We cannot better conclude the account of her blessed death than by subjoining the comments of the same Father whose letter to Cardinal Odescalchi we have just given. After speaking of her heroic abstention from any step which might have relieved her from the galling penury of her existence, especially in her last lingering illness, when but a word on her part would have sufficed to change its whole aspect and bring in most abundant supplies from persons of high station, who would have regarded themselves as obliged and honoured by the permission to assist her, he says, ' Well, a woman replenished with so many merits, virtues, and supernatural gifts, lives unknown and dies abandoned by every one; having round her bed of suffering only a poor family, whom she leaves in destitution and recommends to a priest equally poor, who is to continue collecting daily alms for them. She blesses her children, and leaves them, as her sole bequest, piety, religion, devotion to the Virgin, to the saints, and particularly to St. Philomena, her patroness, whom she constituted the guardian and protectress of her poor and numerous family. After which, recollected in God and animated by the fortitude which resignation imparts, she drinks to the very last drop the bitter chalice of a painful death.

'The forty martyrs of Sebaste merited a crown because they resisted for a few hours the temptation to leave the frozen water for a refreshing bath. What, then, shall be the crown reserved for the martyrdom in spirit, the voluntary martyrdom, long and dolorous, which this pious woman underwent, not for a few hours but for a whole life, and, above all, in the midst of the privations of her last illness, with the ever-present temptation to pass from the frozen waters of indigence and suffering to the soothing bath of ease and consideration for herself and her poor family. Here we see manifested heroic faith, firm hope, and ardent charity. Prudence, justice, temperance, and fortitude reign with absolute sway, attended by the Evangelical counsels and lighted by the seven gifts of the Holy Spirit. Also I entertain no doubt but that the Lord, who willed in His profound wisdom to keep His humble and beloved servant hidden from the world during her life, will deign one day to make known her virtues to serve as an example, and will manifest His mercies by publishing the extraordinary gifts wherewith He enriched her, He whose infinite love takes its delight with the creatures of this miserable earth. "*Ludens in orbe terrarum; et deliciæ meæ, esse cum filiis hominum.*"*

' "Glory be to the Father, to the Son, and to the Holy Ghost, now and for everlasting ages. Amen." '

* Prov. viii. 31.

CHAPTER XXII.

ANNA MARIA'S INTERMENT AND RE-INTERMENTS.

THE cholera was at the gates of Rome at the moment that Anna Maria expired, and indeed was only awaiting the departure of her whose prayers had shielded that city from its ravages during her lifetime, to break forth within its precincts. Meanwhile the rapidity of its advance and the frightful number of its victims—whole families having been well-nigh swept away—had filled the public mind in Italy with indescribable dismay. Quite a panic prevailed in Rome, which had increased tenfold when the epidemic entered the States of the Church. The Pontifical Government had taken the most energetic measures to prevent its introduction, and the terrified people themselves willingly adopted every precaution to escape infection. If they met a body being borne to the grave, albeit enclosed in a coffin, as had lately been enjoined by official regulations, they might be seen hurrying out of the way of the funeral train; while the churches in which any corpse was exposed previously to interment were almost deserted. People shrank from inquiring who had died, or what was the cause of their death, so much did they dread to hear in reply the terrible word, cholera. For this reason, as D. Raffaele himself testified, the death of Anna Maria, which otherwise would have excited the highest interest amongst the population, did not at once become known.

D. Raffaele, who collected alms for her during her long illness, had not been able to reckon upon more than four scudi a month to supply the needs of the family; 'nevertheless,' says Cardinal Pedicini, 'trust-

ing in Providence, he ordered a suitable funeral, with
a leaden coffin, a cast of her head and face in wax, an
act drawn up by a notary, and other expenses, which
together might require two hundred scudi.' D. Raffaele,
we see, had not in vain witnessed for twenty-one years
he results of undoubting confidence in God. 'He
begged me,' continues the Cardinal, 'to lend him fifty
crowns to meet the calls which were most urgent. I
replied that I would send them on the morrow by my
major-domo; but I felt so strong an impulse in my
heart that, before saying holy Mass, I sent for my
major-domo and commissioned him to take the fifty
scudi at once; and I gave them most willingly, in gratitude for the memory of this holy woman, to whom I
was under so many obligations. I was not at the time
aware of the extreme poverty of this family and of the
above-mentioned ecclesiastic. It was not long before
persons resident at Milan and Turin, who knew Anna
Maria only by reputation, sent all the money which
was required.'

Towards the evening of the Saturday, the 10th June,
the body of Anna Maria was placed in a wooden coffin
and removed to the parish church of Santa Maria in
Via Lata, which indeed was nearly opposite, being borne
and accompanied, according to the testimony of her
youngest daughter,* Maria, by the Religious of Ara Cœli;
the priests of that parish also escorting it. The coffin
had been closed in the house previously, and the body
remained during the Sunday exposed in the church,
but still covered, on account of the threats of cholera.
The obsequies having been performed according to the

---

* Ten witnesses were examined in January, 1856, with reference to the burial, disinterment, and translation of the body,
the absence of public *cultus*, &c. &c.

Roman ritual, in the evening it was placed on a mortuary car and transported quietly but with due respect to the new public cemetery of San Lorenzo in the Agro Verano without the walls,* the Vice-Parroco bearing the cross, and a carriage following ' *more nobilium*' (as the Cardinal says), in which were other priests, one of whom was the friend and confidant of Anna Maria, D. Raffaele Natali.   On reaching the cemetery the *De Profundis* was recited, and the body was deposited in the little chapel attached to the burial-ground, there to await the digging of the grave. We subjoin D. Raffaele's brief account given in testimony, as above noticed. 'The corpse of the Servant of God was accompanied to the Cemetery of San Lorenzo fuori le mura by the Vice-Parroco, Signor D. Luigi Antonini, by me, and by another ecclesiastic (I know there was another also, whose name I cannot recall) on the evening of Sunday the 11th June, 1837.   After the absolution, according to the rite of the Holy Roman Church, it was deposited in the chapel of the said cemetery and placed in a leaden coffin, with seals that had been previously affixed in the sacristy of Santa Maria in Via Lata by the Signor Avvocata Rosatini, to await the digging of the grave close to the outer wall of the chapel on the Gospel side, where it was laid on the following morning but without the ceremony of a deed drawn up by an attorney, in order to avoid public notice.' The seals had, however, been affixed to the leaden coffin in presence of three witnesses ; and we shall find that seals had been also affixed to the wooden coffin, when we come to speak of the subsequent disinterment.

* The reason for the interment beyond the walls was a recent prohibition against burying within the precincts of the city, on account of the cholera.

We have recorded these details in order to show the extreme care taken by the Church in cases of this kind; and it is sufficient to cast an eye at the minute interrogatory to which all the persons who were cognisant of any or all particulars relating to her interment were subsequently subjected, to be convinced what securities are taken for the identification of the body of one who, like Anna Maria, dies with the reputation of extraordinary sanctity. Circumstances forbade all display in her case, and even led to the observance of great privacy, but not a single needful precautionary measure was omitted. The precise spot of her burial was indicated by orders transmitted from the Sovereign Pontiff through his Cardinal Vicar, Odescalchi. The servant of God had been laid in the coffin wrapped in her usual garments, and with a brass cross around her neck. A tin tube, containing a statement drawn up by the priest who so long had been her confidant, was also enclosed. A marble slab covered the tomb, with a cornice, or border, of a darker hue, and having at its head a stone cross inserted, of the combined colours worn by the Trinitarian Order, namely, red and blue. Beneath was this simple inscription :—

D. O. M.
Anna-Maria-Antonia Gesualda
Taigi Nata Gianetti in Siena
Il xxx Maggio MDCCLXIX
Morta In Roma Il IX Giugno
MDCCCXXXVII
Terziaria Scalza
Del Ordine Della SSMA Trinità.*

* ' God All-good All-great.
Anna Maria Antonia Gesualda
Taigi, Born Gianetti in Siena the 30th May, 1769,
Died in Rome the 9th June, 1837,
A Discalced Tertiary of the Order of the Most Holy Trinity.'

Moreover, around the coffin, a kind of little vault was constructed supporting the slab; and, although the slab was similar to others in the cemetery, yet the inscription, with its Trinitarian Cross, and the isolation of the tomb, together with the notes taken of its situation and of all particulars regarding the interment, amply sufficed for easy and certain identification at any future time. Here the holy body was to repose for eighteen years.

Soon the report of Anna Maria's death spread through Rome, and D. Raffaele was besieged by the common people with questions innumerable; nor were their superiors in rank less anxious to learn every circumstance regarding the departure of the holy woman. Prelates, bishops, cardinals, nobles vied with each other in the eagerness of their desire to hear the most minute details, questioning him especially as to her predictions respecting future public events. But those could best appreciate her loss who shared her spirit, and were themselves shining examples of holiness. D. Raffaele recalls to memory how one who was himself soon to go, like her, to join the blessed company of the saints, the Canon Gaspar del Bufalo, meeting him accidentally near the door of the Gesù, expressed the deepest sorrow at the loss which Rome had sustained in the decease of Anna Maria Taigi. ' Ah! Don Raffaele,' he exclaimed, ' when the Lord calls to Himself souls dear to Him, it is a sign that He intends to punish. Let us prepare ourselves for scourges.' We have already mentioned how the unconscious husband of the saint became first alive to the exalted holiness of his companion in life from learning the veneration in which she was popularly held. In spite of the prevailing terror of the epidemic which possessed the public mind

her name was on the lips of all. ' The saint is dead !
the saint is dead !' was the exclamation to be heard on
all sides from the devout Roman people. The house
in which she died, and about which the fragrance of
her virtues seemed still to linger, was visited by high
and low ; and numbers of persons, notwithstanding the
very general fear of intermingling with any concourse
of people and of breathing the atmosphere of a burial-
ground in which many of the victims of cholera had
been interred, went to visit and pray at her tomb.

Among the first to give this marked testimony to
her sanctity was one who had loved and revered her
for above thirty years, the Cardinal Pedicini. There,
at this humble gravestone, would he come and kneel,
presenting his requests with the most fervent devotion
and confidence, sure of being heard and aided by her
in the home of bliss, as he had ever been while she
sojourned in this valley of tears. Another eminent
prelate, Cardinal Micara, a man of austere virtue, cultivated mind, and calm judgment, had also so great a
reliance on the power of her intercession that he kept
a picture of Anna Maria by him, having recourse to
her in all his needs, and specially during his last mortal sickness, that he might obtain the grace of a happy
death. This prelate, be it observed, filled the office of
Prefect of the Sacred Congregation of Rites, and was
noted for his exceeding prudence and caution, not to
say severity, where it was question of reputed supernatural gifts. And not only did he himself thus highly
esteem and honour the servant of God, but he frequently exhorted others to recommend themselves to
her prayers in the difficult times through which they
were passing. The Cardinal Ferretti was similarly
devout to Anna Maria, and is said to have died with

her picture in his hand. The Bishops of Mondovi and of Sutri and Nepi might be also seen mingling their homage with that of the common people at her tomb; and many others besides, distinguished for rank, science, and, what is much more, exalted piety joined in the perennial pilgrimage of which her lowly place of interment became and continued to be the object.

The above-mentioned Bishop of Sutri and Nepi, Mgr. Basilici, who was himself a man of eminent piety and, we are told, had a special devotion to St. Philomena, as had Anna Maria, desiring to pray for her when saying Mass after her decease, felt his whole soul immediately filled with the sweetest consolation, as he afterwards confided to one of his friends, and interiorly prompted rather to recommend himself to her prayers than to offer any in her behalf. In like manner, P. Bernardo Clausi, of the Minims, to whose sanctity and possession of eminent gifts we have alluded, having after her death prayed for her, as a testimony of gratitude for the lights and counsels which he had received from her during her life, was nevertheless so convinced that she needed no help from the suffrages of others, that he used these emphatic expressions concerning her: 'If Anna Maria be not in Paradise, then no one is there.' And God Himself meanwhile seemed to be sanctioning the devotion and confidence of the faithful by the many answers made to prayers. The sick were healed, sinners converted, and graces abundantly conceded. She is also said to have appeared to several persons, but concerning these apparitions we have at present no details.

One instance is, however, alluded to in what we are about to relate. We have seen the estimation in which Anna Maria was held, while living, by the servant of

BB

God, Vincenzo Pallotti, Founder of the Pious Society
of Missions; and we find his confidence in her power
with God greatly increased after her blessed death, as
the following passage from Dr. Raphael Melia's Life of
that holy man will show. 'D. Raffaele Natali,' writes
his biographer, 'having heard that the servant of God,
Maria Taigi, had manifested herself to a nun, giving
her some advice, went to Vincent to consult him about
the matter, to know if he were to believe the revelation
asserted by the said nun. Vincent answered him immediately that it was necessary to consult God by
prayer. A few days afterwards, the same priest having
seen Vincent again, Vincent told him that the affair
was not to be despised, and that he himself would put
it to the proof. Then he charged the said priest to tell
the nun to pray to M. Taigi, to give her an answer to
some questions secretly arranged between Vincent and
Natali. The nun did according to the suggestion of
Vincent, though of course she was not aware of the
nature of the questions, and the answers she received
from the servant of God were perfectly in accordance
with the questions Vincent had arranged. The same
witness observes that the said answers could not be
given but by the light of God. Vincent also made
other experiments by which he was able to judge of
the sanctity of the servant of God, Taigi, so that he
made her Plenipotentiary Secretary of the Pious Society
before the throne of the Most Holy Trinity.' By this
name he continued familiarly to call her, and often
experienced the effects of her protection.* Many other

* D. Raffaele Natali makes the following observation in
reply to interrogatories addressed to him and others after the
introduction of her cause, with the object of ascertaining whether due attention had been paid to the prohibition of Urban
VIII. 'I must state, as the simple truth, that whatever I may

testimonies to the fame of her sanctity have been collected, but these, on account of the peculiar distinction of the witnesses, have been specially recorded by her biographers, and suffice for the purpose.

It was in consequence of the high reputation in which she was held by persons so eminent both for their theological science and their personal holiness, and the many recorded miracles granted at her intercession, that the Cardinal Vicar, Odescalchi, commissioned D. Raffaele Natali privately to collect all documents existing relative to the life of the pious woman. It was to this promiscuous collection, which had as yet undergone no sifting scrutiny and was invested with no juridical authority, that Mgr. Luquet had access. Out of this mass of documents, and with the help of whatever other information he could orally gather, that prelate composed his Life of Anna Maria Taigi. Although it was chiefly grounded on the materials to which Mgr.

---

have thought of the sanctity of her life from the knowledge I had of her great virtues, and from the apparitions of the Servant of God, who was seen in glory by an estimable soul now departed, and from the instructions communicated to the aforesaid person, which could not have been known save by extraordinary and supernatural lights—all which were examined into by the Servant of God, Signor Don Vincenzo Pallotti, after having offered prayers on the subject, who thereupon manifested his favourable opinion concerning the said apparitions—nevertheless, out of respect to the Holy See I have not ceased to have Masses of Requiem said in suffrage for the soul of the Servant of God, Anna Maria Taigi, and I always have her present to my mind in my memento for the dead, even as I have other departed souls; and I often remember what St. Francis de Sales said: "These good friends of mine, who knows how long they may make me stay in Purgatory? for they will say he is gone straight to Paradise. I moreover know that souls still undergoing purgation have appeared, and that both favours and counsels have been given by them."'

Raffaele had given him access, yet unfortunately it had
not the benefit of his revision.   The manuscript was
sent to France, and the Cardinal de la Tour d'Auvergne
caused it to be printed in Alby for the Society of Good
Books.   It was translated into Italian by Mgr. Romilli,
Archbishop of Milan, and had a very large circulation,
passing rapidly through several editions both in Rome
and in other Italian cities; amongst which Siena, the
native place of Anna Maria, may be specially mentioned.
In Rome alone seventeen thousand copies were sold.
It was also translated into English and other languages,
and was dispersed through every quarter of the world.
Yet this first compendium not only was incomplete,—
its pious author not feeling himself authorised to publish the highest supernatural gifts with which the servant of God was favoured,—but, what was far more to
be lamented, did her injustice, by imputing to her irre-
gularities in early life of which she was innocent. Mgr.
Luquet, when made aware of his error, would have
wished, had it been possible, to withdraw all the copies
from circulation; but he had it in contemplation to
correct the injurious mistake in a future edition, a
mistake the more painful to him as he was full of zeal
in behalf of the servant of God, and was, in fact, the
first Postulator of her cause.*

* How Mgr. Luquet was led into this error has never been
clearly explained. Probably the strong expressions of contrition for past sins used by Anna Maria helped to deceive
him; but, as these by themselves would not have been deemed
sufficient evidence to authorise him to make the assertion in
question, we are led to conjecture that in collecting information
he must have given credit to some statement injurious to her
moral character. Amongst her other trials, Anna Maria, as we
have seen (p. 156), was a victim of repeated calumnies, for the
repression of which she would never allow any measures to be

The holy body reposed, as we have said, for eighteen years in the Agro Verano; but, as every day the honour in which the servant of God was held increased, people began to complain that it should be left in a common cemetery, and, moreover, in a place inconvenient of access to those whose devotion led them to visit her tomb. Various causes had combined to occasion this apparent neglect: first the ravages of the cholera, and subsequently the other scourges which visited Rome; for we need scarcely remind our readers that the troubles and revolutions of 1848 took place within that period. When peace and quiet were restored, a further obstacle still presented itself in the extreme poverty of Anna Maria's family and the very limited means of the ecclesiastic who took the warmest interest in the matter, Mgr. Raffaele Natali. At this juncture, Mgr. Luquet generously came forward to discharge the expenses consequent on the disinterment and transfer of the body into Rome, for which, as the Postulator of her cause, after the completion of the ordinary Process concerning the virtues of the servant of God (the whole cost of which he had also defrayed), he formally requested authority from the Cardinal Vicar, in May, 1855. He received a favourable answer; his Eminence deputing Canon D. Francesco Annivitti, Fiscal Promoter of the Vicariate, together with a notary, to effect the legal act of recognition, of which full particulars are placed on record in the replies of the witnesses in the interrogatory to which they were subjected. From these replies we will extract as much as will be of general interest to the reader.

taken; but documents founded on the testimony of sworn witnesses have since fully established her innocency of any grave sin.

At the end of May, the delegated judge, D. Giovanni Francesco Cometti, Archbishop of Nicomedia, the
Fiscal Promoter, and the notary, along with the substituted Postulator of the cause and various witnesses,
amongst whom was D. Raffaele Natali, who had been
present at the burial of Anna Maria eighteen years before, proceeded to the Cemetery of San Lorenzo. The
tomb being recognised and verified, the coffin was removed from the grave and borne into a room attached
to the cemetery, known as the Turret. At the four
corners of the leaden coffin, which had upon it an inscription similar to what had been carved on the marble
slab, were the seals of brass affixed by the now defunct
Rosatini, all agreeing with the accurate description recorded of them. The leaden coffin being opened, the
wooden coffin was then extracted. A white strip of
ribbon had been nailed, in the form of a cross, upon
the lid, which was sealed at the four corners with wax
bearing the same impression as the brass seals without.
The lid was raised, and displayed to view the Venerable
Servant of God. The *De Profundis* having been recited and the absolution given, according to the Roman
ritual, by P. Desiderii, one of the Father Ministers of
the Maddalena, they proceeded reverently to examine
the holy body, upon which no taint of corruption had
yet passed. It was, indeed, well-nigh unchanged ; nor
did this result from the exclusion of humidity, of which
there were considerable signs, the same being indicated
by rust on the tube which contained D. Raffaele's
statement and had been laid at her feet. 'All were
agreed,' says one of the witnesses, 'that the corpse was
intact ; I myself saw the fresh colour in the face (la
carnagione).' Her clothes were also in perfect preservation. The coffin was left uncovered for four hours, for

the purpose of removing the humidity, and meanwhile those who had joined in the investigation went to take their midday meal. Such as are unacquainted with the usual proceedings on similar occasions may be surprised at the strict precautions which were taken during that brief absence. The sole window in the Turret was secured within with bars, the door being similarly fastened without, and stamped with four wax seals bearing the impress of the Cardinal Vicar's arms. In the afternoon the witnesses and legal officials returned, bringing with them Signor Gatti, a physician, and Signor Ciccioli, a surgeon, to examine the state of the body. And first we find the seals that had been affixed to the door four hours before inspected, and declared to be perfect and untouched. When we read of such precautions being adopted to secure the identification of the body, we may well conceive how rigorous is the investigation which the Church requires with reference to the far more important subject of the sanctity of the soul which was united to it, and of the consequent claims upon the veneration of the faithful which the departed servant of God shall be declared to possess. The witness already quoted mentions that when they returned to the Turret, it was found that the action of the atmosphere during those four hours had discoloured to a certain degree those portions of the body which alone were uncovered, namely, the face and the hands ; this circumstance accounts for the apparent discrepancy between his previous description and the report given by the doctors in regard to the colour of face and hands; for, although the latter testified to their being essentially unchanged, they added that a certain livid hue had begun to manifest itself, which is the harbinger of decay. They noticed, however, that the face retained

its regular form; that the features were but little altered; that they were all perfectly covered with the
skin; and that the hair and eyes were quite intact.
The skin of the hands was a little dried, but was substantially unimpaired.   In short, the change which had
taken place was very slight, considering the length of
time which had elapsed.   We have seen that, such as
it was, it was chiefly attributable to the exposure of
those four hours; as if God desired to show that it was
no natural cause which had thus shielded the mortal
remains of His servant from corruption, inasmuch as
these influences would, apart from His special protection, have produced their ordinary effect.   We shall
find, in fact, that when her body was again examined
many years afterwards, the covered portions were still
as white as when laid in the grave.   The coffin was
now re-closed, and the Cardinal Vicar's seals were
affixed, as also on the outer leaden coffin, in which it
was replaced.   The room was then carefully secured as
before.

   Great pains had been taken to keep the whole
matter as private as possible, nevertheless various ecclesiastics had heard of what was being done, and
hastened to the spot; they were thus able to add
their testimony to that of the official examiners; Mgr.
Chigi, afterwards Apostolic Nuncio in France, affixing
his own signature to the legal attestation.   It would
seem that the first idea was to transfer the body of the
servant of God to the Church of San Carlo alle Quattro
Fontane.   This would have appeared the most natural
course, particularly as she had herself expressed a wish
to be buried in a church of the Trinitarian Order; but
for some unexplained reason the Cardinal Vicar decided
to have it transported into the Church of Santa Maria

della Pace, which is served by secular clergy, and is one of much resort. Owing to the devotions of the month of May going on in that church, which interfered with the necessary preparation of the tomb, the removal was not effected until the 11th of June; it took place at night, in order to avoid any concourse of people. But a devout population is not easily cheated on such occasions. In spite of all precautions, and notwithstanding the advanced hour, a great crowd was found collected in front of Santa Maria della Pace, when the mortuary car arrived. It consisted of persons of all conditions in life, and behind were a great number of women, who were very pressing to enter, but were kept back, not only to prevent the church being too much crowded, but because it was not the custom to admit women within its walls at that late hour. The body was received by Canon Giacomo Moglia with the usual religious ceremony of the absolution, and, after a repetition of the same legal formalities of which we have spoken, was deposited in a grave under the pavement of the little chapel of San Antonio di Padova, on the sacristy side, before the rail which encloses the altar. A stone marked the spot where the holy body was laid, with this inscription :—

Hic requiescit Serva Dei, Anna Maria Taigi.

It was perhaps permitted by God that she should not at once be deposited in her final and proper resting-place, in order that a subsequent translation should be the occasion of a renewal of honours. Although the prohibition of the Holy See against giving any public *cultus* to those who have not yet been beatified was strictly obeyed in this case, her tomb was a place of constant resort to the devout. One of the witnesses who continually frequented the church says that in the morning, at mid-day, and in the evening he constantly saw people of all classes go and kneel before it, and there silently offer their supplications. Canon Moglia also testifies that persons were continually applying either for a copy of the *Life of Anna Maria* by Mgr. Luquet, or for a picture of her, or for some fragment of the clothes which she had worn.

Ten years having elapsed since the removal of the holy body to Santa Maria della Pace, the two surviving daughters of the Venerable Servant of God (whose cause had been introduced by a decree of the Sacred Congregation of Rites, ratified and signed by the Sovereign Pontiff on the 8th January, 1863), and D. Raffaele Natali, knowing well that her desire had been that she should be interred in a church of the Order to which she was affiliated as Tertiary, joined in addressing a petition to his Holiness, Pope Pius IX., beseeching him to permit the transportation of her body to the Church of San Crisogono of the Trinitarians in Trastevere. Leave being granted, on the 10th July, 1865,* at one o'clock of the afternoon, the Fiscal Promoter the Rev. D. Antonio Ruggeri, the Prefect of the Church of Santa Maria della Pace, Canon Raimondo Pigliacelli, and D. Raffaele Natali, with the notary and several witnesses, amongst whom were two grandsons of Anna Maria, met in the Church of Santa Maria; and, after D. Raffaele had taken a solemn oath that the Venerable Servant of God, while living, had testified her desire to both himself and her daughters that

* P. Calixte, usually accurate, has inadvertently stated that the translation took place on the 18th of August. P. Filippo Balzofiore, an earlier biographer, gives the true date, viz. the 10th of July. The present writer has had occasion frequently to notice the accuracy of this Italian Life.

she should be interred in a church of the Trinitarian
Fathers, the tomb was opened and the coffin identified
with the same legal formalities as before. It was then
provisionally placed in a small room adjoining, called
the little sacristy, and there locked up, the notary
keeping the keys.

At eight o'clock in the evening, in presence of the
same witnesses, the Prefect of the church was desirous
of bidding a solemn farewell to the holy body, which
he and his colleagues had regarded as a dear and precious treasure, and the loss of which they tenderly deplored. His whole voice and manner, as he pronounced
in substance the following words, evinced an emotion
so profound that all present were much affected: '*Bene-
dicta sit Sancta Trinitas atque Indivisa Unitas ; con-
fitebimur Ei, quia fecit nobiscum misericordiam Suam!*'
he exclaimed, as he turned towards the coffin of her
who had been so ardent an adorer of the Blessed
Trinity. ' The affection,' he continued, ' which thou
didst manifest, while living, towards the secular clergy
gives us the hope that thou wilt aid them in Heaven.
We are about to lose thy mortal remains, but we shall
assuredly not be deprived of thy protection. Remember, then, this poor church, which for ten years has
guarded thy remains with so much care. Pray for the
worthy ecclesiastics *qui mecum laborant in ministerio.*
Obtain for them and me an increase of zeal, that in all
things we may act for the glory of God and the salvation of souls. Obedience was thy characteristic virtue,
and it is precisely the obedience which we owe to him
who has authority to command us which constrains us
to part with thee. When it shall have pleased God to
raise thee to the honours of the altar, perhaps none of
us will be able to add to thy glory on earth, but we

pray thee to obtain for us that we may be the companions of that glory in Heaven.' The coffin being then laid on the mortuary car, it was followed by the persons already mentioned, and conveyed to San Crisogono in Trastevere, where the Very Reverend Father Antonio della Madre di Dio, Minister-General of the Trinitarians, and his religious family received it. The notary having drawn up the verbal process of the consignment, and the act having been subscribed by the Fiscal Promoter, the General of the Trinitarians, the parish priest, D. Raffaele Natali, the two grandsons, and other witnesses, it was placed underground at the Epistle corner of the High Altar before the chapel of the Blessed Sacrament, without the rails, having over it a monument, in the form of a sarcophagus, bearing this inscription : '*Hic dormit in pace Venerabilis Serva Dei, Anna Maria Taigi, Conjugata Materfamilias, Ordinis Excalc. SS. Trinitatis Tertiaria Professa, Mortua Romæ ix Junii*, MDCCCXXXVII.'* Although everything had been executed with great privacy, the good people of Trastevere soon became aware of the treasure they had acquired, and the church was thronged during the following day.

In the year 1868 some alterations being about to be effected in the pavement of San Crisogono, permission was granted for the temporary removal of the coffin containing the body of the servant of God into the adjoining Sacristy, known as that of the Relics, where it was laid at the time of its translation, previously to interment. Leave was also given to profit by this oppor-

* 'Here sleeps in peace the Venerable Servant of God, Anna Maria Taigi, Married and Mother of a Family, Professed Tertiary of the Discalced Order of the Most Holy Trinity, who died at Rome the 9th June, 1837.'

tunity for a re-examination of the state of the body and
its translation to a new tomb and coffin prepared for it.
In the beginning of August, the permission of the Holy
Father having been obtained, Mgr. Minetti, the Promoter of the Faith, came accompanied by his Vice-pro-
moter, their assessors, and the Secretary of the Sacred
Congregation of Rites, to be present at the extraction
of the coffin and its removal to the sacristy adjoining.
There, in presence of the prelates, a physician, surgeon,
and other witnesses, the body was again exposed to
view. A white mould covered it like a veil, but, when
this had been removed, little change was found to have
taken place, although thirty-one years had elapsed since
it had been committed to the grave. The face, hands,
and forearm had become of a bronzed hue, but the
throat, which had remained covered, had still preserved
its whiteness; and, though the skin of the hands was
dried, they retained their form and nails, as did also
the feet. The clothes were also in a perfect state of
preservation. A few days later, four nuns, accompanied
by the doctors deputed by the commission, came to re-
clothe the body. One of the daughters of the Venerable
accompanied them, to behold once more the face and
form of her holy mother, upon which the decay of the
tomb had scarce made any inroad. She then withdrew,
and the nuns, after removing the garment of the servant
of God, substituted a silken robe which the Princess
Barberini had made and Pius IX. had blessed. These
Religious deposed that, with the exception of the parts
of the body which had been uncovered, the whole had
preserved the natural whiteness of flesh and was perfectly flexible. They found, it is true, a few worms in
the coffin, but they had as yet respected the uncorrupted
body. In order to satisfy the devotion of the faithful,

of whom a vast concourse flocked to the church, it remained for four days exposed under the guardianship
of the substituted Postulator of the cause, the Trinitarian Religious, and eight soldiers. On the 12th of
August it was placed by the nuns in a coffin of cypress
wood, which had been made to contain it, and which
was sealed with the arms of the Promoter of the Faith,
as was also the outer leaden coffin. The absolution
being again given, the coffin was enclosed in a new
sarcophagus, constructed for it, and deposited near the
Altar of the Most Holy Crucifix, on the Epistle side,
at very little distance from its original situation. On
the external face of the monument was this inscription :—

> Hic quiescunt exuviæ Ven. Servæ Dei
> Annæ Mariæ Taigi
> Matris-familias et Tertiariæ Professæ
> Ord. Discalceat. SSmæ Trinitatis
> Redemp. Captivor.
> Quæ in conjugio fidem
> Inviolate servavit
> Et susceptam prolem pie educavit.*

P. Calixte, writing in 1871, says, 'A letter which
we have received from Rome, dated 15th August of this

---

* ' Here repose the remains of the Venerable Servant of God,
> Anna Maria Taigi,
> Mother of a Family, and Professed Tertiary
> Of the Discalced Order of the Most Holy Trinity
> For the Redemption of Captives,
> Who preserved her conjugal faith inviolate,
> And brought up her children piously.'

The testimony to her conjugal fidelity will here be noticed. The
expression ' Fidelis conjux' is employed in a longer inscription,
with the Promoter of the Faith's attestation of all that had
been done, written on parchment and enclosed in a glass tube,
which was laid at the feet of the holy body within the cypress
coffin.

present year, informs us that the body of the Venerable preserves its flexibility and immunity from all corruption.' From this it would appear that the state of the body has again been verified; but, as he gives no particulars, we have none to offer, neither can we adduce any farther authority for the statement. Her tomb has continued to be frequented, not only by the devout people of Rome and by persons coming from all parts of Italy, but by pilgrims from every land to which the fame of her virtues and wonderful gifts has travelled. Neither are they satisfied with praying at her tomb, but, as P. Calixte tells us, they go and visit the houses in which she dwelt and converse with the surviving members of her family; 'happy to hear from the lips of her daughters, or of the other persons who had known her, some details of so beautiful a life; they examine with respect all the objects which had been used by her, and joyfully carry away some picture or relic of the Venerable.'

D. Raffaele Natali continued to live with this poor family, and kept in his room some remnants of Anna Maria's clothes and other small articles; in particular, part of the haircloth which she had secretly worn, two iron chains, and her discipline made of iron wire cord. In an apartment frequented by the family was another sacred memorial, namely, the identical altar before which the servant of God used to pray in the house where she lived and died. We subjoin the account given by P. Calixte of a visit which he paid, in April of the year 1869, to her surviving descendants. 'Mgr. Natali,' he writes, ' now become Pontifical Chaplain and Abbate of San Vittorio, &c., was still living. He dwelt near the entrance of the Palazzo Barberini, not far from the Quattro Fontane. He had with him the youngest

daughter of the Venerable, Maria, then sixty years of age,
and a granddaughter of Anna Maria, thirty-five years
old, the same whose eye she had healed.   Both seemed
to be deeply pious.   The wax bust of Anna Maria, re-
producing, as we were informed, very faithfully the
features of her face, does not present under a physical
point of view anything which is not very ordinary.
The forehead is narrow and low, the nose is small and
retroussé, but, on the other hand, those eyes, which
seem still to read in the mysterious sun, that indescribable air of suffering mingled with resignation, that
impress of deep humility, all combine to impart to the
countenance of our Venerable an expression of beauty
altogether heavenly.*   Moreover, D. Raffaele assured
us that this bust of Anna Maria will suddenly manifest
a gleam of joy, expressed by a sweet smile, when events
occur favourable to the triumph of the Church.   The
worthy prelate evinced a sober reserve in giving any
information as to the secret details of the life of Anna
Maria, and, above all, as to her prophecies : he was
bound by the secrecy imposed under the sanction of an
oath upon all who are occupied at Rome with this
cause ; but at times he would exclaim, in a tone of
the warmest enthusiasm, " O what beautiful and great
things will be known at the moment of the beatification !" '   P. Calixte also visited with lively emotion the
little room which Anna Maria occupied in the closing

* When we remember that the cast was taken after death,
that Anna Maria was approaching the age of seventy, and was
worn down with illness, sufferings, and austerities, we need
scarcely be surprised that the reputation of beauty which she
enjoyed in youth should not be borne out by her bust.   Great
beauty is quite compatible with features somewhat irregular,
and time plays sad havoc even with the general outline of
the fairest faces.

days of her life. He describes it as having rather the form of a passage, its length being more than three times its width. The apartment was a dependence of the Palazzo Richetti on the Corso, facing the Church of Santa Maria in Via Lata.

The *Univers* of 15th March, 1871, contained the following paragraph in its Roman correspondence :— 'Don Raffaele Natali has just expired, surrounded by the family of Anna Maria, amidst whom he had lived for many years. He was past ninety, and seemed to have preserved his faculties only to speak of the Venerable, whose confidant he had been. The monks of St. Bernard assisted him during the last weeks of his life. Although this holy priest had begged to be buried near Anna Maria at San Crisogono, where he had prepared his place of sepulchre, the Italian law must perforce be obeyed, which required that all interments should take place without the city in the Cemetery of San Lorenzo. This brutal, levelling law respects nothing, and the Religious of every Order, as well as cloistered nuns, must be buried at San Lorenzo.' When this was written, the sacrilegious usurper had not as yet proceeded so far as to expel the consecrated servants of God, while living, from their churches and sacred premises. D. Raffaele, then, lies for the present in the ground where once his beloved and venerated friend so long rested, awaiting the time when that triumph which she predicted, and which he surely expected, as do all the faithful children of Holy Church, shall render possible the execution of his last wishes, and his removal to San Crisogono, there to be laid near to the holy remains of her whom he loved so well on earth, and whose glory we trust he already shares in Heaven.

CHAPTER XXIII

MIRACLES ATTESTING THE SANCTITY OF THE SERVANT OF GOD.

ALL that now remains for us is to notice a few out of the many miracles and favours accorded to persons who have sought the intercession of Anna Maria Taigi. In so doing we need scarcely say that we do not presume to forestal the judgment of the Holy See, to which alone it appertains to pronounce a decision, as upon the virtues, so also upon the gifts and supernatural works of the servants of God. Those miraculous cases which we shall mention have been extracted either from the juridical processes or from letters of undoubted authenticity, written by persons whose veracity can be thoroughly trusted. Every instance of miraculous intervention must be interesting to the true Catholic, not because it furnishes food for curiosity and excites to wonder—indeed admiration, not wonder, is the sentiment which such manifestations of divine power raise in his bosom—but because it speaks to him of his God, of the invisible Ruler and Controller of nature and of natural events, and of the honour He confers upon His servants. Nevertheless, as a long array of miraculous cures is apt to prove wearisome from the very similarity of the facts, we shall content ourselves with a few examples which will suffice for our purpose.

Anna Maria's protection was early displayed in the case of her own family, whom she left in a state of such great poverty and whom, when dying, she had recommended to the care of the priest who had shared their humble dwelling for so many years; promising

that in Heaven, to which she hoped through the merits
of Jesus Christ to be admitted, she would aid them by
her prayers. It seems surprising that they should have
been suffered to remain in want. Devout persons,
rich as well as poor, were continually flocking to her
tomb in the Cemetery of San Lorenzo ; how came it,
then, that it should not have occurred to many that it
would be fitting to testify their love and respect for
this holy woman by inquiring into the circumstances of
those whom she had left behind? Yet so it was to be;
and, indeed, it was chiefly owing to their own abstention, as well as that of D. Raffaele, from making an
appeal to the charity of those who had known and
honoured the departed. In such cases the needs of
sufferers from poverty are not seldom forgotten or overlooked. Besides, the cholera was raging in Rome, and
people's minds were engrossed with the subject; and
God doubtless overruled this and other circumstances
to bring about His purpose of securing to the children
of His servant their inheritance of poverty. But,
whatever may have been the cause of this great indigence, which seems to have lasted for some considerable period, it happened on one occasion that the priest
found himself at the end of his resources, small as those
were at all times. Starvation seemed to be staring him
and his adopted family in the face, when, in their extreme distress, he called upon Anna Maria, reminding
her of her promise. Shortly after, he one day heard a
knock at the door, and, on going to open it, he found
a roll of paper deposited on the threshold. It contained
a considerable sum in gold pieces. The unknown benefactor had disappeared; nor was it till long after
that he ascertained the friendly hand which had supplied this opportune relief. It came from a Milanese

gentleman, who said that he had felt himself strongly moved to send this sum of money to the family of Anna Maria. D. Raffaele also attested that this was by no means a solitary instance, for that he was frequently the subject of like favours; and that without their help he never would have been able to maintain the family dependent upon him.

Persons who interested themselves in her cause also received proofs of her kindness, while others were led to assist in its promotion in consequence of recovery from sickness or being favoured with spiritual graces through her means. A chaplain in Charles Albert's army, having to undergo a severe operation on his eyes, recommended himself to the protection of Anna Maria, and not only was it successfully performed, but he did not suffer the slightest pain. To testify his gratitude, he sent some money to aid in the prosecution of her cause. A Piedmontese lady, who declared she had received a special grace from Anna Maria, also contributed for the same object. Mgr. Luquet himself was indebted to her for the reception of some great favour; he had already shown himself exceedingly liberal in the promotion of her cause, but on this occasion he added a farther sum. A friend of his also contributed, promising that he would give more in the event of his obtaining a much-desired boon. He obtained it, and fulfilled his engagement. A French lady (Madame de Lestainville) is likewise mentioned as having presented a hundred golden crowns to further the cause of her beatification, in gratitude for a signal favour which she said she owed to her intervention.

Many cures were obtained either by simple recourse to her intercession, or as accompanied with the application of her picture or a shred of her garment to the affected part or with an invocation of the Blessed Trinity, for whom her devotion had been so striking. The Minister General of the Capuchins, while Prefect of the College of Missions, was seized in September, 1849, with a violent inflammatory attack. In a few days he was reduced to the last extremity, the medical attendant had given up all hopes of his patient's life, and the patient had similarly given up all trust in his doctor's skill, and had turned his thoughts wholly to preparation for death. He had received the last sacraments, when one of his friends gave him a particle of the haircloth which Anna Maria had worn, exhorting him to recommend himself to her intercession. The good Religious, although well disposed to die, felt moved to act according to his friend's advice, and so, animating his faith, he addressed Anna Maria in these terms :—' Servant of God, if all that is said of you is true, and if you have really power to move the goodness of God, obtain for me the grace of health, provided this be according to His good pleasure.' From the moment he gave utterance to this appeal improvement set in ; he was soon perfectly restored, and able to resume his fatiguing labours ; continuing always to be convinced that he owed his marvellous recovery to the intervention of Anna Maria. Teresa Bresciani, a young woman of twenty-four, had been suffering for six years from a disease in her eyes, which caused the sharpest pain. All medical prescriptions had entirely failed to afford relief. She turned her hopes now exclusively to Heaven; and, having heard of many signal graces accorded through the intercession of Anna Maria Taigi, she began a *triduo* in honour of the Blessed Trinity for the gifts so liberally bestowed on this beloved servant of God. Scarcely had she concluded it when she experienced a complete cure without the help of either doctors or medicine.

Several very remarkable cures are related as having taken place in the island of Malta. One of them is thus recorded in a letter from Mgr. the Canonico Falson to the Postulator of the cause :—' I profit by the present opportunity to give you a very consoling piece of news. A most wonderful miracle has taken place recently, through the mediation of Anna Maria Taigi, in favour of a young Maltese girl named Giuseppa Muscat, of this city of Valletta, who was lame of one of her legs, so that she could not walk. The most skilful physicians had been consulted, but all the various medicaments of the healing art produced no beneficial effect; on the contrary, the malady became more serious, so that the doctors, who had tried every possible remedy, declared the complaint to be quite incurable. The sufferer and her family having thus lost all earthly hope of cure, the girl, who had heard that I had in my possession some pictures and relics of the Servant of God, Anna Maria Taigi, immediately asked me for one, and with lively faith had recourse to her, in a *triduo* of prayers, to obtain the desired boon. On the third day she redoubled her supplications, and a little while before the close of the *triduo*, precisely at noon, she felt a great movement throughout her whole frame, and instantly, without the use of any remedy, she found herself perfectly free from the grievous and incurable malady from which she had suffered for years, to the astonishment of her whole family, and of the doctor himself, who had given up the case and left her, but who hastened to the house in order to verify the fact. And the fact is more than certain, although the physician, a man of advanced age, much experience, and high reputation, before pronouncing his formal opinion, prudently resolved to wait a while that he might see if the marvellous cure, which took place on the 17th of the past month, should prove lasting. The fame of what had occurred having spread abroad, the whole city was moved, and I found myself pestered on all sides by applications for pictures and printed accounts of this Venerable Servant of God. I beg you, therefore, to send me a good store of these pictures, that I may satisfy, at least in part, the devotion of this people towards the said servant of God.' This miracle occurred in 1855, and subsequent letters testified to the permanence of the cure. A process was drawn up in consequence, and forwarded to the Prefect of the Sacred Congregation of Rites. We pass over several other cures in the same island.

In Albano a cure of a boy of sixteen, who was hopelessly afflicted with a spinal complaint, and whose body was covered with ulcers, is recorded. His mother, Anna Maria Guglielmi, full of trust in the intercession of the servant of God, her name-sake, made the youth swallow in water some threads from a gown which she had worn, and gave him one of her pictures to lay on his head, on his breast, and on his wounds. Immediately his recovery commenced. The wounds closed, and he was very shortly restored to perfect health.

Maria Agostina Zabaini, Prioress of the Santissima Annunziata in Rome, who was afflicted with a cancer in the stomach, was delivered from that terrible disease, which Anna Maria had so often healed when on earth, by the same means, the application of her portrait. This cure took place in the year 1859, and her confessor, Ex-General of the Capuchins, afterwards Archbishop and Visitor Apostolic Extraordinary in the In-

dies, attested in 1860 that the Religious continued in
sound health. In Rome a child, ten years of age,
named Alfonso Lazzaroni, lying dangerously ill, rallied
in the course of a few moments through the intercession
of the servant of God, and was soon perfectly restored.

It seems unnecessary to multiply instances. Enough
has been said to show that God has not failed to honour
His servant with abundant testimonies to the power of
her intercession in Heaven, a power which we have seen
to be so great even while she yet abode on earth. It
remains for the authority which alone is competent to
deliver judgment in these matters to add the seal of its
infallible sanction. May this time speedily arrive, and
may it be accorded to our present Holy Father to pronounce the sentence which shall raise the holy matron
of Rome to the honours of our altars. Anna Maria,
constrained by obedience, which, as Cardinal Pedicini
averred, in her floated above all the other virtues, as
oil on water, and bound thereby to make known all her
revelations to the ecclesiastic who was appointed by her
confessor to receive them, declared that the Lord one
day said to her that He willed to make her known to
the whole world as an example of penance and a model
of married women. In concluding her life, therefore,
we have the consolation at least of feeling that, however inadequately our task has been accomplished, we
have been endeavouring, to the best of our ability, to
help forward a work which is agreeable to the designs
of Providence, and may therefore humbly hope for the
Divine blessing upon our labours, and that they may
serve to set forth the example and spread the fame of
the Venerable Servant of God in our own land.

We must add that we have had a further object in
view. Anna Maria, while a pattern of the exercise of

every humble virtue in the world and in the married state, as well as a glorious example of penance, was also the recipient of the most sublime gifts and the depositary of the most awful secrets. These last are as yet but imperfectly known ; yet enough has transpired to lead to very serious reflections, living as we do in such critical times and beholding the persecution of the Church, which she foretold, raging almost in every land. We cannot but call to mind that she also predicted tremendous and unparalleled chastisements ; nor can we suppose that she was prompted thus to speak without a purpose, or that her words ought to be wasted on us any more than her example. True, the Holy See has not as yet passed any judgment on her spirit of prophecy, but her possession of this gift rests on such strong evidence, evidence worthy of such high respect, that we cannot in prudence disregard it. The world is looking on in breathless expectation of the next turn of events in these disordered and perilous times, but it casts no glance towards Heaven—nay, it would scoff at the idea of all things not continuing as they have been since the beginning. We, the children of the Church, and therefore of the light, will do well to be wiser, and to be so prepared that nothing may take us by surprise or shake our hope and confidence. Whatever may happen, the Lord is with us, and after judgment will follow triumph.

'Our God is our refuge and strength, a Helper in troubles which have found us exceedingly. Therefore will we not fear when the earth shall be troubled, and the mountains shall be removed into the heart of the sea. Their waters roared and were troubled, the mountains were troubled with His strength. The stream of the river maketh the City of God joyful :

the Most High hath sanctified His own tabernacle.
God is in the midst thereof, it shall not be removed :
God will help it in the morning early.   Nations were
troubled, and kingdoms were bowed down : He uttered
His voice, the earth trembled.   The Lord of Armies is
with us ; the God of Jacob is our protector.   Come and
behold ye the works of the Lord : what wonders He
hath done upon earth, making wars to cease even to the
end of the earth.   He shall destroy the bow and break
the weapons, and the shield He shall burn in the fire.
Be still, and see that I am God.   I will be exalted
among the nations, and I will be exalted in the earth.
The Lord of Armies is with us : the God of Jacob is
our protector' (Psalm xlv.).

APPENDIX.

APPENDIX.

—————◆—————

FRAGMENTS OF ANNA MARIA TAIGI'S PREDICTIONS. HER PRO-
PHECIES COMPARED WITH THOSE OF OTHER GIFTED SOULS.

WE have not included in the Life of the Venerable Anna
Maria Taigi any prophecies regarding future events except such as can be attributed to her on unquestionable
authority. The authority on which we relied has been
mainly that of D. Raffaele Natali, who not only was cognisant of all her predictions, but had the best opportunities
of understanding them. He was however extremely reserved in his disclosures. As time has gone on further
portions of her prophecies have transpired, but, as they
cannot be so surely traced to their source, we have
omitted them in the text. This omission we will here
supply, premising that we give them under all reserve.

The following fragments were collected by P. Calixte,
and he says that he had them from the lips of persons
worthy of credit.

When the judgment she announced shall overtake the
wicked, the dead bodies round Rome will be as numerous
as the fish which a (then) recent inundation of the Tiber
had carried into that city. All the enemies of the Church,
secret as well as known, will perish during the darkness,
with the exception of some whom God shall soon after
convert. The air shall be infected by demons, who will
appear under all sorts of hideous forms. Blessed candles
will preserve from death, as well as prayers to the Blessed
Virgin and the holy angels. After the darkness, St. Peter

and St. Paul shall descend to preach throughout the earth. A great light emanating from them shall rest upon him whom God has chosen for the future Pope (the *Lumen in Cælo* of St. Malachi's well-known prophecy). St. Michael, appearing on earth, shall chain up Satan until the times of the preaching of Antichrist. Religion will everywhere extend its empire. Russia will be converted, as will also England and China; and all nations will rejoice in contemplating this splendid triumph of the Church. Then will be accomplished the prophecy of our Lord: 'There shall be one fold and one shepherd.' After this, the Santa Casa of Loreto will be transported by angels to Rome into the Basilica of Santa Maria Maggiore. P. Calixte observes that the Blessed Joseph Labre had made a similar prediction, and had also said that it would be transferred before the end of the world to France.

P. Calixte has something of his own to add to these various current reports. 'A pious prelate,' he says, 'a Cameriere Segreto of his Holiness, assured him that Anna Maria foretold the definition of the Immaculate Conception, the holding of the Vatican Council, and the proclamation of Pontifical Infallibility, in spite of the long and insidious opposition of the principal Catholic states. He also said that she announced the sanguinary struggle which has taken place between Prussia and France, and the humiliation and enfeeblement of the latter because she had forgotten her obligations as eldest daughter of the Church. To the horrors of foreign and civil war were to succeed sanguinary conflicts with the revolutionary faction; and this state of desolation was to last until the people of France should cast themselves at the feet of the Sovereign Pontiff, conjuring him to put an end thereto by an act of his supreme authority. The Pope would then send a legate into France to inquire into the state of things, and, on the report made to him, would name a Christian king to occupy its throne.'

To these fragments of reported prophecies we may subjoin a contribution from the Abbé Curicque, who, in his *Voix Prophétiques*, vol. ii. p. 155, says, 'On Monday, the

7th of February, we had gone to assist in the Basilica
of San Crisogono, in Trastevere, at the first Vespers of the
Feast of St. John of Matha, whose Religious serve that
sanctuary. We had then the happiness of praying for a
long time at the glorious tomb of Anna Maria. A little
before the office began, we went into the sacristy, where
we saw the Postulator of the cause of the Venerable, and
we obtained from that Father both some relics of Anna
Maria and some interesting details as to the state of preservation of her mortal remains. We questioned him also
as to the future. The Postulator replied that the Venerable
Servant of God had foretold that Pius IX. would re-enter
at the close of his reign on the integral possession of the
patrimony of St. Peter; and, moreover, those amongst his
enemies who were the fiercest opponents of his temporal
power would not remain alive to witness this glorious
triumph.

There is a general convergence, so to say, and striking
resemblance in the scope of all modern prophecies, which
confer no little importance upon them, taken as a whole,
in the eyes of those who, according to St. Peter's counsel,
are 'looking for and hasting unto the coming of the day of
the Lord.'* But any attempt to illustrate this point would
be quite beyond our present object, which is simply to
compare Anna Maria's prophecy of impending judgment,
and its results with analogous predictions of certain other
souls who were favoured with like revelations. Two women of eminent holiness and supernatural gifts in our days
have made announcements similar to those of Anna Maria,
one of whom was her contemporary, a married woman,
and also a Tertiary of the Trinitarians, Elisabetta Canori
Mora. In the year 1820, she saw in vision an awful
judgment fall upon the world, which in all its particulars
exhibits a marked coincidence with the prophecy on the
same subject attributed to Anna Maria. She first beheld
the heavens opened, and the Prince of the Apostles descend, surrounded with glory and with a number of celestial
spirits singing canticles. He was arrayed in Pontifical

* 2 Peter iii. 12.

garments, and held in his hand a pastoral staff, with which
he traced an immense cross over the earth, the angels
meanwhile singing, ' *Constitues eos principes super omnem
terram*—Thou shalt make them princes over all the earth.'*
She then beheld the faithful gathered, under the image of
a flock of sheep, beneath four sheltering trees, which a
touch of the Apostle's crozier caused to spring out of the
earth at the four extremities of the cross. ' Then,' she
said, ' I understood in my inmost heart that St. Peter had
caused these trees to spring up to serve as a place of refuge
for the faithful friends of Jesus Christ, and to preserve
them from the terrible chastisement which was to overwhelm the earth.' We are reminded of the angel in the
Apocalypse† who is bidden not to hurt the earth until the
servants of God have been sealed in their foreheads, and
of the mysterious Thau spoken of by Ezechiel.‡ After this
symbolical vision, in which the flock of Christ was consigned, under the figure of docile sheep, to the protection
of the chief pastor, he returned to Heaven, and then
quickly followed the judgment. Thick clouds veiled the
firmament, and a terrible wind, like to the roaring of a
furious lion, arose, sweeping the whole earth, and striking
terror into man and beast. Men at that crisis she described as in the height of revolution and engaged in mas-
sacring each other pitilessly. To the vengeance they
were thus mutually exercising on each other was now to
be joined that which the powers of Hell were commissioned
by God to inflict. She beheld legions of demons assuming
the form of men and beasts, and ranging the whole world,
to execute the decrees of God's justice on the wicked—on
their possessions, on the fruits of the earth, on towns, on
villages; ' nothing,' she said, ' will be spared.' In short,
they will fill the earth with ruins, specially devastating
those places where God has been outraged and blasphemed,
and where sacrileges have been perpetrated. Meanwhile
the faithful, under the protection of the holy Apostles,
shall remain uninjured both in person and in property.
After the judgment, she again beheld the heavens brighten,

* Psalm xliv. 17.   † vii. 3.   ‡ ix. 4.

and the chief of the Apostles descend, accompanied by angels singing hymns to his honour, and acknowledging him as the prince of the earth.   Then she saw St. Paul come down from Heaven, commissioned by God to traverse the earth and chain up the demons.   She beheld him drag them before the Prince of the Apostles, who consigned them again to the Hell from which they had been loosed.   After this follow particulars precisely similar to those already given, as contained in Anna Maria's prophecy of the miraculous election of the holy Pontiff, the ' *Lumen in Cœlo*,' and the reconciliation of earth with heaven.

In regard to this prediction we will make one observation, which is susceptible of wider application.   Clearly the opening of this vision is figurative.   The seer herself did not believe that St. Peter literally planted four large trees, under which the faithful gathered in the guise of sheep.   This leads us to ask how much of the remaining portion is also to be taken as symbolical, and how much must be understood literally.   That a great judgment of some kind is described, in which Hell will take a permissive part, and a singular protection be afforded to the faithful, there can be no question.   But are the subsequent apparitions of St. Peter and St. Paul, their preaching to the world and the chaining of Satan, events which the bodily eyes will discern?   Or, if the eyes of some may be opened to behold them, as were the eyes of the servant of the prophet to see the hosts of the Lord fighting for Israel (4 Kings vi. 17), or as those of Attila, the Scourge of God, when he was about to march with his Huns to the destruction of Rome, and the Vicar of Christ went forth to meet him, were opened to see the Apostles St. Peter and St. Paul menacing him in the air, will the vision be patent to all?   This point it seems impossible to decide.   It will be evident that what we have here suggested applies to the parallel announcements of Anna Maria Taigi, though we have given our reasons for inclining to the opinion that the threatened judgment of the three days' darkness is to be literally, not figuratively, understood.

DD

The other holy person who has made similar predictions is a Neapolitan widow still living and now about forty-eight years of age, Palma-Maria-Addolorata Matarelli, a native of Oria in the Terra di Lavoro. She enjoys a great reputation for sanctity, has received the stigmata, and on every Friday has a participation of the agonies of the Passion, including the Sweat of Blood. She is also said to possess the gift of bilocation. Of future events she speaks as confidently as others do of what is passing before their eyes; but on this subject much reserve is practised by her directors—a reserve in every way the more imperative because the subject of these phenomena is still living; and in such cases it is well known what jealous caution the Church prescribes, from the danger of possible illusion. She is greatly revered by the people of Naples, a circumstance naturally irritating to Victor Emmanuel's Government. She was accordingly subjected to a severe inquiry by the civil authorities on the 8th of December, 1865, which in that year fell on a Friday, as also to a medical examination; the result being a more complete establishment of the supernatural facts exhibited in her person. Fragments of her prophecies have been divulged. She is reported to have spoken of republics being set up in France, in Spain, in Italy; of the civil war which was to burst forth afterwards in these countries, simultaneously with other chastisements, such as plague and famine; of the massacre of priests and of some dignitaries of the Church; of the trials through which the City of Peter would have to pass and the sufferings it would endure from the fury of the wicked; of the extermination of the latter; the destruction of Paris; of the dense darkness and infection of the air by devils, and the use of blessed candles as a means of preservation; of supernatural portents which should appear in the heavens; and of a dreadful war which, however, would be of short duration and would be followed by the peace of the world and the triumph of the Church, of which Pius IX. was to see the commencement.*

* The prophecy respecting the three republics and the per

For the authenticity of all the prophecies reported to have been uttered by this holy woman we could not vouch. The following, however, has the sanction of a respected name. We extract it from a letter which the author* of the *Derniers Avis Prophétiques* received from a 'venerable friend,' and which he gives at greater length than is needful for our purpose. It is dated June 20th, 1872.

'You know by reputation the Abbé de Brandt :† he has arrived from Frohsdorf, from Oria, from Naples, from Rome, and from La Salette.   He saw Henri V. for three hours, Pius IX. for two hours at least, Mélanie for half a day, and the holy widow Palma (the Estatica of Oria) twice, and for more than an hour each time.'   Passing by what concerns France and the visit of the Abbé to the Comte de Chambord, we proceed to what the letter relates concerning his interviews with Palma.   'From Frohsdorf, M. de Brandt repaired to Oria.   Thanks to letters of recommendation which he had procured from a Cardinal, he was able to see the Signora Palma.   For more than seven years this stigmatized woman has taken no material nourishment.‡   Three times a day, our Lord communicates Himself to her visibly under the form of an ordinary host, and M. de Brandt saw one of these marvellous communions with his own eyes.   She also communicates every morning from the hand of a priest.   Here are some particulars of the conversation—which this time are most authentic—of this extraordinary woman; for the respected and worthy

---

secution of the Church appeared in the *Osservatore Romano* as early as the year 1863.   See *Les Stigmatisées,* par Le Docteur A. Imbert-Gourbeyre, Professeur à l'Ecole de Médécine de Clermont-Ferrand.   1873.

* Victor C. De Stenay.   His book was published in August, 1872.

† The Abbé de Brandt seems to have been the bearer of a number of letters from the legitimist deputies to the Comte de Chambord at Frohsdorf, in order to secure their safe delivery.

‡ Palma never eats; her sole sustenance being the Blessed Eucharist.   She drinks, however, a considerable quantity of water at intervals of about a couple of days.

M. de Brandt, who has related them to me, is no liar.
First, the seer said to him that she knew that he had had
some difficulties with his bishop in respect to the direction
of souls, but that he had always been in the right way,
and that he was to continue in it. She afterwards said to
him, "There will be dreadful massacres of priests and re
ligious in Spain, in France, in Italy, and especially in
Calabria; this will be soon; we are on the eve of these
things; then, suddenly lighting up, she spoke of the happiness of martyrdom in accents of ineffable joy. M. de
Brandt had laid it down to himself as a rule not to ask
her any question out of pure curiosity, but he thought he
might venture to inquire if these massacres would take
place on the 15th July, as the *Univers** had made her say.
"I said that!" she rejoined; "I know nothing about it. I
retain no recollection of what I may have said when in
ecstasy. I know the time, but I may not willingly reveal
it. There will be three days' darkness: not a single devil
will remain in hell: all will come out, either to urge on
the executioners or to discourage the just. It will be
terrible! it will be terrible! But a great Cross will appear; and the triumph of the Church will soon cause all
miseries to be forgotten."'

These last words recall to mind what P. Bernardo Clausi
said to the nun, his penitent, when speaking of the judgment which she was to live to witness, and of the subsequent joy which should obliterate all memory of sorrow.

It does not enter into our subject to dwell further on
the marvels connected with this extraordinary woman;
we will therefore refer the reader for a circumstantial account of her state to the 2d volume of *Les Stigmatisées* by
Dr. A. Imbert-Gourbeyre. Although the supernatural facts
manifested in her person are his main topic, he also makes
allusion to her prophecies. We may safely add what

* The *Univers*, in a subsequent issue, rectified the error into
which it had fallen through some inaccuracy of its Roman
correspondent. Palma had assigned no date. The reported
prophecies passing from mouth to mouth got embellished and
altered.

he heard from her own lips, on the 25th October, 1871.
'I questioned Palma,' he says, 'concerning Henri V. "I
hope he will come back," she said, "but it will not be yet,
not yet"—making as she spoke a significant gesture with
her arm, as if to put back the time, and added, "Paris must
be purified." "And the Pope," I asked; "what of him?"
"I experience," said the seer, "many alternations concerning him. I know not whether he will be obliged to quit
Rome. I always behold over Rome the Immaculate Conception protecting the Holy Father. The Blessed Virgin," she added, smiling, "owes it, indeed, to the Pope, were
it only from courtesy and gratitude." Such,' says Dr.
Imbert-Gourbeyre, 'are the prophecies which I heard from
Palma's lips. I know from others that she has often spoken
of the woes which will overwhelm France. At the time of
the Prussian war she was heard to say several times that this
was nothing to what was in store for us later. A lady,'
he adds, 'who has seen Palma since my journey to Oria,
wrote to me last June (1872) that she still announces great
woes, but also the triumph of religion. "The blood of the
priests," she said, "will flow like a stream."'

Sister Rosa Colomba, a nun of the Convent of Santa
Caterina of Taggia, near Nice, who died, in 1847, after a
holy life almost entirely spent in the cloister, uttered predictions very similar to those we have recorded. She seemed
to have had a permanent possession of the spirit of prophecy, but she knew so well how to veil her great gifts, as
well as her eminent virtues, under a simplicity almost child-
like, that her companions gave very little heed to what she
said beyond occasionally laughing at some of her utterances; as when she would exclaim, 'Poor Louis Philippe!
you will one day fly from France, and will go and die an
exile in England.' It was only when events began to justify
what their holy sister had said, that they took note of all
that they remembered her to have foretold; and an authentic record was drawn up, which has been kept in the
archives of the diocese. She predicted the chief circumstances of Charles Albert's reign, and described that of his
successor as 'un regno di fanciulli—a reign of babies,'

which would end in his dethronement. When she spoke
of the ' friend' of this new king by name as Napoleon, the
Religious used to be greatly amused, and would ask her if
the exile of St. Helena was to return to life. She announced
a great persecution which, after Napoleon's fall, was to
burst forth against the Church, and which was to be the
work of some of her own children. In the visions which
she had of those times she saw Russian and Prussian armies
invading Italy and the former stabling their horses in the
new Convent of Taggia. For this reason she never would
give her vote for its being built, and said that never would
she hear Mass in the church which should thus be desecrated. And, in fact, she died six days before its consecration. In describing the Revolution, she spoke particularly
of the persecution of the Religious Orders, initiated, as
usual, by an attack upon the Jesuits. Nations were to
march against nations and exterminate each other with the
most murderous weapons ; the Revolution was to spread
throughout Europe, where there would be no tranquillity
until the White Flower should again ascend the throne of
France.

The close connection between the peace of France,
secured by a return to her legitimate government, and this
grand peace of the world, exceeding any it has yet enjoyed
and accompanied by the exaltation of the Church, was, as
we have seen, foretold by Anna Maria Taigi, and has been
the burden of prophecy, we may say, since the days of St.
Remigius, when that holy bishop, in anointing Clovis, declared that France was predestinated by God for the de-
fence of the Church. Hence she was to enjoy greatness
and power co-eval with the world's duration ; but every
time that she should fail in the fulfilment of her vocation
she should meet with terrible punishment. Connected with
this prophecy is one which can be traced as high as the
ninth century ; that which announces that in the latter
days shall arise a great and powerful Monarch of that
illustrious nation, against whom no one would be able to
stand, for the hand of the Lord should be with him. He was
to have dominion in East and West, and subjugate Turks

and barbarians to his sway. 'Doctores nostri dicunt,' wrote
Rabanus Maurus, who was Abbot of Fulda (822), and subsequently Archbishop of Mayence, 'quod unus ex regibus
Francorum Romanum Imperium ex integro tenebit, qui
in novissimo tempore erit, et ipse maximus et omnium re-
gum ultimus.' In his time there was also to be a great and
holy Pontiff, with whom he is ever associated; and so
strong was this ancient belief, which has never died away,
that the non-appearance of this great king was held by a
monk, at the close of the ninth century, as proof that the
world could not be near its end at the commencement of
the tenth.* It is interesting also to note that St. Francis
de Sales expressed a hope that Henri IV. might prove to
be the predicted monarch. An ancient and celebrated prophecy attributed to St. Cesarius, who flourished in the fifth
century, and recorded in a book entitled *Liber Mirabilis*,
printed in 1524, a copy of which exists in what was the
Imperial Library of Paris, after minutely describing the
horrors of the Revolution and the persecution and desolation of the Church, proceeds to say that when the whole
world, and France in particular (Lorraine and Champagne
being specially mentioned), shall have been a prey to great
miseries and tribulations, succour will come from a prince
who shall regain the throne of the lily. This prince will
extend his dominion everywhere. At the same time there
will be a great Pope, a man most holy and of consummate
perfection, who shall have with him this most virtuous
prince sprung from the blood of the Frankish kings. This
king will aid him in reforming the world; and there will
be one only law, one only faith, one only baptism; he will
bring back many from error to the Holy See, and for long
years peace shall endure, because the anger of God shall
be stayed. Examples might be multiplied.

The same traditionary belief prevails, and has prevailed
for ages, throughout the East. The Turks in the height of
their power, and at a time when Asia seemed to menace

* *Liber de Antichristo*, attributed to Alcuin, and appended
to the *Opera S. Augustini*, t. vi. ed. Benedict. See *Le Grand
Pape et le Grand Roi*, p. 47.

Europe much more than Europe to menace Asia, had not forgotten the ancient prophecies, which announced the destruction of the Ottoman Empire by the Christians. With them Christians and Franks are one and the same, seeing that in the East the French represent Christianity. Now these Franks, or French, are to be led by a great king who shall subject the whole East to the religion of Christ. A prophecy well known in the East, and attributed to St. Gregory of Armenia, called the Illuminator, says, 'A valiant nation shall come: it will be that of the Franks; all the world will join itself to this nation, and Asia shall be converted.' 'The East is in expectation,' writes an Oriental traveller; 'tradition has taught it that a great king of France will be at once its conqueror and its liberator.'* So lively have ever been these Oriental traditions that the Arabs and Turks of Jerusalem have walled up the gate by which it is said the Great King of France will enter when he comes to vanquish the East.

The Comte de Maistre, who was gifted with a marvellous sagacity and penetration, almost resembling a prophetic instinct, thus expresses himself in his *Soirées de St. Pétersbourg* : 'The great event of this century will not be a political, but a moral revolution, and it is the French nation which is to be the instrument of this revolution, which will be the greatest of revolutions. Many theologians and great scholars have believed that facts of the highest order and near to their accomplishment are announced in the Apocalypse. More than ever, then, should we study prophecies; for we must hold ourselves prepared for an immense event in the divine order, towards which we are hastening with an accelerated speed which must strike all observers. Religion reigns no longer on earth; the human race cannot remain in this state. There is not perhaps a religious man in Europe (I speak of the educated class) who at this moment is not in expectation of something extraordinary.' How much more cogent do these words seem in our time !

* E. Borée, *Correspondance et Mémoires d'un Voyageur en Orient*, t. ii. p. 80.

Saints of old have, as we said, combined with holy persons in our own days,* in foretelling a great judgment that should come upon the world, in terms which, while they preclude the idea that they are alluding to the end of all and the final judgment, nevertheless point to something entirely unprecedented in times past, which shall introduce the æra of peace and glory to the Church of which we have been speaking.   The grand and leading ideas of tribulation, judgment, and renovation seem embodied in the following words of St. Catherine of Siena, set down from her own lips by her director, the Blessed Raymond of Capua, and reported in the Life which he afterwards wrote of the saint :—' The evil,' she said, ' of which bad Christians will render themselves guilty by persecuting the Holy Church, will bring her honour, light, and the perfume of virtues. After the tribulation and distresses, God, *through a means unforeseen by men*, will purify His holy Church, and renew the spirit of His elect.   Such a reformation of the Church of God and such a renovation of holy pastors shall ensue that the sole thought of it makes my spirit to exult in the Lord.   The spouse of Christ is now, as it were, disfigured and clothed in rags, but then she shall be resplendent in beauty : she will appear adorned with precious jewels and crowned with a diadem of all the virtues.   All the faithful people will rejoice to see her endowed with such holy pastors.   As for the unbelieving nations, they will be attracted by the good odour of Jesus Christ; they will return to the fold of Catholicity ; they will be converted to the true Pastor and Bishop of their souls.   Return, then, thanksgiving to the Lord, because after the tempest He will give to His Church a peace and a joy which shall be extraordinary.'

Of this last triumph to be accorded to the Church on earth before the days of the final persecution and of the appearance of Antichrist St. Hildegarde often spoke.   For

* We may refer all who feel any interest in tracing this catena of evidence to the *Voix Prophétiques* of the Abbé Curicque, and to the little work entitled, *Le Grand Pape et le Grand Roi*, 6me edition.

instance, after relating an awful vision which she had beheld of a horrible beast attacking a woman who symbolises
the Church, and, having described his overthrow by the
vengeance of Heaven, in terms which remind us of the
great judgment which Anna Maria announced, she adds,
' The people, witnesses of this prodigy, exclaimed, " Alas !
alas ! what is this that we see? Ah ! who can save us?
Who will be able to deliver us?   How is it possible that
we have allowed ourselves to be so deceived?   O God most
powerful, have pity on us!   Let us return, let us, then,
return.   Let us hasten to embrace the testament of the
Gospel of Christ. For, alas ! alas ! we have been deceived."
And behold,' continues the saint, ' the feet of the image of
this woman appeared all brilliant with light and resplendent
as the sun.   And I heard a voice from Heaven which said
to me, "Although all things on earth approach to their
doom, so that the world, deprived of all its strength, is declining to its ruin under the weight of its sufferings and
its scourges, nevertheless the spouse of My Son, persecuted
in her children by the precursors of the son of perdition,
will not be shaken, although she will be violently assailed
by them.   On the contrary, at the end of the ages she will
come forth stronger and more vigorous than ever, and, appearing more beautiful and more glorious, she will present
herself to her Spouse with greater sweetness and tenderness to receive His caresses." '

In this mystical language are shadowed forth the evening glories of the Church militant, which F. Faber, in the
Preface to his translation of the Venerable Grignon de
Montfort's treatise on *The True Devotion to the Blessed
Virgin*, calls ' that great age of the Church which is to be
the Age of Mary.'   This age, heralded by the definition of
her Immaculate Conception, shall give special glory to her
by whom God the Father gave His Only-Begotten Son to
the world, that ' rich treasury' of God, as Grignon de Montfort calls her (p. 12), ' in which He has laid up all that
He has of beauty, of splendour, of rarity and of precious-
ness, even to His own Son,—Mary whom the Saints have
named the Treasure of the Lord, out of whose plenitude all

are made rich.' These days of triumph may be brief, but they will be exceedingly glorious, for they will be as it were the earthly coronation of God's most holy Mother. ' Peace will return to the world,' said Marie Lataste, speaking of the same glorious time, ' because Mary shall breathe upon the tempest and calm it; may her name be praised, blessed, and exalted for ever. The prisoners will know that they owe their liberty to her; the exiles, their country; the afflicted, their peace; and all, their welfare. Betwixt thee and thy protected ones there will be a mutual exchange of graces and thanksgivings, of love and attachment, and from North to South, from East to West, all will proclaim Mary—Mary conceived without sin, Mary queen of earth and of heaven.'

Concerning this penultimate age of the Church we find some remarkable passages in the Commentary on the Apocalypse by the Venerable Barthelemi Holzhauser, which exhibit a striking conformity to the more modern utterances, and serve to show that the expectation of the ' Great Pontiff' and the ' Great Monarch' was equally strong in his days as in the present; and, in fact, as we have said, it dates from much farther back. Holzhauser, however, did not profess to be delivering predictions himself, but simply interpreting those of the Apocalypse. Nevertheless, it would seem that he was conscious of receiving special illumination to this end; for, on breaking off his labours at the commencement of the fifteenth chapter, and being questioned by his disciples as to his reason for doing so, he replied that he no longer felt himself enlightened by the same spirit. Holzhauser was, we might say, the Olier of Germany, having dedicated his life to a similar object, the reformation of the secular clergy, and adopted means for that end which bear a strong resemblance to those employed by the great Founder of St. Sulpice. He died as parish priest of Bingen, with the reputation of eminent sanctity, in 1658. Amongst his high supernatural gifts must certainly be reckoned that of prophecy, which gives a singular authority to his Commentary. It is peculiarly interesting to ourselves to know that he foretold that the English would

ultimately return to the bosom of the Church, and would
contribute to the exaltation and progress of Catholicism
even far more efficaciously than had their forefathers. He
also foretold the ravages of Josephism in Germany, the
sanguinary wars which were to be its chastisement at the
time of the first Empire, and the career of the illustrious
Pope Pius VII. He wrote his Commentary on the Apocalypse in the solitudes of the Tyrol, given up the while to
meditation, prayer, and fasting. He divides the history of
the Catholic Church into seven ages, which he considers
to be symbolised by the Seven Churches of Asia. The
first age, which may be styled the period of seed-sowing,
extended from the time of Jesus Christ and the Apostles to
that of Nero; the second age, called that of irrigation, com-
prehended the time of the ten persecutions until the reign
of Constantine; the third age is the illuminative, or that of
Doctors, and extends from the time of Pope Sylvester and
Constantine to that of Leo III. and Charlemagne; the
fourth age, called pacific, reaches to the time of Leo X.;
the fifth age, which is that of affliction, begins with Leo X.
and the reign of Charles V. It includes what we call
modern times, and was inaugurated by the heresy of Luther.
In it Catholics were to be oppressed by heretics and bad
Christians. Everywhere there were to be deplorable calamities and terrible wars. Kingdoms were to be convulsed,
thrones overturned, princes put to death. There were to
be conspiracies formed for the foundation of republics; the
Church and her ministers were to be despoiled. This age
is to be succeeded by the sixth, that of consolation, which
the children of the Church are now expecting; it is the
same of which St. Catherine and St. Hildegarde have spoken
in such glowing terms; it is to be of short duration, and to
terminate with the appearance of Antichrist, which will
usher in the seventh and last age, the age of desolation,
embracing the whole period of Antichrist to the end of the
world.

The sixth age, that of consolation, was to be the witness of a change, the effect of the omnipotent hand of God,
so marvellous, that no one could have conceived it. There

will be a great and holy Pontiff; and a powerful Monarch, sent by God, will arise to put an end to disorder. He will subject all to his power, and will display an ardent zeal for the true Church of Christ, and all heresies will be destroyed; the Empire of the Turks will be broken; and all nations shall come and adore their God in the unity of the true Catholic and Roman faith. Love, concord, peace, and happiness shall reign amongst men. The whole world will be as it were the patrimony of this powerful monarch; for, by the help of the Lord, he shall liberate the earth from wicked men and from the evils with which it is afflicted. Under his auspices a great Council, the greatest of all the Councils, will be brought to a happy conclusion, after it has been subjected to much hostility and opposition. He will use his power to enforce its decrees. God shall bless him, and give all things into his hands.

This great Council, foretold also by Anna Maria, had already been announced in the clearest terms by Sœur de la Nativité, a humble lay-sister in the Ursuline Convent of Fougères, about the year 1792. Her Life and Revelations were first given to the world in 1818. After describing the poisonous effects of the Revolution throughout the world, she said, 'But the assembled Church shall one day condemn and destroy the vicious principle of this wicked constitution. I see in God a numerous assemblage of ministers of the Church, who, strong as an army in battle array and like to a firm and immovable pillar, shall sustain the rights of the Church and of its head, and re-establish her ancient discipline. What a consolation and joy for all the true faithful! I see in God a great Power, which shall restore all to good order. False worships shall be abolished, all the abuses of the Revolution shall be swept away, and religion shall return to be more flourishing than ever.'

We will sum up this subject of modern prophecy in the words of the *Civiltà Cattolica* of May 4th, 1872. They express sentiments which we thoroughly adopt. 'We protest once more that it is not in our mind to put forward as authentic any of the prophecies recorded by us. It belongs to the Church to judge of their supernatural origin.

Nevertheless, it cannot be denied that the agreement of so many and various presages in defining events the expectation of which is in the heart of the greater number of Catholics possesses a persuasive force and is a kind of seal of high probability, if not of certainty. This becomes much clearer if, with the light of right reason and pure faith, we study the present condition of civil society and of the Church. Generally speaking, all intelligent persons, including even the irreligious, with one voice admit that without some remedy the nature of which the human mind cannot divine, the world cannot go on long as it is at present. Either it must be reformed or it will be precipitated into an abyss of barbarism. In like manner, wise Christians are more than unanimous in admitting that the Church is a prey to a diabolical and universal persecution hitherto unexampled; wherefore God must come to her aid with succours proportioned to the need, that is, extraordinary; nor is there any room to doubt that in an opportune time He will do so, in virtue of His infallible promise: "*Portæ inferi non prævalebunt.*" Hence we find ourselves in this extreme case—that the salvation of society, no less than of the Church, requires an unaccustomed intervention of omnipotent power. If this be so, how should we not believe that come it will?'

THE END.

LONDON:
ROBSON AND SONS, PRINTERS, PANCRAS ROAD, N.W.

CPSIA information can be obtained
at www.ICGtesting.com
Printed in the USA
BVHW091512220223
658997BV00003B/167